The Anatomy of Corporate Law

A Comparative and Functional Approach

Second Edition

REINIER KRAAKMAN
JOHN ARMOUR
PAUL DAVIES
LUCA ENRIQUES
HENRY HANSMANN
GERARD HERTIG
KLAUS HOPT
HIDEKI KANDA
EDWARD ROCK

OXFORD
UNIVERSITY PRESS

OXFORD

UNIVERSITY PRESS

Great Clarendon Street, Oxford OX2 6DP

Oxford University Press is a department of the University of Oxford.
It furthers the University's objective of excellence in research, scholarship,
and education by publishing worldwide in

Oxford New York

Auckland Cape Town Dar es Salaam Hong Kong Karachi
Kuala Lumpur Madrid Melbourne Mexico City Nairobi
New Delhi Shanghai Taipei Toronto

With offices in

Argentina Austria Brazil Chile Czech Republic France Greece
Guatemala Hungary Italy Japan Poland Portugal Singapore
South Korea Switzerland Thailand Turkey Ukraine Vietnam

Oxford is a registered trade mark of Oxford University Press
in the UK and in certain other countries

Published in the United States
by Oxford University Press Inc., New York

© R. Kraakman, J. Armour, P. Davies, L. Enriques, H. Hansmann,
G. Hertig, K. Hopt, H. Kanda, and E. Rock, 2009

The moral rights of the authors have been asserted

Crown copyright material is reproduced under Class Licence
Number C01P0000148 with the permission of OPSI
and the Queen's Printer for Scotland

First published 2009

British Library Cataloguing in Publication Data

Data available

Library of Congress Cataloging-in-Publication Data

The anatomy of corporate law: a comparative and functional approach / Reinier
Kraakman ... [et al.].—2nd ed.
p. cm.
Includes index.
ISBN 978-0-19-956583-2 (hardback : alk. paper)—
ISBN 978-0-19-956584-9 (pbk. alk. paper)
1. Corporation law. I. Kraakman, Reinier H.
K1315.A53 2009
346'.066—dc22 2009023537

Typeset by Newgen Imaging Systems (P) Ltd., Chennai, India
Printed in Great Britain
on acid-free paper by
Clays Ltd, St Ives plc

ISBN 978-0-19-956583-2 (Hbk.)
ISBN 978-0-19-956584-9 (Pbk.)

3 5 7 9 10 8 6 4 2

1006070458

Acknowledgements

In preparing this second edition we have had the great benefit of the efforts of the reviewers of our first edition. We should like to mention in particular the review by David Skeel (*Corporate Anatomy Lessons* 113 Yale Law Journal 1519, 2004), from which we learned much, but many reviewers provided insightful comment, which we have tried to take into account.

The process of preparing the second edition was eased by the hospitality which we jointly enjoyed from, in chronological order, New York University Law School, ETH (Zurich), and Yale Law School.

As with the first edition, we have drawn shamelessly on our friends and colleagues for comment on various parts of the book. We list them here and apologize in advance to any whom we have omitted: Marcello Bianchi, Christophe Clerc, Pierre-Henri Conac, Matteo Gargantini, Martin Gelter, Jesse Fried, Henry Hu, Joe McCahery, Federico Mucciarelli, Peter Mülbert, Martine Kloepfer Pelèse, Alain Pietrancosta, Paolo Santella, Rolf Skog, Lorenzo Sasso, Lorenzo Stanghellini, Erik Vermeulen, Dirk A. Zetzsche, and Andrea Zorzi.

Once again, we should like to thank our home institutions for providing financial support to us personally as we worked on this book. We thank the University of Oxford for funding John Armour; the London School of Economics and Political Science for funding Paul Davies and Laura Laborey for research assistance; the Yale Law School for funding Henry Hansmann; the ETH for funding Gerard Hertig; the Harvard Law School John M. Olin Center for Law, Economics, and Business for funding Reinier Kraakman and Alexander Hellgardt and Kaoru Matsuzawa for research assistance; and the Saul Fox Research Endowment for funding Ed Rock.

As ever, we thank our nearest and dearest, who may legitimately wonder why such a short book has involved so much toing and froing.

The Authors

Preface

This book results from a longstanding collaboration among nine authors from six countries, and many more colleagues from around the world who have provided helpful suggestions and criticisms, both for the First Edition and for this, the Second Edition, of *The Anatomy of Corporate Law*. All of us—the authors—have taken principal responsibility for particular chapters of the book, but each of us has also contributed to the structure and content of the entire book. The First Edition of this book took nine years to complete. The Second Edition took less than three, thanks in large part, to the energy and fresh vision of the two new authors who joined our team to rework the *Anatomy*: John Armour, of Oxford University, and Luca Enriques, of CONSOB and the University of Bologna.

As with the First Edition, we can best summarize this book with four words: it is 'international', 'functional', 'neutral', and, not least, it is 'short'. It is international because its authors hail from different jurisdictions, and because it is predicated on the idea of a field of corporate—or company—law, with problems and legal strategies that, at a mid-level of abstraction at least, are independent of the laws of specific jurisdictions. Naturally, we must address particular national corporate laws to make this idea compelling. We therefore focus the book on corporate law in six 'core' jurisdictions: France, Germany, Italy, Japan, the UK, and the U.S. But to the extent that we provide an integrated analysis of the company laws of these jurisdictions, we also provide an analytical framework for investigating corporate law across all jurisdictions.

The framework we develop is also 'functional'. By this we mean that our book highlights the economic logic of corporate law. The corporate form, and the law to which it gives rise, are utilitarian institutions, which must be understood in the first instance in the light of their economic contributions to business life. Of course this point should not be exaggerated. This book's authors do not believe that *every* aspect of corporate law is economically rational, still less that any particular corporate law is optimal. Politics and path dependence affect the law in every jurisdiction, as do the larger legal and business culture in which corporate law operates. Moreover, there are moments—and the financial crisis of 2007–2009 may be one of them—when the future development of corporate law (and of other forms of business regulation) seems especially uncertain. New insight into the interaction of markets and regulation may result in more functional company law, especially in the case of listed companies and financial institutions. Alternatively, the spotlight cast by the financial crisis on matters ranging from executive compensation to limits on directorial liability in the face of staggering financial losses may lead to legal changes that can only be explained as populist backlash. Naturally we hope for the former outcome, and not only because our analytical framework highlights the law's economically rational elements.

This point leads to our third key descriptor: our book is neutral, or at least it attempts to avoid evaluative comparisons among the corporate law systems of our six core jurisdictions. In other words, we do not choose between the UK's City Code or Delaware case law for regulating takeover defenses, or between German and French law that mandate employee representation on the boards of many companies, and the law of Italy, Japan, the UK, and the U.S., which does not. Although all the authors of this book have decided views on these issues, our views are not unanimous. And our project in writing this book is not to decide such contested issues—at least not here—but rather to establish a framework for examining the law that is at once economically grounded (i.e., functional), and sufficiently capacious to accommodate the views of both sides on controversial issues of legal policy.

'Short' is our book's fourth descriptor. To be sure, this Second Edition is slightly longer than the First. Still, we hope that it remains short enough to attract the readers we especially hope to reach: our busy academic colleagues in corporate law and related legal fields; our students, who need a readable and functional overview of diverse corporate law systems; professors of business and economics, who might also need a functional introduction to corporate law; and our academic colleagues in non-corporate fields who might share our interest in private law and the interaction of law and economics. (Sad to say, this book will not aid practising attorneys who require a detailed treatment of substantive law in our core jurisdictions. Such an encyclopedic approach would have required a much longer book. Nevertheless, we hope that practitioners, as well as lawmakers and judges, will find this book a helpful guide to the strategies and policies at play in corporate law.)

The fact that this book remains short, however, is not meant to suggest that it remains unchanged relative to the First Edition. On the structural level, we retain our typology of legal strategies and the rough order of our discussion, beginning with corporate governance and ending with investor protection and interaction between ownership structure and corporate law. Nevertheless, our new edition makes improvements within this structure in a number of ways. First, it broadens the focus of the original edition by addressing enforcement rather than focusing almost exclusively on law-on-the-books, and by considering legal topics—such as insolvency law—that, while clearly relevant to each jurisdiction's corporate law, were somewhat arbitrarily declared off limits in our previous edition. Second, this edition widens the range of core jurisdictions to include Italy, both because Italy's law contains novel features not found among our original jurisdictions and because Italy broadens our sample of continental European jurisdictions. Third, this new edition includes references to recent reforms in corporate law, which have been numerous in all of our core jurisdictions. Fourth, the Second Edition emphasizes empirical literature on corporate law more heavily than did the First, because we believe that much of the next generation of advanced scholarship will be empirical rather than either doctrinal or grounded in *a priori* assumptions about the world, whether economic or otherwise. Finally, the Second Edition includes, as stated previously, the fresh insights and scholarship of our new co-authors, John Armour and Luca Enriques.

It would not be misleading to claim that we have, collectively, reconsidered almost all of the analysis and observations made in our original edition, and that we have rewritten, updated, or otherwise modified more than 70% of the prose in our original edition. We hope that the Second Edition will be as successful as the First in serving the needs of our principal audiences.

Reinier Kraakman
Harvard Law School
20 April 2009

Contents

List of Authors

John Armour is the Lovells Professor of Law and Finance in the Faculty of Law, University of Oxford. His main research interest lies in the integration of legal and economic analysis, with particular emphasis on the impact on the real economy of changes in the law governing insolvency and company law. He has been involved in policy-related projects commissioned by the UK's Department of Trade and Industry, Financial Services Authority, and Insolvency Service. Recent publications include *After Enron: Reforming Corporate Governance and Capital Markets in Europe and the US*, with Joe McCahery (eds.) (Hart Publishing, 2006), *Who Writes the Rules for Hostile Takeovers, and Why?*, with David Skeel, 95 Georgetown Law Journal 1727, 2007, and *Bankruptcy Law and Entrepreneurship*, with Douglas Cumming, 10 American Law and Economics Review 303, 2008.

Paul Davies is the Allen & Overy Professor of Corporate Law in the Faculty of Law, University of Oxford. Between 1998 and 2009 he was the Cassel Professor of Commercial Law at the London School of Economics and Political Science. He was a member of the Steering Group for the Company Law Review which preceded the enactment of the Companies Act 2006, and has been involved recently in policy-related work for the UK Treasury. His most recent works include the 8th edition of Gower and Davies, *Principles of Modern Company Law* (Thomson, 2008) and *Towards a Flexible Labour Market* (Oxford University Press, 2007, with Mark Freedland). He is a Fellow of the European Corporate Governance Institute, a Fellow of the British Academy and an honorary Queen's Counsel.

Luca Enriques is Full Professor of Business Law at the University of Bologna Faculty of Law, where he taught corporate law, corporate governance and securities regulation until 2007. Since then, he has been on leave while serving as a Commissioner at Consob, the Italian Securities and Exchange Commission. Before entering academia in 1999, he worked for the Bank of Italy in Rome. He was advisor to the Italian Ministry of Economy and Finance from 2000 to 2006. An ECGI research associate, he has published four books and several articles in Italian as well as international law reviews on topics relating to corporate law, corporate governance, and securities regulation. Recent publications include *The Uneasy Case for Top-Down Corporate Law Harmonization in the European Union*, with Matteo Gatti (27 University of Pennsylvania Journal of International Economic Law 939, 2006), *Corporate Governance Reforms in Continental Europe*, with Paolo Volpin (21 Journal of Economic Perspectives 117, 2007), *Centros and the Cost of Branching*, with Marco Becht and Veronica Korom (9 Journal of Corporate Law Studies 171, 2009).

Henry Hansmann is the Augustus E. Lines Professor of Law at the Yale Law School. His scholarship has focused principally on the law and economics of organizational ownership and structure, and has dealt not just with business corporations but also with nonprofits, mutuals, cooperatives, condominiums, trusts, and partnerships. He has also been Professor or Visiting Professor at Harvard University, New York University, and the University of Pennsylvania Law Schools. Recent publications include *Law and the Rise of the Firm*, with Reinier Kraakman and Richard Squire (119 Harvard Law Review 1333, 2006), *Corporation and Contract* (8 American Law and Economics Review 1, 2006), and *Globalizing Commercial Litigation*, with Jens Dammann (94 Cornell Law Review 1, 2008).

Gerard Hertig has been Professor of Law at ETH Zurich since 1995. He was previously Professor of Administrative Law and Director of the *Centre d'Etudes Juridiques Européennes* at the University of Geneva Law School (1987–1995). He has been a visiting professor at leading law schools in Europe, Japan, and the U.S. and practised law as a member of the Geneva bar. He is ECGI research associate and a member of the European Shadow Financial Regulatory Committee. Recent publications include *Optional rather than Mandatory EU Company Law*, with Joseph A. McCahery (4 European Company and Financial Law Review 341, 2006), *Basel II and Fostering the Disclosure of Banks' Internal Credit Ratings* (7 European Business Organization Law Review 625, 2006), *On Going Board Reforms: One Size Fits All and Regulatory Capture* (21 Oxford Review of Economic Policy 269, 2005).

Klaus Hopt was Director of the Max Planck Institute for comparative and International Private Law in Hamburg, Germany. His main areas of specialization include commercial law, corporate law, banking and securities regulation. He has been Professor of Law in Tübingen, Florence, Bern, and Munich, Visiting Professor at numerous universities, and judge at the Court of Appeals, Stuttgart, Germany. He served as a member of the High Level Group of Experts mandated by the European Commission to recommend EU company and takeover law reforms. Recent publications include *Corporate Governance in Context* (Oxford University Press, 2005, with Eddy Wymeersch et al (eds.)) and *The European Foundation* (Cambridge University Press, 2006, with Rainer Walz et al (eds.)).

Hideki Kanda is Professor of Law at the University of Tokyo. His main areas of specialization include commercial law, corporate law, banking regulation and securities regulation. He was Visiting Professor of Law at the University of Chicago Law School (1989, 1991, and 1993) and at Harvard Law School (1996). Recent publications include *Corporate Law* (4th ed, Kobundo, 2003, in Japanese), *Comparative Corporate Governance* (Oxford University Press, 1998, with Klaus Hopt et al (eds.)), and *Economics of Corporate Law* (University of Tokyo Press, 1998, with Yoshiro Miwa and Noriyuki Yanagawa (eds.), in Japanese).

Reinier Kraakman is the Ezra Ripley Thayer Professor of Law at Harvard Law School and a Fellow of the European Corporate Governance Institute. He has written numerous articles on corporate law and the economic analysis of corporate liability regimes. He teaches courses in corporate law, corporate finances, and seminars on the theory of corporate law and comparative corporate governance. He is the author, with William T. Allen and Guhan Subramanian, of *Commentaries and Cases in the Law of Business Corporations*, soon to appear in its third edition (Aspen, 2009). His more recent articles include *Law and the Rise of the Firm* (with Henry Hansmann and Richard Squire), 119 Harvard Law Review 1333, 2006, *Property, Contract, and Verification: The* Numerus Clausus *Problem and the Divisibility of Rights,* with Henry Hansmann, 31 Journal of Legal Studies S373, 2002, and *The Essential Role of Organizational Law*, with Henry Hansmann, 110 Yale Law Journal 387, 2000.

Edward Rock is the Saul A. Fox Distinguished Professor of Business Law at the University of Pennsylvania Law School. He also serves as co-director of the Institute for Law and Economics and has written widely on corporate law. He has been Visiting Professor at the Universities of Frankfurt am Main, Jerusalem, and Columbia and has practised law as a member of the Pennsylvania bar. Recent publications include *The Hanging Chads of Corporate Voting* (with Marcel Kahan), 96 Georgetown Law Journal 1227, 2008, and *Hedge Funds in Corporate Governance and Corporate Control* (with Marcel Kahan) 155 University of Pennsylvania Law Review 1021, 2007.

1

What is Corporate Law?

John Armour, Henry Hansmann, and
Reinier Kraakman

1.1 Introduction

What is the *common structure* of the law of business corporations—or, as it would be put in some jurisdictions, company law—across different national jurisdictions? Although this question is rarely asked by corporate law scholars, it is critically important for the comparative investigation of corporate law. Recent scholarship often emphasizes the divergence among European, American, and Japanese corporations in corporate governance, share ownership, capital markets, and business culture.[1] But, notwithstanding the very real differences across jurisdictions along these dimensions, the underlying uniformity of the corporate form is at least as impressive. Business corporations have a fundamentally similar set of legal characteristics—and face a fundamentally similar set of legal problems—in all jurisdictions.

Consider, in this regard, the basic legal characteristics of the business corporation. To anticipate our discussion below, there are five of these characteristics, most of which will be easily recognizable to anyone familiar with business affairs. They are: legal personality, limited liability, transferable shares, delegated management under a board structure, and investor ownership. These characteristics respond—in ways we will explore—to the economic exigencies of the large modern business enterprise. Thus, corporate law everywhere must, of necessity, provide for them. To be sure, there are other forms of business enterprise that lack one or more of these characteristics. But the remarkable fact—and the fact that

[1] See, e.g., Ronald J. Gilson and Mark J. Roe, *Understanding the Japanese Keiretsu: Overlaps Between Corporation Governance and Industrial Organization*, 102 YALE LAW JOURNAL 871 (1993); Mark J. Roe, *Some Differences in Corporation Structure in Germany, Japan, and the United States*, 102 YALE LAW JOURNAL 1927 (1993); Bernard S. Black and John C. Coffee, *Hail Britannia? Institutional Investor Behavior Under Limited Regulation*, 92 MICHIGAN LAW REVIEW 1997 (1994); COMPARATIVE CORPORATE GOVERNANCE: ESSAYS AND MATERIALS (Klaus J. Hopt and Eddy Wymeersch (eds.), 1997); and Mark J. Roe, POLITICAL DETERMINANTS OF CORPORATE GOVERNANCE (2003).

we wish to stress—is that, in market economies, almost all large-scale business firms adopt a legal form that possesses all five of the basic characteristics of the business corporation. Indeed, most small jointly-owned firms adopt this corporate form as well, although sometimes with deviations from one or more of the five basic characteristics to fit their special needs.

It follows that a principal function of corporate law is to provide business enterprises with a legal form that possesses these five core attributes. By making this form widely available and user-friendly, corporate law enables entrepreneurs to transact easily through the medium of the corporate entity, and thus lowers the costs of conducting business. Of course, the number of provisions that the typical corporation statute[2] devotes to defining the corporate form is likely to be only a small part of the statute as a whole. Nevertheless, these are the provisions that comprise the legal core of corporate law that is shared by every jurisdiction. In this chapter, we briefly explore the contracting efficiencies (some familiar and some not) that accompany these five features of the corporate form, and that, we believe, have helped to propel the worldwide diffusion of the corporate form.

As with corporate law itself, however, our principal focus in this book is not on establishing the corporate form per se. Rather, it is on a second, equally important function of corporate law: namely, reducing the ongoing costs of organizing business through the corporate form. Corporate law does this by facilitating coordination between participants in corporate enterprise, and by reducing the scope for value-reducing forms of opportunism among different constituencies. Indeed, much of corporate law can usefully be understood as responding to three principal sources of opportunism: conflicts between managers and shareholders, conflicts among shareholders, and conflicts between shareholders and the corporation's other constituencies, including creditors and employees. All three of these generic conflicts may usefully be characterized as what economists call 'agency problems.' Consequently, Chapter 2 examines these three agency problems, both in general and as they arise in the corporate context, and surveys the range of legal strategies that can be employed to ameliorate those problems.

The reader might object that these agency conflicts are not uniquely 'corporate'. After all, *any* form of jointly-owned enterprise must expect conflicts among its owners, managers, and third-party contractors. We agree; insofar as the corporation is only one of several legal forms for the jointly-owned firm, it faces the same generic agency problems that confront all jointly-owned firms. Nevertheless, the characteristics of this particular form matter a great deal, since it is the form that is chosen by most large-scale enterprises—and, as a practical matter, the only form that firms with widely dispersed ownership can choose in

---

[2] We use the term 'corporation statute' to refer to the general law that governs corporations, and not to a corporation's individual charter (or 'articles of incorporation', as that document is sometimes also called).

many jurisdictions.[3] Moreover, the unique features of this form determine the contours of its agency problems. To take an obvious example, the fact that shareholders enjoy limited liability—while, say, general partners in a partnership do not—has traditionally made creditor protection far more salient in corporate law than it is in partnership law. Similarly, the fact that corporate investors may trade their shares is the foundation of the anonymous trading stock market—an institution that has encouraged the separation of ownership from control, and so has sharpened the management-shareholder agency problem.

In this book, we explore the role of corporate law in minimizing agency problems—and thus, making the corporate form practicable—in the most important categories of corporate actions and decisions. More particularly, Chapters 3–9 address, respectively, seven categories of transactions and decisions that involve the corporation, its owners, its managers, and the other parties with whom it deals. Most of these categories of firm activity are, again, generic, rather than uniquely corporate. For example, Chapters 3 and 4 address governance mechanisms that operate over the firm's ordinary business decisions, whilst Chapter 5 turns to the checks that operate on the corporation's transactions with creditors. As before, however, although similar agency problems arise in similar contexts across all forms of jointly-owned enterprise, the response of corporate law turns in part on the unique legal features that characterize the corporate form.

Taken together, the latter seven chapters of our book cover nearly all of the important problems in corporate law. In each Chapter, we describe how the basic agency problems of the corporate form manifest themselves in the given category of corporate activity, and then explore the range of alternative legal responses that are available. We illustrate these alternative approaches with examples from the corporate law of various prominent jurisdictions. We explore the patterns of homogeneity and heterogeneity that appear. Where there are significant differences across jurisdictions, we seek to address both the sources and the consequences of those differences. Our examples are drawn principally from a handful of major representative jurisdictions, including France, Germany, Italy, Japan, the UK, and the U.S., though we also make reference to the laws of other jurisdictions to make special points.[4]

In emphasizing a strongly functional approach to the issues of comparative law, this book differs from some of the more traditional comparative law scholarship,

---

[3] Only the corporate form is available in many jurisdictions for firms that want access to the capital markets for *equity financing*. Some jurisdictions, however, permit the equity of non-corporate entities to trade in the public markets as well: for example, in the U.S., the equity securities of so-called 'master' limited partnerships and limited liability companies may be registered for public trading.

[4] We focus on developed, rather than developing, economies, because where foundational legal institutions, such as functioning courts and the protection of property rights, are absent or compromised, then the way in which corporate law responds to specific problems is less likely to make a difference to the real economy. A discussion of the ways in which such institutions can be engendered, or replicated by extra-legal means, is beyond the scope of our enquiry.

both in the field of corporate law and elsewhere.[5] We join an emerging tendency in comparative law scholarship by seeking to give a highly integrated view of the role and structure of corporate law that provides a clear framework within which to organize an understanding of individual systems, both alone and in comparison with each other.[6] Moreover, while comparative law scholarship often has a tendency to emphasize differences between jurisdictions, our approach is to focus on similarities. Doing so, we believe, illuminates an underlying commonality of structure that transcends national boundaries. It also provides an important perspective on the potential basis for the international integration of corporate law that is likely to take place as economic activity continues to become more global in scope in the decades to come.

We realize that the term 'functional', which we have used here and in our title, means different things to different people, and that some of the uses to which that term has been put in the past—particularly in the field of sociology—have made the term justifiably suspect. It would perhaps be more accurate to call our approach 'economic' rather than 'functional', though the sometimes tendentious use of economic argumentation in legal literature to support particular (generally laissez-faire) policy positions, as well as the tendency in economic analysis to neglect non-pecuniary motivations or assume an unrealistic degree of rationality in human action, have also caused many scholars—particularly outside the United States—to be as wary of 'economic analysis' as they are of 'functional analysis'. For the purposes at hand, however, we need not commit ourselves on fine points of social science methodology. We need simply note that the exigencies of commercial activity and organization present practical problems that have a rough similarity in developed market economies throughout the world. Our analysis is 'functional' in the sense that we organize discussion around the ways in which corporate laws respond to these problems, and the various forces that have led different jurisdictions to choose roughly similar—though by no means always the same—solutions to them.

That is not to say that our objective here is just to explore the commonality of corporate law across jurisdictions. Of equal importance, we wish to offer a *common language* and a general *analytic framework* with which to understand the purposes that can potentially be served by corporate law, and with which to compare and evaluate the efficacy of different legal regimes in serving those

[5] Compare, e.g., Arthur R. Pinto and Gustavo Visentini (eds.), THE LEGAL BASIS OF CORPORATE GOVERNANCE IN PUBLICLY HELD CORPORATIONS, A COMPARATIVE APPROACH (1998).

[6] Other examples of this trend include Dennis C. Mueller and B. Burcin Yurtoglu, *Country Legal Environments and Corporate Investment Performance*, 1 GERMAN ECONOMIC REVIEW 187 (2000); Rafael La Porta, Florencio Lopez-de-Silanes, Andrei Shleifer, and Robert W. Vishny, *Law and Finance*, 106 JOURNAL OF POLITICAL ECONOMY 1113 (1998); Henry Hansmann and Ugo Mattei, *The Functions of Trust Law: A Comparative Legal and Economic Analysis*, 73 NEW YORK UNIVERSITY LAW REVIEW 434 (1998); Curtis Milhaupt and Katharina Pistor, LAW AND CAPITALISM (2008); Konrad Zweigert and Hein Kötz, INTRODUCTION TO COMPARATIVE LAW (Tony Weir trans., 3rd ed., 1998); Ugo Mattei, COMPARATIVE LAW AND ECONOMICS (1997).

purposes.[7] Indeed, it is our hope that the analysis offered in this book will be of use not only to students of comparative law, but also to those who simply wish to have a more solid framework within which to view their own country's corporation law.

Likewise, we take no strong stand here in the current debate on the extent to which corporate law is or should be 'converging', much less on what it might converge to.[8] That is a subject on which reasonable minds can differ. Indeed, it is a subject on which the reasonable minds that have written this book sometimes differ.[9] Rather, we are seeking to set out a conceptual framework and a factual basis with which that and other important issues facing corporate law can be fruitfully explored.

1.2 What is a Corporation?

As we noted above, the five core structural characteristics of the business corporation are: (1) legal personality, (2) limited liability, (3) transferable shares, (4) centralized management under a board structure, and (5) shared ownership by contributors of capital. In virtually all economically important jurisdictions, there is a basic statute that provides for the formation of firms with all of these characteristics. As this pattern suggests, these characteristics have strongly complementary qualities for many firms. Together, they make the corporation

---

[7] In very general terms, our approach echoes that taken by Dean Robert Clark in his important treatise, CORPORATE LAW (1986), and Frank Easterbrook and Daniel Fischel, in their discussion of U.S. law, THE ECONOMIC STRUCTURE OF CORPORATE LAW (1991). However, our analysis differs from—and goes beyond—that offered by these and other commentators in several key respects. First, and most obviously, we present a comparative analysis that addresses the corporate law of multiple jurisdictions. Second, we provide an integrated functional overview that stresses the agency problems at the core of corporate law, rather than focusing on more particular legal institutions and solutions. Finally, we offer a more expansive account than do other commentators of the functions of central features of the corporate form such as limited liability and the governance structure of the corporate board. Our analysis, moreover, is informed not only by a comparative perspective across jurisdictions, but also, occasionally, by a comparative perspective across legal forms for business enterprise.

[8] Compare Lucian A. Bebchuk and Mark J. Roe, *A Theory of Path Dependence in Corporate Ownership and Governance*, 52 STANFORD LAW REVIEW 127 (1999); William M. Bratton and Joseph A. McCahery, *Comparative Corporate Governance and the Theory of the Firm: The Case Against Global Cross Reference*, 38 COLUMBIA JOURNAL OF TRANSNATIONAL LAW 213 (1999); John C. Coffee, *The Future as History: The Prospects for Global Convergence in Corporate Governance and its Significance*, 93 NORTHWESTERN UNIVERSITY LAW REVIEW 641 (1999); Ronald J. Gilson, *Globalizing Corporate Governance: Convergence of Form or Function*, 49 AMERICAN JOURNAL OF COMPARATIVE LAW 329 (2001); Amir N. Licht, *The Mother of All Path Dependencies: Toward a Cross-Cultural Theory of Corporate Governance Systems*, 26 DELAWARE JOURNAL OF CORPORATE LAW 147 (2001); Mathias M. Siems, CONVERGENCE IN SHAREHOLDER LAW (2007).

[9] The views of the authors of this chapter are briefly set out in Henry Hansmann and Reinier Kraakman, *The End of History for Corporate Law*, 89 GEORGETOWN LAW JOURNAL 439 (2001) and John Armour and Jeffrey N. Gordon, *The Berle-Means Corporation in the Twenty-First Century*, Working Paper (2008), at http://www.law.upenn.edu.

uniquely attractive for organizing productive activity. But these characteristics also generate tensions and tradeoffs that lend a distinctively corporate character to the agency problems that corporate law must address.

1.2.1 Legal personality

In the economics literature, a firm is often characterized as a 'nexus of contracts'. As commonly used, this description is ambiguous. It is often invoked simply to emphasize that most of the important relationships within a firm—including, in particular, those among the firm's owners, managers, and employees—are essentially contractual in character, and hence based on consent, rather than involving some form of extracontractual command-and-control authority. This is an important insight, but it does not distinguish firms from other networks of contractual relationships. It is perhaps more accurate to describe a firm as a 'nexus *for* contracts', in the sense that a firm serves, fundamentally, as the common counterparty in numerous contracts with suppliers, employees, and customers, coordinating the actions of these multiple persons through exercise of its contractual rights.[10] The first and most important contribution of corporate law, as of other forms of organizational law, is to permit a firm to serve this role by permitting the firm to serve as a single contracting party that is distinct from the various individuals who own or manage the firm. In so doing, it enhances the ability of these individuals to engage together in joint projects.

The core element of the firm as a nexus for contracts is what the civil law refers to as 'separate patrimony'. This involves the demarcation of a pool of assets that are distinct from other assets owned, singly or jointly, by the firm's owners (the shareholders),[11] and of which the firm in itself, acting through its designated managers, is viewed in law as being the owner. The firm's rights of ownership over its designated assets include the rights to use the assets, to sell them, and—of particular importance—to make them available for attachment by its creditors. Conversely, because these assets are conceived as belonging to the firm, rather than the firm's owners, they are *unavailable* for attachment by the personal creditors of these persons. The core function of this separate patrimony has been termed '*entity shielding*', to emphasize that it involves shielding the assets of the entity—the corporation—from the creditors of the entity's owners.[12]

---

[10] The characterization of a firm as a 'nexus of contracts' originates with Michael Jensen and William Meckling, *Theory of the Firm: Managerial Behavior, Agency Costs and Ownership Structure*, 3 Journal of Financial Economics 305 (1976), building on Armen Alchian and Harold Demsetz, *Production, Information Costs, and Economic Organization*, 62 American Economic Review 777 (1972).

[11] We use the term 'owners' simply to refer to the group who have the entitlement to control the firm's assets.

[12] The term 'entity shielding' derives from Henry Hansmann, Reinier Kraakman, and Richard Squire, *Law and the Rise of the Firm*, 119 Harvard Law Review 1333 (2006). The centrality of entity shielding to organizational law is explored in Henry Hansmann and Reinier Kraakman,

Where corporations are concerned, entity shielding involves two relatively distinct rules of law. The first is a priority rule that grants to creditors of the firm, as security for the firm's debts, a claim on the firm's assets that is prior to the claims of the personal creditors of the firm's owners. This rule is shared by all modern legal forms for enterprise organization, including partnerships.[13] The consequence of this priority rule is that a firm's assets are, as a default rule of law,[14] automatically made available for the enforcement of contractual liabilities entered into in the name of the firm.[15] By thus bonding the firm's contractual commitments, the rule makes these commitments credible.

The second component of entity shielding—a rule of 'liquidation protection'— provides that the individual owners of the corporation (the shareholders) cannot withdraw their share of firm assets at will, thus forcing partial or complete liquidation of the firm, nor can the personal creditors of an individual owner foreclose on the owner's share of firm assets.[16] This liquidation protection rule serves to protect the going concern value of the firm against destruction either by individual shareholders or their creditors.[17] In contrast to the priority rule just mentioned, it is not found in some other standard legal forms for enterprise organization, such as the partnership.[18] Legal entities, such as the business corporation, that are characterized by both these rules—priority for business creditors and liquidation protection—can therefore be thought of as having 'strong form' entity shielding, as opposed to the 'weak form' entity shielding found in partnerships, which are characterized only by the priority rule and not by liquidation protection.

For a firm to serve effectively as a contracting party, two other types of rules are also needed. First, there must be rules specifying to third parties the individuals who have authority to buy and sell assets in the name of the firm, and to enter into contracts that are bonded by those assets.[19] Whilst of course participants in

---

The Essential Role of Organizational Law, 110 YALE LAW JOURNAL 387 (2000), where the attribute was labelled 'affirmative asset partitioning'.

[13] While even unregistered common law partnerships are subject to this priority rule, the civil law recognizes a class of unregistered 'partnerships' that lack this rule of priority. In effect, such partnerships are just special forms for co-ownership of assets rather than distinct entities for purposes of contracting.

[14] On default rules, see *infra* 1.4.1.

[15] The effect is the same as if the firm's owners had themselves entered into a joint contract and granted non-recourse security over certain personal assets to the counterparty, as opposed to transferring those assets to the corporate patrimony, and then procuring the company to enter into the contract.

[16] Hansmann and Kraakman, *supra* note 12, at 411–13.

[17] Edward B. Rock and Michael L. Wachter, *Waiting for the Omelet to Set: Match-Specific Assets and Minority Oppression in Close Corporations*, 24 JOURNAL OF CORPORATION LAW 913, 918–20 (1999); Margaret M. Blair, *Locking in Capital: What Corporate Law Achieved for Business Organizers in the Nineteenth Century*, 51 UCLA LAW REVIEW 387, 441–9 (2003).

[18] However, it is possible in many jurisdictions to effect liquidation protection by agreement amongst the owners of a partnership.

[19] John Armour and Michael J. Whincop, *The Proprietary Foundations of Corporate Law*, 27 OXFORD JOURNAL OF LEGAL STUDIES 429, 441–2 (2007).

a firm are free to specify the delegation of authority by contract amongst themselves, background rules are needed—beyond such contractual agreement—to deal with situations where agents induce third parties to rely on the mere appearance of their authority. Such rules differ according to organizational form. The particular rules of authority that characterize the corporation are treated below as a separate core characteristic, 'delegated management'. They provide that a board of directors, as opposed to individual owners, has power to bind the company in contract.[20]

Second, there must be rules specifying the procedures by which both the firm and its counterparties can bring lawsuits on the contracts entered into in the name of the firm. Corporations are subject to rules that make such suits easy to bring as a procedural matter. In particular, they eliminate any need to name, or serve notice on, the firm's individual owners—procedures that characterize the rules of suit that, for example, characterized the Anglo-American partnership until the late 19th century.

The outcomes achieved by each of these three types of rules—entity shielding, authority, and procedure—require dedicated legal doctrines to be effective, in the sense that, absent such doctrine, they could not feasibly be replicated simply by contracting among a business's owners and their suppliers and customers. Entity shielding doctrine is needed to create common expectations, among a firm and its various present and potential creditors, concerning the effect that a contract between a firm and one of its creditors will have on the security available to the firm's other creditors.[21] Rules governing the allocation of authority are needed to establish common expectations as to who has authority to transfer rights relating to corporate assets *prior to* entering into a contract for their transfer.[22] And procedures for lawsuits need to be specified by the state, whose third-party authority is invoked by those procedures. This need for special rules of law distinguishes these three types of rules from the other basic elements of the corporate form discussed here, which could in theory be crafted by contract even if the law did not provide for a standard form of enterprise organization that embodies them.[23]

---

[20] Associated rules—such as the doctrine of *ultra vires*—may also prescribe limits as to the extent to which the board may bind the company in contract.

[21] To establish the priority of business creditors by contract, a firm's owners would have to contract with its business creditors to include subordination provisions, with respect to business assets, in all contracts between individual owners and individual creditors. Not only would such provisions be cumbersome to draft and costly to monitor, but they would be subject to a high degree of moral hazard—an individual owner could breach her promise to subordinate the claims of her personal creditors on the firm's assets with impunity, since this promise would be unenforceable against personal creditors who were not party to the bargain. See Hansmann and Kraakman, *supra* note 12, at 407–9.

[22] To leave questions of authority to be determined simply by agreement between the owners of the firm will make it costly for parties wishing to deal with the firm to discover whether authority has in fact been granted in relation to any particular transaction. Authority rules must therefore trade off contracting parties' 'due diligence' costs against preserving flexibility for owners to customize their allocations of authority. See Armour and Whincop, *supra* note 19, at 442–7.

[23] See Hansmann and Kraakman, *supra* note 12, at 407–9.

The concept of the 'separate legal personality' of the corporation, as understood in the legal literature, is in our terms a convenient heuristic formula for describing organizational forms which enjoy the benefit of each of the three foregoing 'foundational' rule types. Starting from the premise that the company is itself a person, in the eyes of the law, it is straightforward to deduce that it should be capable of entering into contracts and owning its own property; capable of delegating authority to agents; and capable of suing and being sued in its own name. For expository convenience, we use the term 'legal personality' to refer to organizational forms—such as the corporation—which share these three attributes. However, we should make clear that legal personality in the lawyer's sense is not in itself an attribute that is a necessary precondition for the existence of any—or indeed all—of these rules,[24] but merely a handy label for a package that conveniently bundles them together. Moreover, although it is common in the legal literature to extend syllogistic deduction from the premise of legal personality to the existence of characteristics beyond the three foundational features we have described in this section, we see no functional rationale that compels this.

1.2.2 Limited liability

The corporate form effectively imposes a default term in contracts between a firm and its creditors whereby the creditors are limited to making claims against assets that are held in the name of ('owned by') firm itself, and have no claim against assets that the firm's shareholders hold in their own names. This rule of 'limited liability' has not, historically, always been associated with the corporate form. Some important corporate jurisdictions long made unlimited shareholder liability for corporate debts the governing rule.[25] Nevertheless, today limited liability has become a nearly universal feature of the corporate form. This evolution indicates strongly the value of limited liability as a contracting tool and financing device.

Limited liability is a (strong) form of 'owner shielding' that is effectively the converse of the 'entity shielding' described above as a component of legal personality.[26] Entity shielding protects the assets of the firm from the creditors of

---

[24] Thus, a common law partnership, which is commonly said by lawyers to lack legal personality, can under English law enjoy each of the three foundational features described in this section: see §§ 31, 33, 39 Partnership Act 1890 (UK); Armour and Whincop, *supra* note 19, at 460–1; *Burnes v. Pennell* (1849) 2 HL Cas 497, 521; 9 ER 1181, 1191; PD 7, para. 5A Civil Procedure Rules (UK).

[25] Limited liability did not become a standard feature of the English law of joint stock companies until the mid-19th century, and in the American state of California shareholders bore unlimited personal liability for corporation obligations until 1931. See Paul L. Davies, GOWER AND DAVIES' PRINCIPLES OF MODERN COMPANY LAW 40–6 (6th ed., 1997); Phillip Blumberg, *Limited Liability and Corporate Groups*, 11 JOURNAL OF CORPORATE LAW 573 (1986).

[26] The term comes from Hansmann, Kraakman, and Squire, *supra* note 12. Note that the owner shielding established by a rule of limited liability is less fundamental than entity shielding, in the sense that it can be achieved by contract, without statutory fiat. *Id.*; Hansmann and Kraakman, *supra* note 12.

the firm's owners, while limited liability protects the assets of the firm's owners from the claims of the firm's creditors. Together, they set up a regime of 'asset partitioning' whereby business assets are pledged as security to business creditors, while the personal assets of the business's owners are reserved for the owners' personal creditors. (By 'creditors' we mean here, broadly, all persons who have a contractual claim on the firm, including employees, suppliers, and customers.) This partitioning can increase the value of both types of assets as security for debt. Creditors of the firm commonly have a comparative advantage in evaluating and monitoring the value of the firm's assets, while an owner's personal creditors are likely to have a comparative advantage in evaluating and monitoring the individual's personal assets. As a consequence, corporate-type asset partitioning can reduce the overall cost of capital to the firm and its owners.

A related aspect of asset partitioning is that it permits firms to isolate different lines of business for the purpose of obtaining credit. By separately incorporating, as subsidiaries, distinct ventures or lines of business, the assets associated with each venture can conveniently be pledged as security just to the creditors who deal with that venture.[27] Those creditors are commonly well positioned to assess and keep track of the value of those assets, but may have little ability to monitor the parent firm's other ventures.

By virtue of asset partitioning—entity shielding and limited liability—the formation of corporations and subsidiary corporations can also be used as a means of sharing the risks of transactions with the firm's creditors, in situations in which the latter are in a better position to identify or bear those risks in relation to the assets shielded by the corporate form. Thus, use of the corporate form can assist in raising debt finance even in situations where there is no need to raise additional equity capital, as in the case of the parent company of a wholly owned subsidiary.[28]

Asset partitioning also permits flexibility in the allocation of risk and return between equity-holders and debt-holders, greatly simplifies the administration of both business and individual bankruptcy, and—by isolating the value of the firm from the personal financial affairs of the firm's owners—facilitates tradability of the firm's shares, which is the third characteristic of the corporate form.[29]

Finally, asset partitioning, and limited liability in particular, plays an important function—but more subtle and less often remarked—in facilitating delegated

---

[27] Conversely, asset partitioning can also be used to reduce transparency as to the location of assets. This concern underlies an important part of corporate law's creditor-oriented rules: see *infra* 5.2.1.3.

[28] See, e.g., Richard Posner, *The Rights of Creditors of Affiliated Corporations*, 43 UNIVERSITY OF CHICAGO LAW REVIEW 499 (1976); Henry Hansmann and Reinier Kraakman, *Toward Unlimited Shareholder Liability for Corporate Torts*, 100 YALE LAW JOURNAL 1879 (1991).

[29] Whilst strong form entity shielding seems essential for free tradability of shares (see Hansmann and Kraakman, *supra* note 12), limited liability does not: so long as shareholder liability for a firm's debts is pro rata rather than joint and several, free tradability of shares is feasible with unlimited personal shareholder liability for corporate debts (see Hansmann and Kraakman, *supra* note 28).

management, which is the fourth of the core characteristics of the corporate form. In effect, by shifting downside business risk from shareholders to creditors, limited liability enlists creditors as monitors of the firm's managers, a task which they may be in a better position to perform than are the shareholders in a firm in which share ownership is widely dispersed.[30]

We should emphasize that, when we refer to limited liability, we mean specifically limited liability *in contract*—that is, limited liability to creditors who have contractual claims on the corporation. The compelling reasons for limited liability in contract generally do not extend to limited liability *in tort*—that is, to persons who are unable to adjust the terms on which they extend credit to the corporation, such as third parties who have been injured as a consequence of the corporation's negligent behavior.[31] Limited liability to such persons is arguably not a necessary feature of the corporate form, and perhaps not even a socially valuable one, as we discuss more thoroughly in Chapter 5.

1.2.3 Transferable shares

Fully transferable shares in ownership are yet another basic characteristic of the business corporation that distinguishes the corporation from the partnership and various other standard-form legal entities. Transferability permits the firm to conduct business uninterruptedly as the identity of its owners changes, thus avoiding the complications of member withdrawal that are common among, for example, partnerships, cooperatives, and mutuals.[32] This in turn enhances the liquidity of shareholders' interests and makes it easier for shareholders to construct and maintain diversified investment portfolios.

Fully transferable shares do not necessarily mean *freely tradable* shares. Even if shares are transferable, they may not be tradable without restriction in public markets, but rather just transferable among limited groups of individuals or with the approval of the current shareholders or of the corporation. Free tradability maximizes the liquidity of shareholdings and the ability of shareholders to diversify their investments. It also gives the firm maximal flexibility in raising capital. For these reasons, all jurisdictions provide for free tradability for at least one class of corporation. However, free tradability can also make it difficult to maintain negotiated arrangements for sharing control and participating in management. Consequently, all jurisdictions also provide mechanisms for restricting

---

[30] See Julian Franks, Colin Mayer, and Luc Renneboog, *Who Disciplines Management in Poorly Performing Companies?*, 10 JOURNAL OF FINANCIAL INTERMEDIATION 209, 225–7 (2001); Hansmann and Kraakman, *supra* note 12.

[31] This category of 'non-adjusting' creditors might include some persons whose relationship with the firm is, in formal terms, contractual. Cf. Lucian Ayre Bebchuk and Jesse M. Fried, *The Uneasy Case for the Priority of Secured Claims in Bankruptcy*, 105 YALE LAW JOURNAL 857, at 885–6 (1996).

[32] See Henry Hansmann, THE OWNERSHIP OF ENTERPRISE 152–5 (1996).

transferability. Sometimes this is done by means of a separate statute, while other jurisdictions simply provide for restraints on transferability as an option under a general corporation statute.

As a matter of terminology, we will refer to corporations with freely tradable shares as 'open' or 'public' corporations, and we will correspondingly use the terms 'closed' or 'private' corporations to refer to corporations that have restrictions on the tradability of their shares. In addition to this general division, two other distinctions are important. First, the shares of open corporations may be listed for trading on an organized securities exchange, in which case we will refer to the firm as a 'listed' or 'publicly traded' corporation, in contrast to an 'unlisted' corporation. Second, a company's shares may be held by a small number of individuals whose interpersonal relationships are important to the management of the firm, in which case we refer to it as 'closely held', as opposed to 'widely held'. It is common to speak, loosely, as if all companies can be categorized as either 'public' or 'close' corporations, bundling these distinctions together (and the widely-used term 'close corporation' itself embodies this ambiguity, being used sometimes to mean 'closed corporation', sometimes to mean 'closely held corporation', and sometimes to mean both). But not all companies with freely-tradable shares in fact have widely held share ownership, or are listed on securities exchanges. Conversely, it is common in some jurisdictions to find corporations whose shares are not freely tradable but that nonetheless have hundreds or thousands of shareholders, and that consequently have little in common with a typical closely held corporation that has only a handful of shareholders, some or all of whom are from the same family.

Transferability of shares, as we have already suggested, is closely connected both with the liquidation protection that is a feature of strong form legal personality, and with limited liability. Absent either of these rules, the creditworthiness of the firm as a whole could change, perhaps fundamentally, as the identity of its shareholders changed. Consequently, the value of shares would be difficult for potential purchasers to judge.[33] Perhaps more importantly, a seller of shares could impose negative or positive externalities on his fellow shareholders depending on the wealth of the person to whom he chose to sell. It is therefore not surprising that strong form legal personality, limited liability, and transferable shares tend to go together, and are all features of the standard corporate form everywhere. This is in contrast to the conventional general partnership, which lacks all of these features.

1.2.4 Delegated management with a board structure

Standard legal forms for enterprise organization differ in their allocation of control rights, including the authority to bind the firm to contracts (discussed above),

---

[33] Paul Halpern, Michael Trebilcock, and Stuart Turnbull, *An Economic Analysis of Limited Liability in Corporation Law*, 30 UNIVERSITY OF TORONTO LAW JOURNAL 117, 136–8 (1980).

the authority to exercise the powers granted to the firm by its contracts, and the authority to direct the uses made of assets owned by the firm.[34] As a default rule, the general partnership form grants power to a majority of partners to manage the firm in the ordinary course of business; more fundamental decisions require unanimity. Both aspects of this allocation are unworkable for business corporations with numerous and constantly changing owners. Consequently, corporate law typically vests principal authority over corporate affairs in a board of directors or similar committee organ that is periodically elected, exclusively or primarily, by the firm's shareholders. More specifically, business corporations are distinguished by a governance structure in which all but the most fundamental decisions are delegated to a board of directors that has four basic features.[35]

First, the board is, at least as a formal matter, separate from the operational managers of the corporation. The nature of this separation varies according to whether the board has one or two tiers. In two-tier boards, top corporate officers occupy the board's second (managing) tier, but are generally absent from the first (supervisory) tier, which is at least nominally independent from the firm's hired officers (i.e. from the firm's senior managerial employees). In single-tier boards, in contrast, hired officers may be members of, and even dominate, the board itself. Regardless of the actual allocation of power between a firm's directors and officers, the legal distinction between them formally divides all corporate decisions that do not require shareholder approval into those requiring approval by the board of directors and those that can be made by the firm's hired officers on their own authority. This formal distinction between the board and hired officers facilitates a separation between, on the one hand, initiation and execution of business decisions, which is the province of hired officers, and on the other hand the monitoring and ratification of decisions, and the hiring of the officers themselves, which are the province of the board. That separation serves as a useful check on the quality of decision-making by hired officers.[36] It also performs

---

[34] We have already observed that an important precondition for a firm to serve as a nexus for contracts is a rule designating, for the benefit of third parties, the individuals who have authority to enter into contracts that bind the firm and its assets (*supra*, text accompanying notes 19–20). Because there is often overlap in practice between the scope of such external authority and the internal division of power to control assets, the latter, unlike the former, cannot be based purely on agreement between participants in the firm, but rather must be designated to some degree by rules of law. Because the underlying problem is one of notice to third parties, the law governing closely held firms often leaves these matters to be designated at will in the firm's charter, while for widely held firms, in which it is advantageous to let public shareholders and creditors know the allocation of authority without having to read the charter, the law is generally more rigid in designating the allocation of authority.

[35] This is not to say that other legal entities, such as partnerships, business trusts, or limited liability companies, cannot have a board structure similar to that of a typical corporation; in fact, they often do. But those forms, unlike the corporation form, do not presume a board of directors as a matter of law. Consequently, they bear the burden of placing third parties on notice that authority to commit the firm differs from the pattern established by the law as a default rule.

[36] See Eugene Fama and Michael Jensen, *Agency Problems and Residual Claims*, 26 JOURNAL OF LAW AND ECONOMICS 327 (1983).

the key function—noted earlier—of permitting third parties to rely on a well-defined institution to formally bind the firm in its transactions with outsiders.

Second, the board of a corporation is elected—at least in substantial part—by the firm's shareholders. The obvious utility of this approach is to help assure that the board remains responsive to the interests of the firm's owners, who bear the costs and benefits of the firm's decisions and whose interests, unlike those of other corporate constituencies, are not strongly protected by contract. This requirement of an elected board distinguishes the corporate form from other legal forms, such as nonprofit corporations or business trusts, that permit or require a board structure, but do not require election of the board by the firm's (beneficial) owners.

Third, though largely or entirely chosen by the firm's shareholders, the board is formally distinct from them. This separation economizes on the costs of decision-making by avoiding the need to inform the firm's ultimate owners and obtain their consent for all but the most fundamental decisions regarding the firm. It also permits the board to serve as a mechanism for protecting the interests of minority shareholders and other corporate constituencies, in ways we will explore in Chapter 4.

Fourth, the board ordinarily has multiple members. This structure—as opposed, for example, to a structure concentrating authority in a single trustee, as in many private trusts—facilitates mutual monitoring and checks idiosyncratic decision-making. However, there are exceptions. Many corporation statutes permit business planners to dispense with a collective board in favor of a single general director or one-person board[37]—the evident reason being that, for a very small corporation, most of the board's legal functions, including its service as shareholder representative and focus of liability, can be discharged effectively by a single elected director who also serves as the firm's principal manager.

1.2.5 Investor ownership

There are two key elements in the ownership of a firm, as we use the term 'ownership' here: the right to control the firm, and the right to receive the firm's net earnings. The law of business corporations is principally designed to facilitate the organization of investor-owned firms—that is, firms in which both elements of ownership are tied to investment of capital in the firm. More specifically, in an investor-owned firm, both the right to participate in control—which generally involves voting in the election of directors and voting to approve major transactions—and the right to receive the firm's residual earnings, or profits, are typically proportional to the amount of capital contributed to the firm. Business

---

[37] This is true not only of most statutes designed principally for nonpublic corporations, such as France's SARL (Art. L. 223–18 Code de Commerce) and SAS (Art. L. 227–6 Code de Commerce) and Germany's GmbH (§ 6 GmbH-Gesetz), but also of the general corporate laws in the UK (§ 154(1) Companies Act 2006), in Italy (Article 2380–2 Civil Code), and in the U.S. state of Delaware, § 141(b) Delaware General Corporation Law.

corporation statutes universally provide for this allocation of control and earnings as the default rule.

There are other forms of ownership that play an important role in contemporary economies, and other bodies of organizational law—including other bodies of
corporate law—that are specifically designed to facilitate the formation of those
other types of firms.[38] For example, cooperative corporation statutes—which
provide for all of the four features of the corporate form just described except
for transferable shares, and often permit the latter as an option as well—allocate
voting power and shares in profits proportionally to acts of patronage, which may
be the amount of inputs supplied to the firm (in the case of a producer cooperative), or the amount of the firm's products purchased from the firm (in the case
of a consumer cooperative). Indeed, business corporations are effectively a special
kind of producer cooperative, in which control and profits are tied to supply of a
particular type of input, namely capital. As a consequence, business corporations
could, in principle, be formed under a well-designed general cooperative corporation statute. But the law provides, instead, a special statutory form for corporations owned by investors of capital ('capital cooperatives', as we might think of
them).[39]

This specialization follows from the dominant role that investor-owned firms
have come to play in contemporary economies, and the consequent advantages
of having a form that is specialized to the particular needs of such firms, and that
signals clearly to all interested parties the particular character of the firm with
which they are dealing. The dominance of investor ownership among large firms,
in turn, reflects several conspicuous efficiency advantages of that form. One is
that, among the various participants in the firm, investors are often the most
difficult to protect simply by contractual means.[40] Another is that investors of
capital have (or, through the design of their shares, can be induced to have) highly
homogeneous interests among themselves, hence reducing—though definitely
not eliminating—the potential for costly conflict among those who share governance of the firm.[41]

Specialization to investor ownership is yet another respect in which the law
of business corporations differs from the law of partnership. The partnership
form typically does not presume that ownership is tied to contribution of capital, and though it is often used in that fashion, it is also commonly used to
assign ownership of the firm in whole or in part to contributors of labor or of

[38] For a discussion of the varieties of forms of ownership found in contemporary economies, of
their respective economic roles, and of the relationship between these forms and the different bodies of organizational law that govern them, see Hansmann, *supra* note 32.

[39] Cooperative corporation statutes, in turn, commonly prohibit the grant of ownership
shares—voting rights and rights to a share of profits—to persons who simply contribute capital to
the firm, thus preventing the formation of investor-owned firms under the cooperative corporation
statutes.

[40] See, e.g., Oliver Williamson, *Corporate Governance*, 93 YALE LAW JOURNAL 1197 (1984).

[41] See Hansmann, *supra* note 32, Ch. 4.

other factors of production—as in partnerships of lawyers and other service professionals, or simply in the prototypical two-person partnership in which one partner supplies labor and the other capital. As a consequence, the business corporation is less flexible than the partnership in terms of assigning ownership. To be sure, with sufficient special contracting and manipulation of the form, ownership shares in a business corporation can be granted to contributors of labor or other factors of production, or in proportion to consumption of the firm's services. Moreover, as the corporate form has evolved, it has achieved greater flexibility in assigning ownership, either by permitting greater deviation from the default rules in the basic corporate form (e.g., through restrictions on share ownership or transfer), or by developing a separate and more adaptable form for close corporations. Nevertheless, the default rules of corporate law are generally designed for investor ownership, and deviation from this pattern can be awkward. The complex arrangements for sharing rights to earnings, assets, and control between entrepreneurs and investors in high-tech start-up firms offer a familiar example.[42]

Sometimes corporate law itself deviates from the assumption of investor ownership to permit or require that persons other than investors of capital—for example, creditors or employees—participate to some degree in either control or net earnings or both. Worker codetermination is a conspicuous example. The wisdom and means of providing for such non-investor participation in firms that are otherwise investor-owned remains one of the basic controversies in corporate law. We address this subject further in Chapter 4.

Most jurisdictions also have one or more statutory forms—such as the U.S. nonprofit corporation, the civil law foundation and association, and the UK company limited by guarantee—that provide for formation of nonprofit firms. These are firms in which no person may participate simultaneously in both the right to control and the right to residual earnings (which is to say, the firms have no owners). While nonprofit organizations, like cooperatives, are sometimes labelled 'corporations', however, they will not be within the specific focus of our attention here. Thus, when we use the term 'corporation' in this book, we refer only to the business corporation, and not to other types of incorporated entities. When there is potential for ambiguity, we will explicitly use the term 'business corporation' to make specific reference to the investor-owned company that is our principal focus.

1.3 Sources of Corporate Law

All jurisdictions with well-developed market economies have a least one core statute that establishes a basic corporate form with the five characteristics

---

[42] Stephen N. Kaplan and Per Strömberg, *Financial Contracting Theory Meets the Real World: An Empirical Analysis of Venture Capital Contracts*, 70 REVIEW OF ECONOMIC STUDIES 281 (2003).

described above, and that is designed particularly to permit the formation of public corporations—that is, corporations with freely tradable shares. Nevertheless, corporate law as we understand it here generally extends well beyond the bounds of this core statute.

1.3.1 Special and partial corporate forms

First, major jurisdictions commonly have at least one distinct statutory form specialized for the formation of closed corporations. These forms—the French SARL, the German GmbH, the Italian Srl, the Japanese close corporation, the American close corporation and (more recent) limited liability company, and the UK private company[43]—typically exhibit all of the canonical features of the corporate form. They differ from open companies chiefly because their shares, though transferable at least in principle, are presumed—and in some cases required—not to trade freely in a public market. Sometimes these forms also permit departure from one of our five core characteristics—delegated management—by permitting elimination of the board in favor of direct management by shareholders.[44] The statutes creating these forms also commonly permit, and sometimes facilitate, special allocations of control, earnings rights, and rights to employment among shareholders that go beyond those permitted in the core public corporation statute.

Second, some jurisdictions have, in addition to these special closed corporation forms, *quasi*-corporate statutory forms that can be used to form business corporations with all of our five core characteristics, though some of these characteristics must be added by contract. One example is the limited liability partnership, which has been provided for recently in the law of the U.S. and some European jurisdictions. This form simply grafts limited liability onto the traditional general partnership. U.S. law now allows the partnership to have something close to strong form entity shielding (by limiting the rights of partners or their creditors to force liquidation).[45] Consequently, with appropriate governance provisions in the partnership agreement, it is effectively possible to create a closed corporation as a limited liability partnership.

Another example is offered by the U.S. statutory business trust. The statutory business trust provides for (unambiguous) strong form legal personality and limited liability, but leaves all elements of internal organization to be specified in the organization's governing instrument (charter), failing even to provide statutory default rules for most such matters.[46] With appropriate charter provisions, a

---

[43] In the case of the UK private company, the standard form is provided not by a separate statute, but by a range of provisions in a single statute with differential application to public and private companies.

[44] See *supra* note 37.

[45] See Hansmann, Kraakman and Squire, *supra* note 12, at 1391–4.

[46] It differs from the common law private trust, from which it evolved, principally in providing unambiguously for limited liability for the trust's beneficiaries even if they exercise control.

statutory business trust can be made the equivalent of a public corporation, with the trust's beneficiaries in the role of shareholders.

The analysis we offer in this book extends to all these special and quasi-corporate forms insofar as they display the five core corporate characteristics.

1.3.2 Other bodies of law

There are bodies of law that, at least in some jurisdictions, are embodied in statutes or decisional law that are separate from the core corporation statutes, and from the special and quasi-corporation statutes just described, but that are nonetheless concerned with particular core characteristics of the corporate form as we define them here. Insofar as they are so concerned, we view them functionally as part of corporate law.

To begin, the German law of groups, or *Konzernrecht,* qualifies limited liability and limits the discretion of boards of directors in corporations that are closely related through cross ownership, seeking to protect the creditors and minority shareholders of corporations with controlling shareholders. Although the *Konzernrecht*—described in more detail in Chapters 5 and 6—is embodied in statutory and decisional law that is formally distinct from the corporation statutes, it is clearly an integral part of German corporate law. Similarly, the statutory rules in many jurisdictions that require employee representation on a corporation's board of directors—such as, conspicuously, the German law of codetermination—qualify as elements of corporate law, even though they occasionally originate outside the principal corporate law statutes, because they impose a detailed structure of employee participation on the boards of directors of large corporations.

Securities laws in many jurisdictions, including conspicuously the U.S., have strong effects on corporate governance through rules mandating disclosure and sometimes, as well, regulating sale and resale of corporate securities, mergers and acquisitions, and corporate elections. Stock exchange rules, which can regulate numerous aspects of the internal affairs of exchange-listed firms, can also serve as an additional source of corporate law, as can other forms of self-regulation, such as the UK's City Code on Takeovers and Mergers.[47] These supplemental sources of law are necessarily part of the overall structure of corporate law, and we shall be concerned here with all of them.

---

[47] We term such self-regulation a source of 'law' in part because it is commonly supported, directly or indirectly, by law in the narrow sense. The self-regulatory authority of the American stock exchanges, for example, is both reinforced and constrained by the U.S. Securities Exchange Act and the administrative rules promulgated by the Securities and Exchange Commission under that Act. Similarly, the authority of the UK's Takeover Panel was supported indirectly until 2006 by the recognition that if its rulings were not observed, formal regulation would follow. Since 2006, it has been directly supported by formal statutory authority in 2006 (Part 28 Companies Act 2006 (UK)), and so is no longer, strictly speaking, 'self-regulatory'.

There are many constraints imposed on companies by bodies of law designed to serve objectives that are, in general, independent of the form taken by the organizations they affect. While we will not explore these bodies in general, we will sometimes discuss them where they are specifically tailored for the corporate form in ways that have important effects on corporate structure and conduct. Bankruptcy law—or 'insolvency law', as it is termed in some jurisdictions—is an example. Bankruptcy effects a shift in the ownership of the firm from one group of investors to another—from shareholders to creditors. By providing creditors with an ultimate sanction against defaulting firms, it casts a shadow over firms' relations with their creditors, and affects the extent to which creditors may need generalized protections in corporate law. We thus consider the role of bankruptcy law in Chapter 5. Tax law also affects directly the internal governance of corporations at various points; the U.S. denial of deductibility from corporate income, for tax purposes, of executive compensation in excess of $1 million unless it is in the form of incentive pay, discussed in Chapter 3, is a clear example.[48] And, beyond providing for board representation of employees, labor law in some countries—as emphasized in Chapter 4—involves employees or unions in the corporate decision-making process, as in requirements that works councils or other workers' organs be consulted prior to taking specified types of actions.

1.4 Law Versus Contract in Corporate Affairs

The relationships among the participants in a corporation are, to an important degree, contractual. The principal contract that binds them is the corporation's *charter* (or 'articles of association' or 'constitution', as it is termed in some jurisdictions). The charter sets out the basic terms of the relationship among the firm's shareholders, and between the shareholders and the firm's directors and other managers.[49] By explicit or implicit reference, the charter can also become part of the contract between the firm and its employees or creditors. Some or all of a corporation's shareholders may, in addition, be bound by one or more shareholders' agreements.

At the same time, corporations are the subject of the large body of law whose various sources we have just reviewed. That body of law is the principal focus of this book. Before examining the details of that law, however, we must address a fundamental—and surprisingly difficult—question: What role does this law play? As we have already seen, with the exception of legal personality, the defining elements of the corporate form could in theory be established simply by contract.

[48] § 162(m) Internal Revenue Code.
[49] The charter may be supplemented by a separate set of bylaws, which commonly govern less fundamental matters and are subject to different—generally more flexible—amendment rules than is the charter.

And the same is true of most of the other rules of law that we examine throughout this book. If those rules of law did not exist, the relationships they establish could still be created by means of contract, just by placing similar provisions in the organization's charter. This was, in fact, the approach taken by the numerous unincorporated joint stock companies formed in England during the 18th and early 19th centuries, before incorporation became widely available in 1844. Those companies obtained their legal personality from partnership and trust law, and created the rest of their corporate structure—including limited liability—by means of contract.[50] Why, then, do we today have, in every advanced economy, elaborate statutes providing numerous detailed rules for the internal governance of corporations?

1.4.1 Mandatory laws versus default provisions

In addressing this question, it is important to distinguish between legal provisions that are merely default rules, in the sense that they govern only if the parties do not explicitly provide for something different, and laws that are mandatory, leaving parties no option but to conform to them.[51]

A significant part of corporate law—more in some jurisdictions, less in others—consists of default provisions.[52] To this extent, corporate law simply offers a standard form contract that the parties can adopt, at their option, in whole or in part. A familiar advantage of such a legally provided standard form is that it simplifies contracting among the parties involved, requiring that they specify only those elements of their relationship that deviate from the standard terms. Corporate law's provision of such standard terms as default is thereby seen in economic terms as a 'public good'. Default provisions can serve this function best if they are 'majoritarian' in content—that is, if they reflect the terms that the majority of well-informed parties would themselves most commonly choose.[53]

Defaults can, however, also serve other functions, such as encouraging the revelation of information. For example, where one contracting party is likely to have superior information relevant to the transaction than is the other (or as economists say, that party has 'private information'), then a default provision may impose a burden, or 'penalty', on the informed party, with the understanding that the default may be waived by disclosure of the information. The purpose of such a rule is to encourage parties to reveal their private information—so that they can avoid the default outcome—and consequently induce explicit bargaining

---

[50] Ron Harris, Industrializing English Law (2000); Hansmann, Kraakman, and Squire, *supra* note 12.

[51] See generally the papers in the symposium edition, entitled *Contractual Freedom and Corporate Law*, in 89 Columbia Law Review 1395–1774 (1989).

[52] They are 'defaults' in the sense that they apply (as with computer settings) 'in *default*' of the parties stipulating something else.

[53] Easterbrook and Fischel, *supra* note 7, at 34–5.

between the parties that will lead to an outcome superior to that which would otherwise be expected.[54] Such a 'penalty default' may not be a majoritarian default.

Default provisions can be supplied in a variety of ways, the choice of which affects the ease and means of 'contracting around' them.[55] A common form of corporate law default is a statutory provision that will govern unless the parties explicitly provide an alternative. The common U.S. requirement that a merger can be approved by a vote of 50% of all outstanding shares is an example. That rule can be displaced by a charter provision that explicitly requires approval by, say, 60% of the shareholders, or 70%, or some other number.

Alternatively, corporate law itself sometimes specifies the rule that will govern if the default provision is not chosen—an 'either-or' provision. An example is offered by French corporate law, which allows companies' charters to opt for a two-tier board structure as an alternative to the default single-tier one.[56] In other words, the law in this case gives the corporation a choice between two statutory provisions, one of which is the default and the other of which is the 'secondary' provision, with the latter applying only if the firm opts out of the default (or, equivalently, 'opts in' to the secondary provision). The law may also impose special procedures for altering a default rule. For example, the law may impose a rule that is highly protective of non-controlling shareholders, and then permit deviation from that rule only with approval by a supermajority of all shareholders, or with separate approval by a majority of the non-controlling shareholders, thereby providing some assurance that the default rule will be altered only if the chosen alternative is superior for all shareholders.[57]

An extension of the binary two-alternative-provisions approach just described is to provide corporations with a choice among a 'menu' of more than two alternative statutorily-specified rules.[58] Although to date this approach is rarely taken within any given corporation statute,[59] it can in effect be seen in the increasing choice among alternative corporate forms, as we discuss below.

[54] See Ian Ayres and Robert Gertner, *Filling Gaps in Incomplete Contracts: An Economic Theory of Default Rules*, 99 YALE LAW JOURNAL 87 (1989).

[55] The ease with which parties can 'contract around' a default provision will affect the way it operates. For example, if the costs of contracting around a provision are high, it may be less useful as an information-forcing 'penalty' default (although this will depend on the size of the 'penalty'), but still capable of functioning adequately as a 'majoritarian' default (as a majority of parties would prefer it anyway). For a nuanced discussion of these and other issues, see Ayres and Gertner, *supra* note 54, at 121–5. For an empirical perspective, see Yair Listokin, *What do Corporate Default Rules and Menus Do? An Empirical Examination*, Working Paper (2006), at http://www.ssrn.com.

[56] See Article 225–57 Code de commerce.

[57] On the latter consideration, see Lucian Bebchuk and Assaf Hamdani, *Optimal Defaults For Corporate Law Evolution*, 96 NORTHWESTERN UNIVERSITY LAW REVIEW 489 (2002).

[58] Michael Klausner, *Corporations, Corporate Law, and Networks of Contracts*, 81 VIRGINIA LAW REVIEW 757, 839–41 (1995).

[59] An exception is the UK's Companies Act 2006, which makes provision for multiple forms of model articles of association to be made available for different types of company: *id.*, § 19(2). Another is Italy's menu of three board systems: a default single-tier one with a separate body in

There are also important rules of corporate law that are mandatory.[60] Large German corporations, for example, have no alternative but to give half of their supervisory board seats to representatives of their employees, and publicly traded U.S. corporations have no alternative but to provide regular detailed financial disclosure in a closely prescribed format.[61] The principled rationale for mandatory terms of these types is usually based on some form of 'contracting failure': that some parties might otherwise be exploited because they are not well informed; that the interests of third parties might be affected; or that collective action problems (such as the notorious 'prisoners' dilemma') might otherwise lead to contractual provisions that are inefficient or unfair.[62] Mandatory terms may also serve a useful standardizing function, in circumstances (such as accounting rules) where the benefits of compliance increase if everyone adheres to the same provision.

Mandatory rules need not just serve a prescriptive function, however. When used in conjunction with a choice of corporate *forms*, they can perform an enabling function similar to that served by default rules. More particularly, mandatory rules can facilitate freedom of contract by helping corporate actors to signal the terms they offer and to bond themselves to those terms. The law accomplishes this by creating corporate forms that are to some degree inflexible (i.e., are subject to mandatory rules), but then permitting choice among different corporate forms.[63] There are two principal variants to this approach.

First, a given jurisdiction can provide for a menu of different standard form legal entities from which parties may choose in structuring an organization. In some U.S. jurisdictions, for example, a firm with the five basic attributes of the business corporation can be formed, alternatively, under a general business corporation statute, a close corporation statute, a limited liability company statute, a limited liability partnership statute, or a business trust statute—with each statute providing a somewhat different set of mandatory and default rules. Most conspicuously, the number of mandatory rules decreases as one moves from the first to the last of these statutory forms. The result is to enhance an entrepreneur's ability to signal, via her choice of form, the terms that the firm offers to other contracting parties, and to make credible the entrepreneur's commitment not to change those terms. Formation as a business corporation, for example, signals simply and clearly—to all who deal with the firm, whether by purchasing shares

---

charge of internal controls ('collegio sindacale'), a new single-tier system with no such separate body, and a two-tier system. See Article 2380, Civil Code.

60 See Jeffrey N. Gordon, *The Mandatory Structure of Corporate Law*, 89 COLUMBIA LAW REVIEW 1549 (1989).

61 See *infra* 3.3.1 (codetermination) and 4.1.4 and 8.2 (disclosure).

62 See generally Michael J. Trebilcock, THE LIMITS OF FREEDOM OF CONTRACT (1993).

63 Larry E. Ribstein, *Statutory Forms for Closely Held Firms: Theories and Evidence From LLCs*, 73 WASHINGTON UNIVERSITY LAW QUARTERLY 369 (1995); John Armour and Michael J. Whincop, *An Economic Analysis of Shared Property in Partnership and Close Corporations Law*, 26 JOURNAL OF CORPORATION LAW 983 (2001).

or simply by contract—that the firm is characterized by a variety of familiar ernance provisions, and that it will continue to have those characteristics u. and until it changes statutory form.[64] Thus, paradoxically, greater rigidity with any particular form may actually enhance overall freedom of contract in structuring private enterprise, so long as there is a sufficiently broad range of alternative forms to choose from.

Second, even with respect to a particular type of legal entity, such as the publicly traded business corporation, the organizers of a firm may be permitted to choose among different jurisdictions' laws. This leads us to the general issue of 'regulatory competition' in corporation law. Before addressing that topic, however, we need to say more about the role of corporation law in general.

1.4.2 Legal rules versus contract

Default rules of corporate law do more than simply provide convenient standard forms, encourage revelation of information, and facilitate choice of the most efficient[65] among several alternative rules. They also provide a means of accommodating, over time, developments that cannot easily be foreseen at the outset.

A contract that, like a corporation's charter, must govern complex relationships over a long period of time, is—to use the word favored by economists—necessarily *incomplete*. Situations will arise for which the contract fails to provide clear guidance, either because the situation was not foreseeable at the time the contract was drafted or because the situation, though foreseeable, seemed too unlikely to justify the costs of making clear provision for it in the contract. Statutory amendments, administrative rulings, and judicial decisions can provide for such situations as they arise, either by adding new rules of corporation law or by interpreting existing rules. This is the *gap-filling* role of corporation law.

Courts can, of course, also fill gaps without making new law, simply by interpreting privately-drafted contractual terms in a corporation's charter. But a firm will get the greatest advantage from the courts' interpretive activity if the firm adopts standard charter terms used by many other firms, since those standard terms are likely to be subject to repeated interpretation by the courts.[66] And the most widely-used standard charter terms are often the default rules embodied in the corporation law. So another advantage of adopting default rules of law, rather than drafting specialized charter terms, is to take advantage of the constant gap-filling activity stimulated by the body of precedents developed as a result of other

---

[64] Third parties dealing with the firm can then ensure that no such change will occur by reserving a contractual veto on it, e.g. in the form of an acceleration clause in a loan agreement.

[65] Here, as elsewhere, we use the term 'efficient', as conventionally used in the economics literature, and as discussed below at 1.5, to refer to an organization of affairs that maximizes aggregate social welfare.

[66] Ian Ayres, *Making A Difference: The Contractual Contributions of Easterbrook and Fischel*, 59 UNIVERSITY OF CHICAGO LAW REVIEW 1391, 1403–8 (1992).

corporations that are also subject to those rules. This is one example of a *network effect* that creates an incentive to choose a common approach.[67]

The problem of contractual incompleteness goes beyond mere gap-filling, however. Given the long lifespan of many corporations, it is likely that some of a firm's initial charter terms, no matter how carefully chosen, will become obsolete with the passage of time owing to changes in the economic and legal environment. Default rules of law have the feature that they are altered over time—by statutory amendments and by judicial interpretation—to adapt them to such changing circumstances. Consequently, by adopting a statutory default rule, a firm has a degree of assurance that the provision will not become anachronistic. If, in contrast, the firm puts in its charter a specially-drafted provision in place of the statutory default, only the firm itself can amend the provision when, over time, a change is called for. This runs into the problem that the firm's own mechanisms for charter amendment may be vetoed or hijacked by particular constituencies in order, respectively, to protect or further their partial interests. Simply adopting the statutory default rules, and delegating to the state the responsibility for altering those rules over time as circumstances change, avoids these latter problems.[68]

However, the quality and speed with which default rules are supplied, interpreted and updated will depend on a range of institutional variables concerning the legislative system, civil procedure, and judicial expertise. In the presence of poorly designed rules of civil procedure, judicial resolution of disputes over the interpretation of statutory provisions can also become a vehicle by which particular constituencies can protect or further their partial interests. Conversely, the design of the procedures for charter amendment will greatly influence the extent to which they can be used for the furtherance of partial interests, as opposed to fostering efficient change.

For example, in the U.S., Delaware, the leading state of incorporation for publicly traded corporations, has a 'rolling' default regime under which changes in default rules of law are applied to all corporations that do not have explicitly inconsistent terms in their charters. One indication that these statutory default rules successfully play a role of 'delegated (re)contracting', is the striking rarity with which U.S. publicly traded corporations deviate from their provisions. It is rare for a U.S. publicly traded corporation to include, in its charter, a provision that is not clearly specified as a default rule in the statutory law of the state in

---

[67] A related network effect that may encourage firms to adopt standardized charter terms, and in particular to accept default rules of law, is that those provisions are more familiar to analysts and investors, thus reducing their costs of evaluating the firm as an investment. Similar network effects may cause legal services to be less expensive for firms that adopt default rules of law. See Marcel Kahan and Michael Klausner, *Standardization and Innovation In Corporate Contracting (or 'The Economics of Boilerplate')*, 83 VIRGINIA LAW REVIEW 713 (1997).

[68] See Henry Hansmann, *Corporation and Contract*, 8 AMERICAN LAW AND ECONOMICS REVIEW 1 (2006).

which the firm is incorporated.[69] In contrast, in the UK, the 'model' articles of association provided by the companies legislation apply on a 'fixed' basis, so that changes to the model provisions do not automatically update the articles of association of companies formed under the previous provisions.[70] Concomitantly, rates of 'opt out' from the UK's model provisions seem to be quite high.[71] However, alteration of the articles of association for a UK company is a more straightforward procedure than for a Delaware-incorporated firm.[72]

It follows from much of the foregoing that, for many corporations, there may often be little practical difference between mandatory and default rules. Firms end up, as a practical matter, adopting default rules as well as the mandatory rules. This suggests that there may be more scope for introducing flexibility into firms' choice of structure through the provision of menus of alternative default rules. There is arguably room for further development of this approach, with corporation statutes providing richer menus of alternative default terms for various aspects of corporate governance, all of which are (re)interpreted and amended over time to keep them current. At present, however, the closest that the law comes to such a menu approach lies in the abilities of participants to select from a range of different business forms—which we have discussed—and of corporations to choose the jurisdiction by whose corporation law they will be governed, which is the subject to which we turn next.

1.4.3 Regulatory competition

The various forms of flexibility in corporate law on which we have so far concentrated—the choice of specially-drafted charter provisions versus default provisions, the choice of one default rule in a given statute as opposed to another, and the choice of one statutory form versus another—can all be provided within any given jurisdiction. As we have noted, however, there can be yet another dimension of choice—namely, choice of the jurisdiction in which to incorporate.

In the United States, for example, the prevailing choice of law rule for corporate law is the 'place of incorporation' rule, which permits a business corporation to be incorporated under—and hence governed by—the law of any of the 50

---

[69] See Listokin, *supra* note 55. The position regarding close corporations is more varied. Many of these have highly specialized charters—arguably reflecting the greater ease of efficiently renegotiating the corporate structure among the small number of parties involved and the fact that structural changes are likely to occur anyway as the firm (hopefully) evolves from a start-up to a listed company.

[70] §§ 19(4), 20(2) Companies Act 2006 (UK).

[71] See Richard C. Nolan, *The Continuing Evolution of Shareholder Governance*, 65 Cambridge Law Journal 92, 115–19 (2006).

[72] In the UK, this is a decision purely for the shareholders, albeit requiring a supermajority vote (75%) (§§ 21and 283 Companies Act 2006 (UK)), whereas in Delaware, a charter amendment must first be proposed by the board, prior to a shareholder vote (§ 242(b) Delaware General Corporation Law).

individual states (or any foreign country), regardless of where the firm's principal place of business, or other assets and activities, are located. Where, as in the U.S., such choice is available at low cost, a given jurisdiction's corporation statute simply serves as an item on a menu of alternative standard forms available to the parties involved. As in the case where there is intra-jurisdictional choice of alternative forms, mandatory rules in any given jurisdiction's corporation law may serve not to constrain choice of form but actually to enhance it, by making it easier for firms to signal, and to bond themselves to, their choice among alternative attributes.

That form of choice, long available within the United States and in a number of other countries as well, is now being extended to corporations throughout the European Union as a consequence of recent decisions of the European Court of Justice that have largely substituted the place of incorporation rule for the 'real seat' doctrine under which, in many European countries, firms were formerly required to incorporate under the law of the state where the firm had its principal place of business.[73]

The consequence of choice across jurisdictions is not just to enlarge the range of governance rules from which a given firm can choose, but also to create the opportunity and the incentive for a jurisdiction to induce firms to incorporate under its law—and thereby bring revenue to the state directly (through franchise fees) and indirectly (through increased demand for local services) by making the jurisdictions' corporate law unusually attractive. Whether such 'regulatory competition' is good or bad has been the subject of vigorous debate. Pessimists argue that it creates a 'race to the bottom' in which the state that wins is that which goes furthest in stripping its law of protections for constituencies who do not control the reincorporation decision. Optimists argue that, on the contrary, regulatory competition in corporate law creates a virtuous 'race to the top' in which—because the capital markets price, more or less accurately, the effects of corporate law on shareholder welfare—the state that wins is that whose law is most effective in protecting the rights of shareholders and other corporate constituencies.[74]

---

[73] Case C-212/97, *Centros Ltd v. Erhvervs-og Selskabssyrelsen* [1999] ECR I-1459; Case C-208/00, *Überseering BV v. Nordic Construction Company Baumanagement GmbH* (NCC) [2002] ECR I-9919; Case C-167/01, *Kamel van Koophandel en Fabrieken voor Amsterdam v. Inspire Art Ltd* [2003] ECR I-10155; Case C-210/06, *Cartesio Oktató és Szolgáltató bt*, Judgment of 16 December 2008. See Jens C. Dammann, *Freedom of Choice in European Company Law*, 29 YALE JOURNAL OF INTERNATIONAL LAW 477 (2004); John Armour, *Who Should Make Corporate Law: EC Legislation versus Regulatory Competition*, 48 CURRENT LEGAL PROBLEMS 369 (2005); Martin Gelter, *The Structure of Regulatory Competition in European Corporate Law*, 5 JOURNAL OF CORPORATE LAW STUDIES 1 (2005).

[74] The classical statements of the two polar views are William Cary, *Federalism and Corporate Law: Reflections Upon Delaware*, 83 YALE LAW JOURNAL 663 (1974), and Ralph Winter, *State Law, Shareholder Protection and the Theory of the Corporation*, 6 JOURNAL OF LEGAL STUDIES 251 (1977). The extensive subsequent literature has debated whether in fact states compete for corporate charters, see Marcel Kahan and Ehud Kamar, *The Myth of State Competition in Corporate Law*, 55 STANFORD LAW REVIEW 679 (2002), whether any competition that does exist leads to law that is better or worse for shareholders, see Roberta Romano, *Law as a Product: Some Pieces of the*

Clearly, the process by which reincorporation is effected will also be an important factor in determining the nature of any such 'race'.[75] The more inclusive the process of parties involved in the firm, the less likely it is that reincorporation will result in a 'race to the bottom'.

Moreover, the effectiveness of regulatory competition presumably depends on the context in which it operates. In contrast to the European Union, for example, the United States offers the advantage of homogeneous property and contract law across its member states and largely federalized bankruptcy and tax law.[76] Even so, only one among the fifty American states—Delaware—has made a sustained effort to attract incorporation by out-of-state firms.[77] It has been quite successful in this effort, now serving as the state of incorporation for roughly half of all U.S. publicly traded corporations, even though few of those corporations do any significant amount of business in Delaware. As part of its effort to remain attractive as a place of incorporation, Delaware's legislature regularly updates its corporation statute, generally deferring to a drafting committee dominated by practising lawyers. The Delaware judiciary, in turn, has a particular court (the 'chancery court') that is largely specialized to deal with corporate law cases, and is a constant source of judge-made law that interprets and supplements the statutory law. This focused attention to law-making clearly has important virtues, although not all agree that the result is an optimal body of corporate law.[78]

Of course, there is dispute as to what constitutes an 'optimal' body of corporate law, even in theory. That is our next topic.

Incorporation Puzzle, 1 Journal of Law Economics and Organization 225, 280–1 (1985); Lucian Bebchuk, *Federalism and the Corporation: The Desirable Limits on State Competition in Corporate Law*, 105 Harvard Law Review 1435, 1441 (1992); and William Carney and George Shepherd, *The Mystery of the Success of Delaware Law*, University of Illinois Law Review 1 (2009), and, if competition leads to more valuable firms, what is the amount of increased value, *see* Robert Daines, *Does Delaware Law Improve Firm Value?*, 62 Journal of Financial Economics 525 (2001), and Guhan Subramanian, *The Disappearing Delaware Effect*, 20 Journal of Law Economics and Organization 32 (2004).

[75] Bebchuk, *supra* note 74, at 1459–61, 1470–5; Simon Deakin, *Regulatory Competition Versus Harmonization in European Company Law*, in Regulatory Competition and Economic Integration, 190, 209–13 (Daniel C. Esty and Damien Geradin (eds.), 2001).

[76] On the implications of non-federalized tax and bankruptcy laws for regulatory competition in European corporate law, see Mitchall Kane and Edward B. Rock, *Corporate Taxation and International Charter Competition*, 106 Michigan Law Review 1229 (2008) (tax) and Horst Eidenmüller, *Free Choice in International Company Insolvency Law in Europe*, 6 European Business Organization Law Review 423 (2005); Armour, *supra* note 73, at 401–11; Luca Enriques and Martin Gelter, *Regulatory Competition in European Company Law and Creditor Protection*, 7 European Business Organization Law Review 417 (2006) (bankruptcy).

[77] In recent years, Nevada has made a modest and largely unsuccessful effort to compete with Delaware. Going back to the beginning of the 20th century, New Jersey was also a competitor.

[78] See, e.g., Jonathan R. Macey and Geoffrey P. Miller, *Toward an Interest-Group Theory of Delaware Corporate Law*, 65 Texas Law Review 469 (1987); Ehud Kamar, *A Regulatory Competition Theory of Indeterminacy in Corporate Law*, 98 Columbia Law Review 1908 (1998).

1.5 What is the Goal of Corporate Law?

What is the goal of corporate law, as distinct from its immediate functions of defining a form of enterprise and containing the conflicts among the participants in this enterprise? As a normative matter, the overall objective of corporate law—as of any branch of law—is presumably to serve the interests of society as a whole. More particularly, the appropriate goal of corporate law is to advance the aggregate welfare[79] of all who are affected by a firm's activities, including the firm's shareholders, employees, suppliers, and customers, as well as third parties such as local communities and beneficiaries of the natural environment. This is what economists would characterize as the pursuit of overall social efficiency.

It is sometimes said that the goals of corporate law should be narrower. In particular, it is sometimes said that the appropriate role of corporate law is simply to assure that the corporation serves the best interests of its shareholders or, more specifically, to maximize financial returns to shareholders or, more specifically still, to maximize the current market price of corporate shares. Such claims can be viewed in two ways.

First, these claims can be taken at face value, in which case they neither describe corporate law as we observe it nor offer a normatively appealing aspiration for that body of law. There would be little to recommend a body of law that, for example, permits corporate shareholders to enrich themselves through transactions that make creditors or employees worse off by $2 for every $1 that the shareholders gain.

Second, such claims can be understood as saying, more modestly, that focusing principally on the maximization of shareholder returns is, in general, the best means by which corporate law can serve the broader goal of advancing overall social welfare. In general, creditors, workers, and customers will consent to deal with a corporation only if they expect themselves to be better off as a result. Consequently, the corporation—and, in particular, its shareholders, as the firm's residual claimants[80] and risk-bearers—have a direct pecuniary interest in making sure that corporate transactions are beneficial, not just to the shareholders, but to all parties who deal with the firm. We believe that this second view is—and surely ought to be—the appropriate interpretation of statements by legal

---

[79] When we speak here of advancing or maximizing the 'aggregate welfare' of society we are using a metaphor that is conceptually a bit loose. There is no coherent way to put a number on society's aggregate welfare, much less to maximize that number—and particularly so when many benefits are in appreciable part non-pecuniary. What we are suggesting here might be put more precisely in the language of welfare economics as pursuing Kaldor-Hicks efficiency within acceptable patterns of distribution.

[80] Shareholders are a corporation's 'residual claimants' in the sense that they are entitled to appropriate all (and only) the net assets and earnings of the corporation after all contractual claimants—such as employees, suppliers, and customers—have been paid in full.

scholars and economists asserting that shareholder value is the proper object of corporate law.

Whether, in fact, the pursuit of shareholder value is generally an effective means of advancing overall social welfare is an empirical question on which reasonable minds can differ. While each of the authors of this book has individual views on this claim, we do not take a strong position on it in the chapters that follow. Rather, we undertake the broader task of offering an analytic framework within which this question can be explored and debated.

1.6 What Forces Shape Corporate Law?

To say that the pursuit of aggregate social welfare is the appropriate goal of corporate law is not to say, of course, that the law always serves that goal. Legislatures and courts are sometimes less attentive to overall social welfare than to the particular interests of influential constituencies, such as controlling shareholders, corporate managers, or organized workers. Moreover, corporate law everywhere continues to bear the imprint of the historical path through which it has evolved, and reflects as well the influence of a variety of non-efficiency-oriented intellectual and ideological currents.[81]

We touch here briefly on several of the most conspicuous of these various forces that help shape corporate law.

1.6.1 Patterns of corporate ownership

The nature and number of corporate shareholders differ markedly even among the most developed market economies, and surely leave a mark on the structure of corporate law.

In the U.S. and the UK, there are large numbers of publicly traded corporations that have *dispersed share ownership*, such that no single shareholder, or affiliated group of shareholders, is capable of exercising control over the firm.[82] Shareholdings among major Japanese firms are also often very dispersed,[83] though in the second half of the 20th century it was common for a substantial fraction of a firm's stock to be held by other firms in a loose group with substantial reciprocal

---

[81] See generally, Mark J. Roe, POLITICAL DETERMINANTS OF CORPORATE GOVERNANCE (2003); Peter A. Gourevitch and James Shinn, POLITICAL POWER AND CORPORATE CONTROL (2005).

[82] Rafael La Porta, Florencio Lopez-de-Silanes, and Andrei Shleifer, *Corporate Ownership Around the World*, 54 JOURNAL OF FINANCE 471, 492–3; Mara Faccio and Larry H.P. Lang, *The Ultimate Ownership of Western European Corporations*, 65 JOURNAL OF FINANCIAL ECONOMICS 365, 379–80; cf. Clifford G. Holderness, *The Myth of Diffuse Ownership in the United States*, REVIEW OF FINANCIAL STUDIES (forthcoming), available at http://www.ssrn.com.

[83] By some accounts, share ownership in Japanese publicly-held corporations is more dispersed than in the U.S.: see Holderness, *supra* note 82; Julian Franks, Colin Mayer, and Hideaki Miyajima, *Evolution of Ownership: The Curious Case of Japan*, Working Paper (2007), at http://www.hbs.edu.

cross-shareholdings.[84] In the nations of continental Europe, in contrast, even firms with publicly-trading shares have traditionally had a *controlling shareholder*, in the form of an individual or family (as in Italy), another firm, a closely coordinated group of other firms (as in Germany),[85] or the state (as in France).

The types of entities by or through which shares are held also differ substantially from one country to another. In the U.S., for example, while individuals continue to hold a substantial amount of stock directly, the majority of stock is now owned by two types of '*institutional investors*'—*mutual funds* and employer-established *pension funds*—though there are many thousands of both types of funds and an individual fund rarely holds a significant fraction of a given company's stock.[86] In England, institutional investors (mainly pension funds and insurance companies) also own a large fraction of corporate stock,[87] but—in contrast to the U.S. pattern—the thirty or so largest funds together hold a sufficiently large share of the stock in many companies to exert substantial control.[88] In Germany, large commercial banks traditionally held substantial blocks of corporate stock on their own account, and also served as custodians for large amounts of stock owned by individuals, whose votes were often effectively exercised by the banks themselves.[89] Recent years have seen the rise of new types of institutional investors as well. Conspicuous among these are *hedge funds*—relatively unregulated collective investment funds that, despite their name,[90] often adopt highly speculative strategies that involve substantial stakes in individual firms, and that sometimes seek to exercise control over those firms—and private equity firms, which are (typically) nonpublic firms that acquire, at least temporarily, complete

[84] See TOKYO STOCK EXCHANGE, 2006 SHAREOWNERSHIP SURVEY, 4 (2007); Hideaki Miyajima and Fumiaki Kuroki, *The Unwinding of Cross-Shareholding in Japan: Causes, Effects, and Implications*, in CORPORATE GOVERNANCE IN JAPAN: INSTITUTIONAL CHANGE AND ORGANIZATIONAL DIVERSITY 79 (Masahiko Aoki, Gregory Jackson, and Hideaki Miyajima (eds.), 2007).

[85] However, there are indications that the traditional position in some jurisdictions, notably Germany, is starting to change in favour of more dispersed stock ownership: see Darius Wojcik, *Change in the German Model of Corporate Governance: Evidence from Blockholdings 1997–2001*, 35 ENVIRONMENT AND PLANNING A 1431; Steen Thomsen, *Convergence of Corporate Governance during the Stock Market Bubble: Towards Anglo-American or European Standards?* in Grandori (ed.), CORPORATE GOVERNANCE AND FIRM ORGANIZATION (2004), 297, 306–12.

[86] Board of Governors of the Federal Reserve System, FLOW OF FUNDS ACCOUNTS IN THE UNITED STATES: ANNUAL FLOWS AND OUTSTANDINGS, 1995–2006, 82 (Table L.213) (2007).

[87] Office for National Statistics (UK), SHARE OWNERSHIP: A REPORT ON OWNERSHIP OF SHARES AS AT 31ST DECEMBER 2006, 9 (2007).

[88] See Geof P. Stapledon, INSTITUTIONAL SHAREHOLDERS AND CORPORATE GOVERNANCE (1996); Armour and Gordon, *supra* note 9, at 29–30.

[89] See e.g., Ralf Elsas and Jan P. Krahnen, *Universal Banks and Relationships with Firms*, in THE GERMAN FINANCIAL SYSTEM 197 (Jan P. Krahnen and Reinhard H. Schmidt (eds.), 2006). This pattern has, however, become less clearly pronounced in recent years, with only private banks still operating in this fashion and many commercial banks finding proxy voting too costly. See also sources cited *supra* note 85.

[90] Marcel Kahan and Edward B. Rock, *Hedge Funds in Corporate Governance and Corporate Control*, 155 UNIVERSITY OF PENNSYLVANIA LAW REVIEW 1021 (2007).

ownership of formerly public companies to effect major changes in the firms' structure, strategy, or management.[91]

Arguably, such differences in patterns of shareholding across countries are the consequence, at least in part, of differences in the structure of corporate law. There is now a large empirical 'law and finance' literature that seeks to demonstrate, in particular, that countries with greater protection for non-controlling shareholders against opportunism by managers and controlling shareholders have less concentrated shareholdings as a consequence,[92] though subsequent studies have sometimes failed to replicate these results,[93] and the conclusions to be drawn from them are much debated.[94]

There can be little doubt, however, that the reverse is (also?) true: the structure of corporate law in any given country is in important part a consequence of that country's particular pattern of corporate ownership, which is in turn determined at least in part by forces exogenous to corporate law.[95] It has been argued, for example, that the fragmented pattern of U.S. shareholdings is to a substantial degree a result of that country's tradition of populist politics, which has produced a number of policies successfully designed to frustrate family and institutional control of industrial enterprise.[96] Correspondingly, it is said that the traditionally more concentrated share ownership patterns in continental Europe and Japan complemented particular patterns of industrial development.[97] In particular, a controlling shareholder may be better placed to make credible long-term commitments to employees, which in turn may facilitate labor relations—and hence

[91] See Brian R. Cheffins and John Armour, *The Eclipse of Private Equity*, 33 DELAWARE JOURNAL OF CORPORATE LAW 1 (2008).

[92] Rafael La Porta, Florencio Lopez-de-Silanes, Andrei Shleifer, and Robert Vishny, *Legal Determinants of External Finance*, 52 JOURNAL OF FINANCE 1131 (1997); Rafael La Porta, Florencio Lopez-de-Silanes, Andrei Shleifer, and Robert Vishny, *Law and Finance*, 106 JOURNAL OF POLITICAL ECONOMY 1113 (1998); Thorsten Beck, Asli Demirgüç-Kunt, and Ross Levine, *Law and Finance: Why does Legal Origin Matter?*, 31 JOURNAL OF COMPARATIVE ECONOMICS 653–75 (2003); Rafael La Porta, Florencio Lopez-de-Silanes, and Andrei Shleifer, *What Works in Securities Laws?*, 61 JOURNAL OF FINANCE 1 (2006).

[93] See Holger Spamann, *On the Insignificance and/or Endogeneity of La Porta et al.'s, 'Antidirector Rights Index' Under Consistent Coding*, Working Paper (2006), at http://www.ssrn.com; John Armour, Simon Deakin, Prabirjit Sarkar, Mathias Siems, and Ajit Singh, *Shareholder Protection and Stock Market Development: An Empirical Test of the Legal Origins Hypothesis*, Working Paper (2007), at http://www.ssrn.com; Howell Jackson and Mark J. Roe, *Public Enforcement of Securities Laws: Preliminary Evidence*, JOURNAL OF FINANCIAL ECONOMICS (forthcoming), available at http://hku.hk/law.

[94] For an overview, see Kenneth A. Dam, THE LAW-GROWTH NEXUS (2006).

[95] Brian R. Cheffins, *Does Law Matter? The Separation of Ownership and Control in the United Kingdom*, 30 JOURNAL OF LEGAL STUDIES 459 (2001); John C. Coffee, Jr., *The Rise of Dispersed Ownership: The Roles of Law and the State in the Separation of Ownership and Control*, 111 YALE LAW JOURNAL 1 (2001).

[96] Mark J. Roe, STRONG MANAGERS, WEAK OWNERS: THE POLITICAL ROOTS OF AMERICAN CORPORATE FINANCE (1994).

[97] See Wendy Carlin and Colin Mayer, *Finance, Investment and Growth*, 69 JOURNAL OF FINANCIAL ECONOMICS 191 (2003).

productivity—where the goal is to motivate workers to use existing technology, rather than to develop new technologies.[98]

These patterns of share ownership, in turn, have helped shape corporate law in two ways. The first, which we might term the 'distributional' effect of corporate ownership on corporate law, is through the influence they give to particular interest groups to shape corporate law in ways that distribute a larger fraction of the fruits of enterprise to themselves. For example, the dispersed share ownership of U.S. publicly traded corporations has given corporate managers substantial autonomy, which they have used—via lobbying, litigation, and choice of their state of incorporation—to help give U.S. corporation law a distinctly managerialist character. Second, in what we might term in contrast the 'efficiency effect', share ownership patterns shape the problems to which reforms designed to facilitate investment respond. Thus the dispersed pattern of U.S. shareholdings has brought changes in corporate law,[99] such as investor-oriented disclosure rules, designed to reassure investors and hence make it less costly for firms to raise capital within that pattern of ownership.[100]

Both the distributional effect and the efficiency effect of corporate ownership on corporate law are likewise evident in other countries. Corporate law everywhere clearly reflects the institutional and political power of a country's dominant corporate interests, whether they be banks, prominent families, investment funds, or unions. At the same time, all of the wealthy countries whose law we focus on have, to a greater or lesser degree, self-consciously shaped their law to enhance the efficiency with which corporations can be financed and managed in the context of the country's particular pattern of ownership.[101]

The distributional effects of ownership patterns often work against efficiency. But that is not necessarily the case. Sometimes the interests of a dominant interest group are aligned with broader social welfare. We turn next to some factors that affect the tradeoff between distributional effects and efficiency effects.

1.6.2 International competition

Dominant ownership groups in a society are likely to be reasonably satisfied with the current corporate law regime if it gives them access to capital on terms more favorable than their competitors. In economies relatively closed to outside competition, the principal competitors of an established firm will be newer and smaller

---

[98] See VARIETIES OF CAPITALISM (Peter A. Hall and David Soskice (eds.), 2001); Barry Eichengreen, EUROPE'S ECONOMY SINCE 1945 (2006).

[99] See, e.g. Raghuram G. Rajan and Luigi Zingales, *The Persistence of Underdevelopment: Institutions, Human Capital, or Constituencies?*, Working Paper (2006), at http://www.ssrn.com.

[100] Coffee, *supra* note 95.

[101] Insightful and informative accounts of the mutual evolution of corporate ownership and corporate law in a variety of countries are collected in Randall K. Morck (ed.), A HISTORY OF CORPORATE GOVERNANCE AROUND THE WORLD (2005). See also sources cited *supra* note 95.

domestic firms. The owners of the established firms therefore have no interest in legal reforms that make it easier for such competitors to obtain capital financing, particularly from public capital markets—something the law might do, for example, by making corporate managers and controlling shareholders more accountable to non-controlling shareholders.[102] Meanwhile, the established firms can themselves rely on other forms of capital financing, such as retained earnings and privileged access to bank loans.[103]

These incentives change, however, in periods such as the present when world tariff levels are low and the most important competitors of a country's dominant domestic firms are no longer other, smaller domestic firms but rather large foreign firms. In such circumstances, it has been argued,[104] established domestic firms are more concerned with raising more capital for themselves, to keep up with their foreign competitors, than they are in denying capital to smaller domestic firms. Consequently, the dominant ownership groups—for example, established industrial families—become more amenable to investor-friendly reforms in corporate law. Hence, the current fervor for corporate governance reform is perhaps in part a consequence of the great success, in recent decades, in reducing barriers to international trade.

1.6.3 Cross-jurisdictional coordination

Self-conscious supranational efforts to coordinate the regulation of corporations across jurisdictions are another important source of both distributional and efficiency pressures on corporate law. To some extent this coordination is being undertaken on a global level—for example, in international efforts to develop common accounting standards.[105] It is currently most conspicuous, however, in the European Union's efforts to further the integration of its common market. Loosely speaking, those efforts take two different—and largely conflicting—forms: harmonization and regulatory competition.

Harmonization was the initial route pursued towards integration of corporate law. These efforts, generally in the form of EC legislation, sought to impose uniform, or at least minimum, rules of corporate law upon all member states. Successful harmonization changes the arena for the exercise of interest group influence from the individual member states to the EC. As such, it encountered a great deal of domestic interest group opposition. The effect so far has largely been

---

[102] Gerard Hertig, *Efficient Fostering of EU Regulatory Competition*, 76 Swiss Review of Business and Financial Market Law 369, 370 (2004).

[103] Mechanisms that rely upon reputation for enforcement also tend to favor incumbent firms and deter market entry, as it is costly to acquire a reputation: see Simon Johnson, John McMillan, and Christopher Woodruff, *Courts and Relational Contracts*, 18 Journal of Law, Economics and Organization 221 (2002).

[104] Raghuram G. Rajan and Luigi Zingales, *The Great Reversals: The Politics of Financial Development in the Twentieth Century*, 69 Journal of Financial Economics 5 (2003).

[105] See *infra* Ch. 5.

deadlock: many of the EC directives that have been adopted, and that are mandatory for the member states, deal with relatively unimportant matters.[106] Whether
that is a bad thing is subject to debate. At least some of the directives adopted to
date—such as uniform minimum legal capital requirements—might be seen as
favoring distributional pressures more than pressures for efficiency, raising the
concern that truly comprehensive harmonization might lock in forms of regulation that are seriously inefficient.

More recently, among the EU states a certain degree of regulatory
competition—which, in contrast to harmonization, is a 'bottom-up' rather than
a 'top-down' process of legal change—has been unleashed by decisions of the
European Court of Justice. As we noted earlier, the Court has struck down various efforts by individual states to impose their rules of corporation law on firms
operating locally but incorporated in other member states.[107] As a mechanism for
market integration, this bypasses the domestic interest groups that have held up
legislative harmonization. However, it too may be susceptible to distributional
pressures if the person(s) choosing a company's state of incorporation stand to
benefit from this decision at the expense of other constituencies. The future path
of European company law will be determined in large part by the relative scope
that harmonization and regulatory competition are given in the years to come.

A similar though more attenuated tug-of-war between the creation of uniform
rules of law at the supra-jurisdictional level and the creation of a uniform *market*
for corporate law across jurisdictions via regulatory competition has long been
playing out as well among the federated states of the United States. The result
has been an uneasy and fluid allocation of corporate law between the federal
government on the one hand and the individual states (led by Delaware) on the
other. A widely-noted step in this process was taken with the Sarbanes-Oxley
Act of 2003 which—in the wake of the Enron series of corporate scandals—
extended federal law to further aspects of corporate governance previously left to
the states.

This is principally a book about the structure and functions of corporate
law, not about its origins. Nonetheless, in the chapters that follow we will here
and there explore, briefly and a bit speculatively, the influence of the forces just
surveyed—and of others as well—in shaping the patterns of corporate law that
we see across jurisdictions.

---

[106] See Luca Enriques, *EC Company Law Directives and Regulations: How Trivial Are They?*,
27 University of Pennsylvania Journal of International Economic Law 1086 (2006).
[107] See sources cited *supra* note 73.

2

Agency Problems and Legal Strategies

John Armour, Henry Hansmann, and
Reinier Kraakman

2.1 Three Agency Problems

As we explained in the preceding chapter,[1] corporate law performs two general functions: first, it establishes the structure of the corporate form as well as ancillary housekeeping rules necessary to support this structure; second, it attempts to control conflicts of interest among corporate constituencies, including those between corporate 'insiders', such as controlling shareholders and top managers, and 'outsiders', such as minority shareholders or creditors. These conflicts all have the character of what economists refer to as 'agency problems' or 'principal-agent' problems. For readers unfamiliar with the jargon of economists, an 'agency problem'—in the most general sense of the term—arises whenever the welfare of one party, termed the 'principal', depends upon actions taken by another party, termed the 'agent'. The problem lies in motivating the agent to act in the principal's interest rather than simply in the agent's own interest. Viewed in these broad terms, agency problems arise in a broad range of contexts that go well beyond those that would formally be classified as agency relationships by lawyers.

In particular, almost any contractual relationship, in which one party (the 'agent') promises performance to another (the 'principal'), is potentially subject to an agency problem. The core of the difficulty is that, because the agent commonly has better information than does the principal about the relevant facts, the principal cannot easily assure himself that the agent's performance is precisely what was promised. As a consequence, the agent has an incentive to act opportunistically,[2] skimping on the quality of his performance, or even diverting to himself some of what was promised to the principal. This means, in turn, that the value of the agent's performance to the principal will be reduced, either

---

[1] See *supra* 1.1.
[2] We use the term 'opportunism' here, following the usage of Oliver Williamson, to refer to self-interested behavior that involves some element of guile, deception, misrepresentation, or bad faith. See Oliver Williamson, THE ECONOMIC INSTITUTIONS OF CAPITALISM 47–9 (1985).

directly or because, to assure the quality of the agent's performance, the principal must engage in costly monitoring of the agent. The greater the complexity of the tasks undertaken by the agent, and the greater the discretion the agent must be given, the larger these 'agency costs' are likely to be.[3]

As we noted in Chapter 1, three generic agency problems arise in business firms. The first involves the conflict between the firm's owners and its hired managers. Here the owners are the principals and the managers are the agents. The problem lies in assuring that the managers are responsive to the owners' interests rather than pursuing their own personal interests. The second agency problem involves the conflict between, on one hand, owners who possess the majority or controlling interest in the firm and, on the other hand, the minority or noncontrolling owners. Here the noncontrolling owners can be thought of as the principals and the controlling owners as the agents, and the difficulty lies in assuring that the former are not expropriated by the latter. While this problem is most conspicuous in tensions between majority and minority shareholders,[4] it appears whenever some subset of a firm's owners can control decisions affecting the class of owners as a whole. Thus if minority shareholders enjoy veto rights in relation to particular decisions, it can give rise to a species of this second agency problem. Similar problems can arise between ordinary and preference shareholders, and between senior and junior creditors in bankruptcy (when creditors are the effective owners of the firm). The third agency problem involves the conflict between the firm itself—including, particularly, its owners—and the other parties with whom the firm contracts, such as creditors, employees, and customers. Here the difficulty lies in assuring that the firm, as agent, does not behave opportunistically toward these various other principals—such as by expropriating creditors, exploiting workers, or misleading consumers.

In each of the foregoing problems, the challenge of assuring agents' responsiveness is greater where there are multiple principals—and especially so where they have different interests, or 'heterogeneous preferences' as economists say. Multiple principals will face *coordination costs*, which will inhibit their ability to engage in collective action.[5] These in turn will interact with agency problems in two ways. First, difficulties of coordinating between principals will lead them to delegate more of their decision-making to agents.[6] Second, the

---

[3] See, e.g., Steven Ross, *The Economic Theory of Agency: The Principal's Problem*, 63 AMERICAN ECONOMIC REVIEW 134 (1973); PRINCIPALS AND AGENTS: THE STRUCTURE OF BUSINESS (John W. Pratt and Richard J. Zeckhauser (eds.), 1984); Paul Milgrom and John Roberts, ECONOMICS, ORGANIZATION AND MANAGEMENT (1992).

[4] These problems become more severe the smaller the degree of ownership of the firm that is enjoyed by the controlling shareholder. See Luca Enriques and Paolo Volpin, *Corporate Governance Reforms in Continental Europe*, 21 JOURNAL OF ECONOMIC PERSPECTIVES 117, 122–5 (2007).

[5] Classic statements of this problem are found in James M. Buchanan and Gordon Tullock, THE CALCULUS OF CONSENT, 63–116 (1962) and Mancur Olsen, THE LOGIC OF COLLECTIVE ACTION (1965).

[6] Frank H. Easterbrook and Daniel R. Fischel, THE ECONOMIC STRUCTURE OF CORPORATE LAW, 66–7 (1991).

more difficult it is for principals to coordinate on a single set of goals for the agent, the more obviously difficult it is to ensure that the agent does the 'right' thing.[7] Coordination costs as between principals thereby exacerbate agency problems.

Law can play an important role in reducing agency costs. Obvious examples are rules and procedures that enhance disclosure by agents or facilitate enforcement actions brought by principals against dishonest or negligent agents. Paradoxically, mechanisms that impose constraints on agents' ability to exploit their principals tend to benefit agents as much as—or even more than—they benefit the principals. The reason is that a principal will be willing to offer greater compensation to an agent when the principal is assured of performance that is honest and of high quality. To take a conspicuous example in the corporate context, rules of law that protect creditors from opportunistic behavior on the part of corporations should reduce the interest rate that corporations must pay for credit, thus benefiting corporations as well as creditors. Likewise, legal constraints on the ability of controlling shareholders to expropriate minority shareholders should increase the price at which shares can be sold to non-controlling shareholders, hence reducing the cost of outside equity capital for corporations. And rules of law that inhibit insider trading by corporate managers should increase the compensation that shareholders are willing to offer the managers. In general, reducing agency costs is in the interests of all parties to a transaction, principals and agents alike.

It follows that the normative goal of advancing aggregate social welfare, as discussed in Chapter 1,[8] is generally equivalent to searching for optimal solutions to the corporation's agency problems, in the sense of finding solutions that maximize the aggregate welfare of the parties involved—that is, of both principals and agents taken together.

2.2 Legal Strategies for Reducing Agency Costs

In addressing agency problems, the law turns repeatedly to a basic set of strategies. We use the term '*legal* strategy' to mean a generic method of deploying substantive law to mitigate the vulnerability of principals to the opportunism of their agents. The strategy involved need not necessarily require legal norms for its implementation. We observed in Chapter 1 that, of the five defining characteristics of the corporate form, only one—legal personality—clearly requires special rules of law.[9] The other characteristics could, in principle, be adopted by contract—for example, through appropriate provisions in the articles of

---

[7] See Hideki Kanda, *Debtholders and Equityholders*, 21 Journal of Legal Studies 431, 440–1, 444–5 (1992); Henry Hansmann, The Ownership of Enterprise, 39–44 (1996).

[8] See *supra* 1.5.   [9] See *supra* 1.2.1.

association agreed to by the firm's owners.[10] The same is true of the various strategies we set out in this section.[11] Moreover, the rule of law implementing a legal strategy may be, as discussed in Chapter 1, either a mandatory or a default rule, or one among a menu of alternative rules.[12]

Legal strategies for controlling agency costs can be divided into two subsets, which we term, respectively, 'regulatory strategies' and 'governance strategies'. Regulatory strategies are prescriptive: they dictate substantive terms that govern the content of the principal-agent relationship, tending to constrain the agent's behavior directly. By contrast, governance strategies seek to facilitate the principals' control over their agent's behavior.[13]

The efficacy of governance strategies depends crucially on the ability of the principals to exercise the control rights accorded to them. Coordination costs between principals will make it more difficult for them either to *monitor* the agent so as to determine the appropriateness of her actions, or to *decide* whether, and how, to take action to sanction nonperformance. High coordination costs thus render governance strategies less successful in controlling agents, and regulatory strategies will tend to seem more attractive. Regulatory strategies have different preconditions for success. Most obviously, they depend for efficacy on the ability of an external authority—a court or regulatory body—to determine whether or not the agent complied with particular prescriptions. This requires not only good-quality regulatory institutions—the hallmarks of which are expertise and integrity—but effective disclosure mechanisms to ensure that information about the actions of agents can be 'verified' by the regulator. In contrast, governance strategies—where the principals are able to exercise them effectively—require only that the principals themselves are able to observe the actions taken by the agent, for which purpose 'softer' information may suffice.

Table 2–1 sets out ten legal strategies—four regulatory strategies and six governance strategies—which, taken together, span the law's principal methods of dealing with agency problems. These strategies are not limited to the corporate context; they can be deployed to protect nearly *any* vulnerable principal-agent relationship. Our focus here, however, will naturally be on the ways that these strategies are deployed in corporate law. At the outset, we should emphasize that the aim of this exercise is not to provide an authoritative taxonomy, but simply to

---

[10] Law can, however, provide useful assistance to parties in relation to these other characteristics through the provision of 'standard forms'. See *supra* 1.4.1.

[11] For evidence on the role of contractual solutions to agency problems adopted by individual firms, see Paul Gompers, Joy Ishii, and Andrew Metrick, *Corporate Governance and Equity Prices*, 118 Quarterly Journal of Economics 107 (2003); Leora Klapper and Inessa Love, *Corporate Governance, Investor Protection, and Performance in Emerging Markets*, 10 Journal of Corporate Finance 703 (2004).

[12] See Chapter 1's discussion of the various forms that rules can take, *supra* 1.3–1.4.

[13] An alternative labelling would therefore be a distinction between 'agent-constraining' and 'principal-empowering' strategies.

Table 2–1: Strategies for Protecting Principals

	Regulatory Strategies		Governance Strategies		
	Agent Constraints	Affiliation Terms	Appointment Rights	Decision Rights	Agent Incentives
Ex Ante	Rules	Entry	Selection	Initiation	Trusteeship
Ex Post	Standards	Exit	Removal	Veto	Reward

offer a heuristic device for thinking about the functional role of law in corporate affairs. As a result, the various strategies are not entirely discrete but sometimes overlap, and our categorization of these strategies does not quadrate perfectly with corporate law doctrine.

2.2.1 Regulatory strategies

Consider first the regulatory strategies on the left hand side of Table 2–1.

2.2.1.1 *Rules and standards*

The most familiar pair of regulatory strategies constrains agents by commanding them not to make decisions, or undertake transactions, that would harm the interests of their principals. Lawmakers can frame such constraints as *rules,* which require or prohibit specific behaviors, or as general *standards,* which leave the precise determination of compliance to adjudicators after the fact.

Both rules and standards attempt to regulate the substance of agency relationships directly. Rules, which prescribe specific behaviors *ex ante,*[14] are commonly used in the corporate context to protect a corporation's creditors and public investors. Thus corporation statutes universally include creditor protection rules such as dividend restrictions, minimum capitalization requirements, or rules requiring action to be taken following serious loss of capital.[15] Similarly, capital market authorities frequently promulgate detailed rules to govern tender offers and proxy voting.[16]

By contrast, few jurisdictions rely solely on the rules strategy for regulating complex, intra-corporate relations, such as, for example, self-dealing transactions initiated by controlling shareholders. Such matters are, presumably, too complex to regulate with no more than a matrix of prohibitions and exemptions, which

[14] For the canonical comparison of the merits of rules and standards as regulatory techniques, see Louis Kaplow, *Rules Versus Standards: An Economic Analysis,* 42 Duke Law Review 557 (1992).
[15] See *infra* 5.2.2.
[16] See, e.g., *infra* 8.2.5.4 (mandatory bid) and 9.2.2 (listing requirements).

would threaten to codify loopholes and create pointless rigidities. Rather than rule-based regulation, then, intra-corporate topics such as insider self-dealing tend to be governed by open standards that leave discretion for adjudicators to determine *ex post* whether violations have occurred.[17] Standards are also used to protect creditors and public investors, but the paradigmatic examples of stand-ards-based regulation relate to the company's internal affairs, as when the law requires directors to act in 'good faith' or mandates that self-dealing transactions must be 'entirely fair'.[18]

The importance of both rules and standards depends in large measure on the vigor with which they are enforced. In principle, well-drafted rules can be mech-anically enforced. Standards, however, inevitably require courts (or other adjudi-cators) to become more deeply involved in evaluating and sometimes moulding corporate decisions *ex post*. In this sense, standards lie between rules (which simply require a decision-maker to determine compliance) and another strategy that we will address below—the trusteeship strategy, which requires a neutral decision-maker to exercise his or her own unconstrained best judgment in mak-ing a corporate decision.

2.2.1.2 Setting the terms of entry and exit

A second set of regulatory strategies open to the law involve regulating the terms on which principals *affiliate* with agents rather than—as with rules and standards—regulating the actions of agents after the principal/agent relationship is established. The law can dictate *terms of entry* by, for example, requiring agents to disclose information about the likely quality of their performance before con-tracting with principals.[19] Alternatively, the law can prescribe *exit opportunities* for principals, such as awarding to a shareholder the right to sell her stock, or awarding to a creditor the right to call for repayment of a loan.

The entry strategy is particularly important in screening out opportunistic agents in the public capital markets.[20] Outside investors know little about public companies unless they are told. Thus it is widely accepted that public investors require some form of systematic disclosure to obtain an adequate supply of infor-mation. Legal rules mandating such disclosure provide an example of an entry strategy because stocks cannot be sold unless the requisite information is sup-plied, generally by the corporation itself.[21] A similar but more extreme form of

---

[17] See *infra* 6.2.5. This is not to say that rules are wholly absent from such situations: some jurisdictions regulate forms of self-dealing judged to merit particular suspicion through rules in combination with a more general standards strategy.

[18] See, e.g., *infra* 5.3.1.1 (managerial liability vis-à-vis creditors).

[19] See *infra* 5.2.1 and 9.2.1.   [20] See *infra* 9.2.1.

[21] The role of disclosure rules in facilitating entry is most intuitive in relation to prospectus dis-closure for initial public offerings, and new issues of seasoned equity. Ongoing disclosure rules may to some extent also facilitate entry, by new shareholders in the secondary market, while at the same time facilitating exit by existing shareholders—an example of a single set of rules implementing

the entry strategy is a requirement that the purchasers of certain securities meet a threshold of net worth or financial sophistication.[22]

The exit strategy, which is also pervasive in corporate law, allows principals to escape opportunistic agents. Broadly speaking, there are two kinds of exit rights. The first is *the right to withdraw* the value of one's investment. The best example of such a right in corporate law is the technique, employed in some jurisdictions, of awarding an appraisal right to shareholders who dissent from certain major transactions such as mergers.[23] As we discuss in Chapter 7,[24] appraisal permits shareholders who object to a significant transaction to claim the value that their shares had *prior to* the disputed transaction—thus avoiding a prospective loss if, in their view, the firm has made a value-reducing decision.

The second type of exit right is *the right of transfer*—the right to sell shares in the market—which is of obvious importance to public shareholders. (Recall that transferability is a core characteristic of the corporate form.) Standing alone, a transfer right provides less protection than a withdrawal right, since an informed transferee steps into the shoes of the transferor, and will therefore offer a price that impounds the expected future loss of value from insider mismanagement or opportunism. But the transfer right permits the replacement of the current shareholder/principal(s) by a new one that may be more effective in controlling the firm's management. Thus, unimpeded transfer rights allow hostile takeovers in which the disaggregated shareholders of a mismanaged company can sell their shares to a single active shareholder with a strong financial interest in efficient management.[25] Such a transfer of control rights, or even the threat of it, can be a highly effective device for disciplining management.[26] Moreover, transfer

more than one strategy. However, the function of ongoing disclosure rules is more general: see *infra*, 2.4 and 9.2.1.4.2.

[22] For example, SEC registration requirements in the U.S. are waived for an issuer whose offers are restricted to 'accredited investors', defined as individuals with net worth in excess of $1m or annual income in excess of $200,000 for each of the last two years (17 C.F.R. §230.501(a), 505, 506 (SEC, Regulation D)). Similarly, in the EU, prospectus disclosure requirements are waived for issues restricted to 'qualified investors', with a securities portfolio of more than €500,000 and knowledge of securities investment (Art. 1(e)(iv), 2, 3(2) Directive 2003/25/EC, 2003 O.J. (L 345) 64 (Prospectus Directive)).

[23] The withdrawal right is a dominant governance device for the regulation of some non-corporate forms of enterprise such as the common law partnership at will, which can be dissolved at any time by any partner. Business corporations sometimes grant similar withdrawal rights to their shareholders through special charter provisions. The most conspicuous example is provided by open-ended investment companies, such as mutual funds in the U.S., which are frequently formed as business corporations under the general corporation statutes. The universal default regime in corporate law, however, provides for a much more limited set of withdrawal rights for shareholders, and in some jurisdictions none at all.

[24] See *infra* 7.2.2, 7.4.1.2.

[25] Some jurisdictions impose limits on the extent to which transfer rights may be impeded. An example is the EU's 'breakthrough rule' for takeovers, implemented in a few European countries. See *infra* 8.3.2.

[26] Viewed this way, of course, legal rules that enhance transferability serve not just as an instance of the exit strategy but, simultaneously, as an instance of the entry strategy and incentive strategy as well. The same legal device can serve multiple protective functions. See also *infra* 8.1.2.4.

rights are a prerequisite for stock markets, which also empower disaggregated shareholders by providing a continuous assessment of managerial performance (among other things) in the form of share prices.

2.2.2 Governance strategies

Thus far we have addressed the set of regulatory strategies that might be extended for the protection of vulnerable parties in any class of contractual relationships. We now turn to the six strategies that depend on the hierarchical elements of the principal-agent relationship.

2.2.2.1 Selection and removal

Given the central role of delegated management in the corporate form, it is no surprise that *appointment rights*—the power to *select* or *remove* directors (or other managers)—are key strategies for controlling the enterprise. Indeed, these strategies are at the very core of corporate governance. As we will discuss in Chapters 3 and 4, moreover, the power to appoint directors is a core strategy not only for addressing the agency problems of shareholders in relation to managers, but also, in some jurisdictions, for addressing agency problems of minority shareholders in relation to controlling shareholders, and of employees in relationship to the shareholder class as a whole.

2.2.2.2 Initiation and ratification

A second pair of governance strategies expands the power of principals to intervene in the firm's management. These are *decision rights,* which grant principals the power to *initiate* or *ratify* management decisions. Again, it is no surprise that this set of decision rights strategies is much less prominent in corporate law than are appointment rights strategies. This disparity is a logical consequence of the fact that the corporate form is designed as a vehicle for the delegation of managerial power and authority to the board of directors. Only the largest and most fundamental corporate decisions (such as mergers and charter amendments) require the ratification of shareholders under existing corporation statutes, and no jurisdiction to our knowledge requires shareholders to initiate managerial decisions.[27]

2.2.2.3 Trusteeship and reward

Finally, a last pair of governance strategies alters the incentives of agents rather than expanding the powers of principals. These are *incentive strategies.* The first incentive strategy is the *reward strategy,* which—as the name implies—rewards

---

[27] See *infra* 3.4. The utility, for reducing agency costs, of separating the initiation of decisions from their ratification was first emphasized by Eugene Fama and Michael Jensen, *Separation of Ownership and Control*, 26 JOURNAL OF LAW AND ECONOMICS 301 (1983).

agents for successfully advancing the interests of their principals. Broadly speaking, there are two principal reward mechanisms in corporate law. The more common form of reward is a *sharing rule* that motivates loyalty by tying the agent's monetary returns directly to those of the principal. A conspicuous example is the protection that minority shareholders enjoy from the equal treatment norm, which requires a strictly pro rata distribution of dividends.[28] As a consequence of this rule, controlling shareholders—here the 'agents'—have an incentive to maximize the returns of the firm's minority shareholders—here the 'principals'—at least to the extent that corporate returns are paid out as dividends. The reward mechanism that is less commonly the focus of corporate law is the *pay-for-performance regime,* in which an agent, although not sharing in his principal's returns, is nonetheless paid for successfully advancing her interests. Even though no jurisdiction *imposes* such a scheme on shareholders, legal rules often facilitate or discourage high-powered incentives of this sort.[29] American law, for example, has long embraced incentive compensation devices such as stock option plans, while more sceptical jurisdictions continue to limit them.

The second incentive strategy—the *trusteeship strategy*—works on a quite different principle. It seeks to remove conflicts of interest *ex ante* to ensure that an agent will not obtain personal gain from disserving her principal. This strategy assumes that, in the absence of strongly focused—or 'high-powered'—monetary incentives to behave opportunistically, agents will respond to the 'low-powered' incentives of conscience, pride, and reputation,[30] and are thus more likely to manage in the interests of their principals. One well-known example of the trusteeship strategy is the 'independent director', now relied upon in many jurisdictions to approve self-dealing transactions. Such directors will not personally profit from actions that disproportionately benefit the firm's managers or controlling shareholders, and hence are expected to be guided more strongly by conscience and reputation in making decisions.[31] Similarly, reliance on auditors to approve financial statements and certain corporate transactions is also an example of

---

[28] See *infra* 4.1.3.2.   [29] See *infra* 3.5.

[30] We use the terms 'high-powered incentives' and 'low-powered incentives' as they are conventionally used in the economics literature, to refer to the distinction between economic incentives on the one hand and ethical or moral incentives on the other. Economic incentives are high-powered in the sense that they are concrete and sharply focused. See, e.g., Williamson, *supra* note 2, 137–41; Bengt Hölmstrom and Paul Milgrom, *The Firm as an Incentive System,* 84 AMERICAN ECONOMIC REVIEW 972 (1994). By referring to moral norms as 'low-powered' incentives we do not mean to imply that they are generally less important in governing human behavior than are monetary incentives. Surely, for most individuals in most circumstances, the opposite is true, and civilization would not have come very far if this were not the case.

[31] On the reputational consequences for independent directors of poor performance, see David Yermack, *Remuneration, Retention, and Reputation Incentives for Outside Directors,* 54 JOURNAL OF FINANCE 2281 (2004); Eliezer M. Fich and Anil Shivdasani, *Financial Fraud, Director Reputation, and Shareholder Wealth,* 86 JOURNAL OF FINANCIAL ECONOMICS 306 (2007).

trusteeship, provided the auditors are motivated principally by reputational concerns.[32] In certain circumstances other agents external to the corporation may be called upon to serve as trustees, as when the law requires an investment banker, a state official, or a court to approve corporate action.

2.2.3 *Ex post* and *ex ante* strategies

The bottom row in Table 2–1 arranges our ten legal strategies into five pairs, each with an '*ex ante*' and an '*ex post*' strategy. This presentation merely highlights the fact that half of the strategies take full effect *before* an agent acts, while the other half respond—at least potentially—to the quality of the agent's action *ex post*. In the case of the regulatory strategies, for example, rules specify what the agent may or may not do *ex ante*, while standards specify the general norm against which an agent's actions will be judged *ex post*. Thus, a rule might prohibit a class of self-dealing transactions outright, while a standard might mandate that these transactions will be judged against a norm of fairness *ex post*.[33] Similarly, in the case of setting the terms of entry and exit, an entry strategy, such as mandatory disclosure, specifies what must be done *before* an agent can deal with a principal, while an exit device such as appraisal rights permits the principal to respond after the quality of the agent's action is revealed.[34]

The six governance strategies also fall into *ex ante* and *ex post* pairs. If principals can appoint their agents *ex ante*, they can screen for loyalty; if principals can remove their agents *ex post*, they can punish disloyalty. Similarly, shareholders might have the power to initiate a major corporate transaction such as a merger, or—as is ordinarily the case—they might be restricted to ratifying a motion to merge offered by the board of directors.[35] Finally, trusteeship is an *ex ante* strategy in the sense that it neutralizes an agent's adverse interests prior to her appointment by the principal, while most reward strategies are *ex post* in the sense that their payouts are contingent on uncertain future outcomes, and thus remain less than fully specified until after the agent acts.

We do not wish, however, to overemphasize the clarity or analytic power of this categorization of legal strategies into *ex ante* and *ex post* types. One could well argue, for example, that the reward strategy should not be considered an *ex post* strategy but rather an *ex ante* strategy because, like the trusteeship strategy, it establishes in advance the terms on which the agent will be compensated.

---

[32] While auditors face reputational sanctions for failure (see, e.g., Jan Barton, *Who Cares About Auditor Reputation?*, 22 Contemporary Accounting Research 549 (2005)), their independence and hence trustee status may be compromised by financial incentives in the form of consulting contracts: see John C. Coffee, *What Caused Enron? A Capsule Social and Economic History of the 1990s*, 89 Cornell Law Review 269, 291–3 (2004).

[33] Compare *infra* 6.2.4 (*ex ante* prohibitions) and 6.2.5 (*ex post* standards).

[34] Compare, e.g., *infra* 5.2.1, 6.2.1.1, 9.2.1 (mandatory disclosure), and 7.2.2 (appraisal).

[35] See *infra* 7.4.

Likewise, one could argue that appointment rights cannot easily be broken into *ex ante* and *ex post* types, since an election of directors might involve, simultaneously, the selection of new directors and the removal of old ones. We offer the *ex post/ex ante* distinction only as a classification heuristic that is helpful for purposes of exposition.

Indeed, as we have already noted, it is in the same heuristic spirit that we offer our categorization of legal strategies in general. The ten strategies arrayed in Table 2–1 clearly overlap, and any given legal rule might well be classified as an instance of two or more of those strategies. Again, our purpose here is simply to emphasize the various ways in which law can be used as an instrument, not to provide a new formalistic schema that displaces rather than aids functional understanding.

2.3 Compliance and Enforcement

Legal strategies are relevant only to the extent that they induce compliance. In this regard, each strategy depends on the existence of other legal institutions—such as courts, regulators, and procedural rules—to secure *enforcement* of the legal norms. In this section, we consider the relationship between enforcement and compliance. We then discuss three modalities by which enforcement may be effected.

2.3.1 Enforcement and intervention

Enforcement is most directly relevant as regards regulatory strategies such as rules and standards. These operate to constrain the agent's behavior; they cannot do this credibly unless they are in fact enforced.[36] This necessitates well-functioning enforcement institutions, such as courts and regulators, along with appropriately-structured incentives to initiate cases.

In contrast, governance strategies rely largely upon intervention by principals to generate agent compliance.[37] Whether this intervention takes the form of appropriate selection of agents and structure of rewards, credible threats of removal, or effective decision-making on key issues, its success in securing agent compliance depends primarily upon the ability of principals to coordinate and act at low cost. To be sure, governance strategies rely upon background legal rules to support their operation; in particular, they rely on rules defining the

---

[36] This point is not new. For early recognition, see Roscoe Pound, *Law in Books and Law in Action*, 44 AMERICAN LAW REVIEW 12 (1910); Gary Becker, *Crime and Punishment: An Economic Approach*, 76 JOURNAL OF POLITICAL ECONOMY 169 (1968).

[37] It is possible to talk of such interventions as a form of 'enforcement', in the sense that they make the impact of the governance strategies credible to the agent. However, to avoid confusion with the more specific sense of enforcement understood by lawyers, we eschew here this wider sense.

decision-making authority of the various corporate actors.[38] They therefore also require legal enforcement institutions to make such delineations of authority effective. However, governance strategies require less sophistication and information on the part of courts and regulators than is required to enforce agents' compliance more directly through regulatory strategies.[39] Enforcement institutions, therefore, are of first-order importance for regulatory strategies, but only of second-order importance for governance strategies.

2.3.2 Modes of enforcement

Turning now to the nature of these 'enforcement institutions', we distinguish three *modalities* of enforcement, according to the character of the actors responsible for taking the initiative: (1) public officials, (2) private parties acting in their own interests, and (3) strategically placed private parties ('gatekeepers') conscripted to act in the public interest. Modalities of enforcement might of course be classified across a number of other dimensions. Our goal here is not to categorize for its own sake, but to provoke thought about how the impact of substantive legal strategies is mediated by different modalities of enforcement. We therefore simply sketch out a heuristic classification based on one dimension—the character of enforcers—and encourage readers to think about how matters might be affected by other dimensions along which enforcement may vary. The categorization we have chosen, we believe, has the advantage that it likely reflects the way in which agents involved in running a firm perceive enforcement—that is, as affecting them through the actions of public officials, interested private parties, and gatekeepers.

2.3.2.1 *Public enforcement*

By 'public enforcement', we refer to all legal and regulatory actions brought by organs of the state. This mode includes criminal and civil suits brought by public officials and agencies, as well as various *ex ante* rights of approval—such as for securities offering statements—exercised by public actors. In addition to formal measures, public enforcement also encompasses reputational sanctions that may accompany the disclosure that a firm is under investigation.[40]

---

[38] For example, decision rights strategies require courts to deny validity to a purported decision made by a process that does not reflect the principals' decision rights.

[39] See Alan Schwartz, *Relational Contracts in the Courts: An Analysis of Incomplete Agreements and Judicial Strategies*, 21 JOURNAL OF LEGAL STUDIES 271 (1992); Edward B. Rock and Michael L. Wachter, *Islands of Conscious Power: Law, Norms, and the Self-Governing Corporation*, 149 UNIVERSITY OF PENNSYLVANIA LAW REVIEW 1619 (2001).

[40] See Jonathan Karpoff and John Lott, Jr., *The Reputational Penalty Firms Face from Committing Criminal Fraud*, 36 JOURNAL OF LAW AND ECONOMICS 757 (1993); Cindy Alexander, *On the Nature of the Reputational Penalty for Corporate Crime: Evidence*, 42 JOURNAL OF LAW AND ECONOMICS 489 (1999); Jonathan Karpoff, D. Scott Lee, and Gerald Martin, *The Cost to Firms of Cooking the Books*, 43 JOURNAL OF FINANCIAL AND QUANTITATIVE ANALYSIS 581 (2008).

Public enforcement action can be initiated by a wide variety of state organs, ranging from local prosecutors' offices to national regulatory authorities that monitor corporate actions in real time—such as the U.S. Securities and Exchange Commission (SEC) monitoring corporate disclosures—and have the power to intervene to prevent breaches.[41] We also describe some self-regulatory and quasi-regulatory authorities, such as national stock exchanges and the UK's Financial Reporting Council, as 'public enforcers'. Such bodies are *enforcers* to the extent that they are able in practice to compel compliance with their rules *ex ante* or to impose sanctions for rule violations *ex post*, whether these sanctions are reputational, contractual, or civil. Moreover, they are meaningfully described as *public* enforcers where their regulatory efficacy is spurred by a credible threat of state intervention, and they can be seen as public franchisees.[42] Where no such credible threat exists, then such organizations are better viewed as purely private.

2.3.2.2 Private enforcement

'Private enforcement' most obviously encompasses civil lawsuits brought by private parties, such as shareholder derivative suits and class actions. Importantly, however, we wish to emphasize that it also should be understood as including informal, or reputational, sanctions imposed by private parties, which might take the form of lower share prices, a decline in social standing, or a personal sense of shame.[43] All of these may be inflicted by private parties on misbehaving corporate actors as private responses to wrongdoing.[44]

As with public enforcement, private enforcement embraces a wide range of institutions. At the formal end of the spectrum, these include class actions and derivative suits, which require considerable legal and institutional infrastructure in the form of a plaintiffs' bar, cooperative judges, and favorable procedural law that facilitates actions through matters as diverse as discovery rights and legal fees. Similarly, at the informal end of the spectrum, market reputation can only 'penalize' misconduct by corporate wrongdoers to the extent that there is a mechanism for dissemination of information about (possible) malfeasance and reasonably

---

[41] On the efficacy of public enforcement of securities laws in promoting deep and liquid markets, contrast Rafael La Porta, Florencio Lopes-de-Silanes, and Andrei Shleifer, *What Works in Securities Laws?*, 61 JOURNAL OF FINANCE 1 (2006) with Howell Jackson and Mark Roe, *Public and Private Enforcement of Securities Laws: Resource-Based Evidence*, Working Paper (2008), at http://www.ssrn.com.

[42] The concept of 'coerced self-regulation' is developed in Ian Ayres and John Braithwaite, RESPONSIVE REGULATION: TRANSCENDING THE DEREGULATION DEBATE 101–32 (1992).

[43] Reputational losses may also be suffered by firms consequent on the announcement of a private lawsuit, in addition to the formal sanction it implies. See, e.g., Amar Gande and Craig Lewis, *Shareholder Initiated Class Action Lawsuits: Shareholder Wealth Effects and Industry Spillovers*, JOURNAL OF FINANCIAL AND QUANTITATIVE ANALYSIS (forthcoming).

[44] Indeed, the source of the sanction may be the actor himself, to the extent that very private internal feelings of guilt are involved.

well-functioning factor and product markets in which the terms on which the firm contracts become less favorable in response to that information.[45]

Unlike public enforcement, the modality we term private enforcement depends chiefly on the mechanism of deterrence—that is, the imposition of penalties *ex post* upon the discovery of misconduct. There are few direct analogs in private enforcement to the *ex ante* regulatory approval we have included within the mode of public enforcement. One example of such enforcement may be the UK's 'scheme of arrangement' procedure, whereby a company wishing to undertake a major restructuring transaction and having obtained requisite votes from share-holders (and creditors, if they are parties) may seek court approval of the arrangement.[46] The court will scrutinize the procedural steps taken at this point, and if its sanction is given to the scheme, it cannot be challenged *ex post*. However, if the focus is widened to include not only enforcement in the strict sense, but means of securing agent compliance more generally, there is an important counterpart: private actors are of course very much involved in *ex ante* governance interventions to secure compliance by agents. Indeed, while the discussion in this section has focused on public and private actors as initiators of the enforcement of legal norms, the same conceptual distinction can also be made in relation to governance interventions. Public actors may also be involved in governance interventions, for instance where the state is a significant stockholder. This position is not observed in most of the jurisdictions we survey, but in some countries—most notably China—state ownership of controlling shares in publicly traded companies is common.[47] Under such circumstances, public actors—namely government agencies—take decisions regarding governance intervention.

2.3.2.3 Gatekeeper control

Gatekeeper control involves the conscription of noncorporate actors, such as accountants and lawyers, in policing the conduct of corporate actors. This conscription generally involves exposing the gatekeepers to the threat of sanction for participation in corporate misbehavior, or for failure to prevent or disclose misbehavior.[48] The actors so conscripted are 'gatekeepers' in the sense that their participation is generally necessary, whether as a matter of practice or of law, to accomplish the corporate transactions that are the ultimate focus of the

---

[45] On the role of reputational penalties in contracting, see Simon Johnson, John McMillan, and Christopher Woodruff, *Courts and Relational Contracts*, 18 JOURNAL OF LAW ECONOMICS AND ORGANIZATION 221 (2002); Franklin Allen, Jun Qian, and Meijun Qian, *Law, Finance, and Economic Growth in China*, 77 JOURNAL OF FINANCIAL ECONOMICS 57 (2005).

[46] Part 26 Companies Act 2006 (UK).

[47] See Lee Branstetter, *China's Financial Markets: An Overview*, in CHINA'S FINANCIAL TRANSITION AT A CROSSROADS 23, 43–57 (Charles W. Calomiris (ed.), 2007).

[48] See Reinier Kraakman, *Gatekeepers: The Anatomy of a Third-Party Enforcement Strategy*, 2 JOURNAL OF LAW ECONOMICS AND ORGANIZATION 53 (1986); John C. Coffee, Jr., GATEKEEPERS: THE PROFESSIONS AND CORPORATE GOVERNANCE (2006).

enforcement efforts. We call the mode 'gatekeeper *control*' to emphasize that it works by harnessing the control that gatekeepers have over corporate transactions, and giving them a strong incentive to use that control to prevent unwanted conduct.

Gatekeeper control is probably best viewed as a form of delegated intervention: principals do not themselves engage in scrutiny of the agent, but leave this to the gatekeeper. Compliance is generally secured through the *ex ante* mechanism of constraint (e.g., auditors refuse to issue an unqualified report) rather than through the *ex post* mechanism of penalizing wrongdoers. Such delegation of course creates a new agency problem between the gatekeeper and the principals. This is dealt with through the application of the basic legal strategies to the gatekeepers themselves, with chief reliance on the standards and trusteeship strategies.

2.4 Disclosure

Disclosure plays a fundamental role in controlling corporate agency costs. As we have already noted,[49] it is an important part of the affiliation rights strategies. Most obviously, prospectus disclosure forces agents to provide prospective principals with information that helps them to decide upon which terms, if any, they wish to *enter* the firm as owners. To a lesser extent, periodic financial disclosure and *ad hoc* disclosure—for example, of information relevant to share prices, and of the terms of related party transactions—also permits principals to determine the extent to which they wish to remain owners, or rather *exit* the firm. However, continuing disclosure also has more general auxiliary effects in relation to each of the other strategies; hence we treat it separately at this point in our discussion.

In relation to regulatory strategies that require enforcement, disclosure of related party transactions helps to reveal the existence of transactions that may be subject to potential challenge, and provides potential litigants with information to bring before a court. In relation to governance strategies, disclosure can be used in several different, but complementary, ways. First, and most generally, mandating disclosure of the terms of the governance arrangements that are in place allows principals to assess appropriate intervention tactics. Second, and specifically in relation to decision rights, mandatory disclosure of the details of a proposed transaction for which the principals' approval is sought can improve the principals' decision. Third, disclosure of those serving in trustee roles serves to bond their reputations publicly to the effective monitoring of agents.

---

[49] See *supra* 2.2.1.2; see also *infra* 9.2.1.

There is of course a need to ensure compliance with disclosure obligations themselves. This is a microcosm of the more general problem of securing agent compliance. For periodic disclosures, where the type of information is expected but the content is not yet known (so-called 'known unknowns'), no additional compliance mechanism may be required beyond a public statement that the disclosure is expected. If the principals are made aware that a particular piece of information (for example, annual financial statements, the structure and composition of the board, or executive compensation arrangements) is expected to be disclosed in a particular format, then non-disclosure itself can send a negative signal to principals, stimulating them to act.[50] The compliance issue with periodic disclosure is not so much whether it happens, but its quality, and hence a trusteeship strategy—in the form of auditors—is typically used to assist in assuring this. For *ad hoc* disclosure, the compliance issues are different, because by definition, principals do not expect particular disclosures in advance (that is, these are so-called 'unknown unknowns'). Here vigorous legal enforcement alone seems to be able to ensure compliance.[51]

2.5 Legal Strategies in Corporate Context

The law does not apply legal strategies in the abstract but only in specific regulatory contexts. For purposes of exposition and analysis, we have grouped those contexts into six basic categories of corporate decisions and transactions. Each of the next seven chapters focuses on one of those categories. Necessarily, the boundaries of these categories are to some degree arbitrary and overlapping. Nevertheless, each category has a degree of functional unity, and the typical deployment of legal strategies in each is at least moderately distinct.

Chapters 3 and 4 examine the legal strategies at play in the regulation of ordinary business transactions and decisions. Not surprisingly, governance strategies predominate in this context. Chapter 5 turns to corporate debt relationships and the problem of creditor protection—a context in which regulatory strategies are common, except when the firm is insolvent, when the emphasis shifts to governance strategies. Chapter 6 examines the legal regulation of related party (or self-dealing) transactions; Chapter 7 investigates the corporate law treatment of 'significant' transactions, such as mergers and major sales of assets, and Chapter 8 assesses the legal treatment of control transactions such as sales of control blocks and hostile takeovers. As the discussion below will demonstrate, jurisdictions adopt a fluid mix of regulatory and governance strategies in all of the

---

[50] This mechanism is used to enforce disclosure of governance arrangements in the UK and elsewhere under so-called 'comply or explain' provisions.

[51] See Utpal Bhattacharya and Hazem Daouk, *The World Price of Insider Trading*, 57 JOURNAL OF FINANCE 75 (2002).

last three transactional contexts. Then, Chapter 9 turns to investor protection and the regulation of issuers on the public market, where regulatory strategies predominate.

While we do not claim that these transactional and decisional categories exhaust all of corporate law, they cover most of what is conventionally understood to be corporate law, and nearly all of the interesting and controversial issues that the subject presents today.

Within each of our seven substantive chapters, our analysis proceeds functionally. In most chapters, our analytic discussion is organized by agency problems and legal strategies: for a given category of corporate decisions, we review the legal strategies that are actively deployed by the key corporate law jurisdictions. In two chapters, however, the analytic discussion is organized somewhat differently—by categories of transactions in Chapter 7 (which concerns significant transactions), and by agency problems in Chapter 8 (which concerns control transactions). This variation in structure responds to the greater heterogeneity of the transactions dealt with in those chapters.

Finally, to the extent that there are significant differences across jurisdictions in the legal strategies employed to regulate a given class of corporate decisions, we attempt to assess the origins of these differences. In particular, in Chapter 10 we ask to what extent these differences can be understood as functional adaptations to differences in institutions, such as trading markets and financial intermediaries (that is 'efficiency effects' of such complementary institutions), and how far they appear to be historical, cultural, or political artifacts driven by distributional rather than functional concerns.[52]

2.6 Systematic Differences

We might expect the use of the various legal strategies for controlling agency costs, and of the associated modes of enforcement, to differ systematically across jurisdictions. In particular, we would expect to see strong complementarities between the structure of share ownership and the types of legal strategies relied upon most heavily to control agency costs. Since the efficacy of governance mechanisms is closely linked to the extent to which principals are able to coordinate, it would be surprising if the structure of share ownership did not affect the extent to which these strategies are employed to control managers. In most jurisdictions around the world, the ownership of shares in publicly traded firms is concentrated in the hands of relatively few shareholders—whether families or institutional investors. With such ownership patterns, owners face relatively low coordination costs as between themselves, and are able to rely on governance

[52] On the distinction between 'efficiency effects' and 'distributional effects' of complementary institutions, see *supra* 1.6.1.

strategies to control managers. Where ownership of shares is more diffuse, however, governance mechanisms are less effective, and there is more need for regulatory mechanisms to take the fore.

Just as the choice of legal strategies for controlling agency problems is likely to complement the pattern of ownership, it will in turn be complemented by the nature and sophistication of the enforcement institutions. In systems relying heavily on regulatory strategies, enforcement institutions will likely have a greater role to play in securing compliance by agents, as opposed to intervention by principals themselves.[53] At a more micro level, particular regulatory strategies complement and are supported by different enforcement institutions. Rules require a sophisticated and quickly responding regulator, if they are not to end up imposing greater hindrance than benefit on parties. Standards, on the other hand, require independent and sophisticated courts and lawyers, if they are to be deployed effectively.

In addition, the appropriate *scope* of continuing disclosure obligations may vary depending on the extent to which particular legal strategies are employed. Thus in the U.S., where regulatory strategies are extensively used, continuing disclosure focuses on self-dealing transactions, and so assists in formal enforcement activities. In the EU, by contrast, where greater reliance is placed on governance mechanisms, disclosure obligations emphasize details of board structure.[54] The necessary *extent* of disclosure will also vary depending on the ownership structure. Where owners are highly coordinated, frequent disclosure may be less important for controlling managers:[55] owners are better able to discover information for themselves, and governance strategies can be used to stimulate disclosure of greater information. This is not to say, however, that effective and adequately enforced disclosure obligations do not matter in systems with coordinated owners. Rather, the problem with coordinated owners is not the first of our three agency problems but the second: ensuring that the information management transmits to powerful owners, and information about how those owners exercise their control rights, makes its way to all owners equally—that is, preventing so-called 'selective disclosure'.

---

[53] The existence of a demand for regulatory, as opposed to governance, strategies may be expected to spur the development of regulatory expertise. Thus in jurisdictions with widely dispersed retail shareholdings, such as the U.S., specialist courts tend to be more active because they are more in demand. See Zohar Goshen, *The Efficiency of Controlling Corporate Self-Dealing: Theory Meets Reality*, 91 CALIFORNIA LAW REVIEW 393 (2003).

[54] See e.g., The High Level Group of Company Law Experts, REPORT OF THE HIGH LEVEL GROUP OF COMPANY LAW EXPERTS ON A MODERN REGULATORY FRAMEWORK FOR COMPANY LAW IN EUROPE 45–6 (2002), at http://ec.europa.eu; Recommendation 2005/162/EC on the role of non-executive or supervisory directors of listed companies and on committees of the (supervisory) board (2005 O.J. (L 52)51), para. 9.

[55] See John Armour and Jeffrey N. Gordon, *The Berle-Means Corporation in the 21st Century*, Working Paper (2008), at http://www.law.upenn.edu.

Many such institutional differences may make little overall difference to the success of firms' control of their agency costs, as various combinations of strategies and associated institutions may be functionally equivalent. However, there are some institutions whose presence or absence is likely to be important in any jurisdiction. In particular, given the fundamental role played by disclosure in supporting both the enforcement of regulatory strategies and the exercise of governance, institutions supporting disclosure—a strong and effective securities regulator and a sophisticated accounting profession, for example—are always likely to make an overall difference to the success of firms in controlling agency costs.[56]

[56] See Bernard Black, *The Legal and Institutional Preconditions for Strong Securities Markets*, 48 UCLA Law Review 781 (2001).

3

The Basic Governance Structure: The Interests of Shareholders as a Class

Luca Enriques, Henry Hansmann, and Reinier Kraakman

The law of corporate governance establishes the 'rules of the game'[1] among corporate constituencies. As we observed in Chapter 2, corporate law must address three fundamental agency problems: the conflict between managers (directors and senior executives) and shareholders, the conflict between controlling and minority shareholders, and the conflict between shareholders and non-shareholder constituencies. This chapter examines how the corporate governance structure mitigates the manager-shareholder conflict; Chapter 4 explores the role of governance in safeguarding minority shareholder and non-shareholder interests. Both chapters focus on publicly traded firms, although much of our discussion applies equally well to companies that are not actively traded.

Corporate governance builds largely on the appointment rights and trusteeship strategies detailed in Table 2–1. We begin by dilating on these strategies, which are *self*-enforcing in the limited sense that they empower a principal, or a disinterested trustee, to safeguard the principal's interests. Thus we focus less on enforcement in Chapters 3 and 4 than in subsequent chapters. We must note, however, that basic shareholder rights are *not* always enforced. Russia's negative experience during the mid-1990s is a cautionary reminder that 'self-enforcing' governance strategies still require an honest judiciary and a strong securities regulator to be effective.[2] Indeed, even in the U.S., there is discomforting evidence of shortcomings in the mechanics of shareholder voting.[3]

---

[1] Lucian A. Bebchuk, *Letting Shareholder Set the Rules*, 119 Harvard Law Review 1784 (2006).

[2] See Bernard Black, Reinier Kraakman, and Anna Tarassova, *Russian Privatization and Corporate Governance: What Went Wrong?*, 52 Stanford Law Review 1731 (2000).

[3] See Marcel Kahan and Edward B. Rock, *The Hanging Chads of Corporate Voting*, 96 Georgetown Law Journal 1227 (2008). While no one suggests that U.S. voting contests are rigged, incumbents often seem to enjoy an edge in closely-matched contests. See e.g. Yair Listokin, *Management Always Wins the Close Ones*, 10 American Law and Economics Review 159 (2008). See also *Hewlett v. Hewlett-Packard Co.*, 2002 WL 818091 (Del. Ch. 2002) (reviewing irregularities in the HP-Compaq proxy contest). The law in some other core jurisdictions appears to do more to allay

3.1 Appointment Rights and Shareholder Interests

Two features of the corporate form underlie corporate governance. The first is investor ownership, which, given the breadth of contemporary capital markets, implies that ultimate control over the firm often lies partly or entirely in the hands of shareholders far removed from the firm's day-to-day operations. The second is delegated management, which implies that shareholder influence is usually exercised indirectly, by electing directors.[4] Thus, a canonical feature of the corporation is a multi-member board—selected (largely or entirely) by shareholders—that is distinct from both the general meeting of shareholders and the firm's managing officers. The law addresses the shareholder-manager agency problem in the first instance by establishing and reinforcing the right of shareholders to appoint the members of the board. The effectiveness of this strategy depends, in turn, on the board's powers and resources, and on the capacity of shareholders to engage in collective action. In addition to this appointment strategy, many jurisdictions rely increasingly on the trusteeship role of independent directors as pillars of corporate governance.

3.1.1 Managerial power and corporate boards

The governance law of public or 'open' corporations is broadly similar in all of our core jurisdictions. It reserves certain fundamental decisions to the general shareholders meeting, while assigning much decision-making power to one- or two-tier boards of directors.

In single-tier jurisdictions such as the U.S., UK, and Japan, one board exercises the legal power to supervise *and* manage a corporation, either directly or through its committees.[5] By contrast, in two-tier jurisdictions, monitoring powers are allocated to elected supervisory boards of non-executive directors, which then appoint and supervise management boards that include the principal executive officers who design and implement business strategy. Germany and the Netherlands mandate two-tier boards for open domestic companies, while Italy and France permit domestic companies to choose between one- and two-tier boards, and firms in every EU jurisdiction may choose between one- and two-tier

concerns about voting irregularities. See, e.g., §§ 342–351 UK Companies Act 2006 (requiring an independent report on shareholder polling upon request of a qualified minority of shareholders).

[4] An exception to this generalization proves the rule. From 1971 until 2004, company law in the Netherlands placed certain large domestic corporations under a so-called *structuur* regime, in which new directors were selected by incumbent directors, subject to review by the commercial court to ensure adequate representation of shareholder and employee interests. For further discussion of the *structuur* regime and its replacement, see *infra* 4.1.3.1.

[5] East Asian jurisdictions heavily influenced by German law and Italy retain vestigial supervisory boards such as the board of auditors (Japan and Italy) or the board of supervisors (China). The powers of these secondary boards are generally limited, however.

boards by opting into the *Societas Europaea* (or SE), which allows either board structure.[6] Although the supervisory and management boards are in a semi-hierarchical legal relationship in the two-tier structure, the management board may be the more powerful of the two in fact. The management board enjoys independent legal status. Under German law, for example, the supervisory board cannot oust the management board without cause, cannot make business decisions reserved to the management board, and—on certain matters—may even be overruled if a recalcitrant management board can obtain the support of a super-majority shareholder vote.[7] In practice, a company's most influential single actor can be the chair of either its supervisory or its management board, depending upon ownership structure and the personalities involved.[8]

In theory, single-tier boards concentrate decision-making power, while two-tier boards favor collective decision-making. For example, a single-tier board permits firms to combine the roles of board chairman and chief executive officer ('CEO'), as commonly happens in the U.S. and France.[9] By contrast, two-tier jurisdictions such as Germany bar supervisory boards from making managerial decisions, and, as a statutory default, requires that management boards make decisions by majority vote.[10] Both approaches to the management of large firms have potential advantages.[11] But two considerations caution against generalizing about these advantages in our core jurisdictions. First, the extent of the distinction between the two board structures is often unclear. Informal leadership coalitions can cross-cut the legal separation between management and supervisory boards;[12] while supermajorities of independent directors and an independent chairman can give single-tier boards a quasi-supervisory flavor.

[6] For France see Art. L. 225–57 Code de commerce. For Italy see Art. 2409–8 to 2409–15 Civil Code. For the SE, see Art. 38 Council Regulation (EC) No 2157/2001 of 8 October 2001, 2001 O.J. (L 294) 1.

[7] §§ 111 IV and 119 II Aktiengesetz (AktG).

[8] For example, a controlling shareholder who chairs a firm's supervisory board is likely to be its dominant actor. In addition, past German practice has sometimes blurred the separation between the two boards by elevating retired members of the management board, and particularly its chair, to the supervisory board. Recently, the non-binding German Corporate Governance Code has limited the number of former management board members on the supervisory board to two, and required 'special reasons' for the election of a former management board member as chairman of the supervisory board (Art. 5.4.2 and 5.4.4).

[9] The UK is the exception among single-tier jurisdictions: Art. A.2.1 of the Combined Code of Best Practices calls for a clear division of responsibility between a company's chairman and chief executive officer.

[10] § 77 Aktiengesetz.

[11] An extensive literature in social psychology explores the systematic differences in group versus individual decision-making and problem-solving. See, e.g., Samuel N. Fraidin, *When Is One Head Better Than Two? Interdependent Information in Group Decision Making*, 93 ORGANIZATIONAL BEHAVIOR AND HUMAN DECISION PROCESSES 102 (2004); Norbert L. Kerr and R. Scott Tindale, *Group Performance and Decision Making g*, 56 ANNUAL REVIEW OF PSYCHOLOGY 623 (2004).

[12] Often, in German companies with no controlling shareholders, the management board de facto picks the supervisory board. See Klaus J. Hopt and Patrick C. Leyens, *Board Models in Europe—Recent Developments of Internal Corporate Governance Structures in Germany, the United Kingdom, France and Italy*, 1 EUROPEAN COMPANY AND FINANCIAL LAW REVIEW 135, 141 (2004).

Second, labor codetermination in Germany, the most prominent two-tier jurisdiction, weakens the supervisory board as a governance organ devoted exclusively
to the interests of the shareholder class. We address the governance features of
codetermination further in Chapter 4. Here we merely note that the two-tier
board structure facilitates strong labor participation in corporate governance in
part because full access to sensitive information and business decision-making
can remain with the management board, thereby mitigating potential conflicts
of interest on the supervisory board.

3.1.2 Nominating directors and the mechanics of voting

In addition to board architecture, the legal aspects of corporate governance
include a wide variety of rules governing director nomination and shareholder
voting.

All of our core jurisdictions apart from the U.S. allow shareholders to nomin-
ate directors. Ordinarily the board proposes the company's slate of nominees,[13]
which is rarely opposed at the annual shareholders meeting. But in most jurisdictions, a qualified minority (usually a small percentage) of shareholders can contest
the board's slate by adding additional nominees to the agenda of the shareholders'
meeting.[14] Insurgent candidates who are nominated in this fashion face the same
up-or-down vote as the company's own nominees. In contrast to this model, however, insurgent shareholders in the U.S. cannot place nominees on the company's
proxy or on the agenda of the shareholders' meeting as of right, but must instead
solicit their *own* proxies and distribute their own solicitations—i.e., ballots, registration statements (subject to SEC review), and supporting materials—to contest
the company's slate of nominees.[15]

Voting rules for board seats at the annual meeting follow a similar pattern.
Our core jurisdictions other than the U.S. follow a majority voting rule, under
which directors are elected by a majority of the votes cast at the shareholders'

---

[13] In Italian listed companies, the incumbents' slate of candidates is formally presented by dominant shareholders, usually in coordination with the managers.

[14] In the UK the default rule is that any shareholder can present her own board candidates in
advance of the meeting (Art. 76, Table A). Similarly, in German companies any shareholder can
add her own candidates up to two weeks before the meeting (§ 127 AktG). In Japan a qualified
minority (1% of votes or 300 votes) may propose its own slate of candidates, which the company
must include in its mail voting/proxy documents. Art. 303 and 305 Companies Act. In Italy the
quorum for the proposal of a slate of candidates varies from 0.5% for the largest companies (by capitalization) to 4.5% for the smaller ones. Art. 144–4 Consob Regulation on Issuers.

[15] See Sofie Cools, *The Real Difference in Corporate Law Between the United States and
Continental Europe: Distribution of Powers*, 30 DELAWARE JOURNAL OF CORPORATE LAW 697, 746
(2005). U.S. securities law allows shareholders to append certain proposals to the company's proxy,
but it expressly excludes resolutions relating to the election of directors. 17 C.F.R. § 240.14a–8
(2008). See also *infra* 3.1.4. The management community has fiercely resisted reform efforts to
allow a qualified minority of shareholders to place their own nominees on the company's proxy.

meeting. By contrast, the statutory default in the U.S. is a 'plurality' voting rule, under which any number of votes suffices to elect a nominee to a board seat.[16] Under this rule, even few favorable votes can elect an entire slate of nominees because dissidents cannot vote *against* the company's nominees: they can only vote a competing slate of nominees, when there is one.[17] Thus, U.S. shareholders cannot block a company's nominees without waging a costly proxy contest. However, U.S. voting practices are currently in flux. Delaware has undertaken a modest statutory reform,[18] and institutional investors have prompted some U.S. companies to opt into majority voting.[19]

Another important aspect of the voting system comprises the rules that regulate—or fail to regulate—the distribution of voting power among classes of shareholders and between nominal and beneficial shareholders. Corporate laws generally embrace the default rule that each stock carries one vote. But all jurisdictions permit some deviations from this one-share/one-vote norm, even while they prohibit or limit others. Thus, all of our core jurisdictions limit circular voting structures[20] and vote buying by parties antagonistic to the interests of shareholders as a class. Germany, Italy, and Japan ban voting caps (i.e., limits on the number of votes a single shareholder may cast) and place limits on dual-class shares that allow controlling shareholders to maintain control while ratcheting down their economic stakes.[21] By contrast, however, all of our jurisdictions

---

[16] See, e.g., § 216(3) Delaware General Corporation Law.

[17] However, U.S. dissidents can withhold favorable votes for board nominees to express dissatisfaction with company policies. Shareholder activists often wage withhold-the-vote campaigns to bring pressure on the board even if they cannot change its composition. Contested elections for U.S. companies' boards are rare. See Lucian A. Bebchuk, *The Myth of the Shareholder Franchise*, 93 Virginia Law Review 675, 688 (2007).

[18] See § 216(4) Delaware General Corporation Law (barring the board from revoking a stockholder bylaw requiring a majority vote for directors).

[19] See Jay W. Verret, *Pandora's Ballot Box, or a Proxy with Moxie? Majority Voting, Ballot Access, and the Legend of Martin Lipton Re-Examined*, 62 The Business Lawyer 1007, 1043 (2007).

[20] Most jurisdictions forbid subsidiaries from voting the shares of their parent companies. Art. L. 233–31 Code de commerce (France); Art. 2359–2 Civil Code (Italy); Art. 308(1) Companies Act (Japan); § 160(c) Delaware General Corporation Law; § 135 Companies Act 2006 (UK). German law bars subsidiaries from owning shares of their parents except in special circumstances (§71d AktG). A number of countries also ban voting in the case of cross-shareholdings by companies that are in no parent-subsidiary relationship. In Italy the relevant threshold (for listed companies only) is 2%, while it is 10% in France, and 25% in Germany. See Shearman & Sterling, LLP, Proportionality Between Ownership and Control in EU Listed Companies: Comparative Legal Study 17 (2007) at http://www.ecgi.de/osov/final_report.php.

[21] For Germany see § 134(1) (voting caps allowed only in non-listed companies), § 12(1) and § 139 (non-voting shares allowed only up to one half of the share capital), and § 12(2) (multiple voting rights banned) Aktiengesetz. For Japan, see Art. 115 Companies Act (shares with restricted voting rights cannot exceed half of the total issued shares); as far as voting caps are concerned, the law is not clear but the Tokyo Stock Exchange is likely to delist companies where ceilings result in an unreasonable restriction of shareholders rights (see Shearman & Sterling, LLP, Proportionality between Ownership and Control in EU Listed Companies: Comparative Legal Study—Exhibit C, Part 2, 357 (2007) at http://www.ecgi.de/osov/final_report.php. For Italy see Art. 2351(2) (non-voting shares cannot exceed half of the outstanding capital), 2351(3) (voting caps allowed only in non-listed companies) and 2351(4) (multiple voting

permit share ownership structures that have effects identical to those of dual-class shares, such as corporate pyramids.[22]

Why is there such disparate treatment of the separation of control from economic interest in shares, both among jurisdictions and within them? One answer is that there is no convincing theoretical or empirical support for a one-share/one-vote rule.[23] Another is that many strategies for separating votes from shares are difficult to regulate. The traditional corporate pyramid illustrates both points. It is arguably efficient insofar as it permits talented controlling shareholders to leverage their own capital by inviting public participation in their enterprises (and it is widely used to finance family-owned businesses throughout the world). In addition, it cannot be banned outright without crippling the partially-held subsidiary as a viable ownership structure.[24]

A less traditional example of separating control rights from cash-flow rights is so-called 'empty voting', in which activists use stock lending, equity swaps, and other derivatives to acquire naked votes in corporations in which they may even hold a net short position.[25] Empty voting is difficult to detect (at least without disclosure reform), and, like vote buying, it can be used to undermine shareholder welfare. Needless to add, it has also attracted the focused attention of corporate lawmakers.[26]

3.1.3 The power to remove directors

Removal rights follow appointment rights. Indeed, one might say that directors are normally 'removed' by dropping their names from the company's slate or by failing to reelect them. It follows that the length of directorial terms can be critical. Longer terms provide insulation from proxy contests, temporary shareholder

---

rights banned) Civil Code. Note also that voting caps can entrench managers as well as protect minority shareholder interests, while circular voting structures and cross-holdings can entrench controlling minority shareholders as well as managers.

[22] See, e.g., Lucian A. Bebchuk, Reinier Kraakman, and George Triantis, *Pyramids, Cross-Ownership, and Dual Class Equity: The Mechanisms and Agency Costs of Separating Control from Cash-Flow Rights*, in CONCENTRATED CORPORATE OWNERSHIP 445 (Randall K. Morck (ed.), 2000).

[23] See e.g. Mike Burkart and Samuel Lee, *The One Share-One Vote Debate: A Theoretical Perspective*, (2007), at http://www.ssrn.com; Renée Adams and Daniel Ferreira, *One Share, One Vote: The Empirical Evidence*, 12 REVIEW OF FINANCE 51 (2008).

[24] Such structures are extremely common but difficult to regulate except, perhaps, through tax law. See, e.g., Randall K. Morck, *How to Eliminate Pyramidal Business Groups: The Double Taxation of Intracorporate Dividends and Other Incisive Uses of Tax Policy*, in TAX POLICY AND THE ECONOMY 135 (James M. Porterba (ed.), 2005). See generally TAX AND CORPORATE GOVERNANCE (Wolfgang Schön (ed.), 2008).

[25] See Henry T. C. Hu and Bernard Black, *The New Vote Buying: Empty Voting and Hidden (Morphable) Ownership*, 79 SOUTHERN CALIFORNIA LAW REVIEW 811 (2006).

[26] Rule 8.3 of the UK Takeover Code, as amended in May 2006, requires 'contracts for differences' (i.e., equity swaps) and similar derivative contracts held during an offer period to be disclosed if they affect more than 1% of the underlying securities.

majorities, and even powerful CEOs. Among our core jurisdictions, directorial terms range from two in the case of Japan, to no limits at all in the case of the UK (where private companies occasionally appoint directors for life).[27] U.S. terms fall somewhere in the middle, with a default of one year and a maximum in most cases of three or four years for staggered or classified boards.[28] By contrast, corporations in Germany and France usually elect directors for five- or six-year terms respectively, the maximum that their statutes permit.[29]

A second aspect of removal rights is the power to remove directors *before* the end of their terms. British, French, Italian, and Japanese law all accord shareholder majorities a non-waivable right to remove directors mid-term without cause.[30] Our remaining jurisdictions provide weaker removal rights. The German default rule allows three-quarters of voting shares to remove a shareholder-elected supervisory board member without cause.[31] The most important U.S. jurisdictions treat the right to remove directors without cause as a statutory default subject to reversal, either by a charter provision on point,[32] or by disallowing removal without cause for classified boards.[33] In addition, Delaware indirectly cabins removal rights by denying shareholders the power to call a special shareholders' meeting unless the company's charter expressly so provides.[34]

Thus, removal rights generally track appointment rights. Jurisdictions with 'shareholder-centric' laws on the books—the UK, France, Japan, and Italy—provide shareholders with non-waivable removal powers as well as robust nomination powers. 'Board-centric' Delaware—the dominant U.S. jurisdiction—weakens removal powers by allowing staggered boards and discouraging special shareholders' meetings. The correlation between appointment and removal powers breaks down principally for German companies, whose shareholders have strong appointment rights (for 'their' supervisory board seats)

---

[27] Art. 332(1) Companies Act (Japan); Paul L. Davies, GOWER AND DAVIES' PRINCIPLES OF MODERN COMPANY LAW 389 (8th ed., 2008) (UK). The maximum term for directors of Italian companies is 3 years. Art. 2383, Civil Code.

[28] In a staggered or classified board, only a fraction of the board is elected each year. For example, Delaware General Corporation Law requires that at least one third of the directors be elected annually (§141(d)) where there is a single class of voting stock. Longer terms are possible, however, where corporate charters provide for multiple classes of voting stock.

[29] § 102 I AktG (Germany); Art. L. 225–18 Code de commerce (France).

[30] § 168 and §303 Companies Act 2006 (UK), Art. L. 225–18 Code de commerce and 225–103 (France); Art. 2383 and 2367, Civil Code and Art. 126–2, Consolidated Act on Financial Intermediation (Italy) (all providing for removal within term and setting minimum thresholds to call special meetings in publicly traded companies). Art. 339(1) Companies Act (Japan) (simple majority required for removal without cause).

[31] § 103 I AktG (Germany).

[32] See § 8.08(a) Revised Model Business Corporation Act.

[33] See § 141(k) Delaware General Corporation Law.

[34] See §§ 211(b) and 211(d) Delaware General Corporation Law. Note that the majority of Delaware companies now going public opt into staggered boards as well as other charter provisions that make the removal of directors difficult. See Lucian A. Bebchuk, John C. Coates, and Guhan Subramanian, *The Powerful Antitakeover Force of Staggered Boards: Theory, Evidence, and Policy*, 54 STANFORD LAW REVIEW 887 (2002).

but can only oust directors from lengthy terms by means of a supermajority vote.[35] (Indeed, German law favors stability on the management board as well, by insulating its members from abrupt removal by the supervisory board.[36])

3.1.4 Facilitating collective action

A final aspect of governance rules is the extent to which they empower dispersed shareholders. Diffuse stock ownership presents shareholders with formidable collective action problems in attempting to exercise their control rights. All of our target jurisdictions address this problem—up to a point.

Voting mechanisms are a conspicuous example. Small shareholders everywhere can exercise their voice at shareholder meetings through one of three mechanisms: mail (or distance) voting, proxy solicitation by corporate partisans, and proxy voting through custodial institutions or other agents. For example, Japanese law allows mid-size and large firms to choose either proxy or mail voting.[37] Mail voting requires the distribution of 'universal ballots', which permit shareholders to vote on all board nominees in lieu of giving proxies to partisan agents who ultimately vote at shareholders' meetings. Likewise, France, Germany, and Italy allow corporations to opt for distance voting,[38] which also enables shareholders to submit universal ballots.[39] By contrast, only the U.S. and the UK rely exclusively on proxy voting among our core jurisdictions.[40] In the UK proxy fights are relatively rare, since prior negotiation among institutional investors often resolves conflicts.[41] It matters in the U.S., however, where shareholders exercise relatively less influence over managers and the costs to insurgents of nominating candidates and soliciting proxies are high.[42]

---

[35] § 103 AktG.   [36] § 84 AktG.

[37] Japanese firms with 1000 or more shareholders must make this choice. Art. 298(1)(iii), 298(2) and 301 Companies Act. Mail voting is also optional for smaller companies, and voting by electronic means is optional for all Japanese companies. Art. 298(1)(iv) Companies Act. In practice most large public Japanese firms adopt mail voting rather than proxy voting.

[38] Art. L. 225–107 Code de commerce (France); Art. 2370(4) Civil Code and Art. 127 Consolidated Act on Financial Intermediation (Italy). For Germany, see the 2001 law on registered shares and on facilitating the exercise of the right to vote (NaStraG).

[39] See Ulrich Noack and Michael Beurskens, *Internet-Influence on Corporate Governance— Progress or Standstill?*, 3 EUROPEAN BUSINESS ORGANIZATION LAW REVIEW 129, 146 (2002).

[40] The NYSE mandates proxy solicitation for 'operating' listed U.S. firms except where solicitation would be impossible (Rule 402.04(A) Listed Company Manual). See also Rules 4350(g) and 4360(g) NASDAQ Marketplace Rules (same). No such law or listing requirement exists in Germany, France, Italy, the UK, or Japan. Note that Art. 12 of the Shareholders' Rights Directive (Directive 2007/36/EC, 2007 O.J. (L 184) 17) will require also the UK to grant all 'traded companies' the right to opt for distance voting, though whether this will change UK corporate practice remains to be seen.

[41] Julian R. Franks, Colin Mayer, and Stefano Rossi, *Ownership: Evolution and Regulation*, THE REVIEW OF FINANCIAL STUDIES (forthcoming 2009) at http://www.ssrn.com.

[42] Heavy regulation of proxy solicitation was a major obstacle to insurgent shareholder action in the U.S. until 1992, when the SEC relaxed many of its filing and disclosure requirements. Regulation of Communication Among Shareholders, Exchange Act Release No. 34-31326 (1992).

Broadly speaking, all institutions that invest in the market on behalf of multiple beneficiaries can be seen as aggregating control rights, and therefore reducing the collective action problems of disaggregated investors. Indeed, many institutions with financial obligations to their beneficiaries or customers— including pension funds, mutual funds, unit trusts, and insurance companies— have long championed shareholder interests in the UK and the U.S.[43] By contrast, purely custodial institutions have no financial interest in the shares they hold, and have traditionally favored company nominees to the extent that they have been empowered to vote custodial shares. For example, U.S. brokerage houses vote their custodial shares in favor of uncontested company nominees,[44] while continental European custodians, such as banks and foundations, traditionally played an even stronger, pro-incumbents role in corporate governance.[45] In Germany, for example, where supervisory boards could not (or did not) engage in partisan proxy solicitation,[46] banks served as depositories for shares, and customarily voted these shares for company nominees by implicit consent.[47] After financial pressures[48] and legal reform[49] largely curbed this practice in the 1990s, voting outcomes in widely held German companies have occasionally become less predictably pro-management.[50]

Indeed, significant barriers to shareholder collective action still remain, including registration and disclosure requirements for any 5% 'group' of shareholders whose members agree to coordinate their votes. See SEC Rule 13d–5 (17 C.F.R. § 240.13d–5 (2008)). Regulation today is not entirely unfavorable for U.S. insurgents, however. The law also benefits them by, for example, forcing extensive corporate disclosure, ensuring that insurgent proxy materials actually reach shareholders, and often allowing small shareholders to piggyback shareholder proposals onto a company's proxy form. Finally, the U.S. is our only core jurisdiction to allow *ex post* compensation of successful insurgents for their campaign expenses. See, e.g., *Rosenfeld v. Fairchild Engine & Airplane Corp.*, 128 N.E. 2d 291 (N.Y. 1955).

[43] See Geof P. Stapledon, INSTITUTIONAL SHAREHOLDERS AND CORPORATE GOVERNANCE (1996).

[44] A proposal to ban this is still pending. See NYSE proposed amendment to Rule 452 (Giving Proxies by Member Organization), at http://www.nyse.com/press/1161166307645.html.

[45] Italy is an exception, because proxy voting by banks was prohibited in 1974 and only became legal again in 1998. There is no evidence today of banks' involvement in shareholder meetings.

[46] See Karsten Schmidt, GESELLSCHAFTSRECHT 854 (4th ed., 2002).

[47] Small shareholders could always instruct their banks as to how to vote their shares. See § 128 Aktiengesetz. But they rarely gave explicit instructions. Mark J. Roe, *Some Differences in Corporate Structure in Germany, Japan, and the United States*, 102 YALE LAW JOURNAL 1927, 1942 (1993).

[48] See Dirk Zetzsche, *Die Aktionärslegitimation durch Berechtigungsnachweis—von der Verkörperungs- zur Registertheorie (Teil 2)*, 4 DER KONZERN 251, 251–2 (2007).

[49] See Eric Nowak, *Investor Protection and Capital Market Regulation in Germany*, in THE GERMAN FINANCIAL SYSTEM 425, 436 (Jan P. Krahnen and Reinhard H. Schmidt (eds.), 2004), which reviews new curbs on proxy voting by banks. Another law reform was the provision for companies to appoint independent shareholder representatives empowered to exercise the proxies of shareholders wishing to vote. § 134(3) AktG.

[50] Anecdotal evidence includes the resignation of Deutsche Börse's Chairmen of the supervisory and management boards after activist investors' pressure made it clear that they would have faced a vote of dismissal at the general meeting. See Norma Cohen and Patrick Jenkins, *D Börse Chiefs Agree to Step Down*, FINANCIAL TIMES (Europe), 10 May 2005, at 1. For evidence of the decline in bank influence in Germany see Dirk Zetzsche, *Explicit and Implicit System of Corporate*

3.2 The Trusteeship Strategy: Independent Directors

Among our core jurisdictions, the principal trusteeship strategy today for protect-ing the interests of disaggregated shareholders—as well as minority shareholders and non-shareholder corporate constituencies—is the addition of 'independent' directors to the board. Of course, 'independence' (and trusteeship) is a matter of degree. At minimum, lawmakers create a measure of trusteeship simply by defining a subset of the firm's managers as 'directors', who are equipped with unique powers and face unique liabilities. Such manager-directors assume more of the credit or blame for company performance than other managers, and are therefore likely to have greater allegiance than other managers to the welfare of the company and its shareholders. At the other extreme, corporate law might rely entirely upon the trusteeship strategy, and entirely abandon the appointment strategy, by mandating that the board be self-appointing with no dependence on, or duty to represent, any constituency other than the corporation in its entir-ety. While the latter approach is not taken today by any of our leading jurisdic-tions—or by any others that we know of—it was until recently approximated by the *structuur* regime in the Netherlands.[51] It is, moreover, the form of governance characteristic of large nonprofit corporations,[52] and the one adopted by the many—generally quite successful—business firms in northern Europe that have been (re)organized as industrial foundations.[53]

The increasingly common requirement that some or all members of a corpor-ation's board of directors not be senior executives of the firm reflects the trustee-ship strategy in that it removes one conspicuous high-powered incentive for directors to favor the interests of the firm's management at the expense of other constituencies. If, however, such non-executive directors are directly appointed by managers, shareholders, or other stakeholders as constituency representa-tives, their independence may be little more than token. For example, although

---

Control—A Convergence Theory of Shareholder Rights, Working Paper (2004), at http://www.ssrn. com. Until recently, the Netherlands went further than any other European jurisdiction in allow-ing a particular kind of custodial intermediary to strip shareholders of their vote. This intermedi-ary, which was in place in many of the largest Dutch listed companies, was the specialized voting trust (*administratie Kantoor*), authorized by statute and established by the corporation itself, which held and voted the corporation's stock and issued the beneficial owners of this stock non-voting trust certificates in its place. A recent law reform restored some voting power to beneficial owners: except in certain circumstances (e.g., when a hostile takeover is imminent), holders of trust certifi-cates in publicly-held corporations now have the statutory right to obtain a proxy to exercise the voting rights on the underlying shares. See e.g. Peter Van Schilfgaarde and Jaap Winter, VAN DE NV EN DE BV 198 (2006).

[51] See *supra* note 4.

[52] See Henry Hansmann, *The Role of Nonprofit Enterprise*, 89 YALE LAW JOURNAL 835–901 (1980).

[53] See Steen Thomsen and Caspar Rose, *Foundation Ownership and Financial Performance: Do Companies Need Owners?*, 18 EUROPEAN JOURNAL OF LAW AND ECONOMICS 343 (2004).

German law excludes top managers from the supervisory board, it reflects a dual appointment strategy rather than a trusteeship strategy to the extent that the board is comprised of shareholder members who depend, financially or otherwise, on shareholder interests, and of labor members similarly dependent on labor interests. France limits the number of employees (and hence managers) on the boards of public companies to one third,[54] but this rule too reflects trusteeship only to the extent that the remaining two-thirds of the board are free of strong ties to large blockholders.

Truly independent directors are board members who are not strongly tied by high-powered financial incentives to any of the company's constituencies but who are motivated principally by ethical and reputational concerns. That is, of course, our definition of a trustee. As noted earlier in this chapter, all of our core jurisdictions including Japan[55] now recognize a class of 'independent' directors in this sense, and most jurisdictions actively support at least some participation by these directors on key board committees. The U.S. is the originator of this form of trusteeship and still its most enthusiastic proponent. U.S. case law generally encourages independent and non-employee directors, while U.S. exchange rules now require that company boards include a majority of independent directors and that key board committees be composed by a majority of independent directors or entirely of them.[56] In addition, the U.S. Sarbanes-Oxley Act requires publicly traded companies to have wholly independent audit committees with the power and the duty to select outside auditors.[57]

Our EU jurisdictions promote independent directors through the less compulsory 'codes of best practices', which we address in Section 3.3 below, except that the EC Audit Directive now requires listed companies (and other 'public-interest entities' such as banks) to have at least one independent director with financial sophistication.[58]

---

[54] See Art. L. 225–22 Code de commerce. See also *infra* 4.2.1.

[55] Japanese law now provides for the trusteeship strategy in the form of a choice between statutory auditors, at least half of whom must be independent, or a tripartite structure of board committees staffed by majorities of independent directors. See *infra* text accompanying notes 85–92. As of this writing, the vast majority of Japanese firms prefer the traditional statutory auditor system over the Western-style system of committees dominated by independent directors.

[56] See Rules 303A.01 (listed companies must have a majority of independent directors) and 303A.04–05 (nominating/corporate governance and compensation committees composed entirely of independent directors) NYSE Listed Company Manual; Rule 4350(c)(1) (majority of independent directors required) and Rules 4350(c)(3)–(4) (compensation and nominations committees comprised solely of independent directors; one out of three members may lack of independence provided that she is not an officer or a family member of an officer) NASDAQ Marketplace Rules. Audit committees must comply with Section 10A, Securities Exchange Act of 1934, 15 U.S.C. § 78a (2008) (each audit committee member shall be independent): see Rule 303A.06 NYSE Listed Company Manual and Rule 4350(d) NASDAQ Marketplace Rules. For Japan, see Art. 2(15) Companies Act (definition of outside director).

[57] Sarbanes-Oxley Act of 2002 [SOX] § 301.

[58] Art. 41(1). Companies may opt to appoint the independent accounting or auditing expert as a member of a separate body (such as the Italian board of auditors) instead of qualifying her as a director.

Thus, trustee-like directors are widely considered to be a key element of good governance. In the U.S., they are most often seen as monitors of managers or controlling shareholders (although this task might be better performed by directors who were *dependent* on shareholder—or minority shareholder—interests[59]). In EU jurisdictions with concentrated ownership structures, independent directors are more likely to be seen as champions of minority shareholders or non-shareholder constituencies.[60] Put differently, trustee-like directors are a wide-spectrum prophylactic. They are potentially valuable for treating all agency problems, but not exclusively dedicated to treating any. Moreover, they come at a price, since there is an inevitable tradeoff between a director's independence and her knowledge about the company.[61] It is, then, not so surprising that the empirical literature has yet to find a significant correlation between independent directors as a percentage of board members and corporate performance.[62]

3.3 Board Structure and International Best Practices

Since both the appointment and trusteeship strategies operate through the board, their success depends in no small part on the board's capabilities—or, more particularly, on its incentives, professionalism, legal powers, committee structure, size, and resources. From the mid-1980s onwards, efforts at governance reform have attempted to increase the board's efficacy along one or more of these dimensions. In particular, commentators tie good governance to a range of so-called

[59] See, e.g., Ronald J. Gilson and Reinier Kraakman, *Reinventing the Outside Director: An Agenda for Institutional Investors*, 43 STANFORD LAW REVIEW 863 (1991).

[60] The NYSE definition of independence excludes large blockholders (Rule 303A.02 NYSE Listed Company Manual); most EU jurisdictions consider large shareholders or their appointees 'dependent' (UK: Art. A.3.1 Combined Code of Best Practices; Italy: Art. 3.C.1 Corporate Governance Code; in France, a stricter evaluation of independence is required for shareholders holding more than 10% of votes or outstanding capital, see AFEP and MEDEF, THE CORPORATE GOVERNANCE OF LISTED CORPORATIONS, § 8.5 (2003)); Japan considers holding company appointees to operating company boards to be independent (see Art. 2(15) Companies Act and TOKYO STOCK EXCHANGE, PRINCIPLES OF CORPORATE GOVERNANCE FOR LISTED COMPANIES 18 (2004)).

[61] For discussion of the tradeoffs between independence and information on the board, see Jeffrey N. Gordon, *The Rise of Independent Directors in the United States, 1950–2005: Of shareholders Value and Stock Market Prices*, 59 STANFORD LAW REVIEW 1465, 1506–7 (2007). Gordon's important article argues that increasingly informed share prices in the U.S. permit increasingly less informed but more independent outside directors. See *id.* at 1541–63. But see Enrichetta Ravina and Paola Sapienza, *What do Independent Directors Know? Evidence From Their Trading* (2006), at http://www.ssrn.com (finding that independent directors do almost as well as insiders in trading company stock, which suggests that they are well informed).

[62] For an extensive review of the literature on independent directors in the U.S., see Gordon, *supra* note 61, at 1500–9. For evidence that firms with more outside directors do not outperform those with fewer in Japan, see Yoshiro Miwa and J. Mark Ramseyer, *Who Appoints Them, What Do they Do? Evidence on Outside Directors from Japan*, 14 JOURNAL OF ECONOMICS, MANAGEMENT & STRATEGY 299 (2005).

'best practices'. Chief among these are size (small is better); committee structure (independent audit, compensation, and nominating committees are good); independence from management, controlling shareholders, or both (more is better); and separation of the roles of board chairman and CEO (independent chairmen are good).

3.3.1 National codes of best practices

Before reviewing these practices in detail, however, we detour slightly to address the remarkable efflorescence of 'soft law' in the form of codes of best practice, which now does much of the work in shaping board structure in European companies.

Following the UK's lead, all EU jurisdictions have now adopted a 'corporate governance code',[63] i.e., guidelines for listed companies that address board composition, structure, and operation, and are drafted by market participants under the aegis of an exchange or regulatory authority. Listed companies are not legally bound to follow these guidelines. Instead, they have an obligation—under listing rules, as in the UK, or under corporate law, as in Germany—to report annually whether they comply with code provisions and, if they do not comply, the reasons for their noncompliance.[64] This device is intended to enlist reputation, shareholder voice, and market pressure to push companies toward best practices, while simultaneously avoiding rigid rules in an area where one size clearly does not fit all.[65]

In general, voluntary codes of best practice seem to be most influential in countries such as the UK, where institutional shareholders are powerful and the financial press is sensitive to governance issues.[66] To be sure, *reported* compliance rates are high and increasing in all jurisdictions that have adopted corporate governance codes.[67] But reported rates may be misleading. Companies may

---

[63] In the wake of several corporate scandals and a consequent fear of direct government intervention the City of London first issued a corporate governance code in 1992 (SIR ADRIAN CADBURY, REPORT OF THE COMMITTEE ON THE FINANCIAL ASPECTS OF CORPORATE GOVERNANCE (1992)).

[64] See LR 9.8.6 UK Listing Rules; for Germany, § 161 AktG.

[65] As one of the coauthors of this book has noticed, however, even corporate governance codes may have a *de facto* one-size-fits-all effect, because market participants may prefer standardization to tailor-made solutions and hence punish deviations from codes recommendations with lower stock prices even when these would be in shareholders' interest. See Gérard Hertig, *On-Going Board Reforms: One Size Fits All and Regulatory Capture*, 21 OXFORD REVIEW OF ECONOMIC POLICY 269, 273–4 (2005).

[66] Formal enforcement of codes is of secondary importance everywhere. See Eddy Wymeersch, *The Enforcement of Corporate Governance Codes*, 6 JOURNAL OF CORPORATE LAW STUDIES 113 (2006).

[67] For the UK see e.g. Sridhar Arcot and Valentina Bruno, *In Letter but not in Spirit: An Analysis of Corporate Governance in the UK* (2006), at http://www.ssrn.com; for France see AMF, *AMF 2008 Report on Corporate Governance and Internal Control* (2009) at http://www.amf-france.org; for Italy and Germany see Eddy Wymeersch, *The Corporate Governance 'Codes of Conduct' Between State and Private Law*, 26–7 (2007), at http://www.ssrn.com.

claim to comply when, in fact, they behave strategically to avoid the 'spirit' or even the letter of national codes. The debacle surrounding the Italian listed company Parmalat provides an illustration. A few months before its collapse, Parmalat declared (among other things) its full compliance with the Italian code principle requiring 'an adequate number' of independent directors—a statement whose obvious inaccuracy went entirely unnoticed at the time.[68] Even in the case of the UK, where full compliance with the combined code hovers in excess of 50% of listed companies, almost 10% choose not to comply and fail to give a reason, in flagrant breach of the FSA's listing rules.[69]

National codes of best practices enforced by the 'comply-or-explain' rule are in place outside the EU as well.[70] Yet, two of our core jurisdictions lack such a code, the U.S. and Japan. In the U.S., the lack of a soft national code of best practices is not particularly puzzling. U.S. 'hard law' has already done much of the work: that is, listing rules, federal law, or the quasi-legislative opinions of the Delaware courts have *already* forced large companies to adopt most of the best practices that the EU codes recommend. Outside directors formed a majority in most U.S. boards from the 1970s onwards; and as early as 1978, the NYSE required listed companies to appoint audit committees staffed by independent directors.[71] Delaware courts and U.S. federal tax law have also encouraged publicly traded companies to increase the numbers and responsibilities of independent directors in the last few decades.[72] And governance requirements were further tightened by the changes in law and listing rules that followed in the wake of the Enron and WorldCom debacles.

In Japan, the Tokyo Stock Exchange has promulgated a limited set of voluntary governance recommendations that do not include a comply-or-explain mandate. These recommendations accommodate both the Western-style independent director model of the board and the traditional Japanese model, in which the board is dominated by inside managers who are monitored by a board of auditors (or a recent variant of this model). Thus, Japan is an outlier among our core jurisdictions to the extent that its norms of best practices do not implicitly encourage

---

[68] The corporate governance statement candidly reported that the board included *three* 'independent' directors out of 13: one the personal accountant (and schoolmate) of the dominant shareholder and CEO; a second a personal lawyer to the CEO; and the third a director in a banking group closely associated with Parmalat. See Guido Ferrarini and Paolo Giudici, *Financial Scandal and the Role of Private Enforcement: The Parmalat Case*, in AFTER ENRON 159, 174 (John Armour and Joseph A. McCahery (eds.), 2006).

[69] See Arcot and Bruno, *supra* note 67, at 3.

[70] For a comprehensive list of corporate governance codes around the world, including codes that are not backed by a 'comply or explain' strategy, see http://www.ecgi.org/codes/all_codes.php.

[71] See e.g. Mark S. Beasley, *An Empirical Analysis of the Relation Between the Board of Director Composition and Financial Statement Fraud*, 71 THE ACCOUNTING REVIEW 447 (1996).

[72] For example, approval by independent directors earns U.S. managers more relaxed judicial review of self-interested decisions, greater leverage over the dismissal of shareholder suits, and even eligibility for favorable tax treatment of management compensation plans. See Gordon, *supra* note 61, at 1480–3.

the large-scale appointment of independent directors.[73] In practice, however, many companies that follow the traditional Japanese model of board composition include independent directors on their boards.

3.3.2 Best practices and board structure

Japan aside, the canon of best practices in corporate governance is remarkably similar across our jurisdictions, whether it is embodied in hard law or semi-voluntary codes. Jurisdictions differ more in the 'severity' of their best practices rather than in the direction of their concerns. One example is international convergence on the standard U.S. triptych of an audit, nomination, and compensation committee within the board, to be staffed—entirely or in part—by independent directors. Here the motivation is clearly to keep control over these crucial functions out of the hands of corporate insiders. As noted above, U.S. listing rules and the Sarbanes-Oxley Act make this board structure mandatory for U.S. listed companies.[74] Somewhat less forcefully, the UK's *Combined Code of Corporate Governance* recommends that independent directors compose one-half of the membership of the board as a whole, that the board's chair be independent on appointment, and that the company's audit committee be entirely independent.[75] France, Germany, and Italy follow suit, albeit with less emphasis on independence.[76] Thus, with the exception of Japan, the composition and committee structure of the boards in our core jurisdictions appear to be converging.

In contrast to directorial independence and committee structure, board size has received less attention in our core jurisdictions, despite its salience in the

---

[73] Bear in mind that very little evidence links most metrics of good governance to corporate performance. See Sanjai Bhagat, Brian J. Bolton, and Roberta Romano, *The Promise and Peril of Corporate Governance Indices*, Working Paper (2007), at http://www.ssrn.com. Note too that the traditional Japanese governance structure retains an elected board of 'statutory auditors', at least half of whom must be from outside the firm.

[74] Only the NYSE requires firms to have nomination and compensation committees composed exclusively of independent directors.

[75] Provision C.3.1 Combined Code of Best Practices. Provision B.2.1. of the most recent, June 2008 Combined Code also requires that the Remuneration Committee be entirely independent, except that it may include the Chairman if she was independent on appointment.

[76] The French code (Principle 8.2) distinguishes between widely held companies (recommending independence for half of the board) and companies with a controlling shareholder (recommending independence for one-third), while the German and Italian codes only recommend an 'adequate number' of independent directors, leaving broad discretion to individual companies. See Recommendation 5.4.2 German Corporate Governance Code; Principle 3.P.1 Italian Corporate Governance Code. The case of independent directors in Germany is particularly delicate, as shareholders may fear that directors who are 'independent' of shareholders might side with labor representatives on a divided board. All three countries recommend an audit committee, and France and Italy a remuneration committee as well. In Germany, 'the majority of the larger listed companies has already installed [nomination and remuneration committees as well].' Klaus J. Hopt and Patrick C. Leyens, *Board Models in Europe—Recent Developments of Internal Corporate Governance Structures in Germany, the United Kingdom, France, and Italy*, 1 European Company and Financial Law Review 135, 141 (2004).

literature on effective governance.[77] No code of best practices limits board size, and only France mandates a maximum size of 18 directors in its company law.[78] Nevertheless, as Table 3–1 illustrates, board size—like committee structure—appears to be converging to the Anglo-American norm of small boards with between nine and twelve directors in all core jurisdictions except Germany.

Table 3–1[79]

	U.S.	UK	Germany	France	Italy	Japan
Average board size	10.7	10.8	≥ 20 for largest companies	10.3	11	13.8
Average per cent of independent directors	81%	59% (excluding chairman)	28%	46%	46%	Between 0%–10%

To be sure, the numbers in Table 3–1 require qualification. To begin, the unusually large size of German boards is an artifact of German codetermination law.[80] Without this constraint, German companies would undoubtedly have supervisory boards in line with international averages—and indeed several major German companies such as Allianz, BASF, and Porsche have converted into the EU-wide SE form expressly in order to reduce the size of their boards to the SE minimum of 12 directors.[81] Similarly, the extent to which 'independent' directors are actually independent differs by jurisdiction. French law, for example, still emphasizes the role of the *président-directeur général* (PDG), a combined chairman of the board and CEO, who typically dominates the board

---

[77] See e.g. David Yermack, *Higher Market Valuation of Companies with a Small Board of Directors*, 40 Journal of Financial Economics 185 (1996); Jeffrey L. Coles, Naveen D. Daniel, and Lalitha Naveen, *Boards: Does One Size Fit All?*, 87 Journal of Financial Economics 329 (2008).

[78] Art. L. 225–17 Code de Commerce.

[79] Sources: Spencer Stuart, 2006 UK Board Index (2006) at http://www.spencerstuart.com; Spencer Stuart, The Changing Profile of Directors (2006) at http://www.spencerstuart.com (U.S.); *id.*, Italia 2006 Spencer Stuart Board Index (2006) at http://www.spencerstuart.com; Heidrick & Struggles, Corporate governance in Europe: Raising the Bar (2007) at http://www.heidrick.com; Tokyo Stock Exchange, TSE-Listed Companies White Paper of Corporate Governance 2007 (2007) at http://www.tse.or.jp (for large companies with 300 or more consolidated subsidiaries—Chart 20; for all listed companies the average is nine). While all of these sources are relatively current as of our writing, the criteria they employ for selecting firms and defining the independence of directors varies. Nevertheless, we believe the table gives a rough idea of actual practice as to board size and independence in each of our jurisdictions.

[80] The supervisory boards of Firms with more than 20,000 employees must contain at least 20 directors. See § 7 Mitbestimmungsgesetz (Codetermination Law).

[81] See Jochem Reichert, *Experience with the SE in Germany*, 4 Utrecht Law Review 22, 27–8 (2008). Available data show a growing interest in the SE form. See also ETUI-REHS, *European Company (SE) Factsheets* (2008) at http://ecdb.worker-participation.eu (listing both established and planned SEs with an indication of the reason for the adoption of the SE statute).

and may even select independent directors with the aid of a controlling share-holder.[82] In Italy, also, blockholders often secure their influence by inflating the board with friendly outside directors.[83]

Finally, the puzzle of Japanese boards is not that they average more direct-ors than other jurisdictions, but that they seem to have so few relative to past decades.[84] Japanese practice traditionally dictated that boards should be large, chiefly in order to create positions for aging but loyal senior executives.[85] But this tradition appears to have changed. Table 3–1 may exaggerate the magnitude of the change because it is based on the average board size of larger compan-ies listed on the Tokyo Stock Exchange, many of which are nonetheless smaller than the same category of companies listed two decades ago (because the number of listed companies has more than doubled during this period). But other fac-tors are also at work. One is that Japanese companies can now adopt a US-style, tripartite committee structure.[86] Another is that innovation has also occurred *within* the traditional Japanese model of the board. Under the so-called *Shikkou-yakuin* system, some Japanese companies now separate strategic decision-making from tactical business decisions by delegating the latter to a new level of corporate officers who might otherwise have served as second-tier directors on a traditional Japanese board.[87] This innovation offers the option of smaller boards without altering the number of honorific positions at the company's apex. (i.e., the sum of directors and executives who serve as *shikkou-yakuin*).

Put differently, in both Germany and Japan, large boards of directors serve organizational functions other than monitoring and managing on behalf of share-holders. This does not mean that traditional Japanese and German companies

---

[82] Eddy Wymeersch, *A Status Report on Corporate Governance Rules and Practices in Some Continental European States,* in COMPARATIVE CORPORATE GOVERNANCE: THE STATE OF THE ART AND EMERGING RESEARCH 1045, 1113–14 (Klaus J. Hopt et al. (eds.), 1998). The *Loi relative aux Nouvelles Régulations Economiques* (NRE) of 15 May 2001 allows French open companies to separ-ate the offices of *président* and *directeur général* in order to align themselves with the international 'good governance' prescription of separating the CEO role from that of chairman of the board. Art. L. 225–51-1 Code de commerce. 15 out the 40 largest French listed companies have done so: see SPENCER STUART, CORPORATE GOVERNANCE IN FRANCE (2007) (http://www.spencerstuart. co.uk/).

[83] Cf. ASSONIME and EMITTENTI TITOLI SpA, *An Analysis of the Compliance with the Italian Corporate Governance Code (Year 2007)* 24 (2008) at http://www.assonime.it) (non-executive, non-independent directors hold on average one-third of board seats in Italian listed companies).

[84] See THE ANATOMY OF CORPORATE LAW 40 note 32 (1st ed., 2004) (listed Japanese firms aver-aged between 19 and 25 directors in the 1990s and earlier).

[85] See Curtis J. Milhaupt, *Creative Norm Destruction: The Evolution of Nonlegal Rules in Japanese Corporate Governance,* 149 UNIVERSITY OF PENNSYLVANIA LAW REVIEW 2083, 2092 (2001).

[86] Sony reduced its board size and began to recruit independent directors in 1997. Soon there-after some other Japanese multinational companies followed suit, ostensibly to enhance efficiency by separating the formulation of policy from its implementation. See, e.g., Ronald J. Gilson and Curtis J. Milhaupt, *Choice As Regulatory Reform: The Case of Japanese Corporate Governance,* 53 AMERICAN JOURNAL OF COMPARATIVE LAW 343, 349 (2005).

[87] See Hideki Kanda, *Understanding Recent Trends Regarding the Liability of Managers and Directors in Japanese Corporate Law,* 17 ZEITSCHRIFT FÜR JAPANISCHES RECHT 29, 32 (2004).

lack effective governance, however. Arguably, real governance in many German companies occurs within the management board,[88] or within supervisory board committees,[89] while the supervisory board as a whole functions mainly to disclose management policy to labor representatives and arbitrate potential labor disputes. Similarly, in Japan, de facto decision-making power traditionally resides not in the board as a whole, but in the hands of informal management committees or a single 'representative' director, who is also the firm's CEO.[90] The separate board of statutory auditors, which monitors management in collaboration with a company's outside auditors,[91] is generally perceived to be relatively ineffective in Japan, as it is in other jurisdictions that maintain this atrophied form of supervisory board.[92]

3.4 Decision Rights and Shareholder Interests

Since the corporate form exists in part to facilitate delegated decision-making,[93] corporate law is sparing in mandating direct decision rights for shareholders. As we explain in later chapters, shareholders obtain mandatory decision rights principally when directors (or their equivalents) have conflicted interests (Chapter 6) or, even more often, when decisions call for basic changes in governance structure or fundamental transactions that potentially restructure the firm (Chapter 7). Moreover, although the law generally discourages shareholders from directly participating in business decisions, there are exceptions. At the level of the individual shareholder, many jurisdictions permit derivative actions, which are not only a species of enforcement device but also a right

---

[88] Thus, German law provides that it is the responsibility of the management board, and the management board alone, to manage the AG. § 76 I AktG. The supervisory board can veto some transactions but—in contrast to a U.S., UK, or French board—cannot instruct the management board to take any action with a minor exception necessary to implement the Co-determination Act. GERMAN STOCK CORPORATION ACT AND CO-DETERMINATION ACT 10 (Martin Peltzer and Anthony G. Hickinbotham (eds. & trans.), 1999).

[89] German supervisory boards, as the Corporate Governance Code itself recommends, may set up committees to which its main tasks, and especially the audit function, can be delegated (§ 5.3 German Corporate Governance Code).

[90] See Gilson and Milhaupt, *supra* note 86, at 349.

[91] Japanese statutory auditors (*kansayaku*) conduct both a financial audit of the company's books and a 'compliance audit' of whether managers are complying with the applicable laws, the company's charter, and their fiduciary duties.

[92] See Gilson and Milhaupt, *supra* note 86, at 348. The board of statutory auditors is also held to have performed poorly in Italy, where it was mandatory until 2003. See Ferrarini and Giudici, *supra* note 68, at 186. Italian publicly traded companies may now choose among a default single-tier structure with a board of statutory auditors, a two-tier structure, and a single-tier board with an audit committee composed of independent directors. See Art. 2380 and 2409–18(2) Civil Code.

[93] Governance costs might be defined as the costs of informing and forging a majority preference among multiple shareholders, as well as the costs of taking mistaken decisions because shareholders are relatively uninformed. These costs are identical to what one of us terms 'ownership costs'. See Henry Hansmann, THE OWNERSHIP OF ENTERPRISE 35 (1996).

granted to individual shareholders to manage a corporate cause of action. We discuss derivative suits further in Chapter 6. Suffice to say here that even in the U.S., the jurisdiction most friendly to derivative suits, courts allow them to proceed only when boards are demonstrably too conflicted or incompetent to manage their corporations' legal claims, especially seemingly plausible claims against corporate insiders.

Jurisdictions also differ at the level of the shareholders meeting. Some jurisdictions allow company charters to authorize the direct participation of the shareholders meeting in making operational business decisions, and all jurisdictions allow shareholders to manage closely held corporations directly. Jurisdictions differ, then, chiefly in the extent to which they accord mandatory or optional decision rights to shareholders of open corporations.

At one end of the spectrum, the UK statutory default permits a qualified majority of shareholders to overrule the board on *any* matter within the board's competence.[94] Thus, shareholders can sell the company or amend the charter even if the board disagrees, provided that the issue is properly noticed and is approved by more than 75% of voting shares.[95] Of course, shareholders seldom overrule a board in this way. A supermajority vote is hard to come by; and, more to the point, a simple majority is generally enough to remove the board. Nevertheless, the latent power to make all business decisions, even in public companies, enhances the UK's position as the most shareholder-centric of our core jurisdictions.

In jurisdictions other than the UK, the shareholders' meeting has less autonomous power. Routine business decisions generally fall within the exclusive competence of the management board or within the single-tier board's exclusive authority to 'manage' the corporation.[96] Nevertheless, continental European jurisdictions and Japan still allow qualified percentages of shareholders to initiate and approve resolutions on a wide range of matters including questions that may have fundamental importance to the company's management and strategic direction, such as amendments to the corporate charter.[97] By contrast, the U.S.—or at least Delaware—law is again the least shareholder-centric jurisdiction. As we discuss in Chapter 7, U.S. shareholders must ratify fundamental corporate

[94] See Schedule 3, Art. 4, Model Articles for Public Companies, Companies (Model Articles) Regulations 2008 No. 3229. Because the shareholders can fire the entire board with a simple majority resolution (§ 168 Companies Act 2006), this is of course irrelevant in practice.

[95] See §§ 314 and 338 (companies are required to circulate shareholder statements and proposed resolutions whenever asked by shareholders representing 5% of voting rights or by 100 shareholders) as well as § 283 (75% consent needed for special resolution to pass) UK Companies Act 2006.

[96] E.g., § 141(a) Delaware General Corporation Law. In Germany, routine business decisions would fall within the exclusive competence of the managerial (rather than supervisory) board (§ 76 Aktiengesetz).

[97] See Dirk Zetzsche, *Shareholder Interaction Preceding Shareholder Meetings of Public Corporations—A Six Country Comparison*, 2 EUROPEAN COMPANY AND FINANCIAL LAW REVIEW 107, 120–8 (2005) (France and Germany). For Italy see Art. 2367 Civil Code and Art. 126–2 Consolidated Act on Financial Intermediation. For Japan, see Art. 303 and 305 Companies Act.

decisions such as mergers and charter amendments but lack the power to initiate them.[98]

Almost all jurisdictions require shareholders to ratify a broader range of corporate decisions than they allow shareholders to initiate. Nevertheless, the pattern of decision rights among jurisdictions is similar at both levels. In general, U.S. law mandates shareholder ratification for a relatively narrow range of decisions, while our other core jurisdictions require shareholder approval for a wider range, including certain routine but important decisions. For example, France, Germany, Italy, the UK, and Japan require the general shareholders' meeting to approve the distribution of the company's earnings.[99] For UK listed companies, the law mandates an advisory shareholder vote on directors' compensation, while the Listing Rules require shareholder approval of a number of 'significant transactions', including substantial sales of corporate assets.[100] Equally important, all EU member states give shareholders the right to appoint and dismiss the auditors of listed and publicly traded companies,[101] while shareholders also elect the 'statutory auditors'—as well as the directors—of Japanese and Italian companies.[102]

Finally, even though shareholder decision rights diverge across jurisdictions in public companies, they converge on flexible and extensive shareholder decision rights in closely held companies. A good example is the closed German limited liability company (GmbH), which may be very large in capitalization and number of shareholders. The GmbH not only mandates shareholder approval of financial statements and dividends, but also authorizes the general shareholders' meeting to instruct the company's board (or general director) on all aspects of company policy.[103] The GmbH form, then, allows shareholders complete authority to manage business by direct voting—unless the company is subject to codetermination law by virtue of the size of its workforce.[104] Similarly, although legal regimes for close companies in France, Italy, Japan, and the U.S. generally

---

[98] See *infra* 7.2 and 7.4.

[99] §§ 58 and 174 AktG (Germany) (the power to decide on the distribution lies with shareholders, but management and supervisory board may limit distributable profit); Art. L. 232–12 Code de commerce (France); Art. 2434 Civil Code (Italy); Art. 454(1) Companies Act (Japan). In the UK, the law does not allocate the power to approve distributions, but the model articles require shareholder approval (Art. 30 Schedule 1, Model Articles for Private Companies Limited by Shares and Art. 70 Schedule 3, Model Articles for Public Companies, Companies (Model Articles) Regulations 2008 No. 3229).

[100] See 6.2.3 (voting on compensation); Ch. 10, UK Listing Rules.

[101] See European Commission, *Green Paper, The Role, the Position and the Liability of the Statutory Auditor within the European Union* 23 (1996), at http://www.europa.eu. However, in most listed companies shareholders merely ratify the choice made by the board (*id.*, 23).

[102] Art. 329(1) Companies Act (directors as well as statutory auditors appointed by general meeting of shareholders) (Japan); Art. 2400 Civil Code (Italy).

[103] Schmidt, *supra* note 46, at 1068; § 46 Gesetz betreffend die Gesellschaften mit beschränkter Haftung (GmbHG) (financial statements, profit distribution), §§ 37, 38, 46 GmbHG (shareholder instructions).

[104] A GmbH subject to codetermination must have a two-tier board and is subject to AG rules on the division of functions between the boards, and between boards and shareholders. Schmidt, *supra* note 46, at 482–3.

identify directors (Italy, the U.S., the UK, and Japan)—or 'managers' (French SARL)—as the default decision-makers, all of these jurisdictions permit closely held companies to opt into full shareholder management.[105]

3.5 The Reward Strategy

Corporate law gives the *well-organized* shareholder majority ample power to protect its interests through appointment and decision rights, which, among other things, allows the shareholder majority to strongly influence management's monetary incentives. But the reward strategy, like the trusteeship of independent directors, is sometimes also said to substitute for direct shareholder monitoring when shareholders are dispersed. The theory, of course, is that optimally-structured pay packages can align the interests of managers with those of shareholders as a class.

The law generally plays into the reward device indirectly, by regulating how, and when, companies can compensate their managers in order to advance the interests of the firm.[106] And the most important reward for managers of publicly traded firms today is one of the many forms of equity compensation—e.g., stock options, restricted stock, and stock appreciation rights—which now comprise major (albeit varying) portions of total compensation for top managers in all of our core jurisdictions.[107]

The U.S. best illustrates the law's role in facilitating—and then curbing—high-powered equity incentives. Although the Delaware courts initially regarded

[105] The French non-publicly traded corporation form, the SARL, vests power to manage the SARL in one or more 'managers', absent a charter provision to the contrary. Art. L. 221–4 and 223–18 Code de commerce. While American non-publicly traded corporation statutes and Italian and UK law generally permit direct shareholder management of the company, this requires a specialized corporate form—the *société par actions simplifiée*—in France. See Art. L. 227–5 and 227–6 Code de commerce. In Japan, non-publicly traded companies are permitted not to have statutory auditors and in that case each shareholder has the same rights as statutory auditors.

[106] The instances in which the law actually mandates equity incentives for directors are largely symbolic, as when French law requires directors to hold at least one share in their companies. Art. L. 225–25 and L. 225–72 Code de commerce.

[107] Even today, however, significant differences remain across countries in the proportion of total remuneration for CEOs that takes the form of long-term equity compensation, annual bonuses, and salary. For example, in the largest U.S. companies between 2002 and 2006, 60% of total direct compensation was equity compensation, slightly over 20% took the form of bonuses, and less than 20% took the form of salary. See Mercer's *2006 CEO Compensation Survey* (covering top U.S. firms) (http://www.mercer.com/pressrelease/details.jhtml/dynamic/idContent/1263210). Curiously, these figures are similar to those for German DAX 30 management boards in 2006, admittedly only the very largest German companies (equity compensation 60%, annual bonuses 25%, salary 15%). Deutsche Börse AG, Remuneration Report 2006, at http://www.deutsche-boerse.com. A broader sample of publicly traded British firms, however, offered much lower levels of long-term equity compensation (equity 28%, annual bonuses 22%, and salary 44%). Martin J. Conyon, John E. Core, and Wayne R. Guay, *How High is US CEO Pay? A Comparison with UK CEO Pay* (2006), at http://www.ssrn.com.

stock options with suspicion,[108] they soon made their peace with option compensation, aided by the wide discretion that U.S. firms enjoy to issue rights and repurchase shares.[109] In addition, a 1994 change in U.S. tax law[110] gave options an enormous (if unintentional) boost by barring corporations from expensing compensation in excess of $1 million per year that was not tied to firm performance. More recently, however, legal reform turned against equity incentives. First, the Sarbanes-Oxley Act of 2002 marginally restricted equity pay by banning corporate loans for top managers to use in acquiring stock or exercising options (a formerly common practice[111]), and by requiring CEOs and CFOs to disgorge returns on equity compensation arising from artificially inflated share prices.[112] Second, just as this chapter is being revised, the U.S. Federal Government has radically restricted the equity compensation of the top executives of all companies that have accepted, or will accept, government capital in order to survive the current financial crisis.[113] These restrictions will persist until the government's investment is redeemed.

Other jurisdictions have taken longer to embrace equity pay and expand board discretion to make incentive awards. In the case of equity compensation, for example, Germany only recently allowed publicly traded companies to repurchase up to 10% of their outstanding shares in order to underwrite stock option compensation plans.[114]

As to board discretion over pay, differences among our jurisdictions are best seen in a comparison of the roughly contemporaneous Delaware civil litigation against Michael Eisner, Disney, Inc.'s former CEO, and other Disney directors, for a termination settlement that awarded $140 million to Disney's President,[115] and the criminal prosecution of Josef Ackermann, Deutsche Bank's CEO and a Mannesmann AG director, and two other members of Mannesmann supervisory board, for paying Mannesmann's CEO, and members of his executive team, 'appreciation awards' (of approximately $20 million for Mannesmann's CEO), for having extracted an extraordinarily high premium from a hostile acquirer (Vodafone) after a drawn-out takeover battle.[116]

The two cases differed importantly on their facts. In *Disney*, the amount at issue was contractually fixed ex ante, and the dispute turned on whether Disney's

---

[108] See e.g. *Krebs v. California Eastern Airways*, 90 A.2d 562 (Del. Ch. 1952).

[109] E.g., § 157 Delaware General Corporation Law.

[110] Internal Revenue Code § 162(m).

[111] See e.g. Kuldeep Shastri and Kathleen M. Khale, *Executive Loans*, 39 JOURNAL OF FINANCIAL AND QUANTITATIVE ANALYSIS 791 (2004).

[112] SOX § 304(a).

[113] See American Recovery and Reinvestment Tax Act of 2009 (enacted 13 Feb. 2009) (barring, *inter alia*, all forms of equity pay for the top five officers and top 20 most highly paid employees below the top five officers in large firms, with the exception of long-term restricted stock valued less than one-third of a covered recipient's ordinary salary).

[114] § 71 Aktiengesetz. Prior rules restricting buy-backs and new share issues had severely restricted equity-based compensation.

[115] *In re Walt Disney Co. Derivative Litigation*, 906 A.2d 27 (Del. 2006).

[116] See e.g. Curtis J. Milhaupt and Katharina Pistor, LAW AND CAPITALISM 69–86 (2008).

directors had been so grossly negligent as to have acted in bad faith, either in negotiating the original contract or in not contesting a 'no fault termination clause' that triggered the $140 million payment to Disney's ex-president, even though shareholders argued that the former president had indeed been at fault. In *Mannesmann*, the payments at issue were gratuitous (*ex post* bonuses granted by Ackermann and one other member of the compensation committee), but made with the full approval of Vodafone—which, by the time of the payout, held 98.66% of Mannesmann's shares.

Despite these factual differences, however, the differing outcomes of the two cases are revealing. The Delaware court deployed the business judgment rule to exonerate Eisner and the Disney board from civil liability despite evidence of negligence and an odor of conflict of interest (the discharged manager had been a close personal friend of the CEO). By contrast, the German Supreme Court, the BGH, ruled that Ackermann might be criminally liable for breach of trust in the form of dissipating corporate assets.[117] From the perspective of Delaware law, it is nearly inconceivable that a disinterested director (Ackermann) would face civil liability for approving a gratuitous bonus ratified by a 98% disinterested shareholder, let alone face criminal liability.[118] Delaware has long permitted disinterested boards to reward departing executives with compensation in excess of their contractual entitlements.[119] For the BHG, criminal liability followed as a matter of course from the penal code, the fact that Mannesmann's independent existence was ending, and the absence of a pre-negotiated golden parachute.

Clearly, the U.S. constrains managerial pay less than Germany does, even if executive pay is controversial in both countries. One issue, then, is whether relatively low-paying jurisdictions such as Germany can compete for top managerial talent in a global market without relaxing constraints on compensation,[120] especially when bordering Switzerland offers U.S.-level compensation.[121] The converse issue, however, is whether U.S. companies (or companies in other high-paying jurisdictions) can continue to offer unprecedented pay packages without

[117] BGH, Decision of 21 December 2005, 3 StR 470/04. Unlike the lower court, the BGH relied on criminal law alone (the criminal equivalent of common law corporate waste doctrine: see § 266 Strafgesetzbuch (Criminal Code)), and, unlike the lower court, did not pin its holding to § 87 AktG, which requires managerial compensation to be reasonable. After the BHG holding, the *Mannesmann* defendants reached a monetary settlement with the public prosecutor.

[118] See Franklin A. Gevurtz, Disney *in a Comparative Light*, 55 AMERICAN JOURNAL OF COMPARATIVE LAW 453, 484 (2007). Under Delaware law, shareholder ratification would also have protected the second member of the Mannesmann executive committee, who, unlike Ackermann, stood to benefit monetarily from the ex post bonuses as a former Mannnesmann officer.

[119] See *Zupnick v. Goizueta*, 698 A.2d 384 (Del. Ch. 1997) (upholding options granted for past services at the end of tenure) and *Blish v. Thompson Automatic Arms Corporation*, Del.Supr., 64 A.2d 581 (1948) (retroactive compensation is not made without consideration where an implied contract is shown to exist or where the amount awarded is not unreasonable in view of the services rendered).

[120] Brian R. Cheffins and Randall S. Thomas, *The Globalization (Americanization?) of Executive Pay*, 1 BERKELEY BUSINESS LAW JOURNAL 233 (2004).

[121] *Schweizer Topverdiener*, BÖRSEN-ZEITUNG, Nov. 22, 2007, at 6 (reviewing study of management compensation in 100 largest Swiss listed companies).

triggering a shareholder revolt or political intervention, particularly during periods of economic stress. As noted above, the UK now mandates a shareholder advisory vote on all executive directors' compensation for listed companies; one wonders whether the U.S. might soon follow suit.[122]

A different question is whether high-powered equity compensation as it is now structured actually motivates managers to maximize long-term corporate value. The empirical literature is again inconclusive.[123] Well-known critics argue that U.S.-style compensation is best explained as low-visibility managerial rents extracted from shareholders rather than as finely-tuned incentives crafted in the course of arms-length bargaining.[124] By contrast, supporters of U.S. pay practices argue that its critics underestimate its incentive properties and misunderstand the bargaining context in which CEO pay must inevitably be set.[125] At bottom, the question is whether incentive compensation is, or might be, a partial substitute for close monitoring by powerful shareholders (or an active market for corporate control), or whether, alternatively, current levels of compensation *result* from insufficient monitoring by shareholders and the market.[126]

3.6 Legal Constraints and Affiliation Rights

Legal constraints and affiliation rights serve as supporting actors rather than as leading players in the structure of corporate governance, at least with respect to protecting the interests of shareholders as a class. All managerial and board decisions are constrained by general fiduciary norms, such as the duties of loyalty and care. Moreover, affiliation rights in the form of mandatory disclosure inform both shareholders and boards of directors by providing a metric for evaluating managerial performance in the form of well-informed share prices.[127] By

---

[122] For evidence that the UK 'say on pay' provision has enhanced sensitivity of CEO cash compensation to negative operating performance see Fabrizio Ferri and David Maber, *Solving the Executive Compensation Problem Through Shareholder Votes? Evidence from the U.K.*, Working Paper (2007), at http://www.ssrn.com. The U.S. has already adopted its own 'say on pay' requirement for firms receiving government capital in the wake of the financial crisis. See *supra* note 113 (2009 Act regulating executive compensation in firms that accept TARP funding).

[123] Compare, e.g., Lucian A. Bebchuk, Martijn Cremers, and Urs. C. Peyer, *Pay Distribution in the Top Executive Team* (2007), at http://www.ssrn.com, with Bhagat, Bolton, and Romano, *supra* note 73, at 54, 56.

[124] See, e.g., Lucian A. Bebchuk and Jesse M. Fried, PAY WITHOUT PERFORMANCE: THE UNFULFILLED PROMISE OF EXECUTIVE COMPENSATION (2004).

[125] See e.g. John E. Core, Wayne R. Guay, and Randall S. Thomas, *Is U.S. CEO Compensation Inefficient Pay Without Performance?*, 103 MICHIGAN LAW REVIEW 1142 (2005).

[126] See, e.g., Marcel Kahan and Edward Rock, *How I Learned to Stop Worrying and Love the Pill: Adaptive Responses to Takeover Law*, 69 UNIVERSITY OF CHICAGO LAW REVIEW 871 (2002) (option compensation as a substitute for takeover pressure). But see, e.g., Lucian Bebchuk, Jesse Fried, and David Walker, *Managerial Power and Rent Extraction in the Design of Executive Compensation*, 69 UNIVERSITY OF CHICAGO LAW REVIEW 751 (2002).

[127] See Gordon, *supra* note 61.

contrast, exit rights are not important to general corporate governance by and large. Corporate law makes use of them only in specialized circumstances that are detailed in later chapters: for example, as a remedy for minority shareholder abuse or as a check on certain fundamental transactions such as mergers.

3.6.1 The constraints strategy

As with exit rights, hard-edged rules and fiduciary standards are poorly suited to protecting the interests of the shareholder majority. Shareholders who can appoint and remove managers have no need to hobble managerial discretion with legal constraints—except, perhaps, in the context of related party transactions, which we address in Chapter 6. Yet, all of our core jurisdictions impose a very broad duty on corporate directors and officers to take reasonable care in the exercise of their offices (duty of care). This duty, while difficult to enforce, is truly part of the wider corporate governance system, and intended to benefit shareholders as a class insofar as their interests are identified with the corporation's interests.

It is tempting to view violations of the director's or officer's duty of care as a kind of corporate 'malpractice', analogous to malpractice committed by other professionals such as doctors or auditors. But the analogy is weak because defining 'reasonable care' is far more difficult for directors than, say, for doctors. The misconduct that violates the duty of care is nominally described as 'negligence' or 'gross negligence'. Yet most jurisdictions recognize a second principle of corporate law, the business judgment rule,[128] which effectively insulates from legal challenge business decisions taken in good faith (that is, without intent to harm the company). This low standard of liability has two principal justifications. The first is that judges are poorly equipped to evaluate highly contextual business decisions. In particular, absent clear standards, hindsight bias can make even the most reasonable managerial decision seem reckless *ex post*. The second is that, given hazy standards and hindsight bias, the risk of legal error associated with aggressively enforcing the duty of care would inevitably lead corporate decision-makers to prefer safe projects with lower returns over risky projects with higher expected returns.[129] Ultimately, shareholders may stand to lose more from such 'defensive management' than they stand to gain from deterring occasional negligence.

---

[128] In Germany, the business judgment rule is embodied in statute law rather than being solely a creation of the courts. § 93(1) para. 2 (AktG) (added in 2005). In the UK, the rule is not stated explicitly but seems to emerge from the courts' lack of willingness to review manager's business decisions in the absence of any conflict of interest: see, e.g., *Howard Smith Ltd v. Ampol Petroleum Ltd* [1974] AC 821, 832. The Companies Act of 2006 introduces an objective standard of due care, but few believe that this will lead UK courts to second-guess business decisions.

[129] See, e.g., William T. Allen, Reinier Kraakman, and Guhan Subramanian, COMMENTARIES AND CASES ON THE LAW OF BUSINESS ORGANIZATION (2nd ed., 2007) Ch. 8.

At least in the U.S., the rare cases in which courts hold directors personally liable for gross negligence in decision-making tend to involve unusual
circumstances, such as a merger or sale of the entire company or the onset of
insolvency.[130] Moreover, even in these cases, the courts often hint at something more than negligence—bad faith or a conflict of interest that is difficult
to prove—as the real basis for liability.[131] The law-on-the-books in continental
European jurisdictions such as Germany appears to offer negligent directors less
protection from liability than U.S. case law, statutory law, and ancillary institutions such as comprehensive D&O insurance.[132] The offset, however, is that the
probability of a suit seeking to impose liability is far higher in the U.S. than in
our other core jurisdictions.

In addition to the global duty of care, many jurisdictions impose specialized
monitoring duties on corporate officers and directors, which play into corporate governance and serve in part to protect shareholder interests. For example,
case law in Delaware and UK holds that the duty of care extends to creating
'information and reporting systems' that can allow the board to assess corporate compliance with all applicable laws.[133] Similarly, EU and Japanese law task
supervisory boards, audit committees, and statutory auditors with ensuring that
publicly traded companies have adequate auditing checks and risk management
controls in place.[134] Section 404 of the U.S. Sarbanes-Oxley Act, a milder version of which was adopted in the EU, requires CEOs and CFOs of U.S. firms to
report on the effectiveness of their firms' internal financial control.[135] However,

---

[130] See *infra* 5.3.1.1.

[131] The famous Delaware example is *Smith v. Van Gorkom*, 488 A.2d 858 (Del. 1985), in which
the Delaware Supreme Court clearly believed that a retiring CEO had a strong personal interest
in selling his company, which added an element of disloyalty to the arguably negligent process followed by the board in consummating the sale.

[132] Thus, § 93(1) para. 2 AktG, the German business judgment rule, appears to protect *non-
negligent* business decisions from legal attack. By contrast, the U.S. rule protects negligent decisions that were made in good faith from judicial review. Allen, Kraakman, and Subramanian, *supra*
note 129, at 252. For similar case law developments in Japan, see Kanda, *supra* note 87, at 30.

[133] See *In re Caremark Int'l Inc. Derivitive Litigation*, 698 A.2d. 959 (Del. Ch. 1996). The *Caremark*
duty of oversight was recently reaffirmed by the Del. Supreme Court in *Stone v. Ritter*, 911 A.2d
362 (Del. 2006). Similarly in the UK, *Re Barings plc (No.5)* [1999] 1 BCLC 433, esp. at 486–9.

[134] See FSA Disclosure Rules and Transparency Rules DTR 7.1 (UK); § 91(2) AktG
(Germany); Art. L. 225–235 Code de Commerce (France); Art. 149 Consolidated Act on
Financial intermediation (Italy). For Japan, auditing requirements are established by Art .328(1),
390(2) and 404(2) of the Companies Act, while internal control requirements are set by Art.
362(4)(iv) and Art. 362(5) of the Companies Act; see also Arts. 24–4–4(1) and 193–2(2) of
the Financial Instruments and Exchange Act. The EC directive on statutory audits (Directive
2006/43/EC, 2006 O.J. (L 157) 87) requires companies to have an audit committee (comprised
of directors or established as a separate body under national law) that shall 'monitor the effectiveness of the company's internal control, internal audit where applicable, and risk management
systems'. Art. 41(2)(b).

[135] SOX § 404. On the costs and benefits of § 404, see e.g. Robert A. Prentice, *Sarbanes-Oxley:
The Evidence Regarding the Impact of Section 404*, 29 CARDOZO LAW REVIEW 703 (2007). Japan
has also adopted a similar provision. See Art. 24–4–4 Financial Instruments and Exchange Act
(effective from April 2008). In the EU, the directive on company reporting (Directive 2006/46/

with the exception of Section 404 and its Japanese analogue, which are enforced by outside auditor attestation,[136] we are unaware of evidence indicating that these narrower monitoring duties are enforced more rigorously than the broader duty of care itself.

3.6.2 Corporate governance-related disclosure

While mandatory disclosure is not itself one of the legal strategies that we defined in Chapter 2, it plays a critical supporting role in the functioning of all legal strategies, and in all aspects of corporate law—at least for publicly traded companies. The structure of the corporate governance system is no exception.

All of our core jurisdictions mandate extensive public disclosure as a condition for allowing companies into the public markets. Firms must make timely disclosure, both periodically and prior to shareholder meetings. Moreover, there is considerable convergence on the content of this disclosure, much of which is governance-related. For example, all of our core jurisdictions require firms to disclose their ownership structure (significant shareholdings and voting trust agreements), executive compensation, and the details of board composition and functioning.[137]

It is quite plausible that such extensive disclosure makes a large contribution to the quality of corporate governance directly, by informing shareholders, and indirectly, by enlisting market prices in evaluating the performance of corporate

EC, 2006 O.J. (L 224) 1) requires that the annual corporate governance statement of listed companies contain a 'description of the main features of the company's internal control and risk management systems in relation to the financial reporting process'. Art. 1(7). However, no assessment of the effectiveness of the internal control structure and procedure has to be made nor, *a fortiori*, have auditors to report on it.

[136] SOX § 404(b). Art. 193–2(2) Financial Instruments and Exchange Act (Japan).

[137] For ownership disclosure requirements, see Art. 9–15, Transparency Directive; US: Section 13d, Securities Exchange Act of 1934; Japan: Art. 27–23 Financial Instruments and Exchange Act. U.S. Regulation S-K, 17 C.F.R. Part 229 Item 601(b)(3)(i)-(ii), requires filing the corporate charter and bylaws as exhibits in Form 10Q (quarterly report) and Form 10K (annual report). In addition, any voting trust agreement or corporate code of ethics must be filed in Form 10Q. See Item 601(b) Exhibit Table. Disclosure of voting trust agreements is also required by the EC Takeover Bids Directive (Art. 10 Directive 2004/25/EC, 2004 O.J. (L 142) 12). As for executive compensation see SEC Executive Compensation and Related Person Disclosure, Exchange Act Release No. 33–8732 (11 Aug. 2006); for EU, see EC Commission, *Fostering an appropriate regime for the remuneration of directors of listed companies* (Recommendation 2004/913/EC, 2004 O.J. (L 385) 55) and the International Accounting Standard No. 24 (Commission Regulation (EC) No 2238/2004 of 29 December 2004, 2004 O.J. (L 394) 1) (disclosure on an aggregate basis). Executive compensation disclosure is required in Japan on an aggregate basis in the annual securities report (to be filed under Art. 24 Financial Instruments and Exchange Act; see Akinobu Shuto, *Executive Compensation and Earnings Management: Empirical Evidence from Japan*, 16 Journal of International Accounting, Auditing and Taxation 1 (2007)) but the annual corporate governance report to be filed under the Tokyo Stock Exchange Securities Listing Regulation requires companies to split the data among categories of beneficiaries (Tokyo Stock Exchange, TSE-Listed Companies White Paper, *supra* note 79).

insiders. Moreover, it is particularly important in firms without powerful inside shareholders, where mandatory disclosure may be the basis on which the shareholder majority can exercise its appointment and decision rights. Arguably the comprehensive nature of U.S. proxy statements, and the large potential liability that attaches to misrepresentations, builds on this assumption. Another indication is the shareholder's right in continental European jurisdictions to void shareholder resolutions if the company withheld material information bearing on the vote at the shareholders' meeting. Litigation of this sort is particularly common in Germany, where courts take voting-related disclosure very seriously, both in publicly traded and privately-held companies.[138]

3. 7 Explaining Jurisdictional Similarities and Differences

A review of major jurisdictions reveals that they often use the same strategies to shape corporate governance in fundamentally similar ways. For example, all of our sample jurisdictions mandate that shareholders elect the decisive majority of directors on the board (or of the managers who serve as director equivalents in non publicly traded corporations); and all require a qualified shareholder majority to approve fundamental changes in the company's legal personality, such as a merger, dissolution, or material change in the company's charter. To a greater or lesser extent, all of our jurisdictions have adopted elements of the now-global norms of good corporate governance. For example, all jurisdictions now require (in their stock exchange listing rules), recommend (in their corporate governance codes) or (in the case of Japan) at least allow companies to opt for the tripartite committee structure—audit, compensation, and nomination committees.[139] Moreover, all single-tier jurisdictions except Japan now require or recommend a significant complement of independent directors on corporate boards and on key board committees (thus embracing the trusteeship device). All major jurisdictions impose a duty of care or prudent management as a legal norm (although nowhere is it rigorously enforced); and all jurisdictions rely on mandatory disclosure to enlist the market as a monitor of the performance of public companies and aid disaggregated shareholders in exercising their appointment rights.

Despite these global similarities, however, there are significant differences in the extent to which the governance *law* of our target jurisdictions is structured to protect shareholder interests against managerial opportunism. Moreover, the law-on-the-books, whether hard or soft, only imperfectly reflects each jurisdiction's distinctive balance of power among shareholders, managers, labor, and the state.

---

[138] See e.g.Ulrick Noack and Dirk Zetzsche, *Corporate Governance Reform in Germany: The Second Decade*, 15 EUROPEAN BUSINESS LAW REVIEW 1033, 1044 (2005).

[139] See *supra* 3.3.2.

Consider the law-on-the-books first. If we were to ask a knowledgeable observer to array our six core jurisdictions on a spectrum from the most to the least empowering for shareholders vis-à-vis managers in publicly traded companies, she would most likely list the UK at one extreme and the U.S. at the other. Despite their common legal heritage, the two Anglo-Saxon jurisdictions mark the ends of the governance continuum. Filling in the middle is trickier. Italy, Germany, and France accord shareholders significant rights that Delaware does not, such as the non-waivable minority right to initiate a shareholder meeting, to initiate a resolution to amend the corporate charter, to place board nominees on the agenda of shareholders' meeting, and to remove directors without cause by a qualified majority vote. However, Japan also has a plausible claim to equally shareholder-friendly law on the basis of its short director terms, easy removal rights, and user-friendly mail and internet voting regimes. The sticking point for Japanese law is that it supports large, insider-dominated corporate boards. This leaves Germany and the U.S. in a dead heat for having the least shareholder-friendly governance law, at least on the books. Delaware law is unmistakably board-centric, while Germany's codetermination statute mandates labor directors on the board with interests that are, on the surface at least, opposed to those of the shareholder class.

In some respects, this legal spectrum accurately depicts the power of shareholders as a class to safeguard their interests vis-à-vis managers. Despite the fact that shareholdings in the U.K. are diffuse, governance in the U.K. is significantly influenced by institutional shareholders, who are well equipped to represent the interests of shareholders as a class.[140] Moreover, one of the most important arbiters of corporate disputes in the UK—the Takeover Panel—developed largely in accordance with the wishes of institutional shareholders.[141] In contrast, the U.S. governance system relies heavily on independent directors, trusteeship, and state courts, none of which are specifically targeted to protect the interests of shareholders as a class. In recent years, however, U.S institutional shareholders—and especially hedge funds—have become increasingly assertive, and U.S. boards have become increasingly attentive to share price.[142] There has been, in other words, a perceptible shift in favor of shareholder interests over board autonomy—albeit it has occurred without major changes in underlying law. Thus, U.S. governance in

[140] For discussion of the political economy of the power of institutional investors in the UK, relative to those in the U.S., see Geoffrey Miller, *Political Structure and Corporate Governance: Some Points of Contrast Between the United States and England*, 1998 Columbia Business Law Review 51; Ronald J. Gilson, *The Political Ecology of Takeovers: Thoughts on Harmonizing the European Corporate Governance Environment*, in European Takeovers: Law and Practice 49 (Klaus J. Hopt and Eddy Wymeersch (eds.), 1992).

[141] See John Armour and David A. Skeel, Jr., *Who Writes the Rules for Hostile Takeovers, and Why?—The Peculiar Divergence of U.S. and U.K. Takeover Regulation*, 95 Georgetown Law Journal 1727, 1767–76 (2007).

[142] See Alon Brav, Wei Jiang, Frank Partnoy, and Randall Thomas, *Hedge Fund Activism, Corporate Governance, and Firm Performance*, 63 Journal of Finance 1729 (2008); Gordon, *supra* note 61, at 1526–35.

practice is more shareholder friendly than the Delaware statute and selected case law might lead one to expect.

Shifting from the U.S. and UK to Italy, France, and Germany changes the landscape of corporate governance in two important respects. First, listed companies on the Continent tend to be controlled by coalitions of stable, large-block shareholders rather than by numerous investors who actively trade in the market.[143] In addition, families hold many large blocks of shares, particularly in France and Italy. This ownership structure largely neutralizes the management-shareholder agency conflict that afflicts large U.S. companies (and would be important in the UK too in the absence of strong shareholder-centric institutions). Large blockholders, like traditional business principals, hire and fire as they wish; they do not need, and probably do not want, anything more than appointment, removal, and decision rights to protect their interests as majority shareholders. It seems natural, then, that jurisdictions dominated by large-block shareholders should have a company law that empowers shareholders as a class, precisely as the law does in France and Italy.

The second way in which the governance landscape shifts on the continent is that, to a greater degree than in the U.S. or UK, corporate governance is a three-party game that revolves around more than the interests of shareholders and managers. In Italy and France, the third party is the state, which is simultaneously an intrusive regulator, a major shareholder,[144] and a defender of 'national champions', in which it may or may not acquire an equity stake.[145] Indeed, in France there is a well-travelled career track between elite state bureaucracies and the corporate headquarters of France's largest companies.[146] The role of the state in corporate governance, we believe, reinforces both shareholder-friendly governance law and concentrated ownership in Italy and France. On one hand, the politicians and civil servants who control the state shareholdings in these

---

[143] See, e.g., Tom Kirchmaier and Jeremy Grant, *Corporate Ownership Structure and Performance in Europe*, 13, 17 (2006), at http://www.ssrn.com (controlled ownership structures appear stable over time in our core jurisdictions).

[144] As of July 2007, the two states still controlled respectively French companies representing 22% of the total capitalization of the blue-chips index (CAC 40) and Italian companies representing 34% of the total capitalization of the blue-chips index (S&P Mib) (source: authors' elaboration, based on market capitalization data available at http://www.euronext.com and http://www.borsaitaliana.it).

[145] Well-known examples include GDF/Suez in France and Autostrada/Abertis in Italy. In the former case, the French government arranged a merger between the French state-controlled firm, GDF and French widely held firm Suez to block a hostile takeover bid for Suez by the (Italian) state-controlled firm ENEL. As a result, the French state became the controlling shareholder in the combined GDF/Suez company. In the latter case, the Italian firm Autostrade, Italy's largest tollroad operator, engaged in merger negotiations with the Spanish firm Abertis, until the decision of the Italian government to review its toll-collecting contract with Autostrade achieved its purpose of torpedoing the deal.

[146] See, e.g., William Lazonick, CORPORATE GOVERNANCE, INNOVATIVE ENTERPRISE AND ECONOMIC DEVELOPMENT, 49–56 (2006) (describing the elite education and civil service experience of typical French CEOs). As French civil servants now tend to join the private sector earlier in their careers, this particular tie between the state and large companies may be weakening.

jurisdictions have a natural incentive to favor strong shareholder rights, both because they represent the state as a shareholder and because they can discreetly act through other large-block shareholders to assure that corporate policies reflect the state's priorities. On the other hand, we suspect that well-connected block-holders might be an economic asset for firms in a politicized environment to the extent that these 'owners' have more legitimacy and resources to protect their companies from political intervention than mere managers backed by dispersed shareholders could muster.[147] Thus, an interventionist state, concentrated owner-ship, and shareholder-friendly law may be mutually reinforcing, especially when the state holds large blocks of stock in its own right.

In contrast to Italy and France, the third actor in German corporate govern-ance is not the state but the strong representation of labor on corporate boards. As noted earlier (and discussed further in Chapter 4), German law provides for quasi-parity codetermination, in which employees and union representatives fill half of the seats on the supervisory boards of large firms.[148] Of course, labor dir-ectors, like shareholder directors, have a fiduciary obligation to further the inter-ests of 'the company' rather than those of their own constituency. Nevertheless, labor's interests have significantly less in common with those of large-block German shareholders than the state's interests might have with those of French and Italian blockholders. In addition, state intervention in corporate governance is likely to be sporadic, while labor directors continuously monitor German firms. We suspect (and we are not the first to do so[149]) that the net effect of Germany's closely-divided supervisory board is to enhance the power of top managers—i.e., of the management board—relative to that of shareholders. Put differently, the modal large German company is likely to be more managerialist than a similar firm in another large blockholder jurisdiction such as Italy or France.[150]

Finally, in Japan the gap in spirit between a shareholder-friendly corporate law and the reality of Japanese corporate governance appears to be larger than in any other core jurisdiction. Japan is a dispersed-shareholder jurisdiction, like the U.S. and UK,[151] but its shareholders are weak, and its managers are strong, even

[147] This observation tracks Mark Roe's similar point that strong labor favors strong capital, in the form of controlling shareholders. See Mark J. Roe, *Legal Origin, Politics, and the Modern Stock Market*, 120 Harvard Law Review 460 (2006).

[148] See *infra* 4.2.1.

[149] See Katharina Pistor, *Codetermination: A Sociopolitical Model with Governance Externalities* 171, in Employees and Corporate Governance (Margaret M. Blair and Mark J. Roe (eds.), 1999).

[150] It can hardly be otherwise if Germany's two-tier board structure functions in part to insu-late companies' business decisions from dissension on their supervisory boards by assigning these decisions to their management boards. A revealing indication of the power of the management board is that often in widely held companies it, rather than the supervisory board, informally nominates the company's *shareholder* nominees to the supervisory board. See *supra* note 12.

[151] One recent study finds that listed companies in the UK and Japan have the most dispersed ownership structures in the world, while the U.S. trails some distance behind. See Clifford G. Holderness, *The Myth of Diffuse Ownership in the United States*, Review of Financial Studies (forthcoming) (2007) at http://www.ssrn.com.

compared to the U.S. Moreover, Japanese boards remain unusually large and—what is more eye-catching—overwhelmingly dominated by inside directors. So how can Japanese corporate law empower shareholders while its governance practice does not? A number of factors help explain this puzzle, including the dispersion of Japanese shareholdings since the Second World War, a statutory law derived from early—and shareholder-friendly—German law, the role of the state in mobilizing Japanese recovery after the war, a strong reliance on debt rather than equity financing, and the continuous increase in Japanese share prices for four decades after the war.[152]

But there is another partial answer that seems especially salient today. Japan has a tradition of stable friendly shareholdings among operating firms that cement business relationships and insulate top managers from challenge. These business-to-business holdings are numerous but generally not large, and they are frequently not even reciprocal. But the important point is that they are stable and management friendly.[153] In prior decades these 'captive' shareholders accounted for a much higher percentage of the outstanding shares of Japanese listed companies than they do today, when they represent around one quarter of outstanding shares—less than the share percentage held by foreign investors in Japanese firms.[154] This change in shareholder identity, as well as the Japanese market's mixed record in recent years, suggests that activist shareholders may resort to the law in order to claim a larger governance role in the future. Indeed, there are already signs of increased activism including attempted takeovers, poison pills,[155] and an upswing in derivative suits. Thus, we conjecture that the gap between the law and the reality of corporate governance in Japan will eventually diminish. We note, however, that this gap might shrink in one of two ways, either because shareholders gain power by exploiting existent shareholder-friendly law, or because the legislator and judiciary change existing law to better support the governance status quo.

---

[152] See Masahiko Aoki, *Toward an Economic Model of the Japanese Firm*, 28 JOURNAL OF ECONOMIC LITERATURE 1 (1990); Ronald J. Gilson and Mark J. Roe, *Understanding the Japanese Keiretsu: Overlaps Between Corporate Governance and Industrial Organization*, 102 YALE LAW JOURNAL 871 (1993); Steven Kaplan, *Top Executive Rewards and Firm Performance: A Comparison of Japan and the U.S.*, 102 JOURNAL OF POLITICAL ECONOMY 510 (1994).

[153] We take no position on the continuing debate about the importance of *Keiretsu*, or networks of companies bound by cross shareholding and relations with a 'main bank'. Compare Curtis Milhaupt and Mark D. West, ECONOMIC ORGANIZATIONS AND CORPORATE GOVERNANCE IN JAPAN: THE IMPACT OF FORMAL AND INFORMAL RULES (2004) with J. Mark Ramseyer and Yoshiro Miwa, THE FABLE OF THE KEIRETSU, URBAN LEGENDS OF THE JAPANESE ECONOMY, Ch. 2 (2006).

[154] As of 2007, foreign investors held 28% of market capitalization; cross-shareholdings ranged between 20% and 25%. See *Going Hybrid. A Special Report on Business in Japan*, THE ECONOMIST, 7–8 (1 December 2007) .

[155] See, e.g., Curtis J. Milhaupt, *In the Shadow of Delaware? The Rise of Hostile Takeovers in Japan*, 105 COLUMBIA LAW REVIEW 2171 (2005); Jack B. Jacobs, *Implementing Japan's New Anti-takeover Defense Guidelines, Part II: The Role of Courts as Expositor and Monitor of the Rules of the Takeover Game*, 3 UNIVERSITY OF TOKYO JOURNAL OF LAW AND POLITICS 102 (2006). See also the Japanese Supreme Court's decision in *Steel Partners v. Bull Dog Sauce* (7 August 2007).

A final puzzle that we have encountered in this chapter is why a single model of best practices (independent directors, a tripartite committee structure, the appointment of an outside chairman, etc.) dominates governance reform in all core jurisdictions when the agency problem that gave rise to this model—managerial opportunism vis-à-vis the shareholder class—is paramount only in diffuse shareholding jurisdictions such as the U.S. and UK. Except in the U.S. and Japan, this model is embedded in the soft law of codes of best governance practices, and tied to the UK's enforcement innovation of a comply-or-explain requirement.

The obvious question with respect to codes of best practices is: why should one size fit all, given the dramatic differences in ownership structure across our target jurisdictions? Here, several conjectures are plausible. One is that international best practices are largely decorative in blockholder jurisdictions, since dominant shareholder coalitions retain the power to hire and fire the entire board, including its nominally independent directors. A second conjecture is that the *same* global good governance recipe of independent directors and independent committees somehow responds effectively to the various agency problems: not only the problem of managerial opportunism, but also the problem of conflict between majority shareholders on one hand, and minority shareholders or non-shareholder constituencies on the other. We explore this issue in Chapter 4. Finally, a third possibility is that the current pan-jurisdictional recipe for best practices means something very different in each jurisdiction. For example, adding independent directors may empower Japanese shareholders and reinforce shareholder dominance in the UK, while it serves to justify reallocating power from shareholders to the board in the U.S. and is largely decorative in continental Europe. The question, then, is whether convergence on the substance of best governance practices is true functional convergence or mere stylistic convergence that hides persistent differences in the actual structure of corporate governance across jurisdictions.[156]

---

[156] Formal convergence that obscures substantive divergence in corporate law is the natural converse of formal divergence that obscures functional convergence. See Ronald J. Gilson, *Globalizing Corporate Governance: Convergence of Form or Function*, 49 AMERICAN JOURNAL OF COMPARATIVE LAW 329 (2001).

4

The Basic Governance Structure: Minority Shareholders and Non-Shareholder Constituencies

Luca Enriques, Henry Hansmann, and Reinier Kraakman

The corporate governance system principally supports the interests of shareholders as a class. Nevertheless, corporate governance can—and to some degree must—also address the agency conflicts jeopardizing the interests of minority shareholder and non-shareholder constituencies. And herein lies the rub. To mitigate either the minority shareholder or the non-shareholder agency problems, a governance regime must necessarily constrain the power of the shareholder majority and thereby aggravate the managerial agency problem. Conversely, governance arrangements that reduce managerial agency costs by empowering the shareholder majority are likely to exacerbate the agency problems faced by minority shareholders and non-shareholders at the hands of controlling shareholders.

Minority shareholders generally lack the extra-corporate protections enjoyed by non-shareholders, including individualized contractual rights and the right to withdraw from the firm altogether.[1] Thus, in this chapter, we first address the protection of minority shareholders, and then turn to governance arrangements that protect the firm's employees—the principal non-shareholder constituency to enjoy such protections as a matter of right in some jurisdictions. Subsequently, in Chapter 5, we address the protections granted to corporate creditors.

4.1 Protecting Minority Shareholders

A growing body of empirical literature documents the private benefits of control—that is, the disproportionate returns—that dominant shareholders

---

[1] That is, unhappy employees can seek alternative employment and unpaid creditors can obtain liquidation of the whole firm through insolvency proceedings. See generally Oliver E. Williamson, *Corporate Governance*, 93 YALE LAW JOURNAL 1197 (1984).

receive, often at the expense of minority shareholders.[2] These benefits are impounded in the control premia charged for controlling blocks and in the price differentials that obtain between publicly traded high- and low-vote shares in the same companies. Both measures are often assumed to be rough indicators of the level of minority shareholder expropriation across our core jurisdictions.[3] The varying degrees of protection accorded to minority shareholders by differing corporate governance systems presumably explain at least some of the variation in these levels.

4.1.1 Minority shareholder appointment rights

Adjustments to shareholder appointment and decision rights can protect minority shareholders either by empowering them, or—almost equivalently—by limiting the power of controlling shareholders.

Consider appointment rights first. Company law enhances minority appointment rights by either reserving board seats for minority shareholders or over-weighting minority votes in the election of directors. An organized minority that selects only a fraction of the board can still benefit from access to information and, in some cases, the opportunity to form coalitions with independent directors.[4] Of course, even without express authorization, shareholder agreements or charters can—and sometimes do—require the appointment of minority directors for individual firms. The law can achieve a similar result on a broader scale by mandating cumulative or proportional voting rules, which allow relatively large blocks of minority shares to elect one or more directors, depending on the number of seats on the board. Moreover, lawmakers can further increase the power of minority directors by assigning them key committee roles or by permitting them to exercise veto powers over certain classes of board decisions.[5]

Significantly, however, legal rules requiring minority directors are relatively *un*common among our core jurisdictions. Only Italy mandates board

---

[2] See Tatiana Nenova, *The Value of Corporate Voting Rights and Control: A Cross-Country Analysis*, 68 Journal of Financial Economics 325, 336 (2003) (employing share price differentials for dual class firms to calculate private benefits); Alexander Dyck and Luigi Zingales, *Private Benefits of Control: An International Comparison*, 59 Journal of Finance 537, 551 (2004) (employing control premia in sales of control blocks to calculate private benefits).

[3] See *infra* note 77 and accompanying text.

[4] One study that appears to confirm the utility of minority board representation finds that minority investors are more likely to have board representation in closed corporations that are managed by controlling shareholders than in those that are not. See Morten Bennedsen, *Why do firms have boards?*, Working Paper (2002) at http://www.ssrn.com.

[5] For example, the Russian Joint-Stock Companies Law requires that major transactions, including those that implicate the interests of controlling shareholders, be unanimously approved by directors. Art. 78. Consequently, 'disinterested' minority directors can block major transactions between the company and its controlling shareholders or managers.

representation for minority shareholders in listed companies.[6] Cumulative voting is the statutory default in Japan, but it is routinely avoided by charter provision.[7] In France, the UK, and the U.S., firms may adopt a cumulative voting rule, but rarely do so;[8] and in Germany, commentators dispute whether cumulative voting is permissible at all in public firms.[9]

Legal devices that dilute the appointment powers of large shareholders to benefit small shareholders are much rarer than devices that enhance minority shareholder power. Perhaps the best known dilution device of this sort is 'vote capping', or imposing a ceiling on the control rights of large shareholders, and, correlatively, inflating the voting power of small shareholders. For example, a stipulation that no shareholder may cast more than 5% of the votes reallocates 75% of the control rights that a 20% shareholder would otherwise exercise to shareholders with stakes of less than 5%.

The UK, the U.S., and France permit publicly traded corporations to opt into voting caps by charter provision, even though today the real motivation for voting caps is more likely to be the deterrence of takeovers than the protection of minority investors. Voting caps survive today chiefly in France.[10] Germany and Italy prohibit them entirely in listed companies,[11] while listing rules and governance culture have eliminated them in the U.S. and UK.[12]

Another class of constraints on controlling shareholders limits the ways in which shareholders may exercise voting rights *in excess of* their economic stakes in their firms. As we note in Chapter 3, such limits include the regulation of dual class equity structures, circular shareholdings, and pyramidal ownership

---

[6] Art. 147–3 Consolidated Act on Financial Intermediation (requiring that at least one director be elected by minority shareholders).

[7] Art. 342 Companies Act.

[8] At the turn of the 20th century, cumulative voting was common in the U.S., See, e.g., Jeffrey N. Gordon, *Institutions as Relational Investors: A New Look at Cumulative Voting*, 94 Columbia Law Review 124 (1994); cf. §§ 708(a) (mandatory cumulative voting) and 301.5(a) (authorizing opt-out from cumulative voting for listed companies) California Corporation Code.

[9] See Mathias Siems, Convergence in Shareholder Law 172 (2008). Even though the majority agrees that proportional voting is permissible, no important German corporation has included such a charter provision.

[10] See *supra* 3.1.2.

[11] Voting caps were banned for German publicly traded (listed) companies in 1998. See § 134 I Aktiengesetz (AktG) (as amended by KonTraG). Still, there was one important exception: Volkswagen AG, which is regulated by a special law, was subject to a 20% voting cap. The European Court of Justice ruled that the voting cap (together with other provisions of the VW Act) impeded the free movement of capital which is guaranteed by Art. 56(1) EC Treaty; see E.C.J., Case C-112/05, *Commission v. Germany*, Judgment of 23 October 2007. Italy banned voting caps in 2003. See Art. 2351 Civil Code (Italy).

[12] We know of no UK or U.S. publicly traded company with voting caps today, although caps were common at the turn of the 20th century in both Europe and the U.S. See Colleen A. Dunlavy, *Corporate Governance in the Late 19th-Century Europe and USA*, in Comparative Corporate Governance: The State of the Art and Emerging Research 5 (Klaus J. Hopt et al. (eds.), 1998).

structures.[13] Regulating these ways to leverage control rights can be viewed either as protecting shareholders as a class, if shares are measured by cash flow rights, or as protecting 'minority' shareholders, if shares are measured by voting rights.

Most jurisdictions ban some strategies for leveraging the voting rights of controlling shareholders, but no jurisdiction—as we note in Chapter 3—bars all of these strategies. Germany, Italy, and Japan go furthest by banning shares with multiple votes and capping the issuance of non-voting or limited-voting preference shares to 50% of outstanding shares.[14] Even these jurisdictions, however, do not regulate pyramidal ownership structures. French law allows corporations to award double voting rights to shareholders who have held their shares two years or more (a mechanism that enhances the power of the state as shareholder).[15] The U.S. and UK permit different classes of shares to carry any combination of cash flow and voting rights, but U.S. exchange listing rules bar recapitalizations that dilute the voting rights of outstanding shares,[16] and UK institutional investors have successfully discouraged dual class shares altogether.[17] Thus, although legal support for a one-share-one-vote norm is limited (probably for sound policy reasons[18]), all core jurisdictions, with the possible exception of the UK, regulate some ways of leveraging voting rights that are seen to be particularly harmful.

4.1.2 Minority shareholder decision rights

As in the case of appointment rights, the law sometimes protects minority shareholders by enhancing their direct decision rights or, alternatively, by diluting the decision rights of controlling shareholders.

Minority decision rights are strongest when the law entrusts individual shareholders (or a small minority of them) with the power to make a corporate

---

[13] See Lucian A. Bebchuk, Reinier Kraakman, and George G. Triantis, *Stock Pyramids, Cross-Ownership, and Dual Class Equity: The Mechanisms and Agency Costs of Separating Control from Cash-Flow Rights*, in Concentrated Ownership Structures 295 (Randall W. Morck (ed.), 2000).

[14] See Art. 2351 Civil Code (Italy); §§ 12 II and 139 II Aktiengesetz AktG (Germany); Art. 108(1)(iii) and 115 Companies Act (Japan). France caps the issue of non-voting shares by listed companies at 25% of all outstanding shares. Art. L. 228–11 to L. 228–20 Code de commerce.

[15] Art. L. 225–123 Code de commerce.

[16] See Rule 313 NYSE Listed Company Manual (voting rights of existing shareholders of publicly traded common stock cannot be disparately reduced or restricted through any corporate action or issuance) and Rule 4351 NASDAQ Marketplace Rules (same). The Tokyo Stock Exchange is considering a similar rule at the time of writing: see Tokyo Stock Exchange, Listing System Improvement FY 2008 15 (2008), at http://www.tse.or.jp.

[17] See Julian Franks, Colin Mayer, and Stefano Rossi, *Spending Less Time with the Family: The Decline of Family Ownership in the United Kingdom*, in A History of Corporate Governance Around the World 581, 604 (Randall K. Morck (ed.), 2005).

[18] See *supra* 3.1.2. See also Guido Ferrarini, *One Share—One Vote: A European Rule?*, in 2 European Company and Financial Law Rev. 147 (2006); Kristian Rydkvist, *Dual-class Shares: A Review*, 8 Oxford Review of Economic Policy, Issue 3, 45, 51 (1992); Lucian A. Bebchuk, A Rent-Protection Theory of Corporate Ownership and Control (1999) (ssrn.com).

decision. Such is the case for instance when the law allows individual share-holders, or a small shareholder minority, to bring suit in the corporation's name against directors or other parties against whom the corporation may have a cause of action.[19]

Minority decision rights that are granted to a majority of minority share-holders are also an effective governance strategy. As we discuss in Chapter 7, hard law and codes of best practices sometimes impose a majority-of-the-minority approval requirement on fundamental transactions between controlling share-holders and their corporations.[20] Indeed, disinterested minority approval is necessary to legitimate all significant self-dealing transactions in some jurisdictions, while in others it has no greater power to insulate self-dealing transactions than does disinterested board approval.[21]

In addition, all of our core jurisdictions fortify minority decision rights over fundamental corporate decisions by imposing supermajority approval requirements. As we discuss in Chapter 7, the range of significant decisions subject to shareholder voting varies, as does the precise voting threshold required for approval.[22] As a practical matter, however, this threshold is always higher than the simple majority of the votes cast at a general shareholders' meeting.[23] Arguably, then, all jurisdictions use decision rights to protect large blocks of minority shares against expropriation via major transactions such as mergers. Several European jurisdictions pursue this end explicitly by awarding a sufficient percentage of minority shares (25% or more of voting shares) a statutory blocking right—to prevent the 'bare majority' from trumping the will of the 'near majority'.[24] But most U.S. states achieve a similar effect by requiring a majority of outstanding shares to approve fundamental transactions such as mergers, which implies a supermajority of the votes that are actually cast.[25] The size of the supermajority in this case depends on the percentage of shares represented at the meeting, which, in turn, reflects the salience of the transaction for minority shareholders.

---

[19] See *supra* 3.4 and *infra* 6.2.5.1.   [20] See *infra* 7.4.2.2.
[21] See *infra* 6.2.3.   [22] See *infra* 7.4 and 7.8.
[23] Germany requires a 75% vote of shares represented at the meeting to approve fundamental transactions. See e.g. § 53 II Gesetz betreffend die Gesellschaften mit beschränkter Haftung (GmbHG) (charter amendment); §§ 50 I, 65 I Umwandlungsgesetz (UmwG) (merger); § 179 II AktG (charter amendment). Similarly, company law in the UK requires a vote of 75% of represented shares to pass 'special resolutions'; §190(1) Companies Act 2006. France requires a two-thirds majority of represented shares for charter amendments in publicly traded corporations (Art. L. 225–96 Code de commerce). In Italy, a two-thirds majority of shares represented at the meeting is required to approve special meeting resolutions of publicly traded companies (including mergers, new issues of shares, etc.) (Art. 2369 Civil Code), while for non-publicly traded companies, approval by a majority of outstanding shares is sufficient (Art. 2479–2 Civil Code). The Japanese Companies Act requires an approving vote of two-thirds of voting shares with a quorum of more than half of all voting shares (the quorum may be reduced to one-third by charter) for the approval of mergers and other basic transactions. See e.g. Art. 466 and 309(2)(xi) (charter amendment); Art. 783, 795, 804 and 309(2)(xii) (merger).
[24] See *infra* 7.2 and 7.4.
[25] See e.g. § 251 Delaware General Corporation Law (merger); § 242 (charter amendment).

Absent a conflict of interest, the costs of granting a blocking or veto power to large minority shareholders are likely to be small. A minority investor holding 25% of her company's equity is unlikely to harm it. But the benefits are limited as well for dispersed shareholders, who are too disorganized or ill-informed to muster a blocking vote without the leadership of a large minority shareholder willing to initiate a proxy fight. In most circumstances, supermajority voting, like voting caps or proportional voting, matters most today in closely held companies and in public companies dominated by coalitions of large shareholders.

4.1.3 The incentive strategy: trusteeship and equal treatment

The incentive strategy for protecting minority shareholders takes two forms. One is the familiar device of populating boards and key board committees with independent directors. As noted in Chapter 3,[26] lawmakers often view independent directors as a kind of broad-spectrum prophylactic, suitable for treating both the agency problems of minority shareholders as well as those of shareholders as a class. The second mode of protecting minority shareholders is strong enforcement of the norm of equal treatment among shares, particularly with respect to distribution and voting rights. This norm applies to both closely held and publicly traded firms, and blurs into an aspect of the constraints strategy: a fiduciary duty of loyalty to the corporation that implicitly extends to minority shareholders and perhaps to other corporate constituencies as well. We first address the role of independent directors as trustees.

4.1.3.1 The trusteeship strategy and independent directors

The addition of independent directors to the board is a popular device for protecting minority shareholders and non-shareholder constituencies alike. Lawmakers implicitly assume that independent directors—motivated by 'low-powered incentives', i.e., morality, professionalism, and personal reputation—will stand up to controlling shareholders in the interest of the enterprise as a whole, including its minority shareholders and, to varying degrees, its non-shareholder constituencies. Strong forms of trusteeship reduce the possibility of controlling the board by shareholders (or by anyone else). In the extreme case, no constituency, including shareholders, can directly appoint representatives to the company's board. This was, in fact, the core principle of the Netherlands' recently abandoned 'structure regime',[27] under which the boards of some large companies

---

[26] See *supra* 3.2.
[27] See e.g. Edo Groenewald, *Corporate Governance in the Netherlands: From the Verdam Report of 1964 to the Tabaksblat Code of 2003*, 6 EUROPEAN BUSINESS ORGANIZATION LAW REVIEW 291 (2005). See also *supra* 3.2.

became self-appointing organs, much like the boards of many nonprofit corporations. Alternatively, investors themselves may contract to give one or more mutually-selected independent directors the decisive voice on the board as a governance solution to intra-shareholder opportunism. This pattern is common in venture capital financing agreements, which often provide rigorous criteria for the appointment of independent directors.[28]

In our core jurisdictions, however, most 'independent' directors are neither self-appointing nor rigorously screened for independence by savvy investors. Instead, director 'independence' typically means *financial* and familial independence from controlling shareholders (and from top corporate officers). A director qualifies as independent under such a definition even if she is vetted and approved by the company's controlling shareholder—and even if she has social ties to the controller—as long as she has no close family or financial ties, such as an employment position or a consulting relationship, with the controller. A conventional example is that an officer of an unrelated, third-party company qualifies as an independent director of the corporation, but an officer of a holding company with a controlling block of stock in the corporation does not.[29]

Finally, the most modest and basic form of a director-based trusteeship strategy abandons all pretence to independence and simply requires board approval for important company decisions. For example, the authority to initiate proposals to merge the company can be vested exclusively in the board of directors, as it is under U.S. and Italian law.[30] Alternatively, shareholders may be barred from directly making any decisions about the company's business without the board's invitation, as they are under German law.[31] These measures constrain the shareholder majority to pursue its policies through directors who, although appointed by the majority, nevertheless face different responsibilities, incentives, and potential liabilities than controlling shareholders.

Of course, how well the director-based trusteeship strategy works, even when some or most directors are financially independent of controlling shareholders, remains an open question. Our core jurisdictions give some reason for skepticism about the efficacy of these directors, at least as trustees for minority

---

[28] See Brian J. Broughman, *The Role of Independent Directors in VC-Backed Firms*, Working Paper (2008) at http://www.ssrn.com.

[29] Such is the case in Italy for listed companies that opt for the two-tier board system: companies controlling them may not appoint their employees as supervisory board members. See Art. 148 Consolidated Act on Financial Intermediation.

[30] See § 251 (b) Delaware General Corporation Law. See *supra* 3.4. Art. 2367 Civil Code (Italy).

[31] § 119 II AktG (shareholder may only vote on management issues if asked by the management board). But in the *Holzmüller* case the BGH held that the discretionary power of the management board, whether to ask the shareholders, converts into a duty to submit a certain matter for decision if the management board 'could not reasonably assume' that it may decide 'solely on its own authority not letting the general meeting participate'. See BGHZ 83, 122, 131.

shareholders.[32] Nevertheless, the U.S. case law provides anecdotal evidence that independent boards or committees can make a difference in cash-out mergers[33] or when controlling shareholders egregiously overreach. A classic example of both the strength and weakness of the strategy is the *Hollinger* case,[34] in which the Delaware Chancery Court backed a majority of independent directors who ousted the dominant shareholder from the board, and prevented him from disposing of his controlling stake in the company as he wished to do. The independent directors in *Hollinger* acted, however, only after the controlling shareholder's misdeeds were already under investigation by the SEC, and the controller had openly violated a contract with the board as a whole to promote the sale of the company in a fashion that would benefit all shareholders rather than the controller alone.

4.1.3.2 *The equal treatment norm*

The equal treatment of shares (and shareholders) of the same class is a fundamental norm of corporate law. Although this norm can be viewed as a rule-based constraint on corporate controllers, it can also be seen as a species of the incentive strategy. To the extent that it binds a controlling shareholder, it motivates her to act in the interests of shareholders as a class, which includes the interests of minority shareholders. As with all abstract norms, however, its functioning is subject to at least two important qualifications. The first concerns the range of corporate decisions or shareholder actions that trigger this norm. The second qualification concerns the meaning of the norm itself. For example, are two shareholders treated equally when a corporate decision has the same formal implications for each, even though it favors the distribution or the risk preferences of the controlling shareholder over those of the minority shareholder? Insofar as shareholder preferences are heterogeneous and controlling shareholders have legitimate power to shape corporate policy, some level of unequal treatment seems endemic to the corporate form.[35]

---

[32] See *supra* 3.2. For a broad discussion of the value of independent directors in U.S. family-controlled listed companies see Deborah A. DeMott, *Guests at the Table: Independent Directors in Family-Influenced Public Companies*, 33 JOURNAL OF CORPORATION LAW 819 (2008).

[33] See *infra* at 7.4.2.2.

[34] See *Hollinger Int'l, Inc. v. Black*, 844 A.2d 1022 (Del. Ch. 2004). For anecdotal evidence on the positive role of independent, minority-appointed directors in Italian listed companies with a dominant shareholder, see Luca Enriques, *Bad Apples, Bad Oranges: A Comment from Old Europe on Post-Enron Corporate Governance Reforms*, 38 WAKE FOREST LAW REVIEW 911, 928 (2003). In addition, there is systematic evidence that an independent board correlates with better performance in companies dominated by a controlling shareholder (see Ronald C. Anderson and David M. Reeb, *Board Composition: Balancing Family Influence in S&P 500 Firms*, 49 ADMINISTRATIVE SCIENCE QUARTERLY 209, 224–6 (2004); Jay Dahya, Orlin Dimitrov, and John. J. McDonnell, *Dominant Shareholders, Corporate Boards and Corporate Value: A Cross-Country Analysis*, 87 JOURNAL OF FINANCIAL ECONOMICS 73 (2008)). However, better performance in companies dominated by a controlling shareholder that have independent directors may well be caused by the quality of the controlling shareholder.

[35] For an instructive U.S. example on point, see the evolution of Massachusetts close corporation case law from *Donahue v. Rodd Electrotype Co.*, 328 N.E. 2d 505 (Mass. 1975), in which the

Our core jurisdictions differ with respect to both qualifications of the equal treatment norm. In general, Civil Code jurisdictions—and particularly those that have been heavily influenced by German law—tend to view equal treatment as a wide-ranging source of law as such rather than as a background norm informing the actual law. For example, Japan frames the principle of equal treatment as a general statutory provision.[36] By contrast, the common law jurisdictions—the U.S. and UK—specify equal treatment by case law or statute in particular contexts, but are less inclined to embrace a general legal standard of equal treatment as distinct from constraint-like standards such as the controlling shareholder's duty to act fairly vis-à-vis minority shareholders.

These jurisdictional differences in the deference accorded to equal treatment have important consequences in a number of areas of corporate law. As we discuss in Chapter 8, respect for equal treatment makes American-style poison pills more difficult to implement in jurisdictions that discourage companies from distinguishing among shareholders in awarding benefits, including stock purchase rights.[37] Indeed, it is arguable that the U.S.—or at least Delaware—law accords the widest latitude for *un*equal treatment of identical shares among all of our core jurisdictions, though there are some isolated areas in which it enforces the equal treatment norm with exceptional vigor. Although most jurisdictions enforce the equal treatment norm most strongly in the area of corporate distributions (i.e., dividends and share repurchases) and share issues, U.S. law limits categorical enforcement only to the payment of dividends. In general, targeted share repurchases, even at prices above market, are permissible in the U.S., and companies may issue shares to third parties without providing preemption rights to incumbent shareholders.[38]

---

court mandates that closely held corporations must purchase shares pro rata from minority and controlling shareholders, to *Wilkes v. Springside Nursing Home, Inc.*, 353 N.E. 2d 637 (1976), in which the court recognizes that controlling shareholders may pursue their right of 'selfish ownership' at a cost to minority shareholders as long as they have a legitimate business purpose.

[36] Art. 109(1) Companies Act. A number of EC directives' provisions more or less broadly impose the equal treatment principle upon EU open companies as well. See Art. 42, Directive 77/91/EEC, 1977 O.J. (L 26) 1; Art. 3(1)(a) Directive 2004/25/EC, 2004 O.J. (L 345) 64; Art. 17(1) Directive 2004/109/EC, 2004 O.J. (L 390) 38; Art. 4 Directive 2007/36/EC, 2007 O.J. (L 184) 17.

[37] Given Japan's strong statutory provision enshrining the equal treatment norm, the evolving Japanese case law on warrant-based takeover defenses is particularly interesting in this regard. See *Bull-dog Sauce v. Steel Partners*, Minshu 61-5-2215 (Japan. S. Ct. 2007) (permitting a discriminatory distribution of warrants where the warrant plan was overwhelmingly approved by an informed shareholder vote and provided compensation for discriminatory treatment to the defeated tender offeror). See *infra* 8.2.3. See also Jeffrey N. Gordon, *An American Perspective on Anti-Takeover Laws in the EU: The German Example*, in REFORMING COMPANY AND TAKEOVER LAW IN EUROPE 541, 551 (Guido Ferrarini et al. (eds.), 2004) (EC directive on capital maintenance protects preemptive rights and limits discriminatory share issuance in a way that makes U.S.-style poison pills unfeasible).

[38] Where deviations from equal treatment in share repurchases are legitimate, these can be used to fend off hostile bidders, whether by selectively buying back the shares held by a potential bidder (greenmail: see *Cheff v. Mathes*, 41 Del. Ch. 494, 199 A.2d 548 (1964)) or via self-tenders

Another area in which deference to the equal treatment norm has important implications is the law of corporate groups (i.e., groups of companies under the common control of another company, often managed as a single, integrated business). As we discuss in Chapters 5 and 6, some jurisdictions provide for special regulation in this area.[39] The idea behind such regulation is that any single intra-group transaction is often part of a larger set of transactions that provides offsetting advantages and disadvantages to particular subsidiaries and to the parent company. Subjecting each individual transaction within this set to all the controls accorded to related-party transactions in general—i.e., assuring that each intra-group transaction does not advantage the group's parent or one of its subsidiaries on a deal-by-deal basis—would needlessly disrupt the group's day-to-day management.

The alternative is to permit judicial evaluation of intra-group transactions in aggregate. In Germany, where the equal treatment norm has wide-ranging application, the equal treatment norm has also been extended to aggregates of intra-group transactions: one of the core provisions of formal German group law is the duty to indemnify group subsidiaries for any losses that stem from acting in the group's interests *on a yearly basis*,[40] which can be viewed as the extrapolation of the equal treatment norm to yearly aggregates of transactions. This contrasts sharply with the U.S. approach in which any particular intra-group transaction between a parent and its partially-held subsidiaries is subject to the full panoply of self-dealing controls. At least on paper, this approach also diverges from the French and Italian approaches. As we show in Chapter 6, these two jurisdictions appear to require 'fair' treatment of minority shareholders within a group by looking at the overall set of interactions among its companies (and without specifying the time frame to be considered). Put differently, France and Italy employ a general fairness standard in group law, which leaves much to a court's discretion, while Germany relies on the more exacting equal treatment norm. However, whether this formal difference in group law among the three jurisdictions makes a real difference in practice is open to question.[41] First, whether German courts effectively enforce 'aggregate' equal treatment within groups is uncertain. Second, with specific regard to France, the indeterminacy of the fairness standard, coupled with the criminal sanction attaching to a negative finding by the courts, may deter abusive behavior by the dominant shareholders of groups even more effectively than a substantive requirement of equal treatment.

Thus, the reach of the equality norm varies greatly, both within and between jurisdictions. However, all jurisdictions rely on this device over at least some

---

excluding the potential bidder form participation (see *Unocal v. Mesa Petroleum Co.*, 493 A.2d 946 (Del. 1985)).

[39] See *infra* 5.2.1.3, 5.3.1.2, and 6.2.5.3.
[40] §§ 302, 311 II AktG.   [41] See *infra* 6.2.5.3.

set of circumstances to align the incentives of controlling and minority shareholders.

4.1.4 Constraints and affiliation rights

We group together the remaining strategies for protecting minority shareholders because there is the least to say about them in a chapter devoted to the governance system. Legal constraints—principally in the form of standards such as the duty of loyalty, the oppression standard, and abuse of majority voting—are widely used to protect the interests of minority shareholders. In fact, these standards are often specific applications of the equal treatment norm, as when courts allow only 'fair' transactions between companies and their controllers—meaning, in effect, that controlling shareholders cannot accept unauthorized distributions from the corporate treasury at the expense of the firm's minority shareholders. We examine these standards more closely in Chapters 6 and 7, although we must stress here that they may help minority shareholders in settings involving neither a related-party transaction nor a fundamental change.[42]

Finally, the affiliation strategy in the guise of mandatory disclosure is at least as important to protecting minority shareholders as it is to protecting shareholders as a class. To the extent that disclosure, as a condition for entering and trading in the public markets, reveals controlling shareholder structures and conflicted transactions, market prices may reflect the risks of controller opportunism and penalize specific instances of it.[43] Moreover, mandatory disclosure provides the information necessary to protect minority shareholders through other mechanisms, such as voting or litigation.

By contrast, the exit strategy is sparingly used to protect minority shareholders. Permanency of investment is a hallmark of the corporate form—unlike the partnership form, in which exit rights are a default governance device. As we address in Chapters 6, 7, and 8, corporate law sometimes provides exit rights, but only upon egregious abuse of power by a controlling shareholder or at the time of a major decision that threatens to transform the enterprise. Examples of this are the possibility of appraisal rights (a mandatory buyout option) upon the occurrence of a fundamental transaction in the U.S., Japan, and elsewhere;[44] or the mandatory bid rule triggered by a sale of control.[45]

---

[42] See *infra* 6.2.5 and 7.4.2. For instance, a minority shareholder in a closely held firm may challenge as oppressive or abusive a controlling shareholder's decision to discharge the minority shareholder as an employee or to remove her from the board when all of the company's distributions to shareholders take the form of employee or director compensation.

[43] See Section 13D Securities Exchange Act of 1934, 15 U.S.C. § 78a (2008); Art. 9–15 Directive 2004/109/EC, 2004 O.J. (L 390) 38. Mandatory disclosure is further discussed in Chapter 9. See *infra* 9.2.1.

[44] See *infra* 7.2.2 and 7.4.1.2.   [45] See *infra* 8.2.5.4.

4.2. Protecting Employees

In addition to protecting minority shareholders, the corporate governance system extends important protections to non-shareholder constituencies. Corporate law in all jurisdictions provides specialized protections to corporate creditors, although it does so primarily through transaction-based rules and standards for solvent firms, or by shifting governance powers wholesale from shareholders to creditors in bankrupt firms. We consider these creditor protections separately in Chapter 5. Here we focus principally on the governance protections accorded to employees.

4.2.1 Appointment and decision rights strategies

The widespread introduction of employee-appointed directors to the boards of large European corporations is the most remarkable experiment in corporate governance of the 20th century. Many west European countries now mandate employee-appointed directors in at least some large companies,[46] although our core jurisdictions are not fully representative in this respect. The U.S., UK, Italy, and Japan have no codetermination requirements. Even French codetermination requirements are tame by the standards of most other European countries, which typically require that employee representatives constitute one-third of the board.[47] France requires some employee representation on the board in companies in which employees own more than 3% of the shares (typically privatized, or partially privatized, firms); but in the vast majority of French companies (with over 50 employees) employees may only select two non-voting representatives to attend board meetings.[48]

By contrast, German law establishes 'quasi-parity co-determination', in which employee directors comprise half the members of supervisory boards in German companies with over 2,000 (German-based) employees.[49] Just as importantly, some of these labor directors must be union nominees, who generally come

---

[46] The only EU countries that have *not* introduced any form of worker board representation are Portugal, Belgium, Italy, and the UK. Many countries, however, provide for codetermination only in state-owned companies.

[47] This is the case for instance in Austria, Denmark, Luxembourg, Hungary, and the Czech Republic. See Norbert Kluge and Michael Stollt, *Übersicht: Unternehmensmitbestimmung in den 27 EU-Mitgliedstaaten*, in Die Europäische Aktiengesellschaft: Eine Einführung in die Europäische Aktiengesellschaft mit Anmerkungen zur grenzüberschreitenden Verschmelzung, 47–50 (R. Köstler (ed.), 3rd ed., 2007).

[48] Art. L. 225–23 and L. 225–71 Code de commerce. Art. L. 432–6 Code du travail. Also, French firms *may* reserve a minority of the board seats to employee directors. Art. L. 225–27 Code de commerce.

[49] §§ 1 and 7 Mitbestimmungsgesetz. See Klaus J. Hopt, *Labor Representation on Corporate Boards: Impacts and Problems for Corporate Governance and Economic Integration in Europe*, 14 International Review of Law and Economics 203, 204 (1994). German companies with

from outside the enterprise.[50] Moreover, only German-based employees and German trade unions have a statutory right to labor directors. Employees and unions based in other countries lack appointment rights, which may—or may not—seem paradoxical,[51] according to one's views of the social functions of codetermination.

Although shareholders and labor appoint equal numbers of directors on the supervisory boards of large German companies (as the term 'quasi-parity' denotes), this does not mean that they share power equally as a formal legal matter, since the board's chairman, who is elected from among the shareholder representatives, has the statutory right to cast a tie-breaking vote in a second round of balloting in case of deadlock.[52] Nevertheless, employee representatives retain considerable power, formally through a statutory right to veto nominees to the management board,[53] and informally, because they are in a position to disrupt the proceedings of the supervisory board. In addition, the German codetermination statute allocates one seat on the management board to a 'human resources director', who often has close ties with unions and employees.[54] Thus, German codetermination gives labor significant leverage over corporate policy by according it influence over the composition of the management board, access to information, and the power to withhold consent from contentious company decisions. This latter point is especially critical, because the usual practice of supervisory boards is to take decisions by unanimous vote.

In contrast to appointment rights, however, corporate law almost never confers direct decision-making rights on non-shareholder constituencies. The same holds true for the EC's Works Council Directive, which, having regard to Community-scale groups or undertakings, requires all EU member states to provide employee information and consultation (but not decision) rights on matters of particular employee concern involving at least two different member states, such as the

---

between 500 and 2,000 employees must grant one-third of their board seats to employees. §§ 1 and 4 Drittelbeteiligungsgesetz.

[50] In the largest companies seven members are elected by employees and three are appointed by trade unions. § 7 II Mitbestimmungsgesetz.

[51] See Christine Windbichler, *Cheers and Boos for Employee Involvement: Co-Determination as Corporate Governance Conundrum*, 6 EUROPEAN BUSINESS ORGANIZATION LAW REVIEW 507, 521–5 (2005). One of the attractions of the *Societas Europaea* (European Company), besides the fact that it allows firms to reduce the supervisory board size to 12 seats (see *supra* 3.1.1), is that it also allows for board representation of employees located outside Germany, thus reducing the grip of German trade unions over the company. See Patrick Jenkins and Tobias Buck, *On the Move: Why European Companies May See Benefits in a Corporate Statute with Fewer Limitations*, FINANCIAL TIMES (Europe), 11 October 2005, at 13 (citing this feature as one of the attractions of the *Societas Europaea* for German companies).

[52] § 29 II Mitbestimmungsgesetz.

[53] Election to the management board is by a two-thirds majority vote of the supervisory board (§ 31 II Mitbestimmungsgesetz). If there is no two-third majority for a candidate, lengthy proceedings are instituted which finally award the tie-breaking vote in a simple majority vote to the chairman of the supervisory board.

[54] § 33 Mitbestimmungsgesetz.

prospective trend of employment, any substantial change in firms' organization and production processes and collective redundancies or sales of undertakings.[55] Other examples include the EC's General Framework Directive, which extends some information and consultation rights to national firms,[56] and rules requiring companies to provide advance notice of decisions on matters seriously affecting employees (e.g. on redundancies and sales of undertakings),[57] thus giving labor time to organize resistance, make its case, or otherwise protect employees' interests. Even if works councils cannot influence major corporate decisions, the information flow that they provide, from top management to the shop floor and vice versa, arguably creates as much trust between companies and their employees as mandatory employee representation on the board, especially since labor representatives on works councils are typically firm employees rather than outside union appointees.[58]

4.2.2 The incentives strategy

Incentive devices are less important in protecting employees than they are in protecting minority shareholders. One might have expected otherwise, at least in the case of independent directors. Yet, only the Netherlands (once again) has attempted a fully developed model of trusteeship to protect employees, in the form of a now-abandoned statute imposing self-selecting boards on certain large Dutch companies that were legally charged with the duty to represent and harmonize the interests of shareholders and labor.[59] The costs of the Dutch experiment in dual trusteeship seem to have been heavy, however. Companies operating under this regime generally performed less well than firms supervised

[55] For example, the European Works Council Directive (Directive 94/45/EC, 1994 O.J. (L 254) 64) requires that member states establish procedures for informing and consulting employees in every firm with at least 1,000 employees, provided that at least the same firm employs at least 150 employees in each of at least two member states. German and Dutch works councils also have limited direct decision rights. §§ 87 *et seq.* Betriebsverfassungsgesetz (Germany) permit works councils to co-decide (with management) matters such as the internal working order of factories, daily working times, health and safety regulations, and local principles of remuneration.

[56] See Art. 4 General Framework Directive (Directive 2002/14/EC, 2002 O.J. (L 80) 29). The directive applies to firms employing more than 50 employees (or to establishments employing more than 20 employees) regardless of the cross-border nature of the firm (Art. 3).

[57] See Art. 2 Collective Redundancies Directive (Council Directive 98/59/EC, 1998 O.J. (L 224) 16); Art. 7 Sale of Undertakings Directive (Council Directive 2001/23/EC, 2001 O.J. (L 82) 16).

[58] Works councils can provide a better framework for information-sharing than the supervisory board because, unlike trade unions, they are usually not involved in negotiations of employment terms: see Annette Van Den Berg, *The Contribution of Work Representation to Solving the Governance Structure Problem*, 8 JOURNAL OF MANAGEMENT AND GOVERNANCE 129 (2004). For a German case study where works council had a greater role than the supervisory board in shaping firm structure see M. Sako and G. Jackson, *Strategy Meets Institutions: The Transformation of Management-Labor Relations at Deutsche Telekom and NTT*, 59 INDUSTRIAL & LABOR RELATIONS REVIEW 347 (2006).

[59] See *supra* text accompanying note 27.

by shareholder-elected boards.[60] This appears to be the principal reason why the Netherlands recently replaced the structure regime with the standard northern European model in which employees elect one-third of the directors of large companies.[61]

Of course independent directors appointed by shareholders may function as weak trustees on behalf of employees, just as they do for minority shareholders, if law and local business culture motivate them to do so. And to some extent the law does encourage weak trusteeship, even in the U.S., where many states other than Delaware permit—but do not require—directors to consider the interests of employees and other non-shareholder constituencies in making important decisions, especially in the context of defending against hostile takeovers.[62]

Unlike minority shareholders, non-shareholder constituencies do not—and usually cannot—enjoy the protection of the equal sharing norm. Employees, lenders, and suppliers generally receive the bulk of their compensation as fixed payments rather than volatile claims on the net income of the firm as a whole. In the case of most employees who invest their human capital in the firm, fixed payments are clearly the dominant risk-sharing arrangement, since the company's stockholders are generally able to diversify their financial investments across firms.

To be sure, the corporate law of many jurisdictions provides that directors owe their duty of loyalty to the company rather than to any of its constituencies, including its shareholders.[63] Such a duty is most naturally understood as a command to maximize the net aggregate returns (pecuniary and non-pecuniary) of *all* corporate constituencies. In theory, implementing this injunction might (or might not) require division of company surplus between shareholders and non-shareholder constituencies such as employees in order to maximize the aggregate private welfare of all corporate constituencies.[64] In practice, however, courts lack the information to determine which policies maximize aggregate private welfare, so the duty to pursue the corporation's interest (in this sense) is unenforceable. Moreover, even fair-minded directors are unlikely to know how best to distribute surplus among multiple corporate constituencies. Thus, the injunction to boards to pursue their corporations' interests is less a species of equal sharing than, at best, a vague counsel of virtue, and, at worst, a smokescreen for board discretion.

---

[60] See William W. Bratton and Joseph A. McCahery, *Restructuring the Relationship between Shareholders and Managers*, in HERPOSITIONERING VAN ONDERNEMINGEN, KONINKLIJKE VERENIGING VOOR DE STAATHUISHOUDKUNDE, PREADVIEZEN 2001, 63 (Hans Schenk (ed.), 2001).

[61] See Groenewald, *supra* note 27, at 299.

[62] See *infra* 8.5. For a trustee-like analysis of the U.S. board, see Margaret M. Blair and Lynn A. Stout, *A Team Production Theory of Corporate Law*, 85 VIRGINIA LAW REVIEW 247 (1999).

[63] E.g. Germany: §§ 76 I and 93 I 2 AktG; Japan: Art. 355 Companies Act.

[64] Note that maximizing the private welfare of all of the firm's current constituencies is not equivalent to maximizing social welfare, which would include, for example, the welfare of potential employees who are never hired because the high wages of current employees limit firm expansion.

No doubt this ambiguity contributes to the continuing popularity of long-term share value as a proxy for the interests of the corporation.

Finally, employee stock ownership might seem to be a weak variant of the equal sharing device. Some jurisdictions encourage firms to share equity ownership with employees, on the theory that this will improve corporate governance and diminish tensions within the firm.[65] But share ownership does not have the same consequences for employees that it has for outside investors with diversified portfolios. For employees, equity ownership severely increases the already large— and largely undiversified—firm-specific risk that employees bear. Moreover, it is unclear whether employee share ownership does protect the interests of employees as a class, since employees generally remain minority shareholders without significant governance rights.

4.2.3 The constraints strategy

The constraints strategy for protecting employees is largely embodied in dedicated regulatory structures, such as labor law, which, perhaps arbitrarily, we exclude from the purview of this book except in the context of fundamental corporate decisions, addressed in Chapter 7 below.[66] Other corporate law constraints for protecting non-shareholders are either toothless or narrowly targeted. For example, in some jurisdictions directors owe a duty of care to all third parties affected by the company's operations,[67] but in practice this duty is principally read to protect the creditors of closely held corporations.[68] Similarly, the UK Companies Act of 2006 imposes a directorial duty to promote 'the benefit of [company] members as a whole, *and in doing so [to] have regard* (amongst other matters) to ... the interests of the company's employees, ... the impact of the company's operations on the community and the environment.'[69] But this language appears to have no constraining force, much like similar language in the typical American other-constituency statute. Finally, a possible constraint for protecting employees is the German requirement that management boards establish 'risk management systems' to identify and contain developments that might threaten the company's survival.[70] Arguably this provision injects the risk preferences of

---

[65] There are also instances of the reward strategy in the form of legally sanctioned sharing regimes. For example, the U.S. has tax-favored employee stock ownership plans, see Henry Hansmann, THE OWNERSHIP OF ENTERPRISE 87 (1996). France mandates both extensive information and limited employee profit-sharing rights in all firms with more than 50 workers. See Art. L. 2322–1, 2323–6 to 2323–26, 3322–2, Art. 3324–1 and 3324–10 Code du travail.

[66] See *infra* 7.4.3.2 and 7.5.2.2.

[67] Art. 429(1) Companies Act (Japan). Art. 2395 Civil Code (Italy). Art. L. 225–251, L. 223–22 Code de commerce (France). However, French courts virtually never impose liability on directors on behalf of third parties as long as the company is solvent. See Maurice Cozian, Alain Viandier, and Florence Deboissy, DROIT DES SOCIÉTÉS, No. 277 (21st ed., 2008).

[68] See *infra* 5.3.1.1.   [69] § 172 Companies Act 2006 (UK).

[70] § 91 II AktG, introduced by the 1998 KonTraG.

non-corporate constituencies, and especially employees, into corporate decision-making. But whether it has this effect in fact must await future litigation.[71]

4.3. Explaining Jurisdictional Differences and Similarities

As with our discussion of the primary manager-shareholder agency problem in Chapter 3, we first rank our core jurisdictions according to the protection that substantive law offers to minority shareholders and employees respectively, and rank them next according to the protection that these constituencies enjoy in practice, considering not only corporate law but also societal and legal institutions more generally. Our rankings are admittedly crude. Jurisdictions vary far more in their treatment of agency problems involving minority shareholders and employees than they do in their approach to the manager-shareholder agency conflict. Nevertheless, this ranking is a useful point of entry into the analysis of inter-jurisdictional differences.

4.3.1 The law-on-the-books

The substantive law-on-the-books gives little guidance as to which jurisdictions place more emphasis on protecting minority shareholders. It does, however, provide an indication of which countries go furthest to protect employees through corporate law.

Consider minority shareholders first. Virtually all minority protection is a matter of corporate law, whether it takes the form of mandatory governance rules or specialized regimes regulating self-dealing transactions. Yet only Italy among our core jurisdictions mandates that minority shareholders appoint a board member in listed firms as a matter of right. Elsewhere the long-term trend is in the opposite direction, i.e., *away* from minority empowerment through devices such as proportional voting and strong supermajority voting rules.[72] In terms of appointment rights, then, Italy qualifies hands down as the most minority-friendly among our core jurisdictions.

Why do other jurisdictions lack mandatory minority-friendly appointment rights for listed companies? One answer is that minority shareholders are a heterogeneous group in publicly traded corporations. On the one hand, retail investors are the most vulnerable minority but, as a consequence of collective action problems, they are also the minority shareholders who are least able to press their interests through appointment and decision rights. On the other hand, the minority shareholders best able to use appointment rights are

---

[71] The scope of this new provision remains unclear and controversial. See Uwe Hüffer, Aktiengesetz, §93 , n.5 and n.8 (8th ed., 2008).
[72] See *supra* 3.1.2 and 4.1.1.

large-block investors, who are also best able to contract for governance protections (say, in a shareholder agreement) even without the addition of mandatory terms in the law. The natural parallel is with labor. To the extent that employees are already organized in union or works council structures, they too—like large-block shareholders—can wield appointment rights effectively. Conversely, they are unlikely to do so if they lack prior organization.

Board representation for minority shareholders might make more sense if, as is relatively often the case in Italy for the largest companies,[73] institutional investors, as opposed to inside blockholders, nominated minority directors. At least in the U.S., however, stringent laws on insider trading and onerous ownership disclosure rules that prevent coordination among shareholders[74] would discourage most institutional investors from exercising appointment rights, making this strategy less appealing. For large-block activist investors such as hedge funds, however, legally protected board representation for minority investors might prove to be a potent tool, even in the U.S.

What, then, of other legal strategies for protecting public minority investors? If independent directors are reliable trustees, then the U.S., followed by the UK, provides minority investors with the most protection by strongly encouraging independent boards. But since controlling shareholders appoint independent directors, even in the U.S. and UK, their allegiance is always suspect unless they expect that their actions will be monitored *ex post*.

Alternatively, consider tough enforcement of the equal treatment norm as a minority safeguard. In this case Japan—followed by Germany, France, and Italy—might be tagged as having the most minority-friendly law-on-the-books. The UK would also qualify, given its preemption rights and minority-protective Takeover Code, while Delaware would be the least minority-friendly member of our core jurisdictions. By contrast, however, if mandatory disclosure best protects minority shareholders, the U.S. rises again to the top of the list of minority-friendly jurisdictions, at least for publicly traded firms. Put differently, all we know from the law-on-the-books is that jurisdictions pursue different strategies to protect minority interests. How well these strategies work in practice must be investigated *in situ*.

The contrast with governance strategies that protect labor's interest could not be more striking. Here, law-on-the-books points to a clear rank order among jurisdictions. Germany's system of quasi-parity codetermination is hands down the governance regime that most aggressively protects employee interests. France follows at a considerable distance behind Germany by mandating a far

---

[73] In 2007, institutional investors nominated around one-third of the minority-appointed directors in companies voluntarily providing such information. See ASSONIME, AN ANALYSIS OF THE COMPLIANCE WITH THE ITALIAN CORPORATE GOVERNANCE CODE 8 (2008), at http://www.assonime.it.

[74] See Mark J. Roe, STRONG MANAGERS, WEAK OWNERS: THE POLITICAL ROOTS OF AMERICAN CORPORATE FINANCE 273 (1994).

more attenuated labor presence on company boards. But all EU jurisdictions—Germany, France, Italy, and the UK—are subject to the Works Council Directive, and emphasize employee participation in structuring the workplace accordingly.[75] Finally, Japan, France, Germany, and Italy all have strong labor law rules governing basic employee interests, ranging from pension rights to terms of dismissal.[76] The U.S. is the least protective of our core jurisdictions, both in direct regulation of employee rights and in structuring the corporate governance system to reflect employee interests.

4.3.2 The law in practice

As we argue above, the law-on-the-books is often an incomplete measure of the protection accorded to corporate constituencies. This is particularly the case for minority shareholders.

4.3.2.1 Minority shareholders

Two prominent empirical papers, using different methodologies, suggest that controlling shareholders obtain private benefits that range from small to negligible in the UK, U.S., and Japan respectively, but are moderately larger in Germany (approximately 10%) and are very large in Italy (30% or more) and—arguably—in France (28%) if the more credible of the studies is accepted.[77] Thus, to the extent that private benefits of control measure the severity of the majority-minority shareholder agency problem, our core jurisdictions differ dramatically in the extent of protection that they offer to minority shareholders, even if these differences were not evident *a priori* from the law-on-the-books. Moreover, these variations follow a clear pattern. The three jurisdictions in which large corporations ordinarily have dispersed ownership also have low private benefits of control, while the three countries in which concentrated ownership dominates have moderate to large private benefits. Put flippantly, our core jurisdictions do best in protecting minority shareholders where the intra-shareholder agency problem is least severe.

---

[75] See Art. 1 Works Council Directive, *supra* note 55.

[76] See e.g, Juan C. Botero, Simeon Djankov, Rafael La Porta, Florencio Lopez-de-Silanes, and Andrei Shleifer, *The Regulation of Labor*, 119 QUARTERLY JOURNAL OF ECONOMICS 1339 (2004) (France displays the most restrictive labor law among our jurisdictions).

[77] The two papers are Tatiana Nenova, *The Value of Corporate Voting Rights and Control: A Cross-Country Analysis*, 68 JOURNAL OF FINANCIAL ECONOMICS 325, 336 (2003) (employing share price differentials for dual class firms to calculate private benefits); Alexander Dyck and Luigi Zingales, *Private Benefits of Control: An International Comparison*, 59 JOURNAL OF FINANCE 537, 551 (2004) (employing control premia in sales of control blocks to calculate private benefits). Although these two papers present similar results across all other jurisdictions, they differ sharply for France (2% vs. 28%). Here Nenova's finding of 28% seems more plausible because it is based on nine observations of French firms, while Dyck and Zingales have only four observations of French control transactions.

This observation suggests that Italy's recent award of appointment rights to minority shareholders is a response—not necessarily a solution—to the mistreatment of minority shareholders. Moreover, it suggests that the strong equal treatment norms found in Civil Code jurisdictions do not necessarily protect minority shareholders, nor does a relatively low percentage of independent directors (as in Japan) necessarily inflate private benefits of control. Even domination by a controlling shareholder is not a reliable predictor, since Scandinavian jurisdictions generally manifest low levels of private benefits despite concentrated ownership structures.[78]

What, then, predicts private benefits of control and, by implication, the efficacy of minority shareholder protection? The literature suggests that many factors matter, from the legal protections to general business culture, and even to the competitiveness of the product markets.[79]

We offer our own supplementary hypotheses building on the analysis of Chapter 3. To begin, pyramids and corporate groups (in the European sense) are rare in the three jurisdictions in which widely held corporate ownership structures prevail. This fact alone removes the most opaque and effective devices for tunneling assets out of controlled companies.

In addition, controlling shareholders are simply not an influential interest group in these three jurisdictions, which is most likely both a cause and an effect of their relative scarcity. In the UK, the interests of institutional shareholders dominate the institutions of lawmaking and enforcement, such as the *FSA* and the Takeover Panel. Institutional investors, although large, are normally passive outsiders with every reason to oppose any form of suspected favoritism toward corporate controllers.

In the U.S., political influence is more evenly balanced between institutional investors and professional managers, with managers enjoying the advantage in the board-centric Delaware courts and institutional shareholders faring slightly better at the federal level of securities regulation. But again, neither managers and institutional investors nor state courts and the SEC have reason to treat controlling shareholders with kid gloves. In the ecosystem of corporate governance, strong managers are natural competitors of controlling shareholders.[80] Stringent U.S. disclosure requirements, holding company regulations,[81] and taxation of intra-corporate distributions[82] are all indications of the comparative weakness of controlling shareholders under U.S. law. The Delaware courts also take a tougher stance toward self-dealing by controlling shareholders than by officers

---

[78] Tatiana Nenova, *supra* note 77 (expropriation in Scandinavian companies is limited to 1% of company value).

[79] See Dyck and Zingales, *supra* note 77.

[80] See Mark J. Roe, Strong Managers, Weak Owners, *supra* note 74, especially at 41.

[81] *Id.*, at 98.

[82] Randall Morck and Bernard Yeung, *Dividend Taxation and Corporate Governance*, 19 Journal of Economic Perspectives 163 (2005).

and directors.[83] Finally, enforcement by the SEC and shareholder class actions are common and often severe.

The case of Japan would seem to be similar in one respect. As we argue in Chapter 3, managers dominate large Japanese companies, and a large percentage of shares still lie in the hands of stable corporate shareholders. As long as strong managers can rely on stable networks of friendly shareholders for support, they have no interest in a corporate law that permits discrimination among shareholders and that, as a consequence, encourages entrepreneurs to aggregate controlling blocks of shares. Little wonder, then, that the equal treatment norm has traditionally been enforced with particular rigor in Japan.[84]

By contrast, in the three continental European jurisdictions in which coalitions of large shareholders control most listed companies, one assumes that controlling shareholders are a potent political influence. In France and Italy, the fact that the state is a major shareholder in many companies—and is often a member of the controlling coalition in the companies in which it holds a non-controlling stake—further compounds the influence of controlling shareholders, as we note in Chapter 3. The empirical evidence suggests that the minority-majority agency problem remains severe in these jurisdictions, despite legal efforts to mitigate it through increased mandatory disclosure,[85] appointment rights for minority shareholders in Italy, and pressure to add independent directors arising from recently-adopted codes of best practice.[86]

Precisely how controlling shareholders obtain private benefits in these three jurisdictions—if the empirical evidence is in fact accurate—is unclear. All three jurisdictions have strong minority protection laws on the books, although there is little private enforcement, especially in Italy.[87] Perhaps the greatest enforcement difficulty, however, lies in policing the terms of related-party transactions among the affiliates of a corporate group. As tax authorities know well, transfer pricing is not easy to regulate. Thus, the principal puzzle posed by the comparative data is *not* why private benefits are large in France and Italy, but rather why they appear to be smaller in Germany (and even more so in Scandinavia).[88] In the

---

[83] See *infra* 6.2.5.2.

[84] Of course, once hostile acquirers become a significant threat despite friendly shareholder support, managers acquire an interest in discriminating among shareholders in order to facilitate warrant or rights-based takeover defenses. See *infra* 8.2.3.2. See also Satoshi Kawai, *Poison Pill in Japan*, 2004 COLUMBIA BUSINESS LAW REVIEW 11 (2004) (shareholder equality, traditionally a key principle in Japan, can be overcome if the board, having adopted a poison pill, bargains in the best interest of all shareholders).

[85] On agency problems in countries where ownership of firms is concentrated see Randall Morck, Daniel Wolfenzon, and Bernard Yeung, *Corporate Governance, Economic Entrenchment and Growth*, 43 JOURNAL OF ECONOMIC LITERATURE 655 (2005). On the role of disclosure in limiting asset diversion see Allen Ferrell, *The Case for Mandatory Disclosure in Securities Regulation around the World*, 2 BROOKLYN JOURNAL OF CORPORATE, FINANCIAL & COMMERCIAL LAW 81 (2007).

[86] See *supra* 3.2 and 4.3.1.

[87] See *infra* 6.2.5.4.

[88] See Ronald J. Gilson, *Controlling Shareholders and Corporate Governance: Complicating the Comparative Taxonomy*, 119 HARVARD LAW REVIEW 1641 (2006).

case of Germany at least, part of the answer may be that managers are stronger, and controlling coalitions of shareholders are weaker on average, than they are in Italy and France. Labor rather than the state is the third-party player in German corporate governance; and German law creates a strong management board, in part with the apparent intention of balancing the influence of shareholders and labor on the supervisory board.[89]

4.3.2.2 Employee protection

In contrast to the weak correlation between formal law and minority share-holder protection, the correlation between law and employee protection is strong. German company law does, in fact, reallocate corporate power to unions and works councils through quasi-parity codetermination, and diluted codetermination in other European jurisdictions does the same, albeit to a much lesser extent. We have already suggested why employees, as opposed to disaggregated shareholders, might stress board representation on their political agenda, if not necessarily on their collective bargaining agenda. Through existing organizational structures such as unions and works councils, employees collectively can make effective use of constituency directors.

What exactly can such directors accomplish apart from the narrow goal of enhancing labor's bargaining power? A cogent argument can be made that labor directors benefit the firm and its shareholders as well as its employees. In Germany, at least, labor directors can influence business policies.[90] But in addition to this, they may also play an important informational role, at least in theory. Mutually wasteful bargaining behavior such as strikes and lock-outs result in part from distrust between firms and employees.[91] By credibly informing employees, labor directors might plausibly limit such costly bargaining behavior. Likewise, by revealing the firm's intentions, labor directors can alert workers about possible future plant closings and accompanying layoffs. Whether employee representation at the board level actually improves industrial relations based on trust between labor and shareholders is impossible to say in the absence of empirical study.[92]

---

[89] See Mark J. Roe, *German Co-Determination and German Securities Markets*, in Klaus J. Hopt et al. (eds.), *supra* note 12, at 361 (weakened supervisory board as a result of a tripartite game among management, labor, and capital).

[90] See *supra* 3.7.

[91] See R.B. Freeman and E.P. Lazear, *An Economic Analysis of Works Councils*, in WORKS COUNCILS: CONSULTATION, REPRESENTATION AND COOPERATION IN INDUSTRIAL RELATIONS 27 (J. Roger and W. Streek (eds.), 1995). See generally, John Kennan and Robert Wilson, *Bargaining with Incomplete Information*, 31 JOURNAL OF ECONOMIC LITERATURE 45 (1993).

[92] We have been unable to find empirical work on the relationship between the extent of labor representation on corporate boards and the incidence of strikes. Indeed, there is even anecdotal evidence that unions have sometimes used board representation to organize strikes in ways that are especially costly for companies. See, e.g., Klaus J. Hopt, *Trusteeship and Conflicts of Interest in Corporate, Banking, and Agency Law—Toward Common Legal Principles for Intermediaries in the Modern Service-Oriented Society*, in REFORMING COMPANY AND TAKEOVER LAW IN EUROPE 51, 52

An alternative theory with some empirical support in the literature argues that codetermination *can* provide German supervisory boards with 'valuable first-hand operational knowledge' that improves board decision-making and increases firm value in the subset of firms in which the need for intra-firm coordination is greatest.[93] Yet there is also evidence that quasi-parity codetermination in larger German firms reduces firm value[94]—and still other, non-comparable, studies finding that codetermination increases (decreases) employee productivity or firm profitability.[95]

Moreover, the question remains: if large efficiencies result from codetermination, why do the parties fail to contract for labor directors voluntarily and divide the surplus? Why do we seldom see labor directors where they are not mandated by law? And if mandatory law is needed to overcome collective action problems associated with the introduction of voluntary codetermination, why is mandatory regulation necessary to sustain codetermination once it has been introduced? Although commentators have offered speculative economic answers to these questions,[96] the empirical literature again remains sparse.

There may also be ideological or cultural explanations for the dearth of employee directors outside of continental Europe. But a competing explanation is that the costs of labor representation exceed its benefits, or at least are feared to do so. One cost is the difficulty of bridging sharply divergent interests between the board's constituent groups of employees and shareholders, or even among employees themselves, in framing policy or supervising management. Voting is a highly imperfect way of making decisions in the presence of such conflicts. Majority decision-making by a divided board risks opportunistic outcomes that diminish the value of the firm as a whole, and is also likely to make for a costly and cumbersome decision-making process.[97]

(Guido Ferrarini et al. (eds.), 2004) (president of the Verdi trade union, Frank Bsirske, served as vice chairman of Lufthansa's supervisory board while organizing an airport strike that was exceptionally costly for his company).

[93] Larry Fauver and Michael E. Fuerst, *Does Good Corporate Governance Include Employee Representation? Evidence from German Corporate Boards*, 82 JOURNAL OF FINANCIAL ECONOMICS. 673, 679 (2006).

[94] See *id.* at 698–701; Gary Gorton and Frank A. Schmid, *Capital, Labor, and the Firm: A Study of German Codetermination*, 2 JOURNAL OF THE EUROPEAN ECONOMIC ASSOCIATION 863 (2004).

[95] For a recent if partisan review, see Simon Renaud, *Dynamic Efficiency of Supervisory Board Codetermination in Germany*, 21 LABOUR 689 (2007). Renaud's own strongly positive findings about the effects of quasi-parity codetermination on profitability and productivity are suspect because they rely on balance sheet data and fail to include the range of control variables found in the finance-oriented literature such as Fauver and Fuerst, *supra* note 93. For a very helpful, if also partisan, review of the wider literature associated with codetermination, see Martin Gelter, STAKEHOLDERS IN EUROPEAN AND US CORPORATE GOVERNANCE (2008) (unpublished S.J.D. dissertation, Harvard Law School) (on file with authors).

[96] See, e.g., Fauver and Fuerst, *supra* note 93, at 679 (proposing that firms may be deterred from adopting codetermination voluntarily by adverse selection in recruiting employees and managers, even if codetermination would increase firm value).

[97] It is nearly always the case that, in any given firm (whether investor-, employee-, customer-, or supplier-owned), the group of persons sharing ownership is remarkable for its homogeneity of

Another cost associated with strong labor representation on the board is that of exacerbating the agency conflict between managers and shareholders as a class. Managerial discretion plausibly increases if shareholder and labor directors split over corporate policy, or if large and divided supervisory boards lack the institutional capacity to monitor managers closely.[98] Indeed, managers may withhold information from boards with the acquiescence of shareholders to limit leaks to employees and competitors.[99] Strong labor may benefit managers, just as strong managers have proven to be loyal protectors of labor's interests in large Japanese companies, even without a regime of codetermination.[100]

So which side of the ledger dominates, the costs or the benefits of codetermination? At least in the case of German-style codetermination, the empirical literature is surprisingly mixed as we have noted above. Certainly large German firms survive and even flourish under the quasi-parity regime of employee representation, and it seems intuitively likely that codetermination has contributed to the heavy orientation of the German economy toward manufacturing exports. Nevertheless, it is difficult to tease out the opportunity costs suffered by the German economy as a result of strong-form codetermination.

Whatever the answers to these basic questions, we expect two concurrent factors to place great pressure on German-style codetermination in the future. On one hand, a growing equity culture throughout the EU is likely to conflict with a governance system that favors collusion between managers and employees.[101] On the other hand, new avenues for regulatory arbitrage, such as the European

interest. Even within investor-owned firms, for example, it is highly unusual for both preferred and common shareholders to share significant voting rights. Likewise, within entirely employee-owned firms it is rare for both managerial and line employees to share control (and voting rights are often given to the line employees, who tend to be more homogeneous). See Hansmann, *supra* note 65, at 62–4 and 91–2. This suggests that the appointments strategy is not easily adapted to resolve significant conflicts of interest.

[98] But see Fauyer and Fuerst, *supra* note 93 (arguing that in some instances employee board representation may increase the monitoring capacity of the supervisory board and thereby *reduce* agency costs).

[99] See Katharina Pistor, *Co-Determination in Germany: A Socio Political Model with Governance Externalities,* in EMPLOYEES AND CORPORATE GOVERNANCE 163, 188–91 (Margaret M. Blair and Mark J. Roe (eds.), 1999). Pistor also provides an illuminating account of the practice of codetermination in German firms as forcing a fractionalization of the supervisory board into employee and management 'benches', which meet separately prior to board meetings (a practice that the German Corporate Governance Code, in the one and only provision addressing codetermination, even recommends: Recommendation 6.3) and always present a common front in formal meetings of the supervisory board. The common practice of forcing supervisory boards to review the auditor's report *at the board meeting,* but not permitting board members to receive a copy for close review, is emblematic of the informational restrictions placed by the management board on the supervisory board. *Id.,* 191.

[100] See Masahiko Aoki, *Toward an Economic Model of the Japanese Firm,* 28 JOURNAL OF ECONOMIC LITERATURE 1 (1990).

[101] See, e.g., Jeffrey N. Gordon, *Pathways to Corporate Convergence? Two Steps on the Road to Shareholder Capitalism in Germany,* 5 COLUMBIA JOURNAL OF EUROPEAN LAW 219 (1999); Michael Bradley and Anant Sundaram, *The Emergence of Shareholder Value in the German Corporation,* Working Paper (2003), at http://www.ssrn.com.

Company and the freedom to incorporate abroad following the European Court of Justice *Centros* case law,[102] may allow German firms to escape codetermination laws that apply only to companies incorporated in Germany.[103] In the long term, the balance of costs and benefits is likely to decide whether strong-form codetermination can survive these challenges.

---

[102] Case C-212/97, *Centros Ltd v Erhvervs- og Selskabsstyrelsen* [1999] ECR I-1459.
[103] See e.g. Jens C. Dammann, *The Future of Codetermination After* Centros: *Will German Corporate Law Move Closer to the U.S. Model?*, 8 Fordham Journal of Corporate & Financial Law 607 (2003).

5

Transactions with Creditors

John Armour, Gerard Hertig, and Hideki Kanda

Every corporate law includes some provisions protecting corporate creditors. All parties who contract with corporations stand to benefit from such protections, for the class of 'creditors' includes not only banks and bondholders, but anyone who accepts a claim on corporate cash flows in exchange for goods or services. Of course, the general law of debtor-creditor relations will apply to such transactions,[1] and of interest for our purposes are only those legal strategies specifically directed at creditors of *corporate* debtors. Such provisions are commonly justified by reference to problems said to be peculiar to corporate creditors, including the power of the firm's shareholders to manipulate limited liability to the detriment of creditors and the power of creditors to seize control of a defaulting firm in a way that prevents the efficient deployment of its assets. This chapter considers the legal strategies employed by our major jurisdictions to address these problems.

5.1 Why Should Corporate Law Deal with Creditors?

A firm's creditors have a dual role in relation to the other participants in the enterprise. Under ordinary circumstances, most creditors are no more than contractual counterparties. However, if the firm defaults on payment obligations, its creditors become entitled to seize and sell its assets.[2] At this point, the creditors

---

[1] Stronger legal protection of creditors' rights is generally associated with more lending to corporate borrowers: Rafael La Porta, Florencio Lopez-de-Silanes, Andrei Shleifer, and Robert W. Vishny, *Legal Determinants of External Finance,* 52 JOURNAL OF FINANCE 1131 (1997); Rainer Haselmann, Katharina Pistor, and Vikrant Vig, *How Law Affects Lending,* Working Paper (2006), at http://www.ssrn.com; Simeon Djankov, Caralee McLiesh, and Andrei Shleifer, *Private Credit in 129 Countries,* 84 JOURNAL OF FINANCIAL ECONOMICS 299 (2007). However, the link is stronger where there are good-quality mechanisms for debt enforcement, which tends to be in developed, rather than developing, economies: Simeon Djankov, Oliver Hart, Caralee McLiesh, and Andrei Shleifer, *Debt Enforcement Around the World,* 116 JOURNAL OF POLITICAL ECONOMY 1105 (2008); Mehnaz Safavian and Siddharth Sharma, *When Do Creditor Rights Work?,* 35 JOURNAL OF COMPARATIVE ECONOMICS 484, 500–2, 506–7 (2007).

[2] See *infra* 5.1.2.

change roles: they become, in a meaningful sense, the owners of the firm's assets. This dual role means that creditors may experience different agency problems at different points in time. As contractual counterparties, they face the possibility of opportunistic behavior by the firm acting in the interests of its shareholders. Yet if the firm defaults, the problem can morph into assuring that one group of owners is not expropriated by another: that is, a creditor-creditor conflict of interest. Moreover, the creditors' contingent ownership will cast a shadow over how relations among participants in the firm are conducted, even if it is financially healthy.

5.1.1 Shareholder-creditor agency problems

Consider first the agency problems arising between firms and their creditors as contractual counterparties. *Ex ante*—before contracting—debtors may lie about their assets to obtain an agreement. *Ex post*—after contracting—they may alter risks in violation of the terms of the agreements with their creditors. Having a legal entity (such as a corporation) as debtor may exacerbate both of these risks.[3] *Ex ante*, it assists shareholders in misrepresenting the value of corporate assets by falsely claiming that the firm holds title to assets that actually belong to other entities or to the shareholders in their personal capacity. *Ex post*, the fact that the shareholders benefit from the firm's successes, but their personal assets are shielded from the consequences of its failure, gives them incentives to engage in actions that benefit them at the expense of creditors. Such actions may take a variety of forms. First, and most basically, the shareholders may siphon assets out of the corporate pool in favor of themselves. This kind of transaction, which is sometimes referred to as 'asset dilution', makes shareholders better off, but harms creditors by reducing the assets available to satisfy their claims.

Second, creditors' interests may be harmed by an increase in the riskiness of the firm's business, in particular through 'asset substitution'.[4] Here shareholders do not take the firm's assets for themselves, but rather sell assets used in low-risk business activities to pay for the acquisition of assets used in high-risk business activities.[5] Shareholders can benefit from an increase in the riskiness—that is,

---

[3] These agency problems also become applicable to individual debtors, especially if bankruptcy law facilitates a discharge of indebtedness ('fresh start') for them.

[4] See Michael C. Jensen and William H. Meckling, *Theory of the Firm: Managerial Behavior, Agency Costs and Ownership Structure*, 3 JOURNAL OF FINANCIAL ECONOMICS 305, 334–7 (1976); Dan Galai and Ronald W. Masulis, *The Option Pricing Model and the Risk Factor of Stock*, 3 JOURNAL OF FINANCIAL ECONOMICS 53 (1976).

[5] However, evidence regarding the empirical significance of such risk-shifting is mixed: see Katherine H. Daigle and Michael T. Maloney, *Residual Claims in Bankruptcy: An Agency Theory Explanation*, 37 JOURNAL OF LAW AND ECONOMICS 157, 182–7 (1994); Gregor Andrade and Steven Kaplan, *How Costly is Financial (not Economic) Distress? Evidence from Highly Leveraged Transactions that Became Distressed*, 53 JOURNAL OF FINANCE 1443 (1998); Assaf Eisdorfer, *Empirical Evidence of Risk Shifting in Financially Distressed Firms*, 63 JOURNAL OF FINANCE 609 (2008).

the volatility—of the firm's cash flows, because if things go well, all the extra goes to them, but if things go badly, they lose no more than they already had at stake. Creditors, however, will be harmed by this increase. It will increase the probability that the firm will not generate sufficient cash to repay them, with no countervailing benefit if things go well, given that creditors' claims against the firm are fixed.[6] To make things worse, such a substitution may be attractive to shareholders even if it reduces the overall value of the firm's assets: that is, the shareholders may prefer a larger slice of a smaller overall pie.[7]

A third way in which shareholders may benefit at creditors' expense is by increasing the firm's overall borrowing. If the 'new' creditors end up sharing the firm's assets with the 'old' creditors in the event of failure, this reduces the expected recoveries of the old creditors should the firm default. This benefits the shareholders by enabling them, in effect, to have the benefit of finance from the old creditors on terms which, in light of the addition of the new creditors, now look too favorable. This effect is sometimes referred to as 'debt dilution'.[8] The ultimate impact on the old creditors will of course depend on what the firm does with the new funds. But because the new borrowing is subsidized (by the old lenders) the new lenders may be persuaded to fund projects that are value-decreasing, and which, without such a subsidy, they would decline to fund.

The intensity of the shareholder-creditor agency problem will be influenced by managerial risk aversion and shareholder control over firm decision-making. Managers of widely held firms who do not have significant equity stakes of their own will share little of the 'upside' payoffs received by shareholders, and may be more averse to increasing the risk of default because of harm to their reputations if the firm becomes financially distressed.[9] As a result, they are less likely to be tempted to take actions that benefit shareholders at the expense of creditors than are managers who are accountable to a controlling shareholder, or who have a significant personal stake in enhancing the firm's share price, as for example

---

[6] The firm need not actually default on its debts for its creditors to be harmed: the value of their claims in secondary loan markets will be reduced immediately by the shareholders' action.

[7] The phenomenon of firms investing in business projects that a rational investor would reject as yielding too low a rate of return is sometimes referred to as 'overinvestment'. The inverse problem—referred to as 'underinvestment'—may also arise in situations where the firm has liabilities exceeding its assets. Such a firm may have growth opportunities that require further investments of capital, but shareholders will be unwilling to make such an investment as the resulting payoffs will have to be shared with creditors: Stewart C. Myers, *Determinants of Corporate Borrowing*, 5 JOURNAL OF FINANCIAL ECONOMICS 147 (1977).

[8] See e.g. Alan Schwartz, *A Theory of Loan Priorities*, 18 JOURNAL OF LEGAL STUDIES 209 (1989).

[9] For example, managers of U.S. firms that go through troubled debt restructurings frequently lose their jobs, and have difficulty securing subsequent employment at a similar level: Stuart C. Gilson, *Management Turnover and Financial Distress*, 25 JOURNAL OF FINANCIAL ECONOMICS 241 (1989); Edith Hotchkiss, *Post-Bankruptcy Performance and Management Turnover*, 50 JOURNAL OF FINANCE 21 (1995); Kenneth M. Ayotte and Edward R. Morrison, *Creditor Control and Conflict in Chapter 11*, Working Paper (2008), at http://www.ssrn.com.

through stock options.[10] In other words, the more successful the various strategies described in Chapter 3 are in aligning managers' interests with shareholders', the stronger will be managers' incentives to act in a way that may benefit shareholders at creditors' expense.

Shareholder-creditor conflicts have the potential to reduce the overall value of the firm's assets.[11] Thus both creditors *and* shareholders can benefit from appropriate restrictions on the ability to divert or substitute assets, because such restrictions are likely to reduce a firm's cost of debt finance.[12] Consistently with this prediction, creditors and corporate borrowers frequently agree to a range of loan covenants in addition to their basic obligations to repay principal and interest. Often these include restrictions on the firm's ability to engage in activities that might conflict with creditors' interests—such as payments of dividends to shareholders, significant asset transactions, or increasing borrowing.[13] Creditors may also take security interests in corporate assets, which restrict the scope for asset substitution by requiring the firm to secure the consent of the creditor before the asset can be alienated free from the creditor's interest.[14] Both of these mechanisms give the creditors a certain amount of control over the debtor's activities.[15]

As creditors and firms frequently expend resources in writing covenants or agreeing upon security interests, one might ask whether corporate law could reduce these transaction costs. However, as we shall see, corporate law largely abjures from regulating transactions with creditors as such.

---

[10] Managers who hold significant blocks of shares in their companies will probably be poorly diversified, and so will be more averse to risk-taking than diversified shareholders. However, stock options can stimulate managers to behave in a less risk-averse fashion, by only paying out if the share price increases. See, e.g., Shivaram Rajgopal and Terry Shevlin, *Empirical Evidence on the Relation Between Stock Option Compensation and Risk Taking*, 33 JOURNAL OF ACCOUNTING AND ECONOMICS 145 (2002).

[11] See e.g. *supra* note 7.

[12] Clifford W. Smith, Jr. and Jerold B. Warner, *On Financial Contracting: An Analysis of Bond Covenants*, 7 JOURNAL OF FINANCIAL ECONOMICS 117 (1979); Michael H. Bradley and Michael R. Roberts, *The Structure and Pricing of Corporate Debt Covenants*, Working Paper (2004), at http://www.ssrn.com.

[13] See Smith and Warner, *supra* note 12; William W. Bratton, *Bond Covenants and Creditor Protection: Economics and Law, Theory and Practice, Substance and Process*, 7 EUROPEAN BUSINESS ORGANIZATION LAW REVIEW 39 (2006). In addition to these *non-financial* covenants, debtors and creditors commonly agree to a range of so called *financial* covenants—that is, promises by the debtor to maintain a certain level of financial health.

[14] Clifford W. Smith, Jr. and Jerold B. Warner, *Bankruptcy, Secured Debt, and Optimal Capital Structure: Comment*, 34 JOURNAL OF FINANCE 247 (1979). For overviews of the literature on secured credit, see Barry E. Adler, *Secured Credit Contracts*, in THE NEW PALGRAVE DICTIONARY OF ECONOMICS AND THE LAW, Vol. 3, 405 (Peter Newman (ed.), 1998); Jean Tirole, THE THEORY OF CORPORATE FINANCE 164–70, 251–4 (2006).

[15] See Ronald J. Daniels and George G. Triantis, *The Role of Debt in Interactive Corporate Governance*, 83 CALIFORNIA LAW REVIEW 1073 (1995); Douglas G. Baird and Robert K. Rasmussen, *Private Debt and the Missing Lever of Corporate Governance*, 154 UNIVERSITY OF PENNSYLVANIA LAW REVIEW 1209 (2006).

This general reliance on contract, rather than legal provisions, calls for explanation. We believe three factors are particularly salient. First, there is a risk of over-kill: having too many restrictions on the firm's behavior can be as harmful as too few. Just as shareholders have incentives to steer the firm to take too *much* risk, creditors have incentives to encourage it to take too *little*.[16] The appropriate balance is likely to vary depending on the firm's business model, and so leaving its determination to contract, rather than the general law, allows it to be set with greater sensitivity.

A second factor is that creditors' interests in the firm—their time and risk horizons—are likely to be much more heterogeneous than those of shareholders.[17] As a result, the provision of standard-form 'terms' to protect creditors may be at once over-protective of some creditors and under-protective of others. Third, the appropriate content of creditor-protective restrictions may change over time, making it necessary to renegotiate them. The ease of renegotiation (and hence the appropriate initial tightness of the restrictions) will depend on the number and identity of the creditors. It is harder for many bondholders, for example, to renegotiate, than for a few bank lenders.[18] Restrictions seeking to govern relations with *all* of a firm's creditors would create significant renegotiation problems unless they are set at a very lax level at the outset—so much so, that in most cases it would not be worth doing so at all.[19]

However, in two particular instances—which we now consider—it appears that these general conditions do not hold, and that the benefits of corporate law responding to shareholder-creditor agency problems relations plausibly outweigh their costs.

5.1.1.1 *The vicinity of insolvency*

All our jurisdictions specifically deal with shareholder-creditor agency problems in relation to corporations that are financially distressed—that is, 'in the vicinity of insolvency'. The incentives for shareholders or managers of such firms to engage in value-decreasing transactions, such as asset substitution, become particularly intense when the firm's future is in doubt. Correspondingly, legal restrictions targeting corporations in financial distress are likely to have benefits. Moreover,

---

[16] Viral V. Acharya, Yakov Amihud, and Lubimor P. Litov, *Creditor Rights and Corporate Risk Taking*, Working Paper (2008), at http://www.ssrn.com.

[17] Hideki Kanda, *Debtholders and Equityholders*, 21 JOURNAL OF LEGAL STUDIES 431, 440–1, 444–5 (1992); Marcel Kahan, *The Qualified Case Against Mandatory Terms in Bonds*, 89 NORTHWESTERN UNIVERSITY LAW REVIEW 565, 609–10 (1995).

[18] Thus bond agreements commonly have fewer (and weaker) covenants than bank lending agreements: compare Bradley and Roberts, *supra* note 12 (loan agreements) with Robert C. Nash, Jeffry M. Netter, and Annette B. Poulsen, *Determinants of Contractual Relations Between Shareholders and Bondholders: Investment Opportunities and Restrictive Covenants*, 9 JOURNAL OF CORPORATE FINANCE 201 (2003) (bonds).

[19] John Armour, *Legal Capital: An Outdated Concept?*, 7 EUROPEAN BUSINESS ORGANIZATION LAW REVIEW 5, 21–2 (2006).

lawmakers may view the costs as modest, because such provisions directly affect only a small subset of the firms in the economy.[20]

A common theme in these restrictions is for the law to seek to encourage managers of distressed corporations—who are, by and large, well-placed to assess the firm's financial situation—to act in the interests of creditors, rather than shareholders, and to initiate, if appropriate, a transition to formal bankruptcy proceedings. In many jurisdictions, this approach is also extended to controlling shareholders, through a variety of mechanisms—liability as de facto or shadow directors; equitable subordination of shareholder loans in bankruptcy, and 'piercing the corporate veil'. Moreover, third parties may be recruited as monitors through the operation of fraudulent conveyance laws and their equivalents. At the same time, the laws in all our jurisdictions give creditors the right to trigger bankruptcy proceedings against firms that are insolvent.

5.1.1.2 Non-adjusting creditors

So-called 'non-adjusting' creditors—those parties who for whatever reason are owed money by a corporate entity, but are unable to adjust the terms of their exposure to reflect the risk that they bear—pose a particular challenge.[21] Most obviously, this group includes victims of corporate torts and the state in right of regulatory claims.[22] Such creditors face particularly severe risks of opportunism, as shareholders know they can avoid personal liability. Shareholders may undercapitalize or shift assets out of risky operating companies precisely in order to minimize their potential tort liability.[23] Put differently, to the extent that the corporate form insulates shareholders from tortious damages or regulatory fines, shareholders are free to opt out of the laws that control the negative externalities of production, including product liability law, environmental law, and tort law generally.[24]

Non-adjusting creditors thus need special protections to a greater degree than creditors of distressed companies and many measures have been proposed to that end. For example, non-adjusting creditors might be given priority over other

---

[20] However this may be a little simplistic, as the *ex post* effects of such provisions will be taken into account in *ex ante* decision-making. Excessive sanctions in financial distress may therefore dull risk-taking in solvent firms: see Michelle J. White, *The Costs of Corporate Bankruptcy: A US-European Comparison*, in CORPORATE BANKRUPTCY: LEGAL AND ECONOMIC PERSPECTIVES, 467 (Jagdeep S. Bhandari and Lawrence A. Weiss (eds.), 1996).

[21] For a taxonomy of such claimants, see Lucian A. Bebchuk and Jesse M. Fried, *The Uneasy Case for the Priority of Secured Claims in Bankruptcy*, 105 YALE LAW JOURNAL 857 (1996).

[22] It is sometimes argued that it should also include contractual creditors with claims too small to merit the costs of adjusting. However, whilst trade creditors frequently do not adjust the *terms* on which they lend, they may nevertheless adjust the *amount* of credit extended according to the riskiness of the borrower: see Mitchell A. Petersen and Raghuram J. Rajan, *Trade Credit: Theories and Evidence*, 10 REVIEW OF FINANCIAL STUDIES 661, 678–9 (1997).

[23] Empirical studies of firms operating in hazardous industries suggest that this occurs: see Al H. Ringleb and Steven N. Wiggins, *Liability and Large-Scale, Long-Term Hazards*, 98 JOURNAL OF POLITICAL ECONOMY 574 (1990).

[24] See Steven Shavell, FOUNDATIONS OF THE ECONOMIC ANALYSIS OF LAW, 230–2 (2004).

creditors in insolvency proceedings.[25] Alternatively, shareholders might be held liable for excess tort liability, either on a *pro rata* basis in every case of tort liability, or to the full extent of damages in cases in which shareholders control risky activities directly.[26]

One regulatory strategy that is adopted in a number of jurisdictions is to require firms pursuing hazardous activities to carry a certain minimum level of insurance. For example, many European countries and Japan have such requirements in relation to automobile and workplace accidents or the processing of toxic waste. These requirements are often supplemented by legislation providing that, on the insolvency of the tortfeasor, entitlement to payment by the liability insurer is automatically transferred to the victim. However, while these requirements make it less attractive for entrepreneurs to opt for the corporate form for the purpose of opportunistically externalizing costs, they are typically not corporation-specific.

5.1.2 Creditor-creditor coordination and agency problems

Transactions with creditors also give rise to a version of the second basic agency problem, namely conflicts between one class of owners and another. As mentioned, creditors have a real option to become the owners of the firm's assets, insofar as is necessary to repay their claims, which becomes exercisable if the firm defaults on its obligations to them.[27] An unpaid creditor may seek a court order enforcing its claim against the debtor's assets, and ordinarily it is the threat of such enforcement that gives the debtor an incentive to repay. It follows that where the firm has defaulted *generally* on its credit obligations, then its creditors have the option, between them, to become owners of all its assets.[28]

However, the creditors will then face a coordination problem. If each acts individually to enforce, this will very quickly result in the break-up of the firm's business. When the firm's assets are worth more kept together than broken up, this is an inefficient outcome and creditors would collectively be better off by agreeing not to enforce, and instead to restructure the firm's debts. Each creditor

[25] David W. Leebron, *Limited Liability, Torts Victims, and Creditors*, 91 Columbia Law Review 1565 (1991).

[26] For a pro rata approach, see Henry Hansmann and Reinier Kraakman, *Toward Unlimited Shareholder Liability for Corporate Torts*, 100 Yale Law Journal 1879 (1991); for a control approach, see Nina A. Mendelson, *A Control-Based Approach to Shareholder Liability*, 102 Columbia Law Review 1203 (2002).

[27] See George G. Triantis, *The Interplay Between Liquidation and Reorganization in Bankruptcy: The Role of Screens, Gatekeepers, and Guillotines*, 16 International Review of Law and Economics 101 (1996); Douglas G. Baird and Robert K. Rasmussen, *Control Rights, Property Rights and the Conceptual Foundations of Corporate Reorganizations*, 87 Virginia Law Review 921 (2001); Robert K. Rasmussen, *Secured Debts, Control Rights and Options*, 25 Cardozo Law Review 1935 (2004).

[28] We assume, as can normally be observed in practice, that equity is wiped out in firms that have generally defaulted on their obligations.

nevertheless has an incentive to enforce individually: those who do so first will get paid in full, rather than a less-than-complete payout in a restructuring. Resolving these problems is bankruptcy law's core function.[29]

As indicated, all our jurisdictions give creditors the right to trigger bankruptcy proceedings against firms that are insolvent.[30] This transforms creditors' individual entitlements to seize or attach particular assets into entitlements to participate in a collective process. Bankruptcy law introduces a new structure for the firm that retains the five basic features of the corporate form described in Chapter 1, with the difference that the *creditors*, rather than the shareholders, are now the owners.[31] First, the assets are subject to strong-form entity shielding: personal creditors of the firm's creditors can no longer seize the corporate assets to which the creditors lay claim, so that the specific value of the assets may be retained.[32] Second, creditors have limited liability for the firm's post-bankruptcy debts, which facilitates continuation of the firm's business if appropriate. Third, creditors' claims are usually freely transferable in bankruptcy, as are those of shareholders in the solvent firm. Fourth, the bankruptcy procedure will typically specify a form of delegated management, distinct from individual creditors and with associated authority rules, usually taking the form of a 'crisis manager' of some description. Fifth, this 'crisis manager' is generally accountable to creditors.

Reflecting the importance of the decision to continue or close down the business, jurisdictions often provide a choice of more than one bankruptcy procedure, with different associated authority and control structures. *Liquidation* procedures are geared towards a sale of the firm's assets by auction, whereas *reorganization*, or 'rescue', procedures seek to facilitate a renegotiation of the firm's obligations to its creditors.[33] Of course, creditors often would rather not have a distressed firm actually go into 'formal' bankruptcy proceedings. This is because a firm's bankruptcy calls its future into question, with the consequence that its suppliers and customers downgrade their expectations about its commitment to performance—which, in turn reduces the value that can be obtained by selling the firm's assets. Hence it is common for firms to seek to effect a 'workout' with their creditors (a restructuring in the shadow of bankruptcy proceedings) rather than go into formal proceedings. Inter-creditor coordination and agency costs mean that the chances of achieving a workout reduce with the number, and

---

[29] Thomas H. Jackson, The Logic and Limits of Bankruptcy Law, 7–19 (1986).

[30] There is variety in the definition of insolvency, but two criteria predominate: a debtor is insolvent when its liabilities exceed its assets ('balance-sheet test', or 'overindebtedness') or when it is durably unable to pay its debts as they fall due ('cash-flow test' or 'commercial' insolvency).

[31] Here we use the term 'owners' not in the technical legal sense (for the corporation is in law the owner of its assets), but in the functional sense articulated in Chapter 1, namely the group entitled to control the firm's assets (see *supra* 1.2.5). The extent to which bankruptcy transfers such control from shareholders to creditors varies across jurisdictions (see *infra* 5.3.2).

[32] This is an important functional difference with bankruptcy laws applicable to individuals, which often do not provide for such effective entity shielding, at least against secured creditors.

[33] See, e.g., UNCITRAL, Legislative Guide on Insolvency Law 26–31 (2005).

heterogeneity, of creditors involved in renegotiation,[34] making bankruptcy law's role correspondingly more important.

Whilst creditors have significant influence over the selection between bankruptcy procedures (for example by agreeing to 'pre-packaged' restructuring plans), few, if any, jurisdictions permit firms to contract with their creditors to use a particular procedure,[35] and none permits firms to design their own.[36] This approach can be supported on the following grounds. *Ex post*, it defines the way in which the control of the firm is allocated if creditors exercise their real option, ideally in a manner that minimizes coordination and agency costs. *Ex ante*, it provides the backdrop to negotiations between creditors and the firm over lending agreements, covenants, and the like. It defines the consequences of the creditors becoming the owners of the firm. Consequently at a step before that, it influences how much creditors will be willing to lend in the first place.[37] In other words, standardization through bankruptcy law is likely to make it easier for parties to determine the background against which they are negotiating. Moreover, mandatory rules prevent parties from agreeing on bankruptcy procedures that benefit them at the expense of non-adjusting creditors.[38] However, this general reliance on mandatory rules has been questioned, on the ground that permitting firms to contract for a particular bankruptcy procedure might allow greater customization to the needs of particular firms.[39]

5.2 Solvent Firms

5.2.1 The affiliation strategy—mandatory disclosure

Creditors generally do not contract without obtaining information from the borrower about its financial performance, unless they can rely on reputation and

---

[34] See, e.g., Stuart C. Gilson, Kose John, and Larry L.P. Lang, *Troubled Debt Restructurings: An Empirical Study of Private Reorganization of Firms in Default*, 27 Journal of Financial Economics 315, 354 (1990); Paul Asquith, Robert Gertner, and David Scharfstein, *Anatomy of Financial Distress: An Examination of Junk-Bond Issuers*, 109 Quarterly Journal of Economics 625, 655 (1994); Antje Brunner and Jan Pieter Krahnan, *Multiple Lenders and Corporate Distress: Evidence on Debt Restructuring*, 75 Review of Economic Studies 415 (2008).

[35] The UK permitted firms to grant a secured creditor the right to enforce against the entirety of their assets, through a procedure known as 'receivership'. This was, however, abolished for most firms by the Enterprise Act 2002.

[36] For 'bankruptcy contracting' to work, a firm must be able to make a choice which binds *all* its creditors, otherwise the coordination problem is not solved: see Alan Schwartz, *A Contract Theory Approach to Bankruptcy*, 107 Yale Law Journal 1807 (1998); Stanley D. Longhofer and Stephen R. Peters, *Protection for Whom? Creditor Conflict and Bankruptcy*, 6 American Law and Economics Review 249 (2004).

[37] See Oliver Hart, Firms, Contracts, and Financial Structure (1995); Alan Schwartz, *A Normative Theory of Business Bankruptcy*, 91 Virginia Law Review 1199 (2005).

[38] See Bebcuk and Fried, *supra* note 21.

[39] Robert K. Rasmussen, *Debtor's Choice: A Menu Approach to Corporate Bankruptcy*, 71 Texas Law Review 51 (1992); Schwartz, *supra* note 36.

other publicly available information. In addition, larger creditors often create exit opportunities for themselves in the form of acceleration clauses (an early stage exit strategy, whereby the debt becomes due and payable upon violation of contractual covenants) and/or security interests (a more robust exit strategy, whereby payment is expedited through enforcement against particular assets).[40]

Corporate law facilitates these transactions by requiring companies to disclose certain basic information. Most obviously, all jurisdictions require that the names of corporate entities reflect their status through a suffix, such as 'Inc.', 'Ltd.', 'GmbH', 'SA', or the like.[41] Companies are also required to file their charters in public registers, which makes available information about company name, legal capital, restrictions on director liability, and the like.[42] Beyond this common core of obligations, there are differences regarding mandatory disclosure to creditors—which increasingly depend on the type of company, rather than the jurisdiction of incorporation.

5.2.1.1 Closely held corporations

Whilst U.S. closely held corporations are required to keep financial accounts, they are under no duty to disclose these to persons other than their shareholders.[43] By contrast, EC jurisdictions and Japan require all companies to prepare financial statements in accordance with the applicable accounting standards and make these available for public inspection.[44] Thus creditors of U.S. closely held companies seem to have less access to financial data than their counterparts in our other jurisdictions.

In practice, however, this difference is less significant than it appears. First, these requirements are often softened for smaller firms, on the basis that the fixed costs of compliance fall disproportionately upon them.[45] Second, several of our

---

[40] See Ronald J. Mann, *Explaining the Pattern of Secured Credit*, 110 HARVARD LAW REVIEW 625 (1997); Robert E. Scott, *The Truth about Secured Financing*, 82 CORNELL LAW REVIEW 1436 (1997); Eilís Ferran, PRINCIPLES OF CORPORATE FINANCE LAW 340–1 (2008).

[41] See Jonathan R. Macey, *The Limited Liability Company: Lessons for Corporate Law*, 73 WASHINGTON UNIVERSITY LAW QUARTERLY 433, 439–40 (1995).

[42] For the EC, see First Company Law Directive 68/151/EEC, 1968 O.J. (L 65/8), Arts. 2–3, as modified by 2003/58/EC2003/58/EC, 2003 O.J. (L 221/13); for the U.S., see, e.g., Revised Model Business Corporation Act § 2.02(a). In Japan, the major items of the charter (but not the charter itself) as well as additional items must be recorded in the commercial registry: Art. 911(3) Companies Act.

[43] See William J. Carney, *The Production of Corporate Law*, 71 SOUTHERN CALIFORNIA LAW REVIEW 715, 761 (1998).

[44] For the EC, see Art. 2(1)(f) First Company Law Directive (disclosure of annual accounts); Fourth Company Law Directive 78/660/EEC, 1978 O.J. (L 222) 11 (accounting standards); for Japan, see Art. 440 Companies Act (disclosure of annual balance sheet by all joint stock companies—kabushikigaisha; disclosure of balance sheet and profit and loss accounts by joint stock companies with legal capital of more than ¥500m or balance sheet debts of ¥20bn or more).

[45] For the EC, see Fourth Company Law Directive, Art. 11 (member states may allow disclosure of abrided accounts for companies satisfying at least two of the following: (1) book value less than €3,650m, (2) annual turnover less than €7.3m, or (3) 50 or fewer employees); European Commission,

major jurisdictions (still) do not enforce disclosure requirements with any rigor when it comes to smaller companies.[46] Third, there are at least partial market substitutes. Many U.S. closely held corporations voluntarily submit detailed financial information to private credit bureaus—who sell credit reports to potential lenders—in order to gain better access to financing in the ordinary course of business.[47] Similarly, whilst U.S. law does not compel 'large' privately-held companies to submit to standardized accounting principles ('GAAP'), providers of capital, such as banks or private equity firms, often do so.

Oddly enough, one area in which some EU member states may claim to provide especially pro-creditor financial disclosure lies in their rejection of EC accounting methodology in favor of an older approach. Germany's closely held companies, for example, are still allowed to disregard the 'true and fair view' approach that underlies the EC's Fourth Company Law Directive in favor of a more conservative approach ('*Vorsichtsprinzip*') that purports to be more protective of creditor interests.[48] How much such accounting differences matter to creditors in comparison to, for example, shareholder guarantees or information about past credit histories remains an open question. We suspect that, overall, the accounts of similarly-sized EU and U.S. closely held companies have more in common with each other than they do with the accounts of public companies, wherever situated.

5.2.1.2 *Publicly-held corporations*

In contrast to closely held companies, disclosure by publicly-held companies is extensively regulated in all our jurisdictions.[49] Under U.S. securities law, a company issuing publicly-traded securities—including bonds—must disclose all material information bearing on the value of the issue and the issuer's financial condition in a registration statement filed with the SEC.[50] In addition, publicly-traded companies must periodically file financial statements that are prepared in accordance with U.S. GAAP, and immediately report on new

---

Report on impacts of raised thresholds defining SMEs (2005, at http://ec.europa.eu). Exempted companies are nevertheless held to higher accounting standards than partnerships. See, e.g., Friedrich Kübler and Heinz-Dieter Assmann, GESELLSCHAFTSRECHT § 19 IV (6th ed., 2006).

[46] Studies estimate that 30% of French SARL and non-listed SA, and 80%–95% of Germany's GmbH, do not disclose their financial statements. See Maurice Cozian, Alain Viandier, and Florence Deboissy, DROIT DES SOCIÉTÉS No. 354 (21st ed., 2008); Mathias Habersack, EUROPÄISCHES GESELLSCHAFTSRECHT § 15 No. 15 (3rd ed., 2006).

[47] On the role of credit bureaus, see Marco Pagano and Tullio Japelli, *Information Sharing in Credit Markets*, 48 JOURNAL OF FINANCE 1693 (1993); CREDIT REPORTING SYSTEMS AND THE INTERNATIONAL ECONOMY (Margaret J. Miller (ed.), 2003). Note that the penalty for misdisclosing to credit bureaus is not the same as for misdisclosing under corporate law, which may affect data quality.

[48] On accounting methodologies, see *infra* 9.2.1.5. Creditor protection is reinforced by the link between the 'conservative' approach and capital maintenance requirements. See *infra* 5.2.2.2.

[49] See also *infra* 9.2.1.   [50] Securities Act 1933 §§ 5–7.

material developments.[51] EU disclosure requirements are increasingly similar to U.S. requirements.[52] To be sure, various member states—including France and Germany—require single firms to prepare their financial statements using accounting standards that differ from U.S. GAAP.[53] Nevertheless, many listed firms in these countries use IFRS—the European 'equivalent' of U.S. GAAP[54]—to prepare single firm financial statements because their *consolidated* financial statements are governed by IFRS.[55] Moreover, single firm accounting standards are converging towards IFRS in many member states.[56] Japan too has undertaken disclosure and accounting reforms that ultimately should result in 'equivalence' to EU and U.S. requirements.[57] When and the extent to which equivalence will be achieved remains open to debate, but there is no doubt that standard-setting authorities in all of our core jurisdictions favor further coordination.[58] On the other hand, as we shall see in Chapter 9, there are still considerable differences in the intensity of enforcement of these disclosure obligations.[59]

Conventional wisdom has it that creditor-oriented accounting disclosure is a phenomenon of jurisdictions with a bank-oriented financial system—

[51] See, e.g., Securities Exchange Act 1934, § 13; Sarbanes-Oxley Act, §§ 401, 409; Regulation S-X; for the SEC's accounting role, see Louis Loss and Joel Seligman, FUNDAMENTALS OF SECURITIES REGULATION 175 (5th ed., 2004).

[52] See, for EU companies traded on regulated markets, Prospectus Directive 2003/71/EC, 2003 O.J. (L 345) 64; Transparency Directive 2004/109/EC, 2004 O.J. (L 390) 38.

[53] See Yuan Ding, Ole-Kristian Hope, Thomas Jeanjean, and Hervé Stolowy, *Differences between Domestic Accounting and IAS: Measurement, Determinants and Implications*, 26 JOURNAL OF ACCOUNTING AND PUBLIC POLICY 1 (2007). Continuing French and German divergence is said to be due to financial statements being used to determine taxable income, albeit German accounting is also biased towards conservatism. See Judy Beckman, Christina Brandes, and Brigitte Eierle, *German Reporting Practices: An Analysis of Reconciliations from German Commercial Code to IFRS or U.S. GAAP*, 20 ADVANCES IN INTERNATIONAL ACCOUNTING 253 (2007).

[54] See European Commission, *Report on Convergence between International Financial Reporting Standards (IFRS) and Third Country Generally Accepted Accounting Principles* (GAAPs) (2008).

[55] See Eva K. Jermakowicz and Sylwia Gornik-Tomaszewski, *Implementing IFRS from the Perspective of EU Publicly Traded Companies*, 15 JOURNAL OF INTERNATIONAL ACCOUNTING, AUDITING AND TAXATION 170 (2006); see also infra 5.2.1.3.

[56] See European Commission, *Planned Implementation of the IAS Regulation (1606/2002) in the EU and EEA* (2005, at http://www.ec.europa.eu).

[57] See Accounting Standards Board of Japan and International Accounting Standards Board, *Tokyo Agreement on achieving convergence of accounting standards by 2011* (8 August 2007, at http://www.asb.or.jp); *New Law Requires Listed Firms to Issue More Transparent Reports*, THE NIKKEI WEEKLY, 14 April 2008 at 29.

[58] Compare *Roadmap for the Potential Use of Financial Statements Prepared in Accordance with International Financial Reporting Standards for U.S. Issuers*, EXCHANGE ACT RELEASE NOS. 33–8982, 34–58960 (2008); European Commission, Decision on the use by third countries' issuers of securities of certain third country's national accounting standards and International Financial Reporting Standards to prepare their consolidated financial statements 2008/961/EC, 2008 O.J. (L 340) 112 and Commission Regulation (EC) No 1289/2008, 2008 O.J. (L 340) 17; *Tokyo Agreement, supra* note 57.

[59] See *infra* 9.3.

Germany, for example—where 'conservative' accounting standards favor the understatement of assets, thus reducing lenders' screening costs. Yet, the capital markets driven convergence in accounting has led to more use of investor-oriented 'true and fair view' standards, under which market prices play a more important role in the evaluation of assets and liabilities and financial statements are more cash-flow oriented.[60] This evolution, however, has been accompanied by an increasing focus on debtors' cash flows by lenders, for screening purposes. It follows that the information provided by modern 'true and fair view' accounting could prove more useful, from creditors' point of view, than information produced under traditional 'conservative' accounting.[61]

5.2.1.3 Groups of companies

Disclosure has particular significance in the context of corporate groups. Arguably, creditors of group companies are more vulnerable to shareholder opportunism than are creditors of independent companies.[62] Shareholders can reduce transparency by blurring divisions between the assets of group members, and lead creditors to infer—wrongly—that the entire group stands behind each member's debts. A group structure also allows controllers to set the terms of intra-group transactions, and thus to assign (and reassign) value within the group. Sometimes an intra-group transaction is designed solely in order to extract value from the creditors of a financially distressed group member or to favor the creditors of one subsidiary to the detriment of the creditors of other group members. Yet creditors may also suffer harm as a by-product of intra-group asset transfers undertaken for other reasons—for example, to secure a tax advantage.

Probably due to its significance, group accounting is the area in which the convergence trend is most visible. Hence, U.S., EU, and Japanese listed groups are required to prepare consolidated accounts in conformity with 'equivalent' GAAP and IFRS standards.[63] However, regulatory efforts to get all listed groups to use IFRS standards still face significant hurdles.[64] In addition, real differences

---

[60] See, e.g., Reinhard H. Schmidt and Marcel Tyrell, *What Constitutes a Financial System in General and the German Financial System in Particular*, THE GERMAN FINANCIAL SYSTEM 19 (Jan P. Krahnen and Reinhard H. Schmidt (eds.), 2004). See also *infra* 9.2.1.5.

[61] See Edgar Löw, *Deutsches Rechnungslegungs Standards Committee*, 13 ZEITSCHRIFT FÜR BANKRECHT UND BANKWIRTSCHAFT 19 (2001). Note that 'true and fair view' accounting may have pro-cyclical effects in a financial crisis situation. See *infra* 9.2.1.5.

[62] See Marianne Bertrand, Paras Mehta, and Sendhil Mullainathan, *Ferreting Out Tunneling: An Application to Indian Business Groups*, 117 QUARTERLY JOURNAL OF ECONOMICS 121 (2002); Simon Johnson, Rafael La Porta, Florencio Lopez-De-Silanes, and Andrei Shleifer, *Tunneling*, 90 AMERICAN ECONOMIC REVIEW, PAPERS AND PROCEEDINGS 22 (2000). The essential aspect of minority shareholder protection is addressed *infra* in Chapters 6 and 7.

[63] See, for the EU, Regulation (EC) 1606/2002 on the Application of International Accounting Standards, 2002 O.J. (L 243) 1.

[64] See Securities and Exchange Commission, *Concept release on allowing U.S. issuers to prepare financial statements using IFRS* (2007, at http://www.sec.org); Report on Convergence, *supra* note 54; Tokyo Agreement, *supra* note 57.

remain when it comes to non-listed groups. In particular, EC law stands alone in extending the consolidation requirement to closely held groups.[65] Moreover, while most jurisdictions require public companies to disclose intra-group transactions, German law curiously provides creditors with less protection than one might expect given the 'conservativeness' of its accounting. In particular, apart from the limited number of companies belonging to so-called 'formal' contractual groups,[66] the German *Konzernrecht* merely obligates controlled firms to provide creditors with an audited *summary* of the extensive report—termed the *Abhängigkeitsbericht* or 'dependence' report—that these companies must deliver to their supervisory board.[67]

5.2.1.4 The role of gatekeepers

The quality of mandated disclosures can be enhanced through verification by trusted third parties, or 'gatekeepers'.[68] Indeed, auditors are universally employed to verify accounting disclosures and credit bureaus have become increasingly important in aggregating and disseminating information salient to borrowers' credit histories. As regards larger borrowers, credit rating agencies have also emerged as a key gatekeeper to whom many of the traditional compliance functions performed by creditors have been delegated, especially when debt is widely dispersed through the use of bonds or securitization of bank loans.[69]

All major jurisdictions require publicly-held companies to use outside auditors to verify their financial statements. Moreover, EC and Japanese law require professional audits for closely held companies, where they are 'larger' in an economic sense.[70] Although there is no similar requirement for closely held U.S. corporations, it is hard to imagine that the detailed financial data demanded by creditors will be considered reliable unless they are subjected to scrutiny by a credible auditor.

In screening debtor financial statements, auditors and credit rating agencies can reduce the cost of capital for borrowers by implicitly pledging their reputational capital. This aspect of gatekeeping is reinforced in all our jurisdictions

---

[65] Seventh Company Law Directive 83/349/EEC, 1983 O.J. (L 193/1).

[66] So-called contractual groups are those listed as such in the trade register: see Uwe Hüffer, AKTIENGESETZ No. 17 § 294 (8th ed. 2008). There is uncertainty about how many groups have opted for the contractual form, but they are deemed to be a minority: see Volker Emmerich and Mathias Habersack, KONZERNRECHT 166 (8th ed., 2005). On *Konzernrecht* distinguishing between contractual and *de facto* groups, see also *infra* 5.3.1.2. Compare Art. 2497–2 Civil Code (Italy), under which controlled firms must disclose the effect of dominance on company management and results.

[67] See § 312 Aktiengesetz; Uwe Hüffer, *supra* note 66, No. 38 § 312. See also *infra* 6.2.1.1 (discussing disclosure requirements for related-party transactions).

[68] See *supra* 2.3.2.3.

[69] See Arnoud W.A. Boot, Todd T. Milbourn, and Anjolein Schmeits, *Credit Ratings as Coordination Mechanisms*, 19 REVIEW OF FINANCIAL STUDIES 80 (2006).

[70] See Art. 51 (EC) Fourth Company Law Directive; Art. 328 Companies Act (Japan).

by auditor licensing requirements, the setting of auditing standards and *ex post* auditor liability which together provide a framework for dealing with gatekeeper 'failure'.[71] Auditors must ensure that a company's financial statements reflect the laws and accounting standards of the jurisdictions in which it is domiciled or its securities trade. Shareholders and creditors also increasingly rely on auditors to play a broader role in monitoring for breaches of fiduciary duties by managers.[72] Auditors, of course, disclaim any duties beyond verifying financial statements, but they are increasingly asked to accept a broader scope of responsibility to the investing public.[73]

Courts have been the principal architects of auditor liability, in particular by finding that creditors were foreseeable users of financial statements, or that they had a special relationship with the auditors, for example because the latter have specifically confirmed their support for the company's accounts.[74] Yet it is difficult to calibrate how much auditor effort is 'optimal'. Partly as a result of such concerns, a number of legislative moves in the 1990s sought to rein in auditor liability.[75] The outcry following Enron, Parmalat and other accounting scandals again led to increases in the scope of the auditor's duties,[76] but the implosion of Arthur Andersen after an Enron-related criminal investigation highlighted the dangers of tampering with auditor reputation and provided new impetus for limiting auditor liability.[77]

Similarly, recent financial scandals—and especially the failure of rating agencies to rate mortgage-based financial products or credit derivatives effectively—should lead to an increase in regulatory scrutiny of credit rating agencies. Whilst they make positive contributions to the mitigation of information asymmetry,[78]

---

[71] See Reinier Kraakman, *Gatekeepers: The Anatomy of a Third-Party Enforcement Strategy*, 2 JOURNAL OF LAW, ECONOMICS, AND ORGANIZATION 53, 70 (1986).

[72] See *infra* 6.2.1.1.

[73] See John C. Coffee, Jr., GATEKEEPERS: THE PROFESSIONS AND CORPORATE GOVERNANCE, at 168 (2006).

[74] See Werner B. Ebke, *Accounting, Auditing and Global Capital Markets*, in CORPORATIONS, CAPITAL MARKETS AND BUSINESS IN THE LAW 113, 126–33 (Theodor Baums, Klaus J. Hopt, and Norbert Horn (eds.), 2000); Paul L. Davies, GOWER AND DAVIES' PRINCIPLES OF MODERN COMPANY LAW 803–9 (8th ed., 2008). See also, for the UK: *Hedley Byrne & Co. v. Heller & Partners* [1964] Appeal Cases 465 (House of Lords 1963); for the U.S: *Rosenblum, Incorporated v. Adler*, 93 New Jersey Supreme Court Reports 324 (1983); for Switzerland: X. *Corporation v. Q*, AMTLICHE SAMMLUNG (AS) 122 III 176 (Federal Tribunal 1996).

[75] See, for the U.S., John C. Coffee, *What Caused Enron?: A Capsule Social and Economic History of the 1990s*, 89 CORNELL LAW REVIEW 269 (2004); for Japan Art. 34–2–2 et seq. Certified Public Accountant Act (revised, 2007); for France, Art. L. 822–18 Code de commerce (three-year limitation period); for Italy, Art. 164 Testo Unico della Finanza; for the UK, Limited Liability Partnership Act 2000.

[76] See §§ 101–109 Sarbanes-Oxley Act 2001 (US); Commission Communication COM(2003) 286, *Reinforcing the Statutory Audit in the EU*, 2003, O.J. (C 236) 2; Directive 2006/43/EC on statutory audits of annual accounts and consolidated accounts, 2006 O.J. (L 157) 87.

[77] See e.g. Commission Recommendation concerning the limitation of the civil liability of statutory auditors and audit firms, 2008 O.J. (L 162) 39 (EC).

[78] See Amir Sufi, *The Real Effect of Debt Certification: Evidence from the Introduction of Bank Loan Ratings*, 22 REVIEW OF FINANCIAL STUDIES 1659 (2009).

credit rating agencies are also subject to conflicts of interest. Hence, regulation intended to introduce licensing requirements and increase transparency in rating methodology and to foster competition in the sector is on the legislative agenda in Europe and the U.S.[79]

5.2.2 The rules strategy: legal capital

If mandatory disclosure helps creditors to protect themselves, then the rules strategy seeks to provide protection for them in a standardized form. The most important rules relate to 'legal capital'.[80] These can apply to at least three separate aspects of corporate finance, which we consider in turn: (1) prescribing a minimum initial investment of equity capital; (2) restrictions on payments out to shareholders; and (3) triggering actions that must be taken following serious depletion of capital.

5.2.2.1 Minimum capital

The rules governing the minimum investment levels for incorporation are termed 'minimum capital' requirements. Amongst our jurisdictions, only those in Europe impose minimum investment thresholds for access to the corporate form. EC law requires *public* corporations to have initial legal capital of no less than €25,000, whereas member states may set higher thresholds if they wish.[81] Although this number is large by Japanese or U.S. standards (which generally require nothing at all),[82] it is actually quite small when compared to the actual capital needs of businesses organized as public firms. As a consequence, minimum capital requirements do not appear to create significant barriers to entry to public corporation status.[83] As regards *non-public* companies, most of our jurisdictions nowadays permit incorporation of a non-public company without any

---

[79] See Proposal for a Regulation on credit rating agencies, COM(2008) 704 final; Amendment to Rules for Nationally Recognized Statistical Rating Organizations, 74 Federal Register 6456 (2009).

[80] In most jurisdictions, legal capital is the aggregate nominal (or par) value of issued shares, which is typically much lower than the actual issue price of these shares. In U.S. jurisdictions that permit 'no par' shares, legal capital is initially set by a company's organizers, and may be any amount less than (or equal to) the issue price of a company's shares. In the UK, the full issue price of shares, including the 'share premium' above the par value, is treated as capital.

[81] See Art. 6 Second Company Law Directive 77/91/EEC, 1977 O.J. (L 26) 1, as amended by 2006/68/EC, 2006 O.J. (L 264) 32, applicable to AG, SA, SpA, plc, etc.

[82] On the U.S., sees Bayless Manning and James J. Hanks, Legal Capital (3rd ed., 1990). Japan abolished initial minimum capital requirement entirely in its Companies Act of 2005. But it maintains distribution regulations based on legal capital and other balance sheet numbers.

[83] KPMG, *Feasibility Study on an Alternative to the Capital Maintenance Regime Established by the Second Company Law Directive 77/91/EEC of 13 December 1976 and an Examination of the Impact on Profit Distribution of the New EU-Accounting Regime: Main Report (2008)*. In theory, capital regulation could go further and require companies to maintain a specific debt-equity ratio. Yet given that different businesses carry different risks, it is hard to see how any such general ratio could be efficient.

minimum capital requirement.[84] Only Italy (still) requires a minimum initial capital investment of €10,000.[85]

It seems unlikely that minimum capital requirements provide any real protection to creditors, as a firm's initial capital is likely to be long gone if it files for bankruptcy. Moreover, the reduction or abolition of minimum capital rules throughout Europe appears to be associated with an increase in entrepreneurship.[86] However, most entrepreneurs appear to invest *some* capital in newly-formed firms, even in the absence of minimum capital rules.[87] This may indicate that the presence of capital is a rough-and-ready proxy for the 'seriousness' of entrepreneurs, by showing that they commit a non-trivial amount of money to their project.[88]

5.2.2.2 Distribution restrictions

Company laws generally restrict distributions to shareholders—including dividends and share repurchases—in order to prevent asset dilution.[89] Although these distribution restrictions vary across jurisdictions, the most common is on the payment of dividends which impair the company's legal capital—that is, distributions that exceed the difference between the book value of the company's assets and the amount of its legal capital, as shown in the balance sheet.[90]

Rules restricting distributions can be viewed as an 'opt-in' set of standard terms. On this view, any firm that has legal capital in excess of minimum requirements does so by choice, not because of a mandatory requirement.[91] In such a

---

[84] Since late 2008, this is true even for Germany, a traditional proponent of minimum capital requirements. See e.g. Alexander Schall, GLÄUBIGERSCHUTZ IM UMBRUCH (forthcoming 2009); Ulrich Noack and Michael Beurskens, *Modernising the German GmbH—Mere Window Dressing or Fundamental Redesign?*, 9 EUROPEAN BUSINESS ORGANIZATION LAW REVIEW 97 (2008). See also, for France, Alain Pietrancosta, *Capital Zéro ou Zéro Capital*, in QUEL AVENIR POUR LE CAPITAL SOCIAL 127 (2004).

[85] Art. 2463 Civil Code (Italy).

[86] See John Armour and Douglas J. Cumming, *Bankruptcy Law and Entrepreneurship*, 10 AMERICAN LAW AND ECONOMICS REVIEW 303 (2008).

[87] See Marco Becht, Colin Mayer, and Hannes F. Wagner, *Where Do Firms Incorporate? Deregulation and the Cost of Entry*, 14 JOURNAL OF CORPORATE FINANCE 241 (2008) (after France removed minimum capital requirements for SaRL form in 2003, 86.8% of new firms set their initial capital below the previous minimum of €7,500, but only 4.9% had a minimum capital as low as €1).

[88] See John Hudson, *The Limited Liability Company: Success, Failure and Future*, 161 ROYAL BANK OF SCOTLAND REVIEW 26 (1989); Horst Eidenmüller, Barbara Grunewald, and Ulrich Noack, *Minimum Capital and the System of Legal Capital*, in Marcus Lutter (ed.), LEGAL CAPITAL IN EUROPE, 1, 25–7 (2006).

[89] See *supra*, text to note 3.

[90] For an overview of a variety of dividend restriction rules, see Brian R. Cheffins, COMPANY LAW: THEORY, STRUCTURE AND OPERATION 534–5 (1997); Holger Fleischer, *Disguised Distributions and Capital Maintenance in European Company Law*, in Lutter, *supra* note 88, 94.

[91] Wolfgang Schön, *The Future of Legal Capital*, 5 EUROPEAN BUSINESS ORGANIZATION LAW REVIEW 429, 438–9 (2004). However, firms have no real choice in jurisdictions where the entire share issue price is treated as capital, as in the UK, and so equity finance cannot be raised without application of distribution restrictions: see Eilís Ferran, *The Place for Creditor Protection on the*

situation, distribution constraints simply reinforce the credibility of the shareholders' promise to retain their capital investment in the firm. From a debtor perspective, such an 'opt-in' has the advantage that when there are multiple creditors, transaction costs are low compared to the repeated negotiation of a (possibly diverse) set of contractual covenants. From a creditor perspective, however, legal capital may not offer sufficient protection. Heterogeneity among creditors will result in some of them demanding covenant protection in addition to 'one size fits all' legal capital, thus reducing transaction cost savings.[92]

The extent to which distribution restrictions restrict payments to shareholders is affected by the scope of the transactions they cover. In Germany and the UK, the restriction on distributions is applied not only to transactions formally structured as dividends or share repurchases, but also to any undervalue transaction between a company and its shareholders, which the courts may recharacterize as having been a 'disguised distribution'.[93] In the U.S., the efficacy of even the basic distribution restriction is undermined by giving the shareholders, or in some cases the board of directors, power to reduce a company's legal capital—and hence the level at which the distribution restriction is set—without creditor consent.[94] By contrast, Japan and many EU jurisdictions require any reduction in legal capital to be preceded by adequate protection—for example, a third party guarantee—for existing creditors.[95]

The efficacy of distribution restrictions depends upon accounting methodology. Whilst conservative accounting provides less information about the ongoing value of the firms, it is more protective of creditors' interests than 'true and fair view' accounting when it comes to reducing the discretion to pay dividends or otherwise transfer assets to shareholders from the pool that bonds the company's debts.[96] Hence, the increasing reliance on 'marking-to-market' in U.S. GAAP may be one of the reasons for the increasing use of profit distribution covenants by U.S. publicly-traded corporations.[97] This, in turn, calls into

---

Agenda for Modernisation of Company Law in the European Union, 3 European Company and Financial Law Review 178, 196 (2006).

[92] See Kanda, *supra* note 17, 440; Kahan, *supra* note 17, at 609–10.

[93] On the UK, see *Re Halt Garage (1964) Ltd* [1982] 3 All England Reports 1016, 1039–44; *Aveling Barford Ltd v. Perion Ltd* (1989) 5 British Company Law Cases 677, 682–3; on Germany, see Fleischer, *supra* note 90. There is no such extension in France and Italy: see Pierre-Henri Conac, Luca Enriques, and Martin Gelter, *Constraining Dominant Shareholders' Self-Dealing: The Legal Framework in France, Germany, and Italy*, 4 European Company and Financial Law Review 491 (2007).

[94] However fraudulent conveyance law will still restrict the payment of dividends when the company is insolvent. See *infra* 5.3.1.3.

[95] See Art. 32 Second Company Law Directive; Art. 447, 449 Japanese Companies Act. These rules are sometimes referred to as 'capital maintenance' in the EU and 'capital unchangeability' in Japan.

[96] See Bernhard Pellens and Thorsten Sellhorn, *Creditor Protection through IFRS Reporting and Solvency Tests*, in Lutter, *supra* note 88, 365; see also Schön, *supra* note 91.

[97] See Joy Begley and R. Freedman, *The Changing Role of Accounting Numbers in Public Lending Agreements*, 18 Accounting Horizons 81 (2004); Christoph Kuhner, *The Future of Creditor*

question the continued utility of legal capital restrictions following the use of IFRS accounting methodology by many listed European firms.[98]

A frequent critique of distribution restrictions is that they constrain changes in capital structure by increasing the costs of corporate restructurings such as leveraged buy-outs and the paying off of dissenting shareholders.[99] To the extent that corporate finance is bank centered and accounting is conservative, such constraints probably pose little burden on financial transactions. On the other hand, they may be more of a handicap when restructuring firms must switch from bank financing and conservative accounting to capital market financing and 'true and fair view' accounting.

5.2.2.3 Loss of capital

In some jurisdictions—particularly in Europe, but not in the U.S.—there are rules governing actions that must be taken following a serious loss of capital. EC law requires public companies to call a shareholders' meeting to consider dissolution after a serious loss of capital, defined as net assets falling below half the company's legal capital.[100] Several European jurisdictions have adopted yet stronger rules, mandating those running the firm either to obtain fresh equity finance or stop trading when a certain proportion of legal capital is exhausted.[101] In some jurisdictions, such as France and Italy, the company must be put into liquidation should the company's net assets fall below the statutory minimum capital,[102] whereas in others, such as Germany and Switzerland, the company must file for insolvency when value of its net assets has fallen to zero.[103]

In theory, such rules could reinforce the credibility of legal capital as a financial cushion for creditors by acting as capital adequacy provisions similar to those governing financial institutions. Yet given low minimum capital thresholds, even

---

Protection through Capital Maintenance Rules in European Company Law-An Economic Perspective, in Lutter, *supra* note 88, 341.

[98] Ferran, *supra* note 91, 200–15. See also *supra* 5.2.1.2.

[99] John Armour, *Share Capital and Creditor Protection: Efficient Rules for a Modern Company Law?*, 63 MODERN LAW REVIEW 355, at 373–5 (2000); Luca Enriques and Jonathan R. Macey, *Creditors Versus Capital Formation: The Case Against the European Legal Capital Rules,* 86 CORNELL LAW REVIEW 1165, 1195–8 (2001).

[100] See Art. 17 Second Company Law Directive. EC law also protects creditors against capital reduction through charter amendments or share repurchases, but not against capital reduction to restore financial soundness—the reasoning being that shareholder opportunism is then less of an issue: Heinz-Dieter Assmann, Barbara Lange, and Rolf Sethe, *The Law of Business Associations,* in INTRODUCTION TO GERMAN LAW 137, 159 (Werner F. Ebke and Matthew W. Finkin (eds.), 1996).

[101] This is a balance-sheet, not a cash-flow test. See *supra* note 30.

[102] See Art. L. 223–42 (for SARL) and 225–248 (for SA) Code de commerce (France); Arts. 2447 and 2482–3 Civil Code (Italy).

[103] §§ 15 and 19 Insolvenzordnung (Germany); Art. 725 Obligationenrecht (public corporations) and Art. 817 Obligationenrecht (closely held corporations) (Switzerland). However, in Germany, a temporary exclusion was introduced (effective from October 2008 until December 2010) for companies which are overindebted but for which the probability of continued operation is otherwise 'highly likely' (§ 19 Insolvenzordnung).

the most stringent loss of capital requirements are concerned more with promoting early filing for bankruptcy than with capital adequacy.[104] To be sure, encouraging earlier liquidation or insolvency proceedings will serve to shorten the 'twilight period' during which shareholder opportunism can harm creditors. Yet the costs of initiating bankruptcy proceedings may be even higher. Whilst such costs can be avoided by a renegotiation, the more heterogeneous the firm's creditors, the less likely this will be to succeed.[105]

5.3 Distressed Firms

5.3.1 The standards strategy

Standards are used widely to protect corporate creditors. While the implementing provisions are variously labeled (examples include *faute de gestion*, wrongful trading, and fraudulent conveyances), each imposes a species of *ex post* liability according to an open-textured standard on persons associated with a distressed company. The *ex post* nature of the standards strategy means that it tends only to be employed if something has gone wrong in a lending relationship—that is, where the debtor company is in financial distress. More particularly, these duties divide into three categories according to whom they target: (1) directors; (2) controlling shareholders; and (3) 'favored' creditors.

5.3.1.1 Directors

In each of our jurisdictions, directors, including *de facto* or shadow directors, may be held personally liable for net increases in losses to creditors resulting from the board's negligence or fraud to creditors when the company is, or is nearly, insolvent.[106] Such duties can be framed and enforced with differing levels of intensity, affecting the extent to which they affect directors' incentives. First, as regards the substantive content of the duty, a less onerous standard is triggered by fraud or knowledge of likely harm to creditors, imposing liability only for actions so harmful to creditors as to call into question directors' subjective good faith. A more intensive standard imposes liability for negligently worsening the financial position of the insolvent company. Second, the intensity can be varied through

---

[104] See Lorenzo Stanghellini, Directors' *Duties and the Optimal Timing of Insolvency: In Defence of the Recapitalize or Liquidate Rule*, Working Paper (2007).

[105] Moreover, a 'guillotine' rule may simply result in creditors, or at least some of them, being forced to accept less of the restructuring surplus in any renegotiation. In the out-of-court restructuring of Ferruzzi in 1993, those in control of the firm (who happened to be the largest creditors) were able, by virtue of the imminent need to file for bankruptcy, to make a 'take it or leave it' restructuring offer that appropriated most of the restructuring surplus at the expense of other creditors: see Alessandro Penati and Luigi Zingales, *Efficiency and Distribution in Financial Restructuring: The Case of the Ferruzzi Group*, Working Paper (1997), at http://faculty.chicagobooth.edu.

[106] See also *supra* 3.6.1.

the trigger for the duty's imposition: the greater the degree of financial distress in which the company must be before the duty kicks in, the more remote will be its effect on incentives. A third dimension over which intensity varies is enforcement. Enforcement is likely to be facilitated if the duties are owed directly to individual creditors, and reduced for duties owed only to the company, which will be unlikely to be enforced unless the company enters bankruptcy proceedings.

The appropriate intensity of such director liability depends on the nature of the debtor firm.[107] Shareholder-creditor agency problems are likely to be most pronounced in firms where managers' and shareholders' interests are closely aligned. For larger firms with dispersed shareholders, managers have fewer incentives to pursue measures that benefit shareholders at creditors' expense; under such circumstances directorial liability based on creditors' interests may over-deter directors, resulting in less risk-taking than is optimal.[108] Directorial liability may therefore be expected to be most useful where shareholders' and managers' interests are aligned. To this there is one important exception. In smaller firms that face financial distress, the owner-managers often have few personal assets beyond their stake in the firm; consequently the threat of liability may not act as a meaningful deterrent. Thus the key factor determining the use of the standards strategy against directors may be expected to be the ownership structure of large firms.

Consistently with these observations, the standard employed for directorial liability to creditors in the U.S. has the lowest intensity amongst our jurisdictions. Most U.S. states employ the technique of a shift in the content of directors' duty of loyalty in relation to insolvent firms and the duty is owed to the corporation, rather than individual creditors.[109] There has been flirtation in some states with a direct tortious claim against directors for 'deepening insolvency',[110] but this has been explicitly ruled out in Delaware.[111]

In the UK, like in the U.S., there is a shift in the content of the duty of loyalty for directors of insolvent firms, this duty being owed only to the company.[112] In addition, however, the UK also imposes negligence-based liability on directors

---

[107] See *supra*, text to note 9.

[108] See also Cheffins, *supra* note 90, 537–48; Henry T.C. Hu and Jay Lawrence Westbrook, *Abolition of the Corporate Duty to Creditors*, 107 Columbia Law Review 1321 (2007).

[109] *Credit Lyonnais Bank Nederland v. Pathe Communications Corporation*, Delaware Chancery Court (1991, reprinted in 17 Delaware Journal of Corporate Law 1099–992); *North American Catholic Education Programming Foundation v. Gheewalla*, 930 Atlantic Reporter 2d 92, 98–102 (Delaware Supreme Court, 2007). *Compare Trustee of Peoples Department Stores Inc. v. Wise* [2004] Supreme Court Reporter 68 (Canada) rejecting such a duty). Note that in the landmark *Credit Lyonnais* case, the 'fiduciary duties towards creditors' issue only arose because directors used the argument as a defense against shareholder damage claims.

[110] See e.g., *Official Committee of Unsecured Creditors v. R.F. Laffertey & Co*, 267 Federal Reporter 3d 340 (3d. Circuit, 2001) (Pennsylvania).

[111] *Trenwick America Litigation Trust v. Ernst & Young LLP*, 906 Atlantic Reporter 2d 168, 204–7 (Delaware Chancery, 2006).

[112] *West Mercia Safetywear Ltd v. Dodd* [1989] 4 Butterowrths Company Law Cases 30, 33; § 172(3) Companies Act 2006 (UK); *Kuwait Asia Bank EC v. National Mutual Life Nominees Ltd* [1991] 1 Appeal Cases 187, 217–19.

for 'wrongful trading' if they fail to take reasonable care in protecting creditors' interests once insolvency proceedings have become inevitable.[113] This duty is, however, only enforceable by a liquidator, and the point at which it is triggered is typically very late—insolvency is usually not 'inevitable' unless the firm is cash-flow, as opposed to balance-sheet, insolvent.[114]

Continental European jurisdictions deploy more intensive standards against directors, consistent with the generally more concentrated ownership structure of their large firms. In these countries, directors of financially distressed firms face negligence-based liability, generally based on duties mediated through the company.[115] Moreover, we noted above that French, German, and Italian directors can be held liable simply for failing to take action following serious loss of capital.[116] The draconian nature of this provision is diluted to some degree by the fact that directors often have substantial discretion over whether a going-concern or liquidation valuation is used in compiling the firm's balance sheet, which can enable them to delay the triggering of the obligation.[117] However, we should not make too much of this, for a court is likely to take a dim view *ex post* of any hint of abuse of this discretion.

In Japan, duties to creditors are triggered even earlier, as creditors have standing to sue directors even if the company is solvent.[118] Although directors of a large Japanese company have rarely been held liable under this provision, it is frequently litigated in the case of closely held companies.[119] In addition, the Supreme Court has developed a 'director's duty to monitor' doctrine, under which non-executive directors are held liable to creditors when they grossly fail to monitor misbehaving managers. Finally, while increased shareholder litigation during the 1990s prompted statutory change to limit director liability, creditor rights have been left unaffected.[120]

Another important difference between our jurisdictions lies in the risk of public enforcement. This is a further way to increase the intensity of deterrence,

---

[113] Insolvency Act 1986 § 214(2) (UK); see also *Rubin v. Gunner* [2004] 2 BUTTERWORTHS COMPANY LAW CASES 110.

[114] See Paul Davies, *Directors' Creditor-Regarding Duties in Respect of Trading Decisions Taken in the Vicinity of Insolvency*, 7 EUROPEAN BUSINESS ORGANIZATION LAW REVIEW 301, 318–20 (2006).

[115] See for France, Art. L. 223–22 (SARL), L. 225–251 (SA) Code de commerce, as well as the feared Art. L. 651–2 (*insuffisance d'actifs*) and L. 652–1 (*obligation aux dettes sociales*) Code de commerce—see *infra* text to note 130; for Germany, § 43 GmbH-Gesetz, §§ 93 and 116 Aktiengesetz; for Italy, Art. 2394 and 2394–2 Civil Code.

[116] See *supra* 5.2.2.3.

[117] See, e.g., Karsten Schmidt, GESELLSCHAFTSRECHT 322–3 (4th ed., 2002); see also Bundesgerichtshof e.AG, 61 ZEITSCHRIFT FÜR WIRTSCHAFTS- UND BANKRECHT 1274 (2007) (managers of start-ups must continuously and seriously verify that the firm is solvent).

[118] Art. 429 Companies Act. This is also true for Italy (Art. 2394 Civil Code), but such suits are unheard of.

[119] Over a hundred cases have been published in the second half of the 20th century, with more than 90% brought by creditors. For the most comprehensive survey, see Yoshiharu Yoshikawa, DIRECTOR'S DUTY TO A THIRD PARTY (1986) (in Japanese).

[120] See Arts. 425–7, 429, 462 Companies Act.

especially when civil liability has limited deterrence value due to its exceeding directors' assets.[121] Most of our jurisdictions have directors' disqualification schemes that permit the state to sanction failure by directors to meet relevant standards of pro-creditor conduct (including breaches of accounting rules or fiduciary duties) by banning them from being involved in the management of a company.[122] Enforcement is most intensive in the UK, where a state-funded investigation into possible misconduct must be launched for every corporate bankruptcy, with a view to initiating possible disqualification proceedings.[123] As a consequence, disqualification is approximately 100 times more common in the UK than is a judgment in a private suit against directors of an insolvent company.[124] Most of the directors disqualified are owner-managers, rather than directors of publicly-traded companies, reflecting the deterrence value of public enforcement when it comes to individuals with limited assets.[125] Disqualification plays a more limited role in other jurisdictions, especially in the U.S., where it is only available for directors of publicly-traded companies, and is not employed as a creditor-protection measure.

Criminal liability is also imposed on directors who worsened the financial position of their company as a consequence of a violation of their statutory duties. In the U.S., as we shall see in Chapter 9, the focus is on antifraud provisions that generally protect investors against losses resulting from negligent misrepresentation in a prospectus or registration statement. The scope of criminal provisions is much more specific in continental Europe. In France, directors who act opportunistically in the vicinity of insolvency face up to five years imprisonment.[126] Germany and Italy adopt an even more inclusive approach, with directors facing criminal sanctions as soon as they violate their duty to call a general meeting (Germany) or recapitalize or liquidate (Italy) when legal capital is lost.[127]

---

[121] *Supra*, text to note 107.

[122] See Art. 653–8 Code du commerce (France); Art. 216–17 Legge Fallimentare (Italy) (limited to criminal prosecutions); Art. 331 Companies Act (Japan); Company Directors Disqualification Act 1986 (UK); Securities Enforcement Remedies and Penny Stock Reform Act of 1990, 15 U.S.Code §§ 77t(e), 78u(d)(2) (U.S.).

[123] Company Directors Disqualification Act 1986, § 7. See Adrian Walters, *Directors' Duties: The Impact of the Company Directors Disqualification Act 1986*, 21 COMPANY LAWYER 110 (2000); Andrew Hicks, *Company Law Director Disqualification: Can it Deliver?*, JOURNAL OF BUSINESS LAW 433 (2001).

[124] See Department of Trade and Industry, *Companies in 2005–2006*, 23 (2006) (on average 1,549 disqualifications per year, 2001–2006); John Armour, *Enforcement Strategies in UK Company Law: A Roadmap and Empirical Assessment*, in RATIONALITY IN COMPANY LAW: ESSAYS IN HONOUR OF DD PRENTICE 71 (John Armour and Jennifer Payne (eds.), 2009).

[125] John Armour, Bernard S. Black, Brian R. Cheffins, and Richard Nolan, *Private Enforcement of Corporate Law: An Empirical Comparison of the US and UK*, Working Paper (2009), at http://www.ssrn.com.

[126] Art. 654–3 Code de commerce.

[127] For Germany, see § 401 Aktiengesetz and § 84 GmbH, as well as Heribert Hirte, KAPITALGESELLSCHAFTSRECHT 135–6 (5th ed., 2006) (providing an overview of leading German cases). In Italy, directors face a low pecuniary sanction of they do not call a general meeting after

5.3.1.2 Shareholders

All jurisdictions offer doctrinal tools for holding shareholders liable for the debts of insolvent corporations, although—not surprisingly—the use of these tools is restricted to controlling or managing shareholders who are found to have abused the corporate form. The three principal tools for imposing liability on shareholders are the doctrine of *de facto* or shadow directors, equitable subordination, and 'piercing the corporate veil'.[128] In addition, specially enhanced standards are applied in the context of corporate groups in some jurisdictions.

The doctrine of *de facto* or shadow directors[129] involves treating a person who acts as a member of, or exercises control over, the board, without formally having been appointed as such, as subject to the same potential liabilities as directors. For example, under French law, a controlling shareholder who directs a company's management to violate their fiduciary duties may be required to indemnify the company its losses (*insuffisance d'actifs*) or even be compelled to pay all the corporation's debts (*obligation aux dettes sociales*).[130] Versions of this doctrine are also applied in our other jurisdictions but for the U.S.[131]

A second form of shareholder liability involves the subordination of debt claims brought by controlling shareholders against the estates of their bankrupt companies.[132] Subordination occurs either because controlling shareholders have behaved inequitably (the so-called '*Deep Rock*' doctrine under U.S. law),[133] or

net assets have fallen below the required threshold and criminal sanctions if the omission leads to, or worsens, the company's financial distress. See Corte di Casszione, Sez. V, 26 May 2005.

[128] These mechanisms directly protect creditors inasmuch as the company being insolvent is a precondition for their availability. Creditors, however, may also be indirectly protected against controlling shareholders looting a solvent company by provisions protecting minority shareholders. See *infra* 6.2.4 and 6.2.5.

[129] Sometimes shadow directors are said to influence directors secretly, as distinguished from *de facto* directors who act openly as directors but are not (see, e.g., *Re Hydrodan (Corby) Ltd* [1994] Butterworths Company Law Cases 161). We use the terms interchangeably.

[130] Art. L. 651–2 and Art. L. 652–1 Code de commerce. These remedies are not available when a restructuring plan has been accepted, providing shareholders with an incentive to contribute to its adoption: see André Jacquemont, Droit des Entreprises en Difficulté No. 904–26 (2007). France is also generally tough on asset diversion: Art. L. 242–6 Code de commerce permits fines up to €375,000 and jail sentences up to 5 years in case of *abus de biens sociaux*. See *infra* 6.2.5.1.

[131] See, for Germany, Bundesgerichtshof Zivilsachen 104, 44; for Italy, Corte di Cassazione, 14 September 1999, No. 9795, 27 Giurisprudenza Commerciale II 167 (2000); for Japan, Art. 429 Companies Act; for the UK, §§ 250–251 Companies Act 2006; *Secretary of State for Trade and Industry v. Deverell* [2001] Chancery Division 340, 354–5.

[132] For an overview of subordination doctrines in Austria, Germany, Italy, Spain, and the U.S., see Martin Gelter and Juerg Roth, *Subordination of Shareholder Loans from a Legal and Economic Perspective*, 5 Journal for Institutional Comparisons 40 (2007). Technically, subordination is a recharacterization of the shareholder's claim from debt to equity, but financially the result is the functional equivalent of liability.

[133] *Taylor v. Standard Gas and Electric Corporation*, 306 United States Reports 307 (1939); *Pepper v. Litton*, 308 United States Reports 295 (1939). The name 'Deep Rock' derives from the debtor in reorganization in *Taylor*, the Deep Rock Oil Corporation. See generally, Robert C. Clark, Corporate Law, 52–67 (1986). Note that subordination sometimes occurs even in the

because controlling shareholders' loans are automatically (in Germany) or under certain conditions (in Italy) subordinated in the insolvency of the company.[134] Both doctrines walk a tightrope between deterring shareholder opportunism and permitting controlling shareholders to make legitimate efforts to rescue failing firms through the injection of new debt capital.[135] This doctrine is not, however, applied in France or the UK.[136]

Finally, all our jurisdictions permit courts to 'pierce the corporate veil' in extreme circumstances; that is, to hold controlling shareholders or the controllers of corporate groups personally liable for the company's debts. To be sure, courts do not set aside the corporate form easily.[137] In no jurisdiction has veil-piercing been directed against publicly-traded companies or passive (non-controlling) shareholders, and most successful cases involve blatant misrepresentation or *ex post* opportunism by shareholders.[138] Nevertheless, U.S. jurisdictions permit veil piercing when (1) controlling shareholders disregard the integrity of their companies by failing to observe formalities, intermingling personal and company assets, or failing to capitalize the company adequately—and (2) there is an element of fraud or 'injustice', as when shareholders have clearly behaved opportunistically. Japan and EU jurisdictions apply the veil piercing doctrine similarly.[139] In France, for example, insolvency procedures can be extended to shareholders that disregard the integrity of their companies (*action en confusion de patrimoine*).[140]

---

absence of shareholder misbehavior. See *Reiner v. Washington Plate Glass Co., Inc.*, 711 FEDERAL REPORTER 2d 414 (D.C. Cir. 1983).

[134] See, for Germany, §§ 39 (applicable to all entities with limited liability) and 135 (subordination for one year) Insolvenzordnung; Dirk A. Verse, *Shareholder Loans in Corporate Insolvency—A New Approach to an Old Problem*, 9 GERMAN LAW JOURNAL 1109 (2008); for Italy, Art. 2467 (close companies) and Art. 2497–5 (within groups) Civil Code (the firm's financial condition would have required an equity contribution rather than a loan).

[135] See Martin Gelter, *The Subordination of Shareholder Loans in Bankruptcy*, 26 INTERNATIONAL REVIEW OF LAW & ECONOMICS 478 (2006); David A. Skeel, Jr. and Georg Krause-Vilmar, *Recharacterisation and the Nonhindrance of Creditors*, 7 EUROPEAN BUSINESS ORGANIZATION LAW REVIEW 259 (2006).

[136] See, for France, Cozian et al., *supra* note 46, No. 241; for the UK, *Salomon v. A. Salomon & Co Ltd* [1897] APPEAL CASES 22.

[137] See e.g. *Adams* v. *Cape Industries* [1990] BUTTERWORTHS COMPANY LAW CASES. 479 (UK); Stephen M. Bainbridge, *Abolishing Veil Piercing*, 26 JOURNAL OF CORPORATION LAW 479 (2001) (U.S.).

[138] See for the U.S.: Robert B. Thompson, *Piercing the Corporate Veil: An Empirical Study*, 76 CORNELL LAW REVIEW 1036 (1991); for Germany: Uwe Hüffer, GESELLSCHAFTSRECHT 341–5 (7th ed., 2007); for the UK: Davies, *supra* note 74, 202–8. In Japan, however, veil piercing is the most litigated issue in corporate law after director liability; see, e.g., Supreme Court Judgment on 27 February 1969, 23 Minshu 511. Similarly, while the rhetoric of English judges suggests otherwise, an empirical study of case outcomes reports that UK courts in fact pierce the corporate veil quite frequently: Charles Mitchell, *Lifting the Corporate Veil in the English Courts: An Empirical Study*, 3 COMPANY, FINANCIAL AND INSOLVENCY LAW REVIEW 15 (1999).

[139] French and German courts tend to discuss public policy considerations in veil piercing analyses, but this appears to have few practical implications: see Cozian et al., *supra* note 46, No. 154 and 166; Kübler and Assmann *supra* note 45, § 23 I 2.

[140] Art. L 621–2 (*sauvegarde*), 631–7 (*redressement judiciaire*) and 641–1 (liquidation judiciaire) Code de commerce (France).

Piercing the corporate veil can be seen as performing a broadly similar function to imposing liability on a shareholder as a *de facto* or shadow director or subordinating a shareholder's loans. However, for the courts of some jurisdictions, 'disregarding' the company's legal personality with regard to one party means that it must be disregarded for all—with the result that veil-piercing acts as a much blunter instrument for controlling opportunism than do the other two doctrines, which by their nature may be targeted more precisely.

Veil-piercing doctrines are also occasionally used to protect the creditors of corporate groups. In the U.S., the doctrine of 'substantive consolidation' gives bankruptcy courts the power to put assets and liabilities of two related corporations into a single pool.[141] Like the French '*action en confusion de patrimoine*', this is a means to respond to debtor opportunism taking the form of concealing assets in different corporate boxes, or of shunting assets around within a group. However, the doctrine makes the creditors of one corporate entity better off at the expense of the creditors of the other and, therefore, is most appropriate where all creditors have been deceived as to the location of assets, or where the creditors that are made worse off acted collusively with the debtor.[142]

Veil-piercing is no more common within groups of companies than it is between companies and controlling shareholders who are individuals.[143] On the other hand, a supplementary set of creditor protection standards covers groups of companies in some jurisdictions, constituting a special law of corporate groups. The German *Konzernrecht* provides the most elaborate example of such a law, attempting to balance the interests of groups as a whole with those of the creditors and minority shareholders of their individual members.[144] In groups based upon a contract of domination, the parent must indemnify its subsidiaries for any losses that stem from acting in the group's interests.[145] Should this fail to happen, creditors of the subsidiary may attach its indemnification claim or sue the parent's directors for damages.[146] More generally, even if a parent company has not entered into a contract of domination (a *de facto* group), it must compensate

---

[141] See, e.g., *In Re Augie/Restivio Baking Co* 860 Federal Reporter 2d 506 (2d Cir. 1988). See also Douglas G. Baird, *Substantive Consolidation Today*, 47 Boston College Law Review 5 (2005); Irit Mevorach, *The Appropriate Treatment of Corporate Groups in Insolvency*, 8 European Business Organization Law Review 179 (2007).

[142] See also Douglas G. Baird, The Elements of Bankruptcy, 170–9 (4th ed., 2006).

[143] In the U.S., Thompson (*supra* note 138, 1056) finds that courts pierce the veil in more than 40% of decided cases to reach the assets of individual shareholders, and in more than 35% of decided cases to reach the assets of corporate shareholders.

[144] See Emmerich and Habersack, *supra* note 66; for a comparative perspective, see Konzernrecht und Kapitalmarktrecht (Peter Hommelhoff, Klaus J. Hopt, and Marcus Lutter (eds.), 2001).

[145] See § 302 Aktiengesetz (subsidiary is an AG); Hüffer, *supra* note 138, 373 (subsidiary is a GmbH) and Bundesgerichtshof Zivilsachen 116, 37 [*Stromlieferung*]. For the distinction between contractual and *de facto* groups, see § 18 Aktiengesetz.

[146] See §§ 302 and 309 Aktiengesetz (subsidiary is an AG); Emmerich and Habersack, *supra* note 66, 446–7 (subsidiary is a GmbH).

any subsidiaries that it causes to act contrary to the subsidiary's own interests.[147] Should the parent fail to do so, creditors may sue the parent for damages.[148]

German law's focus on protecting the interests of the individual entity contrasts with the cooperation-oriented French approach to the same issues. Under French case law, a group's controller is not liable for instructing a subsidiary to act in the interests of the group rather than its own interests as long as the group is (1) stable, (2) pursuing a coherent business policy, and (3) distributing the group's costs and revenues equitably among its members.[149]

The French focus on the 'enterprise' has been perceived as having the advantage of reflecting a more functional approach,[150] while the indemnification requirements of *Konzernrecht* seem more protective of a given subsidiary's creditors. However, there is some evidence that French courts take serious consideration of creditor interests when applying the equitable cooperation doctrine,[151] whereas German courts have recently adopted a more balanced doctrine of 'solvency threatening' parent intervention (*Existenzvernichtungshaftung*) for closely held firms.[152]

5.3.1.3 Creditors and other third parties

The standards strategy is also employed in a variety of guises as regards creditors and other third parties. In these applications, the focus is sometimes on recruiting third parties as gatekeepers, in others on preventing one creditor from getting a better position vis-à-vis the others, and in many cases, both.

The first approach targets third parties who enter into transactions with a debtor in the vicinity of insolvency that are manifestly disadvantageous to the debtor. Such third parties may find that the transaction is set aside *ex post* in the debtor's bankruptcy, and that they are required to return the benefits they received. These results are brought about under the doctrines of *actio pauliana* in continental Europe, fraudulent conveyance in the U.S. and Japan, and 'undervalue transactions' in the UK.[153] The standards strategy recruits third parties

---

[147] See § 311 Aktiengesetz (subsidiary is an AG). Emmerich and Habersack., *supra* note 66, 419–21 (subsidiary is a GmbH). The same approach has been adopted in Italy: see Art. 2497 Civil Code.

[148] See § 317 Aktiengesetz; BUNDESGERICHTSHOF ZIVILSACHEN 149, 10 [*Bremer Vulkan*] and BUNDESGERICHTSHOF ZIVILSACHEN 173, 246 [*Trihotel*].

[149] This is the holding of the well-known *Rozenblum* case (Cour de Cassation, 1985 REVUE DES SOCIÉTÉS 648), a criminal 'abus de biens sociaux' case.

[150] See Wolfgang Schön, *The Concept of the Shareholder in European Company Law*, 1 EUROPEAN BUSINESS ORGANIZATION LAW REVIEW 3, 24–7 (2000); FORUM EUROPAEUM CORPORATE GROUP LAW, *Corporate Group Law for Europe*, 1 EUROPEAN BUSINESS ORGANIZATION LAW REVIEW 165 (2000).

[151] See Marie-Emma Boursier, *Le Fait Justificatif de Groupe dans l'Abus de Biens Sociaux: Entre Efficacité et Clandestinité*, 125 REVUE DES SOCIÉTÉS 273 (2005).

[152] See *supra* note 148 and Mathias Habersack, *Trihotel – Das Ende der Debatte?*, 37 ZEITSCHRIFT FÜR UNTERNEHMENS- UND GESELLSCHAFTSRECHT 533 (2008).

[153] See, for France, Art. L 632–1 and 632–2 Code de commerce; for Germany, § 129 Insolvenzordnung; for Italy, Art. 64–7 Legge Fallimentare; for the U.S., Uniform Fraudulent

as gatekeepers by making them wary of desperate transactions entered into by a distressed debtor, whose shareholders may be engaging in asset substitution.[154] The gatekeeper will only be able to rely on the transaction if they can show they were in 'good faith',[155] or more specifically, that there were reasonable grounds for believing, at the time, that it would benefit the debtor's business.[156]

The second type of application targets 'insider' creditors who influence distressed debtors in a way harmful to other creditors. One version focuses on involvement in management decisions, whereby influential creditors such as banks may be made liable as *de facto* directors or, if an *animus societatis* can be established, as partners of the insolvent firm. In some jurisdictions, such as the UK, liability attaches to any person knowingly carrying on a company's business with the intent to defraud creditors, whereas in others, like Italy or the U.S., there is no shortage of doctrines that impose liability upon lenders who deal with insolvent firms.[157] There is a real risk, however, of over-deterrence: banks may be shy of entering into workout arrangements with failing companies for fear of such liability, even though courts rarely impose liability when banks merely attempt to protect their loans.[158]

Another application of the standards strategy against 'insider' creditors concerns so-called 'preferential' transactions—resulting in a particular creditor being placed in a better position than the others in the debtor's bankruptcy. In continental European jurisdictions, the *actio pauliana* may also be used to challenge such transactions,[159] the principal requirement being that the creditor benefiting from it has acted in bad faith. In the U.S., UK, and Japan, by contrast, there is no need to demonstrate bad faith on the part of the creditor, although the UK requires that the debtor have had some desire to favor the creditor, whereas the U.S. and Japan simply impose liability where the effect of the transaction improves the creditor's position.[160]

Conveyance Act and the Bankruptcy Code; Douglas G. Baird and Thomas H. Jackson, *Fraudulent Conveyance Law and Its Proper Domain,* 38 Vanderbilt Law Review 829 (1985); for Japan, Art. 424 Civil Code; for the UK), §§ 238, 241, 423–425 Insolvency Act 1986.

[154] See John Armour, *Transactions at an Undervalue,* in Vulnerable Transactions in Corporate Insolvency, 46–7 (John Armour and Howard N. Bennett (eds.), 2003).

[155] See § 8(a) Uniform Fraudulent Transfer Act (U.S.) (but primary transferees have no good faith defense under § 548 Bankruptcy Code); Art. 67 Legge Fallimentare (Italy).

[156] See § 238(5) Insolvency Act 1986 (UK).

[157] See, for the UK, § 213 Insolvency Act 1986; *Morris v Bank of India* [2005] 2 Butterworths Company Law Cases 328; for Italy, see Corte di Cassazione, 28 March 2006, No. 7029, Diritto Fallimentare II/630 (2006) (*de facto* director); for the U.S., Lynn M. LoPucki, Strategies for Creditors in Bankruptcy Proceedings 136–7 (3rd ed., 1997).

[158] See for France, Cozian et al., *supra* note 46, No. 269; for Italy, Corte di Cassazione SU, 28 March 2006, No. 7028, 2007 Diritto della Banca e del Mercato Finanziario 149; for the UK, see Davies, *supra* note 74, 219–20; for the U.S. Baird and Rasmussen, *supra* note 15.

[159] See *supra*, note 151.

[160] § 239 Insolvency Act 1986 (UK); Bankruptcy Code (U.S.); 11 U.S.Code § 547; Art. 160 and Art. 162 Bankruptcy Act (Japan). Liability is also imposed on bad faith transferees in Japan.

5.3.2 Governance strategies

If a debtor becomes financially distressed, its assets are probably insufficient to pay all its creditors and permit them a collective exit. Under these circumstances, governance strategies move to the fore. Their application has two phases: first, in the period of transition into bankruptcy, and secondly to the control of firms in bankruptcy procedures.[161] Governance strategies deal largely—but not exclusively—with shareholder-creditor conflicts in the first phase and creditor-creditor conflicts in the second. The understanding that these governance strategies will be employed *ex post* necessarily influences private contracting with creditors, both at the *ex ante* stage of determining debt structure, and later in any renegotiation.

5.3.2.1 Appointment rights

All our jurisdictions give creditors power to initiate a change in the control of the assets of a financially distressed company by triggering bankruptcy proceedings. Jurisdictions commonly allow a single creditor to exercise this power by demonstrating that the debtor is insolvent in the 'cash-flow' sense—that is, unable to pay debts as they fall due.[162] The U.S., however, requires that three creditors bring a petition together.[163] Moreover, the U.S. and, more recently, Germany, France, and Italy, permit managers to trigger bankruptcy proceedings without any requirement that the firm in fact be insolvent.[164]

In most of our jurisdictions, a consequence of transition to bankruptcy is removal of the board from effective control of corporate assets, and its replacement with, or supervision by, an 'administrator' or 'crisis manager' to whom operational managers are accountable.[165] In general, this person is appointed by creditors, rather than shareholders—although in many jurisdictions the court may oversee the appointment,[166] or even have the exclusive power to make it.[167] There are, however, some exceptions to the appointment of a crisis manager.

---

[161] Before it is begun or once it is over, bankruptcy might also be viewed as a form of affiliation strategy, as it permits a collective exit by creditors. Yet, as it unfolds, it is unmistakeably concerned with governance.

[162] See Art. L 631–1 Code de commerce (France); § 14(1) Insolvenzordnung (Germany); Arts. 5 and 6 Legge Fallimentare (Italy); § 123(1)(e) Insolvency Act 1986 (UK); Arts. 15 and 16 Bankruptcy Act (Japan).

[163] 11 U.S. Code §§ 303(b)(1).

[164] See 11 U.S.Code § 301(a) (U.S.); § 18 Insolvenzordnung and Stefan Smid, PRAXISHANDBUCH INSOLVENZRECHT 52 (5th ed., 2007) (Germany). Art. L. 620–1 Code de commerce (France) (*procedure de sauvegarde*); Art. 160 Legge Fallimentare (concordato preventivo).

[165] See Art. 622–1 Code de commerce (France); § 56 Insolvenzordnung (Germany); Art. 21 Legge Fallimentare (Italy); Insolvency Act 1986 Schedule B1 ¶¶ 59, 61, 64 (UK); 11 U.S.Code § 323 (US).

[166] See § 56 *Insolvenzordnung* (Germany); Art. 27 and 37-II Legge Fallimentare (Italy) (court appoints crisis manager but creditors may request replacement); Insolvency Act 1986 § 139 and Schedule B1 ¶ 14 (UK); Bankruptcy Code (US); 11 U.S.Code § 702 (US).

[167] See Art. L. 621–4 Code de commerce (France); Art. 74 Bankruptcy Act (Japan).

Whilst liquidation proceedings under Chapter 7 of the U.S. Bankruptcy Code follow the foregoing pattern, reorganization proceedings under Chapter 11 quite definitely do not. Here board members continue in office and maintain their powers to control the company's assets.[168] Creditors may apply to the court to appoint a trustee to take over control, or to switch the proceedings into Chapter 7, but the default position is that the existing management remains in place and their removal in the hands of shareholders.[169] Japan and, more recently, France and Germany have adopted more modest versions of the U.S. approach. In Japan, courts may forgo the appointment of a crisis manager if petitioned to that effect by a creditor or another interested party, whereas French courts may do so for smaller corporations.[170] In Germany, courts may allow boards to continue to control corporate assets under the surveillance of a custodian, unless insolvency proceedings have been triggered by a creditor who objects to the appointment of a custodian instead of an all-powerful crisis manager.[171]

5.3.2.2 Decision rights

Whilst bankruptcy proceedings generally involve delegated management to a crisis manager of some type, the initiation and veto rights accorded to creditors vary across jurisdictions.

In most jurisdictions, a proposal for 'exit' from bankruptcy proceedings—whether by a sale or closure of the business or a restructuring of its balance sheet—is typically initiated by the crisis manager, subject to veto rights from creditors. There are two significant exceptions. In France, the court adopts the restructuring plan or decides upon a sale or closure of the business, and creditors have no veto power (but their support may, of course, facilitate the adoption of the plan).[172] France thus relies almost exclusively on trusteeship strategy to govern bankruptcy proceedings. Second, in the U.S., the debtor's managers have the exclusive right to initiate a plan for the first 120 days after the relief order associated with the filing for insolvency.[173] Whilst creditors must nevertheless accept the plan for it to be confirmed, the exclusivity period gives shareholders the ability to extract concessions from the creditors so as to avoid delay.[174]

---

[168] Bankruptcy Code (U.S.); 11 U.S.Code § 1107.   [169] *Ibid.*, §§ 1104, 1112.

[170] See Art. 38 and 64 et seq. Civil Rehabilitation Act 1999 (simple general reorganization proceedings) and Art. 67 Corporate Reorganization Act 1952 (more formal proceedings for joint-stock companies, amended in 2002 to introduce debtor-in-possession schemes) (Japan); Art. L. 621–4 and 631–9 Code de commerce (France) (firms with less than 20 employees or turnover below € 3,000,000).

[171] § 270 Insolvenzordnung (Germany).

[172] Art. L. 626–9 (plan de sauvegarde), 631–19 (plan de redressement) and 641–1 (liquidation judiciaire) Code de commerce.

[173] 11 U.S.Code § 1121. This may be extended by the court to 180 days.

[174] William H. Meckling, *Financial Markets, Default and Bankruptcy: The Role of the State*, 41 Law and Contemporary Problems 13, 33–7 (1977); Lucian Ayre Bebchuk and Howard Chang, *Bargaining and the Division of Value in Corporate Reorganization*, 8 Journal of Law, Economics, and Organization 253 (1992).

Deciding upon a plan for exiting bankruptcy runs into problems of inter-creditor conflicts.[175] Creditors who are in a junior class that is 'out of the money' will, analogously to shareholders in a financially distressed firm, tend to prefer more risky outcomes. Creditors who are in a senior class that is 'oversecured'—that is, the assets are more than enough to pay them off—will prefer a less risky plan. Giving either group a say in the outcome will at best add to transaction costs and at worst lead to an inappropriate decision about the firm's future. Jurisdictions that give veto rights to creditors over the confirmation of a restructuring plan try to reduce this problem by seeking to give only those creditors who are 'residual claimants' a say in the process. Hence, most jurisdictions do not allow voting by either creditors who will recover in full or by junior creditors who are 'out of the money' under the plan.[176]

5.3.2.3 Incentive strategies

The trusteeship strategy plays a more important role in our jurisdictions for creditor than for shareholder protection purposes, whereas the converse is true for the rewards strategy. There seem to be two reasons for this. The first reflects basic differences in the payoffs to creditors and shareholders. The rewards strategy, which incentivizes agents to act in principals' interests by sharing the payoffs, cannot function so effectively in relation to agents acting for creditors, for the creditors' maximum payoffs are fixed by their contracts.[177] Instead, creditors are more concerned about the possibility of losses—hence a trusteeship strategy, which relies upon the reputational rather than financial incentives of the decision-maker, seems a more natural fit. The second reason stems from the problems of inter-creditor agency costs that arise once a firm moves under the control of its creditors. Because the value of a firm's assets is uncertain and creditors are often grouped in differing classes of priority, it is unlikely to be clear to which group any reward should be offered.

Courts are the principal trustee involved in the governance of bankrupt firms. As we have seen, France relies most on this strategy. Courts alone take the decision concerning the future deployment of the firm's assets, creditors having no veto right. By contrast, courts in our other jurisdictions are not primarily responsible for making the decision how to exit the proceedings.[178] They essentially confirm

---

[175] See Philippe Aghion, Oliver Hart, and John Moore, *The Economics of Bankruptcy Reform*, 8 Journal of Law, Economics, and Organization 523 (1992).

[176] See §§ 237 Insolvenzordnung (Germany); Art. 127 and 177 Legge Fallimentare (Italy); Schedule B1 ¶ 52 Insolvency Act 1986 (UK); 11 U.S.Code §§ 1126(f)–(g) (U.S.).

[177] Compensation structures may, however, mitigate the asset substitution problem. See James Brander and Michel Poitevin, *Managerial Compensation and the Agency Problem*, 13 Managerial and Decision Economics 55 (1992); Kose John and Teresa John, *Top-Management Compensation and Capital Structure*, 48 Journal of Finance 949 (1993).

[178] See, for Germany, § 248 Insolvenzordnung (confirmation of plan); for Japan, Patrick Shea and Kaori Miyake, *Insolvency-Related Reorganization Procedures in Japan: The Four Cornerstones*, 14 University of California at Los Angeles Pacific Basin Law Review 243 (1996)

significant decisions and resolve questions and disputes arising between different classes of claimant. Whilst courts lack the high-powered financial incentives of market participants, which may make their valuations less careful, their lack of financial interest also means that their actions are less likely to be motivated by strategic considerations. Consistently with this, there is some empirical evidence that bankruptcy procedures controlled by courts achieve no worse returns for creditors, on average, than do decisions made by market participants.[179]

Despite the general focus on trusteeship, the reward strategy is applied in relation to the resolution of shareholder-creditor agency problems in the U.S. and Japan. As we have seen,[180] U.S. Chapter 11 proceedings allow the incumbent managers to remain in control of the firm and give them initiation rights regarding the plan of reorganization. Similarly, Japanese law does not force managers to enter insolvency proceedings, but makes doing so more attractive by allowing the board to remain in office after these proceedings are initiated. To be sure, U.S. managers often lose their jobs in the aftermath of an insolvency filing.[181] However, given that the debtor can go into bankruptcy proceedings without being actually insolvent, the U.S. and Japanese approach can be understood as offering shareholders a reward for early filing. It gives them the chance to emerge from bankruptcy with a continued stake in the firm, rather than having their claims extinguished, thus reducing the need for shareholders to engage in asset substitution in the vicinity of insolvency.[182] Such retention of claims by shareholders in firms emerging from Chapter 11 was a well-documented phenomenon.[183] However, more assertive creditor bargaining in recent years has meant it has practically vanished,[184] taking with it the idea that the reward strategy plays a meaningful role in relation to creditors.

(applicable to Chapter 11-type procedures only); for the UK, Insolvency Act 1986 Schedule B1 ¶¶ 63, 68 (administrator may apply to court for directions); 70–3 (authorize sale of assets subject to security); 76–9 (extension or termination of administration proceedings); for the U.S. Bankruptcy Code (US); 11 U.S.Code §§ 1129 (confirmation of plan); 1104 (appointment of trustee or examiner where requested).

[179] See Edward R. Morrison, *Bankruptcy Decision Making: An Empirical Study of Continuation Bias in Small-Business Bankruptcies*, 50 JOURNAL OF LAW AND ECONOMICS 381 (2007); Régis Blazy, Bertrand Chopard, Agnès Fimayer, and Jean-Daniel Guigou, *Financial Versus Social Efficiency of Corporate Bankruptcy Law: The French Dilemma?*, Working Paper (2007), at http://ideas.repec.org.
[180] See *supra* 5.3.2.1.   [181] See *supra* note 9.
[182] See Julian R. Franks, Kjell G. Nyborg, and Walter N. Torous, *A Comparison of U.S., UK, and German Insolvency Codes*, 25 FINANCIAL MANAGEMENT 86 (1996); Alan Schwartz, *The Absolute Priority Rule and the Firm's Investment Policy*, 72 WASHINGTON UNIVERSITY LAW QUARTERLY 1213 (1994).
[183] See, e.g., Lawrence A. Weiss, *Bankruptcy Resolution: Direct Costs and Violation of Priority Claims*, 27 JOURNAL OF FINANCIAL ECONOMICS 285 (1990); Julian R. Franks and Walter N. Torous, *An Empirical Investigation of US Firms in Reorganization*, 44 JOURNAL OF FINANCE 747 (1989).
[184] See Lawrence A. Wiess and Vedran Capkun, *Bankruptcy Resolution: Priority of Claims with the Secured Creditor in Control*, Working Paper (2007), at http://www.bepress.com; Sreedhar T. Bharath, Venky Panchapegesan, and Ingrid Werner, *The Changing Nature of Chapter 11*, Working Paper (2007), at http://www.ssrn.com.

In sum, courts play a central role in resolving the creditor-creditor coordination and agency problems following a debtor company's entry into formal bankruptcy proceedings. Their most extensive use is in France, where the court completely pre-empts creditor governance. Courts also play a significant role in overseeing the process in most other jurisdictions, whereas UK courts have less of an over-sight role, greater discretion being thus granted to the crisis manager.

5.4 Ownership Regimes and Creditor Protection

Corporate law in every jurisdiction supplements debtor-creditor law in facilitating transactions between corporations and their creditors. All our jurisdictions, more-over, have adopted the same set of broad legal strategies: regulatory strategies in relation to firms not in default (primarily mandatory disclosure, with some rule-based controls, and a range of standards applied to firms that are in financial diffi-culties), coupled with governance strategies for firms which are in default.

However, this framework similarity masks variations at a more micro level. One way of characterizing these variations is to describe countries' legal regimes as being 'debtor-friendly' or 'creditor-friendly', according to the extent to which they facilitate or restrict creditor enforcement against a financially distressed debtor.[185] Thus, the U.S., and to a lesser extent, Japanese, approach is said to reflect debtor-friendliness, while the UK and, to a lesser extent, German approaches are on this view characterized as creditor-friendly. However, the existence of different classes of creditors suggests that a binary division into pro-creditor or pro-debtor may be too simplistic,[186] and a taxonomical division simply begs the question as to the factors that determine particular jurisdictions' orientation. Whilst some have sought to attribute differences in creditor protection to the civil law or com-mon law origins of a jurisdiction,[187] this account is called into question not only by the framework similarities *across* jurisdictions that we document in this chap-ter, but also the considerable micro-level variation in creditor rights *within* the civil and common law families.[188]

As indicated in Chapter 1, legal strategies appear to be significantly related to ownership structures, although perhaps less directly in relation to creditor rights

---

[185] See, e.g. Franks et al., *supra* note 182; Sefa Franken, *Creditor- and Debtor-Oriented Corporate Bankruptcy Regimes Revisited*, 5 European Business Organization Law Review 645 (2004).

[186] For example, is the presence or absence of an automatic stay of secured creditors' claims in bankruptcy proceedings 'creditor friendly'? The answer likely depends on whether the 'creditor' one has in mind is secured or unsecured.

[187] See Djankov et al., *Private Credit*, *supra* note 1.

[188] See Erik Berglöf, Howard Rosenthal, and Ernst-Ludwig von Thadden, *The Formation of Legal Institutions for Bankruptcy: A Comparative Study of Legislative History,* Working Paper (2001), at http://www.vwl.uni-mannheim.de; John Armour, Simon Deakin, Priya Lele, and Mathias Siems, *How Do Legal Rules Evolve? Evidence from a Cross-Country Comparison of Shareholder, Creditor and Worker Protection,* 57 American Journal of Comparative Law (forthcoming 2009).

than when it comes to the basic governance structure and minority shareholder rights. This is because the size of their aggregate financial interest and their relative concentration allow banks to influence politics as much as any other constituencies, including shareholders or managers in borrower firms.[189] Banks' interest group activism, however, is likely to vary with the nature of the financial system as well as with the structure of share ownership.[190] We can see this in the following case studies.

5.4.1 Regulatory or contractual controls?

Germany and Italy have traditionally relied most on providing standard terms to facilitate contracting with creditors. They have strong records of imposing credit-oriented accounting principles and legal capital rules upon larger as well as smaller corporations. The U.S. has adopted the opposite approach in recent decades, having adopted bondholder-oriented disclosure requirements and left the design of accounting and capital constraints to market participants. France, Japan, and the UK lie somewhere in between, France being closer to Germany and the UK closer to the U.S.

The German approach is typical of an ownership regime where controlling shareholders have a strong voice. In such a regime, concentrated share ownership and concentrated lending generally go hand in hand, reducing creditor heterogeneity and increasing the advantages of one-size-fits-all mandatory standard terms. In the U.S., by contrast, share ownership is widely dispersed and banking concentration has been restricted.[191] In such a regime, corporate debt also tends to be more dispersed, increasing creditor heterogeneity and reducing the advantages of one-size-fits-all standard terms. Consequently, creditors derive few benefits from firms' adherence to such provisions, but debtors still bear their

---

[189] See Enriques and Macey, *supra* note 99, 1202–3; see also Bruce G. Carruthers and Terence C. Halliday, Rescuing Business: The Making of Corporate Bankruptcy Law in England and the United States (1998).

[190] See John Armour, Brian R. Cheffins, and David A. Skeel, *Corporate Ownership Structure and the Evolution of Bankruptcy Law: Lessons from the United Kingdom*, 55 Vanderbilt Law Review 1699 (2002); Jan Mahrt-Smith, *The Interaction of Capital Structure and Ownership Structure*, 78 Journal of Business 787 (2005).

Note that differences in patterns of share ownership and debt structure may also be complementary to countries' industrial structure. Industries for which long-term capital investments are required may be better complemented by concentrated equity ownership (with concentrated creditors); whereas industries in which a large number of innovations are explored and amongst which capital redeployment must be effected rapidly may be better served by a (dispersed) equity-oriented financial structure, with correspondingly dispersed creditors. See Wendy Carlin and Colin Mayer, *Finance, Investment, and Growth*, in Corporate Governance Regimes: Convergence and Diversity (Joseph A. McCahery, Piet Moerland, Theo Raaijmakers, and Luc Renneboog (eds.), 2002), 325; Franklin Allen, Laura Bartiloro, and Oskar Kowalewski, *Does Economic Structure Determine Financial Structure?*, Working Paper (2006), at http://www.ssrn.com.

[191] Mark J. Roe, Strong Managers, Weak Owners: The Political Roots of American Corporate Finance 54–9 (1994).

costs. Hence managers may be expected to favor their removal, and banks are unlikely to oppose this.

France, like Germany and Italy, has concentrated ownership, although the importance of the state as both equity and debt holder (through state-owned banks) allows for a more relaxed approach to the mandating of standard terms. Whilst the UK and Japan, like the U.S., have relatively dispersed share ownership, it is a much more recent phenomenon in these jurisdictions and blockholdings remain more common than in the U.S.[192] Associated with this, lending for UK and Japanese firms has tended, until recently, to be more concentrated. This has been associated with a greater use of mandatory standard terms than in the U.S.

5.4.2 The role of bankruptcy law

If firms have few creditors, then corporate bankruptcy law need only perform the role of liquidating failed firms: firms that have businesses worth saving can be restructured by a private 'workout'.[193] However, as the dispersion of creditors increases, so does the difficulty of achieving a private solution, and it becomes increasingly valuable to have the option of a bankruptcy procedure that uses governance strategies to help creditors take ownership of a firm that continues to operate.

As we have seen, Chapter 11 of the U.S. Bankruptcy Code adopts a 'debtor-friendly' stance that is almost unique in our jurisdictions, giving managers of distressed companies the discretion to orchestrate a court-supervised turnaround while remaining at the helm. At the same time, large U.S. firms have tended to raise debt finance from a wider number of creditors—relying more on bonds and less on bank debt—than has been the case in other jurisdictions.[194] This corresponds with an environment in which banks have traditionally been fragmented, and consequently posed no real opposition to the passage of the 'manager-friendly' bankruptcy code in 1978.[195]

The UK is at the opposite pole. It has traditionally been very favorable to the enforcement of individual creditors' security with almost no judicial involvement,

---

[192] See, e.g., Brian R. Cheffins, CORPORATE OWNERSHIP AND CONTROL: BRITISH BUSINESS TRANSFORMED (2008).

[193] In such a milieu, the absence of any governance strategies in bankruptcy law geared towards the continuation—as opposed to the closure—of a distressed firm can actually serve to increase the chances of a successful workout. The knowledge that the consequences of failing to agree will be highly destructive can focus creditors' minds.

[194] See, e.g., Jenny Corbett and Tim Jenkinson, *How is Investment Financed? A Study of Germany, Japan, the United Kingdom and the United States*, 65 MANCHESTER SCHOOL 69, 74–5, 80–1, 85 (1997); William R. Emmons and Frank A. Schmid, *Corporate Governance and Corporate Performance*, in CORPORATE GOVERNANCE AND GLOBALIZATION 59, 78 (Stephen S. Cohen and Gavin Boyd (eds.), 1998) ('Simply put, firms in the United States and Canada issue significant amounts of bonds but nowhere else in the G7 countries is this true').

[195] See Roe, *supra* note 191; on banks' weak opposition to the 1978 Act, see Carruthers and Halliday, *supra* note 189, 166–94; David A. Skeel, Jr., DEBT'S DOMINION, at 180–3 (2001).

so much so that until recently, a bank holding a security interest covering the entirety of the debtor's assets was permitted to privately control the realization of the assets of the distressed firm.[196] This has corresponded to a strong, concentrated, banking sector, with relatively low use of bonds, as opposed to bank, finance.[197] As a consequence, private workouts play a significant role even for large public firms, with the threat of 'tough' bankruptcy proceedings acting as a powerful mechanism for securing compliance from recalcitrant debtors *ex ante* and creditors unwilling to negotiate *ex post*. Bankruptcy has, in this environment, tended to be reserved for more severe failures—an outcome reflecting the interests of both the debtor's institutional owners and its banks.[198] Germany, Italy, and Japan also follow a similar pattern. In France, bankruptcy proceedings have tended to be used more frequently, corresponding not with greater bank power, but with greater state involvement. The state has played a significant role in the ownership of French banks, reducing their ability to oppose a bankruptcy regime introduced in 1985 that strongly favored employees, promoting their interests over those of other creditors.[199]

5.4.3 Managerial incentives

The standard employed for directorial liability to creditors has the highest intensity in Japan and the lowest in the U.S., continental Europe being closest to the Japanese regime and the UK to the U.S. regime.

In Japan, creditors have standing to sue directors even if the company is solvent, in particular if they fail to properly monitor managers. Closely held companies are the primary target here, reflecting the concentrated ownership and debt structure of that category of firms. Banks have, obviously, an interest in getting managerial incentives aligned with their interests in the vicinity of insolvency. Controlling shareholders, for their part, have no strong reasons to oppose such an outcome as it does not interfere with contractual arrangements or the use of private workouts.

The U.S. is at the opposite pole, with directorial liability to creditors having the lowest intensity amongst our jurisdictions. There is a shift in the content of directors' duty of loyalty in relation to insolvent firms, but its practical impact

---

[196] See John Armour and Sandra Frisby, *Rethinking Receivership*, 21 Oxford Journal of Legal Studies 73 (2001).

[197] See Peter Brierley and Gertjan Vleighe, *Corporate Workouts, the London Approach and Financial Stability*, 7 Financial Stability Review 168, 175 (1999).

[198] See Sitjn Claessens and Leora F. Klapper, *Bankruptcy Around the World: Explanations of Its Relative Use*, 7 American Law and Economics Review 253, 262 (2005) (U.S. bankruptcy rate—proportion of firms filing for bankruptcy proceedings—was higher than all our other jurisdictions: U.S. 3.65%, France 2.62%, UK 1.65%, Germany 1.03%, Italy 0.54%, and Japan 0.22%).

[199] In recent years, diminishing state ownership has been accompanied by increasing creditor influence over restructuring plans.

remains limited.[200] Once more, this reflects both widely dispersed ownership in large public firms and a fragmented banking industry. Managers have no interest in high intensity liability and creditor heterogeneity makes it unattractive for banks to lobby for a more stringent approach.

In France, Germany, and Italy, the approach is similar to the one adopted in Japan, albeit creditors do not have standing to sue directors of solvent companies. Directors of financially distressed firms can be held liable simply for failing to take action following serious loss of capital, an across-the-board outcome which is also consistent with the generally more concentrated ownership and debt structure of large continental European firms. In the UK, on the other hand, there is a U.S.-like shift in the content of the duty of loyalty for directors of insolvent firms. In addition, however, the UK imposes a negligence-based liability on directors for 'wrongful trading', albeit this duty is usually only triggered when the firm is cash-flow insolvent.[201] This approach is, again, in line with the less dispersed ownership and more concentrated debt structure in the UK's large public firms.

---

[200] See *supra* note 109.

[201] See Paul Davies, *Directors' Creditor-Regarding Duties in Respect of Trading Decisions Taken in the Vicinity of Insolvency*, 7 European Business Organization Law Review 301, 318–20 (2006).

6

Related-Party Transactions

Luca Enriques, Gerard Hertig, and Hideki Kanda

In Chapters 3 and 4, we reviewed the response of company law to agency problems in the context of the ordinary governance of the corporation. Chapter 5 has shown that all jurisdictions have adopted legal strategies targeting transactions that siphon off assets to the detriment of creditors. Value diversion is, of course, also a core issue in the relationship between managers and shareholders and between controlling and other shareholders.

This chapter centers upon straightforward techniques for value diversion: related-party transactions. This category includes both transactions in which related parties such as directors and controlling shareholders deal with the corporation—traditional self-dealing and managerial compensation—as well as transactions in which related parties may appropriate value belonging to the corporation—the taking of corporate opportunities and trading in the company's shares.[1]

In traditional self-dealing, the law's concern is that an influential manager or a controlling shareholder will transact with the company on terms less favorable than could be obtained in an arm's length negotiation. Self-dealing typically refers to purchases or sales of assets by related parties, as when a CEO purchases land from her company. But it also refers to other transactions, such as company guarantees in favor of its controlling shareholder and transactions with close relatives of managers or with companies owned by their families. In such cases, the conflicts of interest are acute. Compensation agreements, while technically a form of self-dealing, are unavoidable for companies and thus less suspect. Nevertheless, as hinted at in Chapter 3, there is an obvious risk of collusion among senior managers and the board in setting compensation levels. For example, directors might approve excessive compensation because they are richly compensated themselves, or because they fear losing their seats on the board if they refuse.[2]

---

[1] See Robert C. Clark, CORPORATE LAW 141–5 (1986).

[2] See Lucian Bebchuk and Jesse Fried, PAY WITHOUT PERFORMANCE 25–7 (2004); Eliezer M. Fich and Lawrence J. White, *Why Do CEOs Reciprocally Sit on Each Other's Board?*, 11 JOURNAL OF CORPORATE FINANCE 175 (2005).

In corporate opportunity cases, related parties take business opportunities that should have been offered to their companies instead.[3] Similarly, when trading in the company's shares on the basis of price-sensitive corporate information (so-called insider trading), officers, directors or controlling shareholders appropriate part of the value of yet undisclosed company information by selling or buying before it is reflected in stock prices.

Related-party transactions include the routine forms of abusive insider behavior that have come to be dubbed 'tunneling' in the economic literature,[4] a category that includes all forms of misappropriation of value (assets, cash flows, or the company's equity itself) by corporate insiders.[5] We cover other, more specialized forms of tunneling in later chapters, including misappropriation associated with significant corporate actions in Chapter 7, misappropriation accompanying control transactions in Chapter 8, and misappropriation arising from securities fraud other than insider trading in Chapter 9.

6.1 Why Are Related-Party Transactions Permitted at All?

As a threshold matter, we must ask why related-party transactions are permitted at all, given their vulnerability to abuse by corporate insiders. The answers differ, according to the nature of the transaction and to the size of the firm, i.e., small, closely held companies or larger, publicly-traded corporations.

Consider first traditional self-dealing transactions and the taking of business opportunities. Directors, officers, and controlling shareholders are often the only parties with whom small companies *can* transact, either because outsiders cannot evaluate their prospects or because these companies would be forced to reveal trade secrets or confidential plans to deal with them. More generally, a self-dealing transaction may be entered into in more favorable terms with an insider who knows the company and the risks involved than with an unrelated but distrustful party. Similarly, other firms in a group of companies may be better able to take advantage of a business opportunity than the company which first encountered it.

Even more intuitively, prohibiting the other two kinds of related-party transactions (managerial compensation and trading in the company's shares) would simply be absurd. Just as no one would agree to work for the corporation for free,

---

[3] A famous example is the acquisition of Pepsi-Cola by an executive of another beverage company. See *Guth v. Loft, Inc.*, 5 ATLANTIC REPORTER, SECOND SERIES (A.2d) 503 (Delaware Supreme Court 1939).

[4] See Simon Johnson, Rafael La Porta, Florencio Lopez-de-Silanes, and Andrei Shleifer, *Tunneling*, 90(2) AMERICAN ECONOMIC REVIEW 22 (2000) (reporting that the term was 'coined originally to characterize the expropriation of minority shareholders in the Czech Republic (as in removing assets through an underground tunnel)').

[5] See Vladimir Atanasov, Bernard Black, and Conrad S. Ciccotello, *Unbundling and Measuring Tunneling*, Working Paper (2008), available at http://www.ssrn.com.

managers cannot reasonably be prevented from investing in their companies, or controlling shareholders from selling their company's shares.

Equally important, per se prohibitions of related-party transactions may not accomplish much.[6] They are unlikely to reduce the incentives to engage in one-shot expropriations of firm assets (steal-and-run transactions), these being in any event unlawful under general private or criminal law. And they are arguably unnecessary for more modest forms of abusive self-dealing that may be deterred by civil liability or a credible threat to the wrongdoer's continuing employment.

This is why jurisdictions permit related-party transactions even when conflicts of interests are especially acute because of the dispersion of shareholder ownership or the use of control-enhancing mechanisms, such as pyramids and dual class shares.[7] All jurisdictions, however, subject such transactions to legal constraints.[8]

6.2 Legal Strategies for Related-Party Transactions

Corporate law adopts a wide range of legal strategies to constrain related-party transactions which cover four of the five sets of legal strategies set forth in Chapter 2: affiliation terms (mandatory disclosure and dissolution rights), agent incentives (trusteeship in particular), decision rights (shareholder approval), as well as agent constraints (rules and standards).

6.2.1 The affiliation strategy

6.2.1.1 Mandatory disclosure

Mandatory disclosure that alerts shareholders and the market to related-party transactions is among the most significant controls against expropriation by managers or controlling shareholders. The strategy has obvious advantages. It enlists the capital and labor markets as well as financial analysts and the media in deterring suspect transactions with the threat of lower share prices and the risk of reputational harm. Mandatory disclosure also increases the likelihood of actions against the extraction of private benefits: compliance with the requirement conveys information about suspect transactions to approval and enforcement actors, while culpable failure to disclose is easier to punish given that no proof of harm has to be given.[9] Best of all, mandatory disclosure imposes virtually

---

[6] See Luca Enriques, *The Law on Company Directors' Self-Dealing: A Comparative Analysis*, 2 INTERNATIONAL AND COMPARATIVE CORPORATE LAW JOURNAL 297, 305–6 (2000).

[7] See *supra* 4.1.1.

[8] See also Zohar Goshen, *The Efficiency of Controlling Corporate Self-Dealing: Theory Meets Reality*, 91 CALIFORNIA LAW REVIEW 393 (2003).

[9] See, e.g., Bernard S. Black, *The Core Fiduciary Duties of Outside Directors*, 2001 ASIA BUSINESS LAW REVIEW 3, 10.

no constraints on legitimate self-dealing, compensation contracts, or trading in shares. Mandatory disclosure may, however, lead to some over-enforcement because enforcement actors will be more likely to challenge even legitimate related-party transactions, either because they believe in good faith that the transaction is harmful to the corporation or just to obtain a lucrative settlement, relying on the fact that courts may well err in judging a transaction's legality.[10]

While all of our jurisdictions require public disclosure of at least some self-dealing transactions, of managerial compensation, and of trading in the company's shares, the regulatory intensity varies and has traditionally been, and still is, highest in the U.S.

Let us start with self-dealing. U.S. securities law imposes disclosure duties to all companies, U.S. and (to some extent) foreign, that trade in the U.S. public market.[11] These companies must report annually all transactions that exceed U.S. $120,000 in value and in which directors, executive officers, or a shareholder of more than 5% of any class of their voting securities has a 'material interest'.[12] U.S. Generally Accepted Accounting Principles ('U.S.-GAAP') complement this requirement by imposing annual disclosure of all 'material' transactions between the company and its officers, directors or controlling shareholders.[13]

European Community (EC) requirements, as distinct from the law of member states, used to be much less demanding. In recent years, however, the EC has made significant steps in the direction of greater disclosure of related-party transactions. With adoption of International Financial Reporting Standards (IFRS),[14] European Union (EU) listed companies now have to disclose annually any transaction with directors, senior executives and controlling shareholders.[15] Other EC accounting law provisions complement these disclosure mandates by requiring that member states, at a minimum, oblige companies (other than smaller ones) to reveal all material related-party transactions that have not been concluded under 'normal' market conditions.[16]

---

[10] Mandatory disclosure can also prove costly for other reasons, for example if it makes competitors aware of strategic changes or forces firms to set up information collection systems that are disproportionate to their size. All jurisdictions tackle the issue by limiting the addressees or scope of disclosure requirements. For a discussion, see *infra* 9.2.1.

[11] Registration, and thus disclosure requirements, are applicable to U.S. corporations listed on an exchange as well as to those with assets in excess of $10,000,000 and with 750 or more shareholders (§ 12(g)(1) 1934 Securities Exchange Act); for registration and comparable disclosure requirements applicable to non-U.S. corporations, see Louis Loss and Joel Seligman, FUNDAMENTALS OF SECURITIES REGULATION 209–19 (5th ed., 2004).

[12] SEC Regulation S-K, Item 404.

[13] See Statement of Financial Accounting Standards (SFAS) 57, Related Party Disclosure.

[14] Regulation on the Application of International Accounting Standards [2002] O.J. L. 243/1.

[15] See IAS 24. The Transparency Directive ([2004] OJ L 390/38) provides for half-yearly disclosure of 'major related parties transactions' (Art. 5(4)). For consistency, many listed firms that must prepare consolidated financial statements governed by IFRS also use IFRS to prepare single firm financial statements. See *supra* 5.2.1.2.

[16] Art. 43(1)(7b) Fourth Company Law Directive 78/660/EEC, 1978 O.J. (L. 222) 11 and Art. 34(7b) Seventh Company Law Directive 83/349/EEC, 1983 O.J. (L. 193) 1, as amended by

Member states impose further disclosure requirements. Single firm accounting standards are converging towards IFRS in many member states.[17] In addition, UK listed companies must circulate a form (circular) prior to entering into material related-party transactions.[18] Italy similarly requires public firms to immediately disclose such transactions.[19] In France, statutory auditors of *sociétés anonymes* must provide a specific report on related-party transactions entered into in the previous financial year that were neither 'ordinary' nor entered into at market conditions ('non-routine transactions').[20] Further, shareholders can obtain a list of related-party transactions that are not included in the report because they are routine.[21]

By contrast, Germany has remained lenient towards controlling shareholders. While the Corporate Governance Code recommends that listed companies inform the annual meeting about any conflict of interests that arose within the supervisory board,[22] corporate law does not require an *Aktiengesellschaft* (*AG*) or a *Gesellschaft mit beschränkter Haftung* (*GmbH*) to disclose transactions with a controlling shareholder.[23] In addition, while parent companies must disclose the share of their profits and losses that is attributable to their subsidiaries taken as a whole,[24] *Konzernrecht* limits the information rights of minority shareholders in these subsidiaries to a summary of the legally required annual report on intra-group transactions (*Abhängigkeitsbericht*).[25] However, shareholders of German companies have a broad-sweeping right to ask questions, either at any time (for GmbHs) or at general meetings (AGs), which may force managers to provide detailed information on the relationships between the company and its parent, subsidiary, or controlling shareholder.[26]

Directive 2006/46/EC, 2006 O.J. (L 224) 1. Larger companies are those that satisfy at least two of the following criteria: (1) a balance-sheet total of more than €17.5 million, (2) an annual net turnover of more than € 35 million, or (3) 250 or more employees. See Art. 27 Fourth Company Law Directive, as amended. This provision might, however, be self-defeating, because admitting that a transaction has not been concluded under 'normal' market conditions could have adverse tax consequences—especially in jurisdictions where there is no distinction between corporate and tax accounting.

[17] See European Commission, Report on the operation of IAS Regulation 1606/2002 COM(2008) 215 final (2008), available at http://www.ec.europa.eu.

[18] See Listing Rules, Section 11.1.7 (non-routine transactions by listed firms); §§ 188–226 Companies Act 2006 (various property, credit, and compensation transactions).

[19] See Art. 71–2 Commissione Nazionale per le Societa e la Borsa (Consob) Regulation on Issuers.

[20] Art. L. 225–40 Code de commerce.   [21] Art. L. 225–115 Code de commerce.

[22] See Section 5.5.3 Corporate Governance Code.

[23] The balance sheet of a closely held GmbH must disclose aggregate claims and liabilities vis-à-vis owners (§ 42(3) Gesetz betreffend die Gesellschaften mit beschränkter Haftung (GmbHG)), but this provides no information about self-dealing transactions initiated and completed within the accounting year. The fact that neither the Corporate Governance Code nor corporate law recommend or require the disclosure of transactions with controlling shareholders most probably reflects their political influence. See *infra* 6.3.

[24] § 307(2) Handelsgesetzbuch (HGB).

[25] § 312(1) Aktiengesetz (AktG). See also *supra* 5.2.1.3.

[26] See § 131(1) AktG; § 51a GmbHG. There are various restrictions to the right to ask questions, especially when transactions are deemed confidential or not significant. See Gerald Spindler,

Finally, in Japan, all companies are required to disclose details of their transactions with directors, officers, or third parties acting on their behest.[27] Japanese accounting regulations complement these disclosure mandates by requiring companies to list material transactions with controlling shareholders.[28]

Disclosure of managerial compensation is also an area in which, with the exception of Japan, jurisdictions have broadly converged in requiring disclosure of individual managers' compensation. In the U.S., companies traded on a public market must disclose all compensation paid to the CEO, the CFO and the three most highly compensated other executive officers.[29] European Community rules are more lenient, because IFRS impose annual disclosure of *aggregate* compensation to directors and key managers of listed companies.[30] Individual member states, however, go beyond EC requirements. In accord with European Commission recommendations, all major member states mandate that listed companies disclose individual directors' compensation,[31] with continental European jurisdictions lagging behind the U.S. and the UK in terms of required details. On the other hand, only Japan limits disclosure to aggregate director compensation (distinguishing between inside and outside directors), not the terms of individual compensation packages.[32]

Finally, convergence can also be observed in the area of disclosure of trading in the company's shares, especially by managers and directors. The U.S. and Japan require officers, directors, and beneficial owners of more than 10% of any class of equity security of a listed company to disclose transactions in the company's shares (and holdings too in the case of the U.S.).[33] Similarly, EU listed companies' directors and senior executives are required to disclose their transactions

in Karsten Schmid and Marcus Lutter (eds.), Aktiengesetz Kommentar, No. 37 § 131 (2008); Marcus Lutter and Peter Hommelhoff, No. 13–20 §50a, in GmbH-Gesetz Kommentar, Walter Bayer, Peter Hommelhoff, Detlef Kleindick, and Marcus Lutter (eds.), (16th ed., 2004). Shareholders' right to ask question is reported to be actively enforced, but data on the importance of related-party litigation seems unavailable.

[27] Art. 128 Ministry of Justice (MOJ) Companies Act Implementation Regulation (for all joint-stock companies); Accounting Standards Board of Japan (ASBJ), Disclosure of Related Party Transactions (17 October 2006) (applicable to reporting companies under the Financial Instruments and Exchange Act—FIEA).

[28] See Art. 128 MOJ Companies Act Implementation Regulation (for all joint-stock companies). Regarding voluntary compliance with U.S. GAAP by closely held corporations, see *supra* 5.2.1.1.

[29] SEC Regulation S-K, Item 402.

[30] See IAS 24.

[31] See, for the EC, Commission Recommendation fostering an appropriate regime for the remuneration of directors of listed companies 2004 O.J. (L 385) 55; for France, Art. L. 225–102–1 Code de commerce (*sociétés anonymes* (SA)); for Germany, *Vorstandsvergütungs-Offenlegungsgesetz* (listed companies); for Italy, Art. 78 Consob Regulation on Issuers (listed companies); for the UK, ss 420–1 Companies Act 2006 (listed companies).

[32] Art. 121(iv)(v) and Art. 124(v)(vi) MOJ Companies Act Implementation Regulation; see also Financial Services Agency Regulation on Disclosure of Corporate Affairs, as amended in March 2003 (similar requirement for reporting companies).

[33] § 16(a) 1934 Securities Exchange Act. Art. 163 FIEA (Japan).

in company shares, whereas their shareholders must disclose such transactions when they cross thresholds ranging from 5% to 75% of voting rights.[34] Italy is the only EU jurisdiction in our sample to have extended the duty to report all transactions in company shares to controlling shareholders and beneficial owners of more than 10% of the shares.[35]

There has thus been substantial convergence in the treatment of related-party transactions in *listed* companies and that trend is likely to continue in coming years. Many jurisdictions are subjecting their major firms to IFRS and regulators everywhere are tightening their supervision of the reporting of insider trades. Even more importantly, auditors around the world are tightening their scrutiny of transactions that may reflect asset diversion or profit manipulation.

To begin with, the International Standards on Auditing, a set of non-binding principles on how to conduct audits issued by the International Federation of Accountants, require auditors to pay special attention to related-party transactions.[36] In addition, many jurisdictions have adopted statutory provisions that strengthen this gatekeeper mandate. Within Europe, Italy requires boards of auditors of listed companies to monitor self-dealing transactions.[37] In Germany, auditors of *AG*s must verify the management board's annual report on intra-group transactions.[38] France, as indicated above, goes a step further by requiring auditors of *SA*s to provide shareholders with a special report on all non-routine self-dealing transactions.[39] Similar requirements have been adopted outside Europe as well. Japan obliges auditors to report to shareholders whether the related-party transaction information they get is true.[40] In the U.S., the Private Securities Litigation Reform Act of 1995 contains a provision on self-dealing, according to which auditors must ensure that material transactions are disclosed in companies' financial documents.[41] However, it remains to be seen whether this is a permanent development, especially in jurisdictions where audit fees or auditor liability risks are comparatively low and in firms that have controlling shareholders.[42] We will return to this issue in Chapter 9.

---

[34] For managers, see Art. 6(4) Market Abuse Directive 2003/6/EC, 2003 O.J. (L 96) 116, as implemented by Directive 2004/72/EC, 2004 O.J. (L 162) 70. For shareholders, see Art. 9 Transparency Directive (the acquisition and disposal of voting rights must be disclosed at the 5%, 10%, 20%, 25%, 30% or 1/3, 50% and 2/3 or 75% thresholds).

[35] See Art. 114(7) Consolidated Act on Financial Intermediation.

[36] See International Standard on Auditing 550 (under review as of writing).

[37] Art. 149–50 Consolidated Act on Financial Intermediation.

[38] § 313 Aktiengesetz; see also *supra* 5.2.1.3.

[39] See *supra* note 20 and accompanying text.   [40] Art. 193–2(1) FIEA.

[41] See Section 10A Securities Exchange Act (the audit must in fact include 'procedures designed to identify related party transactions that are material to the financial statements or otherwise require disclosure therein').

[42] See Yasuyuki Fuchita, *Financial Gatekeepers in Japan*, in Financial Gatekeepers, Can they Protect Investors? 13, 23–9 Yasuyuki Fuchita and Robert E. Litan (eds.) (2006) (low auditor fees are a major quality constraint); European Commission, Recommendation concerning the limitation of the civil liability of statutory auditors and audit firms, 2008 O.J. (L 162) 39; John C. Coffee Jr., Gatekeepers. The Professions and Corporate Governance 89–93

When it comes to *ex post* enforcement, the machinery is still much more effective in the U.S. than elsewhere. A failure to disclose related-party transactions, if detected, can give rise to SEC enforcement actions, criminal prosecution and, inevitably, a private securities fraud class action on behalf of shareholders. The case of Conrad Black, the dominant shareholder in newspaper company Hollinger International, is illustrative. In December 2007, Black was sentenced to 6 1/2 years in prison for fraud and obstruction of justice in connection with the company's failure to disclose self-dealing transactions with entities related to Black and with Black himself, by which tens of millions of dollars were diverted from Hollinger International.[43]

Outside the U.S., the use of securities fraud provisions to attack related-party transactions has thus far been much less common, although it might become more so in the future with the increased legislative focus on their disclosure, the strengthening of supervisory authorities, and an institutional environment more favorable to private enforcement.[44] In the meantime, listed companies can opt into the more severe U.S. disclosure rules and enforcement apparatus by cross-listing their shares in a U.S. stock market, thus bonding to more stringent securities laws and signaling that insiders will not abuse their control powers.[45]

The law on the books is less comparable for *non-listed* companies, with more lenient requirements in the U.S. than elsewhere. In practice, however, convergence may be much greater. While U.S. law does not impose mandatory disclosure requirements on non-public companies, they tend to reveal related-party transactions through voluntary compliance with U.S. GAAP.[46] In Europe and Japan, on the other hand, it is difficult to tell how strictly larger non-listed firms comply with the requirement to disclose material self-dealing transactions and unclear whether smaller firms voluntarily reveal such information.[47]

(2006) (gatekeepers are better placed to police managerial misbehavior in the form of earnings management than controlling shareholders' extraction of private benefits).

[43] See *U.S. v. Conrad M. Black*, 2007 U.S. District Court, LEXIS 81777; Stephanie Kirchgaessner and Hal Weitzman, *Black Sentenced to Six and a Half Years*, FINANCIAL TIMES, 11 December 2007, at 1; *In re Hollinger International, Inc. Securities Litigation*, 2006 U.S. Dist. LEXIS 47173 (N. D. Ill.).

[44] See also *infra* 6.2.5.4.

[45] See John C. Coffee, Jr., *Law and the Market: The Impact of Enforcement* 156 UNIVERSITY OF PENNSYLVANIA LAW REVIEW 229 (2007) (bonding hypothesis for cross-listings); Michal Barzuza, *Lemon Signaling in Cross-Listing*, Working Paper (2007), available at http://www.ssrn.com (signaling hypothesis for cross-listings); Edward Rock, *Securities Regulation as Lobster Trap: A Credible Commitment Theory of Mandatory Disclosure*, 23 CARDOZO L. REV. 675 (2002) (bonding hypothesis for cross-listing). The bonding hypothesis has been subject to criticism: see Jordan Siegel, *Can Foreign Firms Bond Themselves Effectively by Renting U.S. Securities Laws?*, 75 JOURNAL OF FINANCIAL ECONOMICS 319 (2005); Amir N. Licht, *Cross-Listing and Corporate Governance: Bonding or Avoiding*, 4 CHICAGO JOURNAL OF INTERNATIONAL LAW 141 (2003).

[46] See AMERICAN INSTITUTE OF CERTIFIED PUBLIC ACCOUNTANTS, PRIVATE COMPANY FINANCIAL REPORTING TASK FORCE REPORT 8 (2005) (many private companies prepare their financial statements in accordance with U.S. GAAP).

[47] See *supra* 5.2.1.1.

As an aid to private enforcement against abusive related-party transactions, targeted disclosure is sometimes available to shareholders suspicious of a given transaction. European jurisdictions allow minority shareholders to file a request for the designation of a business expert or special auditor to investigate specific transactions, and usually self-dealing ones. These court-appointed experts are a means for shareholders to obtain the data needed to bring liability suits or otherwise challenge unfair self-dealing. This can prove especially important in the absence of U.S.-style discovery mechanisms, which makes it harder for plaintiffs to obtain evidence on insiders' wrongdoings. But while this information gathering mechanism is of increasing importance in France and Germany, it seems less effective elsewhere.[48] On the other hand, U.S. law is not only favorable to plaintiffs with its discovery rules, but it also grants shareholders the right to inspect a company's books and records, provided they prove 'a proper purpose'.[49]

6.2.1.2 Dissolution and exit rights

Voting power and influence over management make it possible for those in control to appropriate corporate profits, e.g. in the form of salaries to the members of the controlling family. When such practices take the form of egregious abuse and occur systematically, most of our major jurisdictions give the minority a right to force a corporate dissolution.[50] This exit strategy, however, is limited to *closely held* companies and, even in that context, actual dissolution is rare.[51] Courts tend

---

[48] See, for France Maurice Cozian, Alain Viandier, and Florence Deboissy, Droit des Sociétés No. 399 (21st ed., 2008) (the number of petitions to designate an *expert de gestion* is on the increase); for Germany, Spindler, note 25, No. 1 § 142 (2008) (same). Compare for the UK, Paul L. Davies, Gower and Davies, Principles of Modern Corporate Law 635 (8th ed., 2008); for Italy, Luca Enriques, *Scelte Pubbliche e Interessi Particolari nella Riforma del Diritto Societario*, 2005 Mercato Concorrenza Regole 145, 170 (the 2003 corporate law reform emasculated a similar protection tool).

[49] Delaware GCL §220; for more details, see Willliam T. Allen, Reinier Kraakman, and Guhan Subramanian, Commentaries and Cases on the Law of Business Organization 193 (2nd ed., 2007).

[50] For France, Art. 1844-7 Code Civil; for Germany, §61 GmbH-Gesetz (shareholders with 10% of the shares can seek dissolution); for Japan, see Art. 833 Companies Act (10% shareholder can seek dissolution before the court); for the UK, s 122(1)(g) Insolvency Act 1986; for the U.S., § 14.30(2) RMBCA; § 40 Model Statutory Close Corporation Supplement. No such right exists under Italian law.

[51] See, for France, Maurice Cozian, Alain Viandier, and Florence Deboissy, Droit des Sociétés, No. 447–51 (21st ed., 2008) (courts do not grant dissolution lightly); for Germany, Marcus Lutter and Detlef Kleindiek, No. 8 §61, in Bayer et al., *supra* note 26 (dissolution will only be granted in exceptional circumstances); for the UK, Davies, *supra* note 48, at 704–7 (the unfair prejudice remedy has crowded out winding-up petitions); for the U.S., compare Frank H. Easterbrook and Daniel R. Fischel, The Economic Structure of Corporate Law 239 (1991) (courts grant dissolution sparingly) with Edward B. Rock and Michael L. Wachter, *Waiting for the Omelet to Set, Match-Specific Assets and Minority Oppression*, 23 Journal of Corporate Law 913, 923 (1999) (courts have become more willing to order dissolution).

to protect the going-concern value of companies by encouraging or requiring their controllers to buy out minority shareholders.

In practice, then, minority shareholders in closely held corporations typically get a kind of put option, conditional upon serious oppression: they can exercise a contractual or equitable right to sell their shares to the controller. Exercise of this right normally involves litigation to determine the share price for the buy-out. Because litigation involving valuation issues is costly, the dissolution right is mainly a negotiating tool in situations of minority 'oppression', thus discouraging extreme forms of abuse *ex ante*.

6.2.2 Agent incentives strategies

Asset diversion is constrained everywhere through reward strategies. Minority shareholders are generally protected against discriminatory cash dividends through the pro rata rule, as we have seen in Chapter 4.[52] In some European countries, minority shareholders are also indirectly protected by creditor-oriented provisions on concealed distributions. In Germany and the UK, 'undervalue transactions' between the corporation and its controlling shareholder can be recharacterized by courts as a 'disguised' and, therefore, unlawful distribution.[53] In most jurisdictions, however, trusteeship strategies play a more central role than reward strategies. In fact, all jurisdictions traditionally enlist the board to review at least some conflicted transactions.

6.2.2.1 The board as a trustee

Requiring or encouraging disinterested director approval of conflicted transactions has several virtues: first, compliance is (relatively) cheap; second, fair, value-increasing transactions will likely be approved and thereby insulated from outside attack;[54] third, disinterested directors may well raise questions at least about the most suspicious related-party transactions.

The principal costs of a board approval requirement are just the inverse of its virtues. Independent directors may not be the disinterested trustees that the law contemplates. For the most part, they are selected with the (interested) consent of top executive officers, controlling shareholders, or both. If they are unlikely to intervene to derail fair transactions, they may also be unlikely or unable to object to unfair ones, especially at the margins. Unfair, value-decreasing related-party transactions may be erroneously approved: rampant self-dealing approved

---

[52] See *supra* 4.1.3.2.

[53] See Holger Fleischer, *Disguised Distributions and Capital Maintenance in European Company Law*, in Marcus Lutter (ed.), Legal Capital in Europe 94 (2006).

[54] See Robert B. Thompson and Randall S. Thomas, *The Public and Private Faces of Derivative Law Suits*, 57 Vanderbilt Law Review 1747, 1787 (2004).

by disinterested directors appears to have been an important contributor to the Enron debacle.[55]

The advantages of board approval are deemed to exceed its costs. Jurisdictions generally require the board to be informed about transactions with major insiders, in particular directors[56]—which amounts to implicitly subjecting them to a weak form of board authorization or ratification. In addition, many jurisdictions require or strongly encourage *explicit* board approval of at least some related-party transactions.[57]

France (for *SAs*), Germany (for *AGs*), Italy (for *società per azioni*) and Japan (for all companies) mandate disinterested board approval of managerial self-dealing, while the UK in effect imposes it by requiring boards to send a form (circular) to shareholders. However, this requirement has a more limited scope in Italy, Germany, and the UK. Italian law mandates board approval merely for self-dealing transactions in which executive directors otherwise having the authority to decide on them are self-interested.[58] German requirements mainly apply to lending to, and significant services provided by, supervisory board members.[59] (German law also imposes company representation by a member of the supervisory board for transactions with members of the management board.)[60] Under UK law, listed companies' boards *de facto* approve all non-routine transactions with directors, but for other companies such approval is limited to some of them, in particular substantial property transactions and credit transactions.[61] By contrast, French and Japanese laws mandate disinterested board authorization for all non-routine transactions between a company and its directors or general managers.[62]

---

[55] See William C. Powers, Raymond S. Trough, and Herbert S. Winokur, *Report of Investigation by the Special Investigative Committee of the Board of Directors of Enron Corp* (1 February 2002).

[56] See, for Germany, Corporate Governance Code §4.3.4 (2006); for Italy, Art. 2391 Civil Code; for the UK, s 177 Companies Act 2006.

[57] To reinforce its effectiveness, board approval is generally considered invalid if marred by materially incomplete disclosure, bad faith, waste of assets or decisive voting by a conflicted director.

[58] Article 2391, Civil Code (self-interest can also be indirect, e.g. when the controlling shareholder has an interest and the director has a sufficiently strong link with her, such as an employment relationship with the parent company).

[59] §114 Aktiengesetz (transactions regarding the provision of significant services or work by supervisory board members must be approved by the board); and §89 and §115 AktG (requiring supervisory board approval for loans to management and supervisory board members).

[60] See §112 AktG. Note that Switzerland, which also requires that a disinterested director represent the company when it transacts with a board member, does not impose board approval: see Peter Böckli, SCHWEIZER AKTIENRECHT 1628–9 (3rd ed., 2004) and *Erbengemeinschaft J. M. v. K. AG*, AMTLICHE SAMMLUNG 127 III 332, 334–5 (Federal Tribunal, 2001).

[61] See ss 188–226 Companies Act 2006 (also covering payments for loss of office and long term service contracts). Boards *de facto* approve all such transactions, because Listing Rules and/or the Companies Act require that they be approved by shareholders (see *infra* 6.2.3), which will usually be the case upon the board's proposal.

[62] For France, see Art. L. 225–38 Code de commerce (also applicable to third parties acting for directors or general managers) and Art. L. 225–39 (exempting routine transactions); for Japan, see Art. 356(1)(ii)(iii) Companies Act (all transactions, with no exemption).

France and the UK subject transactions between, respectively, a *SA* or a listed company, and a major shareholder to the same approval requirement as managerial self-dealing.[63] Japanese courts, for their part, require board approval for transactions between companies with interlocking directors.[64]

Although U.S. jurisdictions stop short of mandating board approval of self-dealing, they strongly encourage it. State law incentivizes interested managers to seek board approval by usually according transactions that are authorized (or ratified) by the board *business judgment* protection.[65] Board approval also plays a crucial role for transactions with controlling shareholders, which are always subject to the stringent 'entire fairness' standard. As an incentive for independent director approval, Delaware law shifts the burden of proof to the party challenging a transaction with a controlling shareholder when the board vests the task of negotiating the transaction in a committee of substantively independent directors and gives them the necessary resources (like access to independent legal and financial advice) to accomplish its task.[66] But while this may be *necessary* to pass the 'entire fairness' test applied by Delaware courts,[67] it may not be *sufficient*, as Delaware courts tend to look at a wider range of facts.[68]

6.2.2.2 Increasing reliance upon disinterested board approval

Overall, the significant development in past years has been convergence in jurisdictions' reliance on board approval, at least when it comes to listed companies. Not only is internal disclosure of managerial self-dealing the norm everywhere, but jurisdictions that traditionally did not mandate board approval have largely achieved that result through corporate governance codes. Hence, the German Corporate Governance Code recommends board approval for important transactions with members of the management board or persons they are close to.[69] In Italy, the Corporate Governance Code recommends that companies identify

---

[63] For France, see Art. L. 225–38 Code de commerce (the provision more precisely requires board approval for transactions involving a shareholder with more than 10% of the voting rights and, if such shareholder is a company, the entity controlling it). However, as a matter of practice, transactions between companies of the same group are often deemed to be routine ones. See Dominique Schmidt, Les conflits d'intérêts dans la société anonyme 120 (2nd ed., 2004). For the UK, see *infra*, 6.2.3.

[64] Case law interpreting Art. 356(1)(ii)(iii) Companies Act.

[65] See § 8.31 Model Business Corporation Act; *Flieger* v. *Lawrence,* 361 A.2d 218 (Delaware Supreme Court 1976); *Kahn* v. *Lynch Communications Systems, Incorporated,* 638 A.2d 1110 (Delaware Supreme Court 1994).

[66] See Allen et al., *supra* note 49, at 323; *Kahn v. Lynch Communications Systems, Inc.,* 638 Atlantic Reporter, Second Series (A.2d) 1110 (Delaware Supreme Court 1994); *Weinberger v. UOP, Inc.,* 457 Atlantic Reporter, Second Series (A.2d) 701 (Delaware Supreme Court 1983).

[67] See *infra* 6.2.5.2.

[68] On the intricacies of Delaware case law on procedural fairness in parent-subsidiary transactions, see William J. Carney and George B. Shepherd, *The Mystery of Delaware Law's Continuing Success,* 2009 University of Illinois Law Review 1.

[69] Corporate Governance Code §4.3.4 (2006).

classes of significant transactions, including related-party ones, to be examined and approved by the board.[70]

Further, regardless of the treatment of traditional managerial self-dealing, all major jurisdictions nowadays require boards of listed companies to approve the compensation of top executive officers.[71] As stock options have become more common, regulatory and investor pressure has prompted listed companies to adopt implementation measures, such as assigning compensation decisions to specialized committees on the board staffed entirely by independent directors—a trend that has been reinforced by post-Enron reforms.[72] Judges tend to defer to boards' decision-making on compensation matters even more than for other related-party transactions: courts everywhere review it under the board-friendly business judgment doctrine. Board approval of compensation is least likely to be questioned in the U.S.[73] But even in Germany, where there is evidence of a more aggressive judicial approach towards compensation, courts are unlikely to question board approval unless there is gross inadequacy between compensation levels and job characteristics.[74]

Finally, jurisdictions increasingly encourage their managers to obtain board approval prior to the exploitation of information that could be of use to their corporation. In the U.S., directors who exploit a 'corporate opportunity' to their personal advantage are deemed to have acted fairly only if they properly disclosed the business prospect to disinterested directors and took it with their approval.[75] The UK and Japan currently follow a similar approach: directors may appropriate business opportunities within the company's line of business as long as they receive the disinterested directors' informed consent.[76] Virtually

---

[70] Corporate Governance Code § 1.C.1(f) (2006). As of 2007, 82% of the largest listed companies in Italy declared that their boards approve related-party transactions. See ASSONIME AND EMITTENTI TITOLI, *An Analysis of the Compliance with the Italian Corporate Governance Code* 20 (2008).

[71] See, for the U.S., §8.11 Model Business Corporation Act; for France, Art. L 225–45 and L. 225–46 Code de commerce; for Germany, §87 AktG; for Italy, Art. 2389(3) Civil Code; for Japan, Art. 404(3) Companies Act (in 'committee' companies, the compensation committee decides the individual amount of compensation for each director and officer). In the UK, board approval is a default rule (see § 84 Table A, Companies Regulations 1985, as amended), but it is unusual for firms to opt out of it, both for historical reasons (the alternative used to be shareholder approval) and, for listed firms, because the Combined Code recommends approval by a remuneration committee on a comply or explain basis (B.2.2).

[72] For the U.S., see Larry E. Ribstein, *Market vs. Regulatory Responses to Corporate Fraud: A Critique of the Sarbanes-Oxley Act of 2002*, 28 JOURNAL OF CORPORATION LAW 1, 12 (2002); for the EU, see Guido Ferrarini and Niamh Moloney, *Executive Remuneration and Corporate Governance in the EU: Convergence, Divergence and Reform Perspectives*, 1 EUROPEAN COMPANY AND FINANCIAL LAW REVIEW 251 (2004).

[73] See also *supra* 3.5 for an account of the deployment of the business judgment rule in the *Disney* case. One of the few cases where compensation has been judged unreasonable is *Rogers v. Hill*, 289 U.S. 582 (1933).

[74] § 87 AktG (supervisory board approval for compensation of executives that are members of the *Vorstand*). See also *supra* 3.5 for an account of the (quite unusual) *Mannesmann* case.

[75] See e.g. Allen et al., *supra* note 49, at 352.

[76] For the UK, see s 175 Companies Act 2006; for Japan, see Art. 356(1)(i) Companies Act.

the same doctrine has also gained acceptance in Germany (under the rubric of the *Geschäftschancen* doctrine), in Italy, and even in France (as a possible *abus de biens/pouvoirs sociaux* or violation of the duty of loyalty).[77]

Differences persist for transactions with controlling shareholders. Board approval is crucial in France and especially in the U.S. (where lack of approval by independent directors means the certainty of a shareholder suit and a high risk of a costly settlement for the controlling shareholder). By contrast, board approval is mainly limited to intra-group transactions in Germany and Japan, while the UK and Italy only require that transactions with a controlling shareholder be disclosed to the board.[78]

To sum up, the broad reliance upon board approval does not mean that jurisdictions have unlimited faith in the carefulness and independence of the board. There is, however, a discrepancy between laws 'on the books' and the richness of case law. In Japan, where director's breach of duty is even presumed,[79] and in continental European countries (with the exception of Germany) statutes are more stringent, but cases are sparse and the liability risk low. In the U.S., on the other hand, statutory intervention is less visible, but case law richer and the liability risk correspondingly higher. That being said, the financial consequences of inadequate board approval are generally limited and confined to the interested related party.[80]

6.2.3 Shareholder voting: the decision rights strategy

As an alternative or complement to disinterested board approval of related-party transactions, jurisdictions may require or encourage shareholder approval. Shareholders, after all, are the parties who lose from managerial or controlling shareholder opportunism. Outside directors are *disinterested*, while shareholders are affirmatively *interested* in preserving corporate value. It might therefore appear that the shareholders meeting should screen conflicted transactions. But, of course, this reasoning runs counter to the logic of the corporate form, which fosters delegation of decision-making to the board in order to avoid the

---

[77] See, for Germany, Thomas E. Abeltshauser, LEITUNGSHAFTUNG IM KAPITALGESELL-SCHAFTSRECHT 373 (1998); for Italy, Art. 2391(5) Civil Code; for France, see Art. L. 225–251 and Art. L. 242–6 Code de commerce, Cozian et al., *supra* note 51, No. 617 (causing the loss of a profit opportunity is potentially abusive) and Laurent Godon, *Jurisprudence Commentée*, 120 REVUE DES SOCIÉTÉS 702 (2002).

[78] For the UK, see s 177 UK Companies Act 2006 (albeit some transactions are subject to shareholder approval: see *infra* 6.2.3); for Italy, see also *supra* notes 58 and 70.

[79] See Art. 423(3) Companies Act.

[80] See Marcus Lutter, *Limited Liability Companies and Private Companies*, in XII INTERNATIONAL ENCYCLOPEDIA OF COMPARATIVE LAW 2–267, 2–273 (1997). In our jurisdictions, the remedy for a conflicted transaction entered into without effective approval is either to void the transaction or to compensate the company for any resulting harm. Jurisdictions diverge in the extent to which they encourage one or another of these remedies.

costs and the collective action problems associated with direct governance by shareholders.

No jurisdiction mandates across-the-board shareholder approval for related-party transactions, not even with controlling shareholders. This is because doing so might be excessively cumbersome (especially for companies that are integrated into groups, where such transactions can be very frequent) and could also raise conflicted voting issues.[81] In addition, most of our sample jurisdictions are reluctant to mandate minority shareholder approval, perhaps out of concern for the control rights of shareholder majorities. Indeed, 'majority of the minority' voting is a well-established institution in the U.S. and UK,[82] two jurisdictions in which large companies typically lack a controlling shareholder, but is much less developed in continental Europe, where controlling shareholders have significant voting (and lobbying) power.

There is greater convergence among our jurisdictions in the selected related-party transactions that require shareholder approval.[83] Nowadays, all of our jurisdictions require listed firms to submit some forms of director and senior officer compensation to shareholder approval.[84] This is a direct consequence of considerable increases in executive remuneration levels around the world and the controversies they generated.[85] U.S. stock exchanges require a shareholder vote on all equity compensation plans whereas some states mandate shareholder approval of stock option plans.[86] In the EU, where the European Commission has recommended that member states adopt legislation aimed at giving shareholders in listed companies a say regarding director and senior officer remuneration, most member states have adopted rules on prior shareholder approval of share-based incentive schemes (Germany, Italy, the Netherlands, and the UK being the most demanding by mandating such a vote without limitations).[87] While shareholders

---

[81] See *supra* 4.1.2 and *infra* 7.4.2.   [82] See *infra* note 93 and accompanying text.

[83] See also Simon Djankov, Rafael La Porta, Florencio Lopez-De-Silanes, and Andrei Shleifer, *The Law and Economics of Self-Dealing*, 88 JOURNAL OF FINANCIAL ECONOMICS 430 (2008) (advocating approval by disinterested shareholders of large related-party transactions coupled with full disclosure as a key corporate governance reform).

[84] For Germany, see § 113 AktG (overall compensation of members of the management board); for France, Art. L 225–45 Code de commerce (overall compensation of directors); for Italy, Art. 2389 (same) and Art. 114–2 Consolidated Act on Financial Intermediation (stock-based compensation for directors and employees); for Japan, see Art. 361(1) Companies Act (overall compensation of directors and stock option plans).

[85] See *supra* 3.5. A study reports that in the U.S. shareholder voting on compensation plans has evolved since the 1990s, with shareholders becoming increasingly aggressive over compensation plans that they consider harmful. See Angela Morgan, Annette Poulsen, and Jack Wolf, *The Evolution of Shareholder Voting for Executive Compensation Schemes*, 12 JOURNAL OF CORPORATE FINANCE 715 (2006).

[86] See § 303A.08 New York Stock Exchange Listing Rules; Jeffrey N. Gordon, *Executive Compensation: If There's a Problem, What's the Remedy? The Case for 'Compensation Discussion and Analysis'*, 30 JOURNAL OF CORPORATION LAW 675, 699 (2005).

[87] See Commission Recommendation on fostering an appropriate regime for the remuneration of directors of listed companies [2004] O.J. L 385/55; Commission Staff Working Document,

generally vote on the remuneration policy for supervisory board members, member states have been much less keen to give shareholders a specific say about the remuneration criteria for, or individual compensation of, one-tier board members or senior executives.[88]

Beyond that, France and the UK appear to be most inclined to give shareholders a say on related-party transactions. French statutory law requires shareholder ratification of all non-routine self-dealing transactions entered into during the prior financial year.[89] The UK mandates *ex ante* shareholder approval for non-routine transactions with directors and large shareholders of listed companies.[90] For other companies, the Companies Act requires shareholder approval of some transactions with directors, in particular substantial property transactions and credit transactions.[91]

While the French approach seems very encompassing, in practice, it may not have a substantially larger scope than UK law. As in the UK for listed companies, it leaves corporate decision-makers with some discretion in deciding whether a transaction is non-routine and, thus, needs to be approved by shareholders.[92] In contrast with France, further, the UK shares with the U.S. a judicial tradition of accepting minority shareholder approval as the most reliable method of screening conflicted transactions with controlling shareholders.[93]

Other jurisdictions are less insistent on shareholder approval. German law requires minority approval in non-publicly-traded corporations, but only when the articles of association or the firm's management submit a related-party transaction to shareholder vote.[94] Italy, for its part, requires shareholder approval when a director of a publicly-traded corporation wants to sit on the board of a competing corporation.[95]

It is worth noting (and somewhat surprising) that the timing of shareholder consent is not an important consideration anywhere. Shareholder approval

Report on the application of the Commission Recommendation on directors' remuneration, Brussels, SEC (2007) 1022.

[88] See *id.*, Table 2. The most demanding jurisdiction is France, where shareholders of listed companies ratify each director's total compensation by voting on the annual report (Art. L. 225–102–1 Code de commerce) and vote on individual golden parachutes and some retirement benefits for the chairman of the board and general managers (Art. L. 225–42–1); the UK provides for a shareholders advisory vote on the directors' remuneration report (s 439 Companies Act 2006), basically a confidence vote on the work of the compensation committee.

[89] Art. L. 223–19 (SARL) L. 225–40 and 225–88 (SA) Code de commerce. Conflicted shareholders or managers are forbidden from voting their shares to approve their own transactions—the outcome being nullified if they are found to have voted.

[90] See Davies, *supra* note 48, 549–50.   [91] See *supra* note 61.

[92] See Schmidt, *supra* note 64, at 117–21 (criticizing the French regime because it grants insiders too much discretion).

[93] On Delaware law see e.g. Leo E. Strine, Jr., *The Delaware Way: How We Do Corporate Law and Some of the New Challenges We (and Europe) Face*, 30 Delaware Journal of Corporate Law 673, 678 (2005).

[94] See § 47 GmbHG; Lutter and Hommelhoff, No. 22–3 § 47, in Bayer et al., *supra* note 26 (requirement also applicable to groups of companies).

[95] Art. 2390 Civil Code.

appears to have the same legal effect, whether it precedes or follows a conflicted transaction, although intuitively *ex ante* approval might seem to be more effective in screening self-dealing transactions. Indeed, shareholder ratification shifts the burden of proof in U.S. courts not only after self-dealing occurs, but also after it is discovered and challenged in court. Even France, a jurisdiction that particularly values shareholder consent, allows *ex post* validation of conflicted transactions that required *ex ante* board authorization by law but were never actually submitted to the board.[96] The UK goes further still by permitting post-transaction ratification by shareholders to protect directors against most liability claims and, if ratification takes place 'within a reasonable period', to validate their substantial property transactions and loans.[97]

6.2.4 Prohibiting conflicted transactions: the rules strategy

Sweeping prohibitions of related-party transactions were once common in company law.[98] Today they apply only to a handful of transactions, namely credit transactions, third party employment contracts and some forms of trading by insiders.[99]

Only France and the U.S. currently prohibit loans between a company and one of its directors. The French prohibition can be seen as a historical curiosity—Italy and the UK abolished similar rules in recent years.[100] By contrast, the U.S. prohibition is a newcomer. In the 1990s and early 2000s, company loans were used by some managers to leverage their ownership of company shares, thus increasing their incentives to engage in questionable practices aimed at bolstering the share price. Further, they were often used as 'stealth compensation', as managers often failed to repay the loans and companies forgave them.[101] As a response to Enron and other scandals, Congress prohibited public companies from making personal loans to executives.[102] While the U.S. reaction is understandable, it remains unclear why loans to managers should be more suspect than other conflicted contracts (for example, consulting contracts). At best, the logic must be that these

---

[96] See Art. L. 225–42 Code de commerce. Germany adopts a similar approach: see Abeltshauser, *supra* note 77, 359.

[97] See Davies, *supra* note 48, 546, 581–4; ss 196 and 214 Companies Act 2006.

[98] See Bernhard Grossfeld, *Management and Control of Marketable Share Companies,* in XIII INTERNATIONAL ENCYCLOPEDIA OF COMPARATIVE LAW 4–302 (1971); Harold Marsh, *Are Directors Trustees? Conflict of Interest and Corporate Morality,* 22 BUSINESS LAWYER 35 (1966). But see Norwood P. Beveridge, *The Corporate Director's Fiduciary Duty of Loyalty: Understanding the Self-Interested Director Transaction,* 45 DEPAUL LAW REVIEW 729 (1996) (arguing that U.S. jurisdictions never prohibited self-dealing per se).

[99] Of course, specific rules on conflicted transactions, usually not banning them outright, exist for certain industries, such as banking, investment services, and insurance.

[100] See Art. L. 223–21 (SARL) and Art. L. 225–43 (SA) Code de commerce (loans, credit lines, guarantees to directors—except when they are legal entities—and general managers) For SARL, the prohibition also applies to shareholders, but only when they are individuals.

[101] See Bebchuk and Fried, *supra* note 2, at 112–7.   [102] § 402 Sarbanes-Oxley Act.

loans are especially *unlikely* to generate efficiencies significant enough to offset their risks.

Apart from bans on loans, prohibitions tend to focus on transactions between managers and third parties that are thought to divert the value of information that the law assigns, implicitly or otherwise, to the company or its shareholders. One example is Germany's non-compete rule for top executives in closely held companies.[103] Of course, barring executives from competing with their companies often makes sense, as executives who serve two competing firms will inevitably favor one over the other in allocating time and sensitive information. Nevertheless, there may be circumstances in which companies will reasonably prefer to allow their managers to compete. For example, smaller companies may need to permit competition to attract competent executives, and larger firms may benefit from the know-how gathered by their executives as directors of competitors in the same industry. For this reason, most jurisdictions deal with competition issues through standards rather than prohibitions.

'Insider trading'[104] is a third—and much more important—class of transactions that jurisdictions typically subject to per se restrictions. In brief, there are two sorts of rules against trading by insiders: prophylactic restrictions on short-term trading and direct bans on trading on material inside information. The most important prophylactic rules are restrictions on 'short swing' (within less than six months) purchase-and-sale or sale-and-purchase transactions by 'statutory insiders' of U.S. and Japanese registered companies, including directors, officers, and holders of 10% or more of a company's equity.[105] These rules effectively prohibit short-term trading by allocating the resulting profits (or losses avoided) to the corporate treasury, on the theory that these gains are likely to derive from nonpublic corporate information. The UK adopts similar restrictions in their listing requirements for the same reason.[106]

Still more significant, all major jurisdictions now impose some kind of direct ban on insider trading on the basis of nonpublic price-sensitive information about the issuer. European jurisdictions and Japan bar the officers, directors and controlling shareholders of listed companies from trading in their companies' securities prior to the disclosure of material nonpublic information.[107]

---

[103] See Peter Hommelhoff and Detlef Kleindiek No. 20 Anhang § 6 in Bayer et al., *supra* note 26. By contrast, the supervisory boards of German public companies may allow top managers to compete. See § 88 AktG.

[104] Remember that, at the beginning of this chapter, we defined 'insider trading' as trading based on price-sensitive inside information. Therefore, the prohibition is not on trading by insiders per se.

[105] For the U.S., see § 16(b) 1934 Securities Exchange Act; for Japan, see Art. 164 Financial Instruments and Exchange Act.

[106] See the minimum requirements set by the UK Listing Authority's Model Code (Listing Rules 9, Annex 1): a director may only deal in securities of the listed company after clearance by the board chairman, but clearance must not be given on considerations of a short-term nature (§ 8(b)).

[107] For the EU, see Art. 2 Market Abuse Directive [2003] O.J. L 96/16; for Japan, Art. 166 Securities and Exchange Act. Various EU member states have extended the insider trading ban to

The U.S., by contrast, bars insider trading on undisclosed information in '*any* security',[108] which includes not only the securities of public companies but also those of closely held ones.[109] Although all jurisdictions mandate stiff civil and/or criminal sanctions for illegal insider trading (e.g., disgorgement of profits, treble damages, and prison sentences),[110] the U.S. has traditionally mounted a much larger enforcement effort than other jurisdictions.[111] Lower enforcement levels in Europe and Japan probably reflect the higher burden of proof faced by prosecutors due to a (fading) statutory preference for criminal over civil sanctions and more limited public enforcement resources.[112]

As an empirical matter, it is unclear how effective direct bans on trading based upon material nonpublic information are. Even in the U.S., the ban seems to have had limited effect on the overall volume and profitability of trading by insiders, albeit they have become less likely to trade immediately before earnings announcements and corporate takeovers—possibly due to public

securities that are traded on non-regulated markets such as multilateral trading facilities. See, for Germany, § 12(1) Wertpapierhandelsgesetz; for the UK, s 118(1) Financial Services and Markets Act 2000.

[108] This is the wording in §10(b) 1934 Securities Exchange Act and in Rule 10b-5, the general antifraud provisions from which the insider trading prohibition has been derived in the U.S.

[109] This means that some close corporation disputes are governed by Rule 10b-5, litigated in federal court and can even, in theory, trigger criminal liability such as when a controlling shareholder/manager buys back the stock of a departing employee without disclosing material information about the financial condition of the company.

[110] For the U.S., see Loss and Seligman, *supra* note 11, 1054–60 (also discussing special sanctions such as disgorgement, civil penalties, and bounty provisions); for France, see Daniel Ohl, DROIT DES SOCIÉTÉS COTÉES No. 498 (2nd ed., 2005) (criminal sanctions and administrative fines); for Germany, see Rolf Sethe, *Insiderrecht* No. 8–13, in Heinz-Dieter Assmann and Rolf A. Schütze, HANDBUCH DES KAPITALANLAGERECHTS 587 (3rd ed., 2007) (criminal sanctions and disgorgement of profits); for the UK, see Davies, *supra* note 48, 1123–7 (criminal sanctions, administrative fines, disgorgement of profits).

[111] There was a high number of successful U.S. civil cases in the 1990s, compared to a handful of criminal convictions in Europe and Japan, but the latter jurisdictions' record seems to have improved in recent years. For example, Italy's Consob filings for public prosecution resulted in 33 court decisions in 2006 (against 16 for the whole 1991–1997 period), with convictions in 6 cases (against 2 for 1991–1997) (Annual Report 2006); similarly, Germany's *Bundesanstalt für Finanzdienstleistungsaufsicht* (BaFin) filings for public prosecutions resulted in 11 convictions in 2006 (there were none in the 1990s) (Annual Report 2006). Another indication of increased European activism is provided by the increase in cross-border exchange of insider trading information; for example, France's *Autorité des Marchés Financiers* (AMF) has made 182 such requests in 2006 while receiving 50 (Annual Report 2006). In Japan, the Securities and Exchange Surveillance Commission (SESC) has filed 5 cases for public prosecution in 2006 compared to 7 for the whole 1992–1999 period (see SESC Annual Reports 2005–2006), whereas the Tokyo District Court's 19 July 2007 judgment sentencing an investment fund manager to two years imprisonment and a U.S.$9,4 million fine was perceived as a stiff signal by market participants (see *Court Hands Murakami Stern Ruling*, THE NIKKEI WEEKLY, 23 July 2007 at 7). This is the tenth criminal prosecution in Japan for the violation of Art. 167 FIEA (prohibiting insider trading).

[112] See Peter Jan Engelen, *Difficulties in the Criminal Prosecution of Insider Trading—A Clinical Study of the Bekaert Case*, 22 EUROPEAN JOURNAL OF LAW AND ECONOMICS 121 (2006); Howell E. Jackson and Mark J. Roe, *Public and Private Enforcement of Securities Laws: Resource-Based Evidence*, Working Paper (2008), available at http://www.ssrn.com; Coffee, *supra* note 45.

companies commonly imposing blackout periods to minimize the securities fraud liability risk.[113] Studies of insider trading outside the U.S. reach contradictory results. For example, one study, based on data from 38 jurisdictions, finds that the cost of equity decreases significantly after the first prosecution for insider trading violation,[114] apparently because even minimal enforcement increases the attractiveness of the equity market to outside investors. Similarly, another study, based on data from 33 jurisdictions, finds that stock price informativeness and market liquidity are higher in more prohibitive jurisdictions.[115] However, two other multi-jurisdictional studies conclude that legal prohibitions generally fail to control insider trading, and only serve to make takeovers more expensive.[116]

Another question is why direct bans are the strategy of choice for select transactions by insiders. The reason must be that potential benefits are much less visible, and therefore less plausible, than those resulting from self-dealing transactions subject to less intrusive regulation. Mutually advantageous transactions between directors and small corporations are easy to imagine: for example, the director with superior information may be the only party willing to transact with her firm. To date, lawmakers remain unpersuaded that trading based on undisclosed information, especially in the public market, might sometimes have similar benefits. Some academics have argued that lawmakers underestimate the advantages it has as an efficient form of incentive compensation or as a superior channel of nonpublic information into share prices.[117] Other scholars, however, have questioned the informational benefits of trading based upon nonpublic information and provided evidence that it may have a negative impact on market liquidity by

---

[113] See Alan D. Jagolinzer and Darren T. Roulstone, *The Effects of Insider Trading Regulation on Trade Timing, Litigation Risk, and Profitability,* Working Paper (2007), at http://www.kellogg. northwestern.edu; H. Nejat Seyhun, *The Effectiveness of Insider-Trading Sanctions,* 35 JOURNAL OF LAW AND ECONOMICS 149 (1992). See also Olaf Stotz, *Germany's New Insider Trading Law: The Empirical Evidence after the First Year,* 7 GERMAN ECONOMIC REVIEW 449 (2006) (trading by insiders is very profitable).

[114] Utpal Bhattacharya and Hazem Daouk, *The World Price of Insider Trading,* 57 JOURNAL OF FINANCE 75 (2002).

[115] Laura Beny Nyantung, *Insider Trading Laws and Stock Markets Around the World: An Empirical Contribution to the Theoretical Law and Economics Debate,* 32 JOURNAL OF CORPORATION LAW 231 (2007).

[116] Arturo Bris, *Do Insider Trading Laws Work?,* 11 EUROPEAN FINANCIAL MANAGEMENT 267 (2005); Javier Estrada and J. Ignacio Peña, *Empirical Evidence on the Impact of European Insider Trading Regulations,* 20 STUDIES IN ECONOMICS AND FINANCE 12 (2002).

[117] See, e.g., Henry G. Manne, INSIDER TRADING AND THE STOCK MARKET (1966); Dennis W. Carlton and Daniel R. Fischel, *The Regulation of Insider Trading,* 35 STANFORD LAW REVIEW 857 (1983); Ian Ayres and Joe Bankman, *Substitutes for Insider Trading,* 54 STANFORD LAW REVIEW 235 (2001); Kristoffel R. Grechenig, *The Marginal Incentive of Insider Trading: An Economic Reinterpretation of the Case Law,* 37 UNIVERSITY OF MEMPHIS LAW REVIEW 75 (2006); Jonathan Macey, *Getting the Word Out about Fraud: A Theoretical Analysis of Whistleblowing and Insider Trading,* 105 MICHIGAN LAW REVIEW 1899 (2007). See also the empirical study by Nihat Aktas, Eric de Bodt, and Hervé Van Oppens, *Legal Insider Trading and Market Efficiency,* 32 JOURNAL OF BANKING AND FINANCE 1379 (2008).

increasing bid-ask spreads—a conclusion that the mentioned multi-jurisdictional studies seem to support.[118]

6.2.5 The standards strategy: the duty of loyalty and group law

If nowadays rules are rarely used to regulate conflicted transactions, standards are pervasive. All jurisdictions impose standards—which we group under the umbrella phrase 'duty of loyalty'—to control related-party conflicts and limit the risk of asset or information diversion. In essence, the duty of loyalty is a fairness standard which requires judges to determine *ex post* whether shareholders—as a class or as a minority—are worse off as an outcome of the related-party transaction.

Duty-of-loyalty doctrines have a variety of labels across jurisdictions, such as the duty of entire fairness, the prohibition against 'wrongful profiting from position', or the ban on *abus de biens sociaux*. Continental European jurisdictions define it differently in the context of groups of companies. Whatever the labels and the details, these doctrines have a similar thrust: unfair related-party transactions are unlawful and it is for the courts to determine unfairness after the fact. The strictness of enforcement varies. Some courts, like Delaware's, tend to be very strict, and only consider fair those transactions in which the company obtains deal terms comparable to those it would have obtained in a transaction with a non-related party. For other courts, like Italy's, it is enough that the transaction is not harmful to the company (e.g. the sale price is no lower than the company's reservation price). Finally, some courts, like the UK's, focus on the existence of a conflict of interest as defined by law, with the fairness of the transaction only relevant to the measure of damages.[119]

In addition, rules allocating the burden of proof are central to how effective the fairness standard will be in protecting shareholders' interests. In Delaware, defendants have the burden of proving the transaction's fairness, unless procedural steps have been taken to mimic the dynamics of an arms' length negotiation (such as entrusting a committee of independent directors with the power to negotiate with the controlling shareholder).[120] Other jurisdictions usually allocate the burden of proving unfairness of related-party transactions upon plaintiffs.

---

[118] Reinier Kraakman, *The Legal Theory of Insider Trading Regulation in the United States*, in EUROPEAN INSIDER DEALING 39 (Klaus J. Hopt and Eddy Wymeersch (eds.), 1991); Zohar Goshen and Gideon Parchomovsky, *On Insider Trading, Markets, and 'Negative' Property Rights in Information*, 87 VIRGINIA LAW REVIEW 1229 (2001). See also the empirical study by Raymond P.H. Fishe and Michel A. Robe, *The Impact of Illegal Insider Trading in Dealer and Specialist Markets*, 71 JOURNAL OF FINANCIAL ECONOMICS 461 (2004).

[119] See Davies, *supra* note 48, at 531: If there is a conflict of interest of the type covered by self-dealing law, British courts will find a breach of duty on the part of the director, even if the transaction is fair.

[120] See e.g. Allen et al., *supra* note 49, at 317–23.

Finally, enforcement significantly varies in terms of compliance mechanisms (private and public action, non-judicial intervention), remedies (transaction nullification, damages, and administrative or criminal sanctions), and frequency and ease by which shareholders can obtain redress.

6.2.5.1 Directors and officers

As we described in Section 6.2.2, all jurisdictions assign responsibility for ensuring compliance with the duty of loyalty to disinterested directors, through the widely required—or encouraged—screening of related-party transactions. Thus, the standards strategy frequently operates in conjunction with the trusteeship strategy. Jurisdictions differ, however, in the extent to which the standards strategy functions independently of other strategies.

The duty of loyalty plays the largest autonomous role in the U.S., where courts generally review the fairness of transactions with directors that have not been preapproved by independent directors. Delaware courts, in particular, are well-known for their pro-shareholder stance in this area,[121] and aggressively articulate norms of fair corporate behavior including admonishing managers when the transaction's terms are not in line with those of an arms' length transaction.[122] However, while such procedures can be costly for directors in terms of time and reputation, and inside directors are frequently held liable, personal liability of independent directors is exceedingly rare.[123]

European and Japanese courts, by contrast, seldom question the 'fairness' of conflicted transactions and even self-interested managers are unlikely to be sued, let alone held liable, for breaches of the duty of loyalty.[124] This has often been attributed to higher procedural thresholds for shareholder litigation.[125] It is true that a modest Japanese procedural reform sparked an explosion in derivative suits

---

[121] Delaware courts are said to use a so-called 'smell test': 'if the terms of the underlying transaction stink badly enough, the courts will find a way to abrogate any procedural protections supplied by the business judgment rule.' Charles M. Yablon, *On the Allocation of Burdens of Proof in Corporate Law: An Essay on Fairness and Fuzzy Sets*, 13 Cardozo Law Review 497, 502 (1991).

[122] See Edward B. Rock, *Saints and Sinners: How Does Delaware Corporate Law Work?*, 44 UCLA Law Review 1009 (1997).

[123] See Bernard Black and Brian R. Cheffins, *Outside Director Liability Across Countries*, 84 Texas Law Review 1385 (2006). Indemnification provisions and insurance protection make the liability risk even lower. See §8.51 RMBCA (indemnification) and Bernard Black, Brian Cheffins, and Michael Klausner, *Outside Director Liability*, 58 Stanford Law Review 1055 (2006).

[124] See also Marcus Lutter, *Limited Liability Companies and Private Companies*, in XII International Encyclopedia of Comparative Law 2–267, 2–273 (1997).

[125] Germany and Italy are often cited as evidence. According to §148 AktG, only shareholders of German *AG*s with at least 1% or a €100,000 holding (in par value) may sue directors for damages; Art. 2393–2 Civil Code sets the threshold for derivative suits against Italian listed and publicly traded companies at 2.5 and 20% respectively (but the bylaws can provide for a lower threshold and, in non-listed companies, for a higher one, up to one third of the shares). There is no such threshold for non-publicly-traded companies nor for claims based on group law (see *infra* 6.2.5.3) in either country.

in the early 1990s,[126] but there is evidence that derivative litigation remains low even in jurisdictions where any shareholder can sue directors derivatively.[127] The higher incidence of shareholder litigation in the U.S. is best explained by the presence of a specialized plaintiffs' bar that emerged out of a unique combination of contingent fees, discovery mechanisms, pleading rules, generous attorney's fee awards, and the absence of the 'loser pays' rule.[128]

There are two exceptions to the traditionally low level of formal enforcement of the law on managerial transactions outside the U.S.[129] First, as already hinted, derivative suits against directors have become relatively more frequent in Japan. In the absence of discovery mechanisms similar to U.S. ones, most Japanese suits concentrate on misbehavior identified by public prosecutors, and rely on the evidence unearthed in criminal proceedings.[130] The second exception is France, where self-dealing managers face a significant risk of criminal sanctions. Prosecutions for *abus de biens sociaux*, most often upon minority shareholders' demand, are common.[131]

6.2.5.2 Controlling shareholders

In all jurisdictions, controlling shareholders may be held accountable for having engaged in 'unfair' self-dealing. The liability risk is highest in U.S. jurisdictions. Courts apply tough standards, the 'entire fairness' test (in Delaware) and the 'utmost good faith and loyalty' test (in some other states), to self-dealing by controlling shareholders, even when such transactions have been preapproved by independent directors.[132] Europe and Japan have adopted a more lenient approach, at least once enforcement is taken into account. Limitations to standing to sue, such as minimum ownership thresholds, make it hard for minority shareholders

---

[126] See Mark D. West, *Why Shareholders Sue: The Evidence from Japan*, 30 JOURNAL OF LEGAL STUDIES 351 (2001).

[127] See, for France, Art. L. 223–22 (SARL) and Art. L. 225–252 (SA) Code de commerce; for Japan, Art. 847 Companies Act; Mark D. West, *The Pricing of Shareholder Derivative Actions in Japan and the United States*, 88 NORTHWESTERN UNIVERSITY LAW REVIEW 1436 (1994).

[128] On U.S. derivative litigation being driven by attorney's fees, see e.g. Roberta Romano, *The Shareholder Suit: Litigation Without Foundation?*, 7 JOURNAL OF LAW, ECONOMICS AND ORGANIZATION 55 (1991). See also *infra* 9.3.1 for a discussion of shareholder class actions.

[129] Litigation, however, can be expected to increase in Europe following recent reforms, in particular in Germany, Italy, and the UK. As to Germany and Italy, see e.g. Pierre-Henri Conac, Luca Enriques, and Martin Gelter, *Constraining Dominant Shareholders' Self-Dealing: The Legal Framework in France, Germany, and Italy*, 4 EUROPEAN COMPANY AND FINANCIAL LAW REVIEW 491, 507–9 (2007); as to the UK, see Arad Reisberg, DERIVATIVE ACTIONS AND CORPORATE GOVERNANCE: THEORY AND OPERATION (2008). See also *infra* 9.3.1 on securities fraud litigation.

[130] See West, *Why Shareholders Sue, supra* note 126, 378.

[131] See Art. L. 241–3 and Art. L. 242–6 Code de commerce (jail up to 5 years, fine up to €375,000). See also Conac, Enriques and Gelter, *supra* note 129, 518–9 (highlighting the propulsive role played by shareholders as some sort of 'private prosecutors' and providing data on the frequency of such cases).

[132] See *Kahn v. Lynch Communications Systems, Inc.*, 638 ATLANTIC REPORTER, SECOND SERIES (A.2d) 1110 (Delaware Supreme Court 1994); *Weinberger v. UOP, Inc.*, 457 ATLANTIC REPORTER, SECOND SERIES (A.2d) 701 (Delaware Supreme Court 1983).

to challenge non-managing controlling shareholders' self-dealing, especially in Germany and Italy. And even in France, where conflicted transactions are subject to specific constraints and minority shareholders face fewer limitations on standing to sue, controlling shareholders are not much at risk if the transaction has been properly approved.[133]

The European approach reflects a general reluctance to hold controlling shareholders liable so long as they are not directly involved in the company's management. But when controlling shareholders assume actual control, European jurisdictions become more demanding. Controlling shareholders who actively intervene in corporate affairs may become *de facto* or 'shadow' directors and face civil liability as directors and even criminal sanctions, for example, under the French *abus de biens sociaux* provisions.[134] Moreover, several European jurisdictions apply special standards to transactions between subsidiary companies and their parents or other entities within the group.

6.2.5.3 Groups

Taking as a starting point that companies belonging to a group enter into transactions with each other as a matter of routine, and that the efficiency of the group structure depends on such transactions, Germany, France, and Italy require courts to evaluate whether the overall operations of an individual subsidiary, and especially its interactions with the parent and other affiliates, are fair as a whole.[135] Of course, this implies that individual transactions harming a subsidiary cannot be successfully challenged, unless the plaintiff proves that the overall management of the group was itself harmful to the subsidiary, an extremely difficult task outside bankruptcy.

The German law of corporate groups (*Konzernrecht*) is the most elaborate, but ultimately relies on a simple fairness standard. Corporate parents in contractual groups have the power to instruct their subsidiaries to follow group interests rather than their own individual ones.[136] But, as a *quid pro quo*, they must indemnify their subsidiaries for any losses that stem from acting in the group's interests.[137] Should a parent fail to indemnify its subsidiaries accordingly,

---

[133] See Cozian et al., *supra* note 51, No. 379 (courts assess the legality, not the fairness of decisions that allegedly reflect an *abus de majorité*). French statutory provisions require disinterested approval of self-dealing by both directors and shareholders.

[134] Art. L. 241–9 (SARL) and Art. L. 246–2 (SA) Code de commerce. In Germany, AG shareholders using their influence on the company to instruct supervisory or management board members to act to the detriment of the firm or its shareholders may be liable for damages. § 117(1) AktG.

[135] For the argument that focusing on each single transaction to prevent controlling shareholders' abuse, as most jurisdictions (and especially Delaware) do, may lead to inefficient allocation of control rights by systematically disfavoring control by business partners, see Jens Dammann, *Corporate Ostracism: Freezing-Out Controlling Shareholders*, 33 JOURNAL OF CORPORATION LAW 681 (2008).

[136] See *supra* 6.2.5.3.   [137] See §302 AktG.

minority shareholders may sue in a derivative action.[138] In *de facto* groups, the parent company similarly cannot force its subsidiaries to act contrary to their interests without providing compensation.[139] Should a parent fail to do so, any minority shareholder would have the right to sue directors and the parent company for damages on behalf of the subsidiary.[140] Whether the German regime is effective in protecting minority shareholders remains unclear.[141] In the past, parent companies generally ignored the indemnification or compensation requirements—unless the subsidiary was insolvent, in which case not much was left for minority shareholders.[142] Nowadays, improvements in business practices and an increase in litigation risks seem to have resulted in a more adequate treatment of minority shareholders.

Italy's approach to corporate groups is less articulate than Germany's, but still recognizes the specific properties of this organizational form. It allows parent companies to manage their subsidiaries as a mere business unit and provides for *ex post* review of the overall fairness of a subsidiary's management. Minority shareholders of subsidiary corporations can sue the parent company and its directors for pro rata damages if they abuse their powers in managing the subsidiary's business. However, the parent cannot be held liable if there is no damage 'in light of the overall results of the management and co-ordination activity'.[143]

Similarly, according to French law, parent companies may instruct their subsidiaries to sacrifice their own interests for those of the corporate group.[144] The *Rozenblum* doctrine holds that a French corporate parent may legitimately divert value from one of its subsidiaries if three conditions are met: the structure of the group is stable, the parent is implementing a coherent group policy, and there is an overall equitable intra-group distribution of costs and revenues. As a practical matter, judges tend to consider the distribution of costs and revenues overall equitable so long as intra-group transactions do not pose a threat to the company's solvency.[145]

The French and Italian focus on the 'enterprise', rather than on a particular legal entity, has been considered to have the advantage of being a more functional

---

[138] See e.g. Uwe Hüffer, Aktiengesetz, No. 20 §302 (8th ed., 2008).

[139] §311 AktG. In practice, it is often difficult to establish whether the subsidiary has been harmed or not. The main tests are whether parent-subsidiary transactions are at arm's length and whether the subsidiary's directors have otherwise exceeded their business discretion: Hüffer *supra* note 138, No. 29–36 § 311 AktG.

[140] § 317 AktG.

[141] See Jochen Vetter, in Schmid and Lutter, *supra* note 26, No. 8 §311 (2008) (for AGs); Volker Emmerich and Mathias Habersack, Konzernrecht 423 (8th ed., 2005) (for GmbHs).

[142] See Forum Europaeum Corporate Group Law, *Corporate Group Law for Europe*, 1 European Business Organization Law Review 165, 202–4 (2000).

[143] Art. 2497 Civil Code.

[144] (1985) Revue des Sociétés 648 (Cour de Cassation); see also Cozian et al., *supra* note 51, N°1456.

[145] See Marie-Emma Boursier, *Le Fait Justificatif de Groupe dans l'Abus de Biens Sociaux: Entre Efficacité et Clandestinité*, 2005 Revue des Sociétés 273.

approach.[146] For this reason, some European legal scholars view this approach as the model for European harmonization.[147]

6.2.5.4 Enforcement of the standards strategy

In its core content (fairness), the duty of loyalty is similar in common and civil law jurisdictions, but its bite crucially depends on how courts enforce it. Managers and dominant shareholders face greater risk in the U.S. than in most other jurisdictions, with Japan and France falling somewhere in between.[148]

U.S. (and especially Delaware) courts are much more willing than elsewhere to review conflicted transactions for fairness even when it requires second-guessing the merits of business choices that are tainted by self-interest.[149] Further, U.S. law greatly facilitates shareholder lawsuits. Not only are the procedural hurdles for shareholder suits relatively low in the U.S., but a combination of civil procedure rules (e.g. on discovery) and generous rulings on attorney's fees is also available to support a specialized plaintiff's bar.[150] But why doesn't public enforcement make up for weaker private enforcement in other jurisdictions (with the exception of France, where criminal prosecutions are generated at low costs by aggrieved shareholders)?[151]

Other factors must be considered. First, where ownership in publicly-held companies is concentrated, as in continental Europe, managerial self-dealing is not an issue, because controlling shareholders can curb it effectively. As to controlling shareholders' extraction of private benefits of control, dominant owners' political influence is likely to be an effective constraint on public enforcement. Second, the U.S. experience seems to indicate that high levels of private litigation can prompt public enforcers to be more active themselves: prosecutors and the SEC risk public criticism if they cannot show that they are doing as much as the private bar. Increased public enforcement, in turn, spurs private litigation that piggybacks on the evidence unearthed.[152] In sum, competition between private and public enforcers seems to lead to an overall higher level of enforcement. Outside the U.S., then, the absence of a specialized plaintiffs' bar has a negative impact on public enforcement too.

---

[146] See Wolfgang Schön, *The Concept of the Shareholder in European Company Law,* 1 EUROPEAN BUSINESS ORGANIZATION LAW REVIEW 3, 24–27 (2000).

[147] Forum Europaeum, *supra* note 142, 205–6.

[148] See also Klaus J. Hopt, *Common Principles of Corporate Governance in Europe,* in Basil S. Markesinis (ed.), THE COMING TOGETHER OF THE COMMON LAW AND THE CIVIL LAW 105, 109 (2000).

[149] Cf. Luca Enriques, *Do Corporate Law Judges Matter? Some Evidence from Milan,* 3 EUROPEAN BUSINESS ORGANIZATION LAW REVIEW 765, 795–801 (2002) (describing Italian courts' reluctance to second-guess business decisions, even when tainted by conflicts of interest).

[150] See *supra* 6.2.5.1.   [151] See *supra* note 133 and accompanying text.

[152] See James D. Cox, Randall S. Thomas, and Dana Kiku, *SEC Enforcement Heuristics: An Empirical Enquiry,* 53 DUKE LAW JOURNAL 737, 761 (2003).

6.3 Ownership Regimes and Related-Party Transactions

With the exception of the U.S., jurisdictions tend to have a more lenient approach towards transactions with controlling shareholders than those with managers. This may be because unlike managers, controlling shareholders commonly have a large share of their own wealth invested in their companies—even when they take advantage of control enhancing mechanisms—and therefore have a stronger financial interest in long-term firm performance.

Even when controlling shareholders do not manage the company, they are likely to exercise far more influence over corporate affairs than anyone else, by virtue of their power to appoint board members. As a result, they are generally better placed than managers to extract private benefits through related-party transactions.[153] This is a pervasive problem, given that controlled companies are the norm internationally.[154] Although all major jurisdictions can boast at least a few widely held *listed companies* (usually their very largest), only Japan, the UK and the US have a large number of companies that are widely held without a *controlling* shareholder.[155] This suggests that the more lenient approach towards controlling shareholders in continental Europe may be explained by their stronger political clout.[156]

Yet a third explanation may be that controlling shareholders are often business partners of their company, with the two (and possibly other companies) forming a business group (or *group of companies*). When this is the case, related-party transactions between the subsidiary and the parent can be a matter of routine. While such frequent interactions increase the risk of expropriation, they may also generate synergies. Stringent legal requirements for individual transactions may make it more difficult to obtain such synergies, and in turn may negatively affect the market for corporate control, by disfavoring (partial) control by business partners.[157] This is the reason why some jurisdictions provide an overarching

---

[153] Controlling shareholders' ability to extract benefits varies from country to country. For a survey of international comparisons of private benefits of control see Renée Adams and Daniel Ferreira, *One Share, One Vote: The Empirical Evidence*, 12 REVIEW OF FINANCE 51 (2008).

[154] See Fabrizio Barca and Marco Becht (eds.), THE CONTROL OF CORPORATE EUROPE (2001); Stijn Claessens, Simeon Djankov, and Larry H. P. Lang, *The Separation of Ownership and Control in East Asian Corporations*, 58 JOURNAL OF FINANCIAL ECONOMICS 81 (2000); Rafael La Porta, Florencio Lopez-de-Silanes, and Andrei Shleifer, *Corporate Ownership Around the World*, 54 JOURNAL OF FINANCE 471 (1999).

[155] See *supra* note 154 and Mara Faccio and Larry H.P. Lang, *The Ultimate Ownership of Western European Corporations*, 65 JOURNAL OF FINANCIAL ECONOMICS 365 (2002); Clifford G. Holderness, *Myth of Diffuse Ownership in the United States*, 22 REVIEW OF FINANCIAL STUDIES 1377 (2009). Note, however, that blockholders often form *ad hoc* controlling coalitions in Japan and the UK.

[156] On the U.S. being tough on controlling shareholders because they are politically weak due to the ownership structure of listed firms, see *supra* 4.3.2.1. Compare Mark J. Roe, POLITICAL DETERMINANTS OF CORPORATE GOVERNANCE (2002).

[157] See Dammann, *supra* note 135.

set of rules to deal with intra-group relationships. The prototypical example is Germany, where the law of corporate groups aims to strike a balance between minority shareholders (and creditor) protection and the nimble management of the group.[158]

In broad outline, our major jurisdictions rely heavily on approval—by disinterested directors, shareholders, or both—as the primary check on managerial transactions and on standards as the primary check on controlling shareholders transactions. In addition, when it comes to listed companies, all jurisdictions nowadays follow the lead of U.S. securities law in providing for the mandatory disclosure of related-party transactions and prohibiting trading on price sensitive non-public information by corporate managers and controlling shareholders.

The extent to which corporate law constrains managerial and controlling shareholder opportunism may be less far-reaching than one could expect. In part, this is because shareholders can protect themselves, either through charter provisions (in closely held companies) or by applying a discount when buying an equity stake (in listed companies).[159] In part, this reflects an awareness that some forms of related-party transactions are necessary (for example, management compensation contracts) and other forms efficient, especially in the context of closely held firms. Finally, some methods of protecting minority shareholders, such as granting them veto rights over the conflicted transactions of controlling shareholders, give rise to a risk of strategic behavior—including opportunistic hold-ups of innocent transactions.[160]

There are also differences among our jurisdictions in the extent to which the extraction of private benefits via related-party transactions is constrained. One might argue that this mostly reflects variations in prevailing ownership regimes. Shareholdings in listed companies are more concentrated in continental Europe than in Japan, the UK, or (especially) the U.S.[161] In theory, given that opportunistic managerial behavior is more likely in the U.S. (lower ownership concentration should go hand-in-hand with reduced shareholder monitoring), one might expect courts or lawmakers to have addressed the issue by imposing tougher constraints on managers than those prevailing in continental Europe. Conversely, given the higher risk of minority shareholder expropriation by controlling shareholders, one might expect courts or lawmakers in continental Europe to have subjected controlling shareholders to more stringent constraints than their U.S. counterparts. At first glance, this is also what we observe. The fairness of a transaction with a manager is more likely to be questioned in the U.S. than in

---

[158] Emmerich and Habersack, *supra* note 141, 9–11.

[159] See Art Durney and E. Han Kim, *To Steal or not to Steal: Firm Attributes, Legal Environment, and Valuation*, 60 JOURNAL OF FINANCE 1461 (2005).

[160] Minority opportunism (also called *abus de minorité*—abusive practices by minority shareholders) is of particular concern in Europe: see Klaus J. Hopt, *Shareholder Rights and Remedies: A View from Germany and the Continent*, 2 COMPANY FINANCIAL AND INSOLVENCY LAW REVIEW 261, 267–9 (1997); more generally, see Easterbrook and Fischel, *supra* note 51, 238.

[161] See *supra* 1.6.1.

continental Europe, whereas continental European jurisdictions have adopted specific provisions for groups of companies.

The distinction, however, is not a clear-cut one, for two reasons. One is that managers (in the U.S. and Japan) and large shareholders (in Europe) have used their political clout to minimize regulatory constraints and, thus, blur the distinction. Hence, while U.S. courts do not shy away from imposing liability on managers for self-dealing transactions, lower powered self-dealing, such as management entrenchment, is largely unregulated. Conversely, group law is generally lenient and not significantly enforced—so much so that constraints on controlled transactions can be considered weaker in continental Europe than in the U.S. The other reason is that ownership regimes are not static. Hence, recent increases in institutional investor ownership around the world has gone hand-in-hand with related-party transaction litigation becoming more frequent in non-U.S. jurisdictions.[162]

Our discussion of regulatory strategies has provided specific evidence of this relationship between ownership regimes and the regulation of related-party transactions. Disclosure requirements used to be more demanding for U.S. and UK public companies than in continental Europe and Japan, reflecting differences in ownership and political power of institutional investors and controlling shareholders. More recently, expansion and family succession considerations have forced continental European and Japanese firms to compete for institutional investor equity investments. This has prompted reforms that bring disclosure requirements broadly in line with Anglo-Saxon disclosure requirements—and, hence, globally equivalent disclosure requirements at least for listed companies.

Turning to approval requirements, most company laws rely on directors to police the fairness of transactions with top managers. But jurisdictions differ in their expectations about the board's independence. In Germany and Italy, where families have long controlled many public firms, corporate law defers most to directors' and managers' judgment. In France, where the state has traditionally been a controlling shareholder, and the UK, where institutional investors are politically powerful blockholders, corporate law allows the board to play an evaluation role, but supplements it by mandating a shareholder vote on all non-routine transactions by companies that are publicly traded (in France) or listed (in the UK). In the U.S. and, to a lesser extent, Japan, where blockholders are smaller or less politically powerful than in the UK when it comes to larger publicly traded companies, corporate law requires board approval, with a backstop of judicial review: appropriate board approval typically leads courts to review authorized or ratified transactions under the business judgment rule.

No jurisdiction relies entirely on the board to screen interested transactions by controlling shareholders. In practice, however, challenges to board-approved

---

[162] See *supra* 1.6.1.

transactions are more likely to be successful in the Anglo-Saxon jurisdictions than in continental Europe, reflecting the political power of controlling shareholders in the latter. Hence, U.S. courts will review the fairness of controlled transactions even when they have been approved by a board committee with special bargaining powers and outside advisers or a majority of minority shareholders, although such measures will shift the burden of proof, as a doctrinal matter, and hence significantly increase the likelihood of court approval, as a practical matter. By contrast, French requirements for additional shareholder approval are perfunctory, while German and Italian group law leaves considerable discretion to the board unless the firm becomes insolvent—in which case shareholders are unlikely to benefit from it.

Finally, formal enforcement of standards via shareholder suits is significant only in the U.S. As discussed, board approval of transactions with managers or controlling shareholders is more likely to be subject to judicial review in the U.S. than elsewhere. Similarly, the use of securities fraud provisions for failure to disclose transactions with related parties is much more common in the U.S. This reflects both the uniqueness of the U.S. institutional framework and the greater *informal* enforcement capability of large blockholders in other jurisdictions. With the growing importance of U.S. institutional investor ownership, both formal and informal enforcement of standards can be expected to increase in Europe and Japan.

7

Fundamental Changes

*Edward Rock, Paul Davies, Hideki Kanda, and
Reinier Kraakman*

In Chapters 3 and 4, we discussed the basic governance structure of the
corporation. In this chapter, we discuss fundamental changes in the relationship
among the participants in the firm, and how corporate law mitigates the opportunism that can accompany these changes.

Collective action problems, asymmetric information, and contractual
incompleteness in long-lived corporations make midstream changes in the
fundamental relationships among the firm's participants ripe for abuse. As a
result, corporate law everywhere provides for the special regulation of these
changes. Centralized management exercises most decision-making power
in the corporate form, but this rule does not extend to decisions that fundamentally reallocate power among the firm's participants.[1] No jurisdiction, for
example, authorizes the board of directors to amend the company's charter in
a material way or to effect unilaterally a merger that alters the company's legal
identity. The board's power over such basic decisions is always circumscribed,
usually by shareholder decision rights and sometimes by other forms of legal
regulation as well. Even a board-centered jurisdiction such as Delaware must
grapple with the problem of protecting settled expectations against attempts by
managers to take power allocated to shareholders, by majority shareholders to
take advantage of minority shareholders, and by shareholders to benefit at the
expense of creditors. Indeed, in Chapter 6, we have already reviewed the limits
on board authority to approve transactions involving high-powered conflicts of
interest between the company and its directors or controlling shareholders.[2] In
this chapter, we address how corporate law limits board authority to change the
fundamental allocation of power.

---

[1] See *supra* 3.4.
[2] See *supra* 6.2.2 and 6.2.3.

7.1 What are Fundamental Changes in the Relationship Among the Participants in the Firm?

As noted above, boards of directors in all jurisdictions lack the power to reallocate power unilaterally among the firm's major participants, including in particular the board and the shareholders' meeting. Although there is no single set of characteristics that marks the limits of the board's power to decide unilaterally, either across jurisdictions or within them, there are general tendencies. Corporate law seldom limits board discretion *unless* corporate actions or decisions share the following two characteristics: (1) they are large relative to the participants' stake in the company, and (2) they create a possible conflict of interests for directors, even if this conflict does not rise to the level of a self-dealing transaction.[3]

Although these two characteristics largely describe the limitations on board discretion, there is an important complication. Because jurisdictions weigh the interests of shareholders, minority shareholders, and stakeholders differently, and because the dominant agency problem will differ depending on the prevailing pattern of share ownership (dispersed v. concentrated), jurisdictions inevitably diverge to some extent in how they select and regulate 'fundamental changes'. With this caveat in mind, let us turn to the two key characteristics associated with significant corporate transformations.

Consider first the *size* of a corporate action. At first glance, it is not obvious why size should matter to board discretion. One might suppose that if the board's expertise is critical in ordinary business decisions, it is even more so for decisions that involve very large stakes for participants or for the company. The response to this point, however, is that the relative size of a corporate action also increases the value of any legal intervention that increases the quality of the company's decision-making. To take the classic example, given that shareholders meetings to authorize corporate transactions are costly, they are more likely to be efficient (if they are efficient at all) for large transactions than for small ones. In addition, shareholders meetings are more likely to be effective if the stakes are large enough to overcome the shareholder's collective action problem.[4] On the other hand, it seems that the size of a decision alone does not trigger heightened regulation; corporate law generally delegates even the largest investment and borrowing decisions to the board alone.

The second key characteristic of corporate actions that is often associated with constraints on board discretion is a risk of *self-interested* decision-making by the

---

[3] Finally, at least in some cases, the actions or decisions involve general, non-firm specific, investment-like judgments that shareholders are arguably equipped to make for themselves.

[4] Edward B. Rock, *The Logic and (Uncertain) Significance of Institutional Shareholder Activism*, 79 GEORGETOWN LAW JOURNAL 445 (1991).

board. Low-powered conflicts of interest frequently dog major transactions, even without signs of flagrant self-dealing. For example, directors and officers who negotiate to sell their companies enter a 'final period' or 'end game', in which their incentives turn less on the interests of their current shareholders than on side deals with, or future employment by, their acquiring companies.[5] Even such low-powered conflicts of interest can seriously harm shareholders, and are thus a focus of regulation.

In this chapter, we consider several corporate transformations that trigger special scrutiny, including charter amendments, mergers, corporate divisions and asset sales, share issues and corporate distributions, reincorporations, delistings and deregistrations, and voluntary liquidation. As we shall see, many of these corporate-level restructurings can be used to freeze out minority shareholders. In addition, controllers can employ a simple compulsory share exchange to freeze out minority shareholders even without a corporate-level restructuring. Given this, and the fact that the legal strategies used to protect minority shareholders in corporate-level freeze-outs often track those used in shareholder-level restructurings, we extend our discussion to treat freeze-out transactions more generally.[6]

Interestingly, despite the vulnerability of minority shareholders in freeze-out transactions, no modern jurisdiction prohibits controllers from taking public corporations private, or parent companies from forcing the sale of minority shares in their subsidiaries. The reason may be that freeze-out transactions can plausibly generate efficiency gains despite the deep conflicts that they entail. First, freeze-outs eliminate the chronic conflicts of interest between parent companies and partly-owned subsidiaries that arise from intra-group self-dealing transactions and allocations of business opportunities.[7] Second, they may sometimes motivate controllers to allow minority shareholders to cash out of otherwise illiquid investments. Third, the power to effect freeze-outs may encourage controlling shareholders to risk additional capital, after buying out minority shareholders, that they would not have invested if forced to share their returns with minority investors.[8] Finally, freeze-out transactions eliminate the costs of being a public company, such as preparing disclosure documents and the opportunity costs of disclosing information of value to the firm's competitors.

---

[5] See Ronald J. Gilson and Reinier Kraakman, *What Triggers Revlon?*, 25 WAKE FOREST LAW REVIEW 37 (1990).

[6] However, we postpone full discussion of post-public offer squeeze-outs until Chapter 8.

[7] See *supra* 4.1.3.2.

[8] This rationale for freeze-outs requires additional assumptions to be plausible. Imagine, for example, a risk-averse controlling shareholder with private information about a prospect of lucrative but risky returns from expanding the company's operations. Such a controller might not be able to raise outside capital without jeopardizing his control, and might not be willing to provide additional capital himself.

7.2　Charter Amendments

Although many of the relationships among participants in the firm are structured by contract, including contracts with creditors and shareholder agreements,[9] corporate law contains a special sort of contractual device that allows for flexibility, constitutional commitments and publicity: the corporate charter.[10] Like other constitutions, corporate charters serve three main purposes: they establish a basic governance structure; they allow the entrenchment of terms, typically through a special amendment process; and they are public. Unlike ordinary contracts, corporate charters can be amended with less than unanimous approval by the parties to the charter, and must be filed and are generally available to anyone who asks. Each of these features serves important functions.

Under Delaware law, for example, a charter amendment must be proposed by the board and ratified by a majority of the outstanding stock.[11] By contrast, in European jurisdictions, including the UK, and Japan, the charter can normally be amended by a supermajority shareholder vote, without board initiative.[12] The U.S. rule creates a bilateral veto, i.e., neither the board nor the shareholders can amend the charter alone. By contrast, requiring only supermajority shareholder approval allows large minority shareholders to veto proposed charter amendments, but gives management no formal say in the matter. Both sets of amendment rules permit corporate planners to entrench governance provisions in the charter—an option that is particularly valuable since our core jurisdictions allow any charter provision not in conflict with the law. By means of charter provisions, shareholders can make credible pre-commitments. For example, under the Delaware approach, dispersed shareholders who approve an antitakeover provision in the charter—such as a classified board—strengthen the bargaining role of the board in an attempted takeover by reducing the likelihood that they would accept, or that an acquirer would make, a takeover offer with the approval of the board.[13] Under the supermajority shareholder approval mechanism, shareholders bond themselves to consider (large) minority interests.

---

[9] See Chapter 5 above for discussion of the extent to which contracts with financial creditors shape the governance of the firm.

[10] Marcel Kahan and Edward Rock, *Corporate Constitutionalism: Antitakeover Charter Provisions as Precommitment*, 152 University of Pennsylvania Law Review 473 (2003). Note that what we term the 'charter' often has another name according to jurisdiction, such as the 'certificate of incorporation', the 'article', the 'statutes' on the 'constitution'. See, e.g., Delaware General Corporate Law (hereafter 'DGCL') § 102.

[11] Delaware General Corporation Law (hereafter DGCL) § 242.

[12] UK Companies Act 2006, s. 21; France: Commercial Code, Art. L. 225–96; Germany: Aktiengesetz (hereafter 'AktG') § 119(1) no 5; Italy: Civil Code Art. 2365; Japan: Companies Act, Art. 466. These systems may permit changes to be effected in exceptional cases by the board alone, but, generally only where the change is regarded as minor or there are strong public policy reasons for board-alone decision-making. Of course, in practice most proposals for charter amendments originate from the board.

[13] See Kahan and Rock, *supra* note 10.

The extent to which charter provisions entrench governance rules depends on the structure of share ownership. As described above, where shareholdings are dispersed, the Delaware approach creates a bilateral veto between managers and shareholders, which allows current shareholders to guard against uninformed decision-making by future shareholders (through charter provisions such as the staggered board), at the risk of facilitating management entrenchment.[14] While Delaware's board-centred corporate law system views the bilateral veto as an attractive feature of corporate law, shareholder-centred systems, such as the UK, are more concerned with management entrenchment, and the charter-amendment rule is thus one which formally excludes management from the process of amending the charter.

In a system with concentrated holdings, by contrast, a bilateral board-shareholder veto is likely to be empty since controlling shareholders can generally choose boards that will do their bidding. In these systems, however, a supermajority voting requirement gives (large) minority shareholders a veto, thus creating a bilateral veto among shareholders. In this way the majority may be able to make credible pre-commitments to the minority through appropriate provisions in the charter, providing that minority shareholders can ensure that their holdings are not diluted below the veto threshold. Perhaps to obviate this risk, some corporate law systems permit the shareholders to increase the supermajority requirement for certain provisions, perhaps even to the level of unanimity.[15]

Of course, shareholder agreements existing separately from the charter can be used to entrench governance provisions as well. One disadvantage of a shareholder agreement is that, like other contracts, it would ordinarily require unanimous consent to amend, but it is usually possible to structure a shareholder agreement so that amendments are binding on all upon approval by a majority. Ultimately, the great advantage of entrenchment in the charter is that it operates more smoothly, by automatically binding new shareholders, than an extra-charter agreement. However, because many jurisdictions do not require the disclosure of shareholder agreements, at least if the company is not listed, that may be perceived as a countervailing advantage. Of course, a shareholder agreement to which only some shareholders are party may also operate as a mechanism for entrenching control rather than for protecting the minority.

In recognition of the governance and publicity functions of charters, jurisdictions typically regulate certain aspects of corporate structure by mandating the inclusion of specific provisions in the charter, if the company is to make use of them. For example, 'dual class' capital structures in which some shares have more votes than others, where permitted, may be required to appear in the charter; similarly, where permitted, limitations on directorial liability.[16]

---

[14] Of course management entrenchment can be constrained in other ways. See *infra* 8.2.3.1.
[15] See, for example, Companies Act 2006, s 22 (UK). The commitment must be present on formation or be introduced later with the unanimous consent of the shareholders.
[16] DGCL 102(b)(7); Arts. 426 and 427 of the Companies Act (Japan). Even in jurisdictions which do not insist that such requirements appear in the charter, the charter provides a convenient

All jurisdictions require corporate charters to deal with the company's share capital in a significant way, for example, by stating the number of authorized shares, the number of share classes, their par value, and the powers, rights, qualifications, and restrictions on these shares. The extent to which such terms constrain the board in the issuance of shares depends, however, on a larger set of rules. Thus, in Delaware, while the charter must state the number of authorized shares, the board has exclusive authority to issue stock below the number of shares fixed in the charter.[17] Japan has a so-called 'one-fourth rule' for public corporations: authorized shares are limited to a maximum of four times of the number of issued shares. This limit does not apply to close corporations, in which shareholders instead enjoy preemptive rights.[18] By contrast, European jurisdictions contain at least statutory default rules requiring shareholder authorization of share issues or pre-emption rights on cash issues. These provisions address more directly the board/shareholder balance of power in equity capital raising, which also makes authorized capital rules insignificant, albeit this time by providing shareholders with a veto.[19] These provisions also make U.S.-style poison pills considerably more difficult to put in place.[20]

The mandatory content of corporate charters differs across our major jurisdictions in two respects. The first concerns the fine structure of the board of directors. In several European jurisdictions, matters of board structure, such as the number of board seats (but not the number or function of board committees) must be memorialized in the corporate charter, and may thus be changed only

way of making them public or giving them binding force. See, for example, Art. 3 of the Second EU Company Law Directive, requiring certain information about shareholder rights to appear 'in either the statutes or the instrument of incorporation or a separate document published in accordance with the procedure laid down in the laws of each Member State...' Restrictions on the transfer of shares, in Delaware, may be in the charter, the bylaws or a shareholder agreement. Del. 202(b). The UK does not insist on the rights of classes of shareholders being set out in the charter (as opposed to the terms of issue of the shares), though they often are dealt with in the articles of association.

  [17]   *Grimes v. Alteon*, 804 ATLANTIC REPORTER 2d 256 (Del. 2002).
  [18]   Arts. 37(3), 113(3) Companies Act (Japan)
  [19]   Both these additional sets of rules are discussed below. For this reason the Companies Act 2006 in the UK removed the concept of authorized capital from company law. However, the charter remains important in this area for the Second EU Directive, laying down minimum requirements for issuance and preemption, permits these shareholder rights to be modified or excluded, inter alia, in the charter.
  [20]   See *infra* 8.2.3. In Delaware, the charter's limitation on authorized shares, in some circumstances, will be illusory. When a charter contains an authorized but unissued series of preferred stock ('blank check preferred'), the board's power under DGCL 152 to fix the terms of the preferred stock upon issue gives the board the effective power to issue ownership and voting interests that may, in some unusual circumstances, even allow the board to transfer control. This occurred in the U.S. bailout of AIG. Steven M Davidoff and David T. Zaring, *Big Deal: The Government's Response to the Financial Crisis* (24 November 2008), available at SSRN: http://ssrn.com/abstract=1306342 at 29–33. The power conferred on the board by authorized but unissued preferred stock also provides the foundation for the board's power to issue 'poison pill' shareholder rights plans without shareholder approval.

by a supermajority shareholder vote.[21] By contrast, in the U.S., such provisions are typically included in the 'bylaws'—the rules for the day-to-day running of the corporation, typically adopted by the board—although they can be placed in the charter, if desired.[22] UK law has also traditionally regarded board structure (including committees) and composition to be quintessentially matters of 'internal management', that may either be enshrined in the charter or left to rules made by the board itself. In Japan any departure from a default setting of corporate organs must be stated in the charter.[23] These differences in mandatory content are of decreasing importance, however, because of the trend in all major jurisdictions to mandate, by law or rules of best practice, that key board committees in listed companies, especially the audit committee, be independent and follow specific procedures.[24]

The second difference among jurisdictions concerns a statement of the corporation's subscribed *legal capital*, which must be made in the corporation's charter in some European jurisdictions, but not in the U.S. and Japan.[25] This requirement is linked to the minimum capital rules of the Second Company Law Directive and of particular national systems. We discuss the importance of minimum capital requirements in Chapter 5.[26]

---

[21] The charter must specify the number of supervisory board seats for German AGs if it is to comprise more than the mandatory minimum (§ 95 AktG) and when the charter of a French SARL establishes a board of directors with limited terms, it must also specify the number of board seats (Art. L. 223–18 Code de commerce). For the French SA, the charter only sets a maximum number of seats within the range (3–18) allowed by law (Art. L. 225–17 Code de commerce). By contrast, the law allows German GmbHs great freedom regarding the number of board seats: the charter may, e.g., specify a number, set a range, or leave the decision to another body. Except in relation to audit committees, where EU law requires, at least as a default, an audit committee for companies listed on regulated markets, the boards of French SAs, Italian SPAs (Art. 2381, Civil Code), and of German AGs (§ 107 AktG) remain free to decide whether to have committees or not, but for French boards the committees' powers are only advisory (see M. Cozian, A. Viandier, and F. Deboissy, Droit des Sociétés (20th ed., 2007) § 522).

[22] Bylaws, under Delaware law, have a curious status. Formally, if the certificate of incorporation is thought of as the corporate constitution, the bylaws can be understood to be the corporate statutes: they govern the day-to-day operation of the firm but when the certificate of incorporation and the bylaws conflict, the certificate of incorporation governs. DGCL § 109. An odd provision of the Delaware law has made bylaws a focus of shareholder activism. While the power to adopt bylaws may be, and typically is, delegated to the board of directors, that delegation does not divest shareholders of the power to adopt, amend or repeal bylaws. DGCL § 109. This has sparked a variety of conflicts over the permissible scope of bylaws and left unanswered some fundamental questions such as what happens if the board, pursuant to its delegated power, repeals a shareholder-adopted bylaw.

[23] See generally Art. 326(2) Companies Act (Japan).   [24] See *supra* 3.3.2.

[25] § 23 AktG and § 3 GmbH-Gesetz (Germany); Art. L. 210–2 Code de commerce (France, applicable to all corporate forms); cf. s 9 Companies Act 2006 (UK), no longer requiring the share capital to be stated in the charter but nevertheless requiring a 'statement of capital' to be publicly filed on formation—see Gower and Davies, Principles of Modern Company Law (8th ed., 2008) § 4–15. For a more extended discussion of legal capital see *supra* 5.2.2. Generally speaking, legal capital does not include reserves and subordinated debt, but jurisdictions often also require the accumulation of non-distributable reserves as a safety cushion.

[26] *Supra* 5.2.2.1. In fact, the Second Directive does not require the initial subscribed capital to be stated in the charter (the 'instrument of incorporation' will do instead) nor does it set a level of

7.2.1 The management-shareholder conflict in charter amendments

Charter provisions can be used to entrench management vis-à-vis shareholders. For example, a charter provision establishing a classified board gives the directors a temporary veto over efforts by shareholders to oust them in response to a bid for control (unless directors are mandatorily subject to removal by an ordinary majority of the shareholders, irrespective of what the charter says).[27] The shareholder approval strategy is used to control the management-shareholder shareholder agency costs: any midstream charter change must be approved by shareholder vote. When a consensus emerges among shareholders that a particular provision, e.g., a classified board, is unduly entrenching of management, charter amendments to adopt such provisions are no longer proposed, as is currently the case in the U.S.

7.2.2 The majority-minority shareholder conflict in charter amendments

Although the supermajority vote may provide a degree of protection for minorities, most jurisdictions go further. In many systems, a charter amendment that adversely affects a class of shareholders must be approved by a majority of that class voting together.[28] Such a provision is particularly important for preferred shareholders, who often lack voting rights and who rely in consequence on the charter, and the rules governing the amendment of the charter, to protect their interests. Such protection, however, must be carefully drafted to protect the preferred stockholders.[29] For example, although charter changes can be effected by means of a merger as well as by means of a charter amendment, Delaware case law provides that unless the preferred stock clearly states that class approval is required for changes to the terms, whether by charter amendment *or* by merger, the protection offered is illusory.[30] Equally, the British courts have drawn a sharp distinction between variations of the formal rights of a class of shareholders (requiring separate approval) and changes in the charter reducing the value of those rights but not changing them formally (not requiring class approval). Thus, increasing the voting rights of another class of shares or even eliminating preference shares entirely through a reduction of capital (provided the preference

---

minimum capital for incorporation of a public company provided that level is met before the company begins trading.

[27] See *supra* 3.1.3.

[28] See, e.g., DGCL § 242; Article 2376, Civil Code (Italy); Art. L. 225–99, Commercial Code (France); Companies Act 2006, Part 17, ch. 9 (UK). Aktiengesetz § 179(3) (Germany); Art. 322 Companies Act (Japan).

[29] William Bratton, *Venture Capital on the Downside: Preferred Stock and Corporate Control*, 100 Michigan Law Review 891, 922–39 (2002).

[30] *Id.*

shareholders are treated in accordance with the rights they would have on a liquidation of the company) have been held to fall outside the class protection.[31]

Most jurisdictions also have some fall-back standard allowing courts to review the most egregious examples of self-interested charter changes, whether involving class rights or not, but these standards are rarely invoked successfully.[32] However, a more common protection is the appraisal right. Italy and most U.S. states, though not Delaware, provide appraisal rights for charter amendments that materially affect the rights of dissenting shareholders (e.g., altering preferential rights, limiting voting rights, or establishing cumulative voting).[33] France too provides a potential appraisal right in respect of changes to the charter. The right can arise only in the case of a company that is quoted on a regulated market and has a controlling shareholder or controlling group of shareholders. When the controllers propose to alter the charter in a significant way and 'in particular the provisions concerning the company's legal form or [the] disposal and transfer of equity securities or the rights pertaining thereto', they must inform the market regulator (the Autorité des Marchés Financiers—hereafter AMF) in advance, which may require the controllers to make a buy-out offer, on terms agreed with the AMF, for the minority's shares.[34]

Charter provisions can also be used to solidify control by a controlling shareholder. A dual class capital structure (either high voting and low voting, or voting and non-voting, stock), which must be in the charter to be valid, will allow shareholders with a minority of the cash-flow rights to retain control. As such, it is a powerful entrenchment device. While permitted under Delaware law, it is rarely included in charters at the stage of the initial public offering. Midstream recapitalizations have a more interesting history. For a period of time during the 1980s,

---

[31] See Gower and Davies, *supra* note 25, paras. 19–11 ff. The preference shareholders can contract for more extensive protection but, as in the U.S., need to do so clearly. For a successful extension see *Re Northern Engineering Industries plc* [1994] 2 BUTTERWORTHS COMPANY LAW CASES 704, CA. As a result, most investors rely on the preferred contract for protection, rather than statutory provisions, giving preferred stock a legal status that is closer to debt than equity.

[32] For example, *abus de majorité* in France (see Cozian et al., *supra* note 21, paras. 378–81); provisions prohibiting 'unfair prejudice' in the UK (see Gower and Davies, *supra* note 25, Ch. 20). The AktG § 243(2) permits a challenge by an individual shareholder to any decision of the general meeting on the grounds that another voting shareholder has acquired through the resolution 'special benefits for himself or another person to the detriment of the company or other shareholders'. See Art. 831(1)(iii) Companies Act (Japan) (similar rule). Potentially more important, the UK has also developed a review standard in the specific context of charter changes i.e. the requirement that the change be effected 'bona fide in the interests of the company'. This rather opaque formula tends to require simply that the majority act in good faith, except in cases of expropriation of shares where it has a larger impact. See *Gamlestaden Fastigheter AB v. Baltic Partners Ltd* [2008] 1 BCLC 468 and *infra* 7.4.2.3.1.

[33] Art. 2437 Civil Code (appraisal right granted for, e.g., charter amendments regarding voting rights or significant changes in the scope of business); § 13.02 REVISED MODEL BUSINESS CORPORATION ACT (hereafter 'RMBA')(U.S.).

[34] General Regulation of the AMF, Art. 236–6. There is considerable debate as to what amounts to a 'significant' change. See A Viandier, OPA, OPE ET AUTRES OFFRES PUBLIQUES (3rd ed., 2006) paras. 2593ff.

U.S. boards sought to amend their charters to include such provisions, and often manipulated the process through 'agenda control' or by adding 'sweeteners' to induce shareholders to approve the amendments. Eventually, a consensus formed that these sorts of tactics were best understood as efforts by would-be controlling shareholders (often current managers) to exploit non-controlling shareholders' collective action problems to induce them to approve value-reducing amendments. In response, the Securities Exchange Commission (hereafter 'SEC') enacted rule 19c-4 which required exchanges to refuse to list firms which had engaged in midstream dual class recapitalizations, whether implemented by charter amendment, share exchange or other technique.[35] Although the SEC rule was ultimately held to be beyond its regulatory authority,[36] the exchanges, which had already adopted conforming rules, left them in place. Japan is similar and stock exchanges generally do not permit midstream dual class recapitalizations that would exploit existing non-controlling shareholders.[37]

In Europe, dual-class capital structures are controversial although generally permitted;[38] and they are regulated differently than in the U.S. Even if the charter confers on the board the discretion to issue classes of share with widely differing cash-flow or governance rights attached, mandatory rules of corporate law, derived from the Second Directive, require shareholder consent to any particular exercise of the power and also require pre-emptive rights to be given to the existing shareholders in the case of the issue of equity shares for cash, at least as the default rule.[39] Consequently, dual class recapitalizations have been handled not through specific rules implementing the proportionality principle but rather through the general rules on charter amendments and share issuance.[40]

7.3 Share Issuance

Transactions in the capital of the corporation can also realign interests: issuance of new shares can dilute the ownership of existing shareholders; repurchase of

---

[35] Voting Rights Listing Standards, Release No. 34–25891, 53 Fed. Reg. 26376 (1988).
[36] *Business Roundtable v. SEC*, 905 FEDERAL REPORTER 2d 406 (D.C. Cir. 1990).
[37] See Tokyo Stock Exchange, Listing System Improvement FY2008, 27 May 2008.
[38] See Arman Khachaturyan, *Trapped in Delusions: Democracy, Fairness and the One-Share-One-Vote Rule in the European Union*, 8 EUROPEAN BUSINESS ORGANIZATION REVIEW 335 (2007); see also Christian At, Mike Burkart and Samuel Lee, *Security-Voting Structure and Bidder Screening*, ECGI Finance Working Paper No. 158 (2007); Mike Burkart and Samuel Lee, *The One Share—One Vote Debate: A Theoretical Perspective*, ECGI Finance Working Paper No. 176 (2007).
[39] See below.
[40] The European Commission recently rejected proposals to make the proportionality principle mandatory at Community level. See COMMISSION STAFF WORKING DOCUMENT IMPACT ASSESSMENT ON THE PROPORTIONALITY BETWEEN CAPITAL AND CONTROL IN LISTED COMPANIES, SEC (2007) 1705, December 2007.

shares can entrench managers, create a controlling shareholder, provide an exit to an advantaged shareholder, and injure creditors.[41]

7.3.1 The manager-shareholder conflict

We argued above that shareholders as a class have an interest in maintaining direct control over large decisions that can realign their interests, in part to prevent the dilution of their cash flow or voting rights in major transactions such as corporate mergers.[42] The same concerns about share dilution arise whenever companies issue new equity or repurchase outstanding stock. EC law responds to these concerns in part by mandating that any reduction in subscribed legal capital in public companies must be ratified by a qualified majority of shareholders—a requirement that various member states have also extended to nonpublic corporations.[43] By contrast, most U.S. jurisdictions permit companies to reduce their legal capital without seeking shareholder approval[44]—an approach that reflects the U.S. view of legal capital as a vestigial concept rather than a useful trigger for shareholder decision rights.[45] Japan falls somewhere in the middle. While the minimum capital requirement was abolished entirely under the Companies Act of 2005, the notion of legal capital is maintained for the regulation of distributions, and the reduction of legal capital requires supermajority shareholder decision.[46]

Whatever their approach to legal capital, however, all jurisdictions regulate some aspects of the corporate decision to issue new shares. Like the merger decision, the decision to issue shares can significantly affect shareholder interests. As with mergers, managers' incentives are also problematic: share issuances can be used to build empires, entrench managers, and dilute control. Not surprisingly, then, we find the familiar requirements of board and shareholder approval.

Jurisdictions such as the U.S. and Japan draw a sharp distinction between the number of shares authorized by the charter and the number of shares that are actually issued and outstanding. In these jurisdictions, an increase in the amount of *authorized* capital of a company is an organic change that must be approved

---

[41] Note, too, that some of these adjustments to capital are also organic changes, since they require material amendments to company charters.

[42] See *supra* 7.1.

[43] See Art. 30 Second Company Law Directive, applicable to public companies; see also §§ 3, 53 GmbH-Gesetz (Germany); Art. L. 223–30 and Art. L. 223–34 Code de commerce (France, SARL); Companies Act 2006, Part 17, Ch. 10 (UK—also requiring court confirmation or, in the case of a private company, a solvency statement from the directors); Art. 2479 and 2479-II Civil Code (Italy, SRL).

[44] § 244 DGCL (the reduction of the legal capital can be made by a decision of the board of directors).

[45] On the very limited role of legal capital in the U.S., see *supra* 5.2.2.

[46] Art. 447(1) Companies Act (Japan).

by a qualified vote of the company's shareholders. By contrast, a new issue of shares that leaves the number of issued shares below the charter's authorization limit lies within the discretion of the board. Since most companies have actually issued only a fraction of their authorized shares at any particular point, the decision to issue shares is effectively a board decision that does not require a shareholder vote.[47] The principal exception occurs under U.S. listing requirements for exchange-traded firms, which require a shareholder vote when there is a new issue of shares large enough to shift voting control over a listed company's board of directors, unless the new issue takes the form of an offering to dispersed public shareholders.[48]

By contrast, the original six member states of the European Community (other than the Netherlands) did not distinguish between authorized and issued capital, so that the requirement for shareholder approval was attached by the Second Directive to the issuance of capital.[49] The practical difficulties to which this rule gave rise, however, were met by Community law permitting the company's charter or the shareholders in general meeting to delegate that decision to the board, for periods of up to five years.[50] In practice, the position may not be very different from that which obtains in the U.S. as far as fund-raising is concerned, but the European regime gives the shareholders more control over shareholder rights plans.[51]

Share issuances and repurchases, especially when targeted or discriminatory, can also be used by managers to entrench themselves. We discuss preemption rights and share repurchases in the next subsection.

---

[47] Japan has a so-called 'one-fourth rule' for public corporations. See supra text attached to note 18.

[48] See § 312.03(c) NYSE Listed Company Manual and §§ 712, 713 American Stock Exchange Company Guide (requiring shareholder vote when the company makes an issue of more than 20% of outstanding shares, unless shares are issued as a public offering for cash). The qualifications of the exchange listing requirements in the U.S. make clear that they are directed at control transfers rather than at dilution. Japan and the UK lack parallel exchange rule, although Japan has an unusual corporate law provision requiring that two-thirds of existing shareholders approve a targeted offering made to an investor at a 'particularly favorable' price. Arts. 199(2), 201(1), 309(2)(v) Japanese Companies Act.

[49] Second Directive, Art. 25. On this point see Vanessa Edwards, EC Company Law (1999), 77–8.

[50] *Ibid.* Member states may determine the majority required for such shareholder authorization and also add further limitations on the authority that may be delegated to the board, e.g. no more than half the par value of the existing capital in Germany: AktG § 202(3). As we have noted above at note 19, the UK has now abolished the concept of authorized share capital in its recent reforms, but institutional shareholder guidance in the UK indicates that such shareholders will vote in favor of giving boards authorization to issue more than one third of the existing share capital (and in any event no more than two thirds) only on the basis that the whole board should stand for re-election at the following general meeting. In addition, the actual use of this authorization should comply with the preemption requirements, discussed below. See Association of British Insures, *Directors' Powers to Allot Share Capital and Disapply Shareholders' Pre-emption Rights*, December 2008.

[51] See *infra* 8.2.3.

7.3.2 The majority-minority conflict

Although shareholders risk dilution from new equity and corporate distributions, minority shareholders face the largest risk because they are typically not protected by shareholder decision rights. Instead, minority shareholders must depend on other legal strategies for protection, such as the sharing norms, rules, and standards.

Preemptive rights are a paradigmatic example of the sharing strategy. By allowing existing shareholders to purchase new shares pro rata before any shares are offered to outsiders, preemptive rights permit minority shareholders to safeguard their proportionate investment stakes and discourage controlling shareholders from acquiring additional shares from the firm at low prices.

Jurisdictions differ in their approaches to preemptive rights. In the case of closely-held companies, Germany mandates preemptive rights; the UK grants them as the statutory default; and France, Japan, and the U.S. only enforce preemptive rights that are enshrined in company charters.[52] In the case of public companies, however, preemptive rights are a default option in all European jurisdictions.[53] Nevertheless, shareholders may opt out of this default by a qualified shareholder vote if shareholders delegate the power to issue the shares to the board.[54] Consequently, the strength of the preemption rule depends in part on the willingness of the shareholders to waive it. In the UK, institutional shareholders strongly support it and have developed Preemption Guidelines narrowly identifying the situations in which they will routinely vote in favor of disapplication resolutions put forward by listed companies.[55] In France the default rule is strengthened through regulation rather than shareholder activism: the market regulator will in effect require that for listed companies a 'priority subscription' period for existing shareholders is made available, even if preemption rights proper are removed.[56] In U.S. jurisdictions, by comparison, the statutory default is a rule of no preemptive rights for public as well as close companies. If shareholders are

---

[52] For Germany, see Karsten Schmidt, GESELLSCHAFTSRECHT (4th ed., 2002) 1174 (GmbH shareholders are considered as having the same preemptive rights as AG shareholders); for France see Cozian et al., *supra* note 21, para 1067 (French doctrine considers that SARL shareholders have preemptive rights only when the charter or other contract so provides); similarly in Italy for SRLs: Art. 2481-II Civil Code; for Japan, see Art. 202(1) Companies Act; for the UK, see Part 17, Ch. 3 of the Companies Act 2006 (opt-out regime); for the U.S., see § 6.30 RMBCA (shareholders do not have preemptive rights unless the articles of incorporation so provide).

[53] See, e.g., Art. 29 Second Company Law Directive (shareholders must be offered shares on a preemptive basis when capital is increased by consideration in cash, a right that cannot be restricted by the statutes but only by decision of the general meeting).

[54] Second Directive, Arts. 25(4) and 40.

[55] See Gower and Davies, *supra* note 25, 842–5: no more than 5% of the issued common shares in any year or more than 7.5% over a rolling period of three years. The Guidelines are available at: http://www.pre-emptiongroup.org.uk/principles/index.htm.

[56] Cozian et al., *supra* note 21, para. 823.

to receive preemptive rights, a company's charter must provide for them. Japan is the same for public companies.

Like other devices for protecting minority shareholders, preemptive rights have a cost. They delay new issues of shares by forcing companies to solicit their own shareholders before turning to the market.[57] They also limit management's ability to issue blocks of shares with significant voting power. These constraints may also explain why both Japan and the U.S. states have abandoned preemptive rights as the statutory default, and why Japanese and U.S. shareholders almost never attempt to override this default by writing preemptive rights into their corporate charters.[58]

In lieu of preemptive rights, U.S. jurisdictions rely on a standards strategy, the duty of loyalty, to thwart opportunistic issues of shares. Enforcing the duty of loyalty is costly and litigation-intensive, but it is likely to provide small minority shareholders with better protection than preemptive rights do. Even in the UK, in small companies where the minority shareholder may not be able to block the disapplication of preemption rights, they may file a petition alleging 'unfair prejudice' and seeking a right to be bought out at a fair price.[59] Japan combines the standards and the decision-rights strategy here. Shareholders in non-public companies enjoy preemptive rights, and all companies, including public ones, must receive supermajority shareholder approval to issue new shares to third parties at 'especially' favorable prices.[60] In addition, the issuance of stock may be enjoined by the court if it is 'significantly unfair' (even where the price is not favorable).[61]

The European preemption rules apply only to share issues for cash. In non-cash issues the minority are also at risk if shares are issued to the majority or persons connected with them at an undervaluation. Again, the approach of Community law is to address the problem through detailed rules, notably by requiring potentially expensive independent valuation of the non-cash consideration in public companies.[62]

---

[57] In particular, the shares of the company making the rights issue may come under pressure from short-sellers, even when the shares are issued at a substantial discount to the market price, at least where the issuer is seen to be in a weak financial position. This occurred in the recent round of rights issues by British banks hit by the 'credit crunch'. Nevertheless the Government proposed to maintain the preemption principle whilst seeking to reduce the timetable for such issues. See Office of Public Sector Information, *Report of the Rights Issue Review Group*, November 2008. This reflects a consistent governmental policy in favor of preemption. See, for example, Department of Trade and Industry, *Pre-Emption Rights: Final Report*, 2005 (URN 05/679).

[58] See Robert C. Clark, Corporate Law 719 (1986) (U.S. public corporations very rarely recognize preemptive rights). By contrast, it seems that preemptive rights are more often granted in U.S. closely-held corporations: see Robert W. Hamilton, The Law of Corporations 196 (5th ed., 2000).

[59] On unfair prejudice see *supra* note 32.

[60] Arts. 199(2), 201(1), 309(2)(v) Companies Act (Japan).

[61] Art. 210 Companies Act (Japan).

[62] Second Directive, Art. 10, somewhat relaxed by Art. 10A, introduced in 2006.

7.4 Mergers

The relationships among the participants in the firm can be revolutionized by a merger. A shareholder's ownership stake can be diluted, transformed, or, in some jurisdictions, cashed out. A preferred stockholder's accrued dividends can be wiped out. A shareholder in a widely-dispersed firm can find itself a shareholder in a controlled firm. A shareholder in a firm with no antitakeover protections can wake up a shareholder in a company that is effectively takeover-proof. A shareholder in a privately-held company can end up a shareholder of a publicly-held company or vice versa. The overwhelming problems, however, are related to price: a shareholder can miss the opportunity to sell its shares at a high price or be forced to sell at too low a price.

Because mergers can so fundamentally realign the relationships among the firm participants, every jurisdiction accords special treatment to mergers and other modes of consolidation. Although some mergers result in no realignment of interests (and are typically exempted from the shareholder approval requirement), many mergers exhibit the functional characteristics of fundamental transformations: they are large; and they often give rise to agency problems.[63]

Mergers and consolidations pool the assets and liabilities of two or more corporations into a single corporation, which is either one of the combining entities (the 'surviving company'), or an entirely new company (the 'emerging company'). Most jurisdictions require supermajority shareholder authorization for a merger or consolidation. In the EU, the Third Company Law Directive sets a minimum approval requirement of at least two-thirds of the votes at the shareholders meeting (or, as an alternative, one half of outstanding shares).[64] Some member states impose even higher voting thresholds. For example, Germany and the UK[65] require 75% of voting shareholders to approve a merger, while France and Japan require at least a two-thirds majority of voting shares with a minimum quorum

---

[63] The jobs of the weaker merging firm's managers are often as much at risk as those of managers in the targets of hostile takeovers (see *infra* 8.1.2.1), even if the merger is officially called a 'merger of equals'. Regarding the similarity between hostile and friendly transactions, see G. William Schwert, *Hostility in Takeovers: In the Eyes of the Beholder?*, 55 JOURNAL OF FINANCE 2599 (2000).

[64] Art. 7 Third Company Law Directive [1978] O.J. L 295/36, applicable to public companies. This article also requires the consent of each class of shareholders whose rights are affected, voting separately, not just of the shareholders' meeting. On 'class rights' see *supra* 7.2.2.

[65] The UK is technically peculiar in not having a free-standing statutory merger procedure. Instead, the 'scheme of arrangement' (dealt with in Part 26 of the Companies Act 2006) can be used to this end. However, a 'scheme' may be used to adjust the mutual rights of shareholders and/ or creditors and the company, whether or not another company is involved in the scheme. It was originally designed (in the 19th century) for the adjustment of creditors' rights in insolvency. If the scheme is used to effect a merger or division, it may attract the additional regulation of Part 27, implementing the Third and Sixth EC Directives in the UK, though some mergers and divisions fall outside those Directives and so outside Part 27. Although the scheme is increasingly often used to effect a control shift (see *infra* 8.1.1), scheme mergers are relatively uncommon in the UK. See generally Gower and Davies, *supra* note 25, Ch. 29.

of one-third of the outstanding shares for the SA.[66] By contrast, most U.S. jurisdictions, including Delaware and the RMBCA states, require a simple majority
of outstanding shares to approve a merger or other organic change, although this
might easily translate into 70% or more of shares that are actually voted.[67]

These shareholder ratification requirements ordinarily apply to both (or all)
participants in a merger or consolidation.[68] The fact that shareholders of acquiring companies must often authorize mergers (*even* if there is no alteration of their
charters) suggests that corporate law is less concerned with formal legal identity
than with the sheer size of these transactions, and the possibility that they can
radically alter the power and composition of the acquiring corporation's management. Consistent with this focus on transactions that fundamentally re-order
relations is the fact that some jurisdictions *do not* require the acquirer's shareholder authorization when it is much larger than the company it targets, as long
as the merger does not alter the surviving corporation's charter.[69] Here the implication is that a shareholder vote is unnecessary because the boards of acquiring
companies are merely making modest purchases for pocket change that, for tax
reasons or otherwise, are conveniently structured as a merger rather than as asset
purchases or acquisitions of subsidiaries.

7.4.1 The management-shareholder conflict in mergers

The two principal management-shareholder agency conflicts that potentially arise
in mergers are (a) management's self-interested refusal to agree to a merger that

---

[66] § 50 Umwandlungsgesetz (for GmbH) and § 65 Umwandlungsgesetz (for AG, unless the
charter sets a higher threshold) (Germany); ss. 899 and 907 of Companies Act 2006 (UK); Arts.
L. 236–2, L. 223–30 and L. 225–96 Code de commerce (requiring two-thirds majority, now for
SARLs formed after 3 August 2005 as well as for SAs and setting a one-third quorum) (France).
For Japan, see Arts. 783, 784, 795, 796, 804, 309(2)(xii) Companies Act (requiring two-thirds
majority of voting shares, and setting a majority quorum that can be reduced to one-third by charter). Similarly, Italy requires a two-thirds majority of shares representing at least one-third of the
outstanding capital for public companies (SPA) (in non-listed public companies, a simple majority
of the outstanding shares may, however, approve the merger) (Art. 2368–2369 Civil Code); in private companies, a majority of the outstanding shares is required (Art. 2479-II Civil Code (SRL)).
[67] § 251(c) DGCL; § 11.04(e) RMBCA. If only 70% of shareholders vote, more than 71 % of
voting shareholders must approve a transaction to provide a majority of outstanding shares.
[68] The UK scheme procedure (above note 65) does not require the consent of the shareholders
of the surviving company in a merger 'by absorption', if the rights of those shareholders are not
affected by the merger (as they normally will not be). This 'rights-based' approach to shareholder
approval is qualified in the case of mergers to which the Third EU Directive applies, but even that
Directive (Article 8) permits member states to shift the burden of convening a meeting in such
cases to the shareholders. The UK has taken advantage of this permission: if the holders of at least
5% of the voting capital of the surviving company do not ask for a meeting, none need be held:
Companies Act 2006, s. 918.
[69] See § 251(f) DGCL (Delaware) (voting not required if surviving corporation issues less than
20% additional shares); Art. 796(3) Companies Act (Japan) (voting not required if surviving
corporation pays consideration of 20% or less of its net worth, with some exceptions). Compare
Art. L. 236–11 Code de commerce (France) (shareholders of surviving companies must always
authorize mergers, even when parent company merges with a small, 100%-owned subsidiary).

shareholders support and (b) self-interested attempts by management to build empires or to negotiate their future job status or compensation with an acquiring company at the expense of their shareholders.[70] Because these agency problems primarily arise in dispersed ownership structures, we focus here primarily on the U.S., the UK, and Japan.[71]

7.4.1.1 Managerial 'entrenchment'

What is to be done when managers resist a merger proposal which shareholders would like to accept? How can a system distinguish between resistance that is driven by a sincere, well-founded belief that a merger is not in the interests of shareholders from resistance that is driven by self-interest? Different systems address this problem differently. In a board-centered system such as the U.S., managerial entrenchment is addressed through a combination of a trusteeship strategy (boards dominated by independent directors) combined with a rewards strategy (high-powered incentive compensation for managers triggered by a change in control) and a decision rights strategy (although a poison pill allows boards to say 'no' to a merger proposal, shareholders can vote in a new slate of directors) with residual standards-based *ex post* judicial review under the heading of fiduciary duties.

More shareholder-centric systems strike the balance differently. Thus, in the UK, an acquirer can shift the form of the transaction to a straight share acquisition. By this shift the acquirer avoids the de facto block which the management of the target can exercise over the convening of the target shareholder meeting which is necessary to secure approval of the merger.[72] Having removed the need for positive cooperation from the target management, in most cases the acquirer can then invoke the City Code's ban on frustrating action to neutralize any negative action the target management might take against the tender offer without shareholder approval.[73] Japan is similar to the UK.

7.4.1.2 Managerial nest-feathering

A second manager-shareholder agency problem arises if managers, in negotiating a merger agreement, put their own interests in building an empire through acquisitions or in securing employment with the surviving firm ahead of shareholders' interests in maximizing share value. Here, interestingly, the strategies adopted by different jurisdictions are rather more similar. First, the shareholder approval

---

[70] A third conflict arises in management buyouts when managers, with a financial sponsor, seek to acquire the company from the public shareholders. It is discussed below in the context of freeze-outs.

[71] For majority/minority shareholder conflict see *infra* 7.4.2.

[72] For the difficulties an acquirer has in using the UK-style merger against a hostile target see *Re Savoy Hotel Ltd* [1981] Ch 351, discussed in Gower and Davies at para. 29–5.

[73] These issues are discussed more fully in Chapter 8 in the context of control shifts.

requirement[74] gives shareholders a means of challenging a merger driven by managerialism. Large-block shareholders or coalitions of block holders, including of late hedge funds and institutional investors, will sometimes have the voting power to block corporate actions, especially when there is a clearly better alternative transaction proposed.[75]

Second, to increase the efficiency of shareholder voting, many jurisdictions require approval by gatekeepers of the terms of mergers, consolidations, and other organic changes (a trusteeship strategy). For example, EC law requires public companies which merge to commission independent experts' reports on the substantive terms of mergers prior to their shareholder meetings.[76] Other jurisdictions promote third-party review in less formal ways. In Japan, the stock exchanges require a third party to analyse whether the proposed mergers are fair to shareholders.[77] And in the U.S., public companies pursuing a merger customarily seek to protect themselves from shareholder suits by soliciting fairness opinions from investment bankers,[78] which shareholders can peruse before they vote.

Some jurisdictions use other trusteeship strategies. For example, in the UK, court approval of the scheme is mandatory, though in the case of schemes to effect mergers it is likely that this traditional requirement has been displaced in functional terms by the more recent Community requirement for an expert's report, except in the case of mergers not covered by the Community rules.[79]

Third, the U.S. and Japan also protect shareholders through an exit strategy—the appraisal remedy—that allows dissatisfied shareholders to escape the financial effects of organic changes approved by shareholder majorities by selling their shares back to the corporation at a 'reasonable' price in certain circumstances. Although Community law does not require appraisal as an element of the merger process, France, Germany and Italy offer it on a limited basis. The provisions on appraisal in

[74] *Supra* note 66.
[75] For examples, see Marcel Kahan and Edward Rock, *Hedge Funds in Corporate Governance and Corporate Control*, 155 U. PA. L. REV. 1021 (2007).
[76] Art. 10 Third Company Law Directive (requires third-party reports on the fairness of merger terms, though the holders of voting securities in the company can waive this requirement on the basis of unanimity). Experts may be natural or legal persons depending on the laws of each member state but must in any case be appointed or approved by a judicial or administrative authority. The EC law does not harmonize the requirements experts need to satisfy in order to be appointed or approved, but our EU jurisdictions require that they be accountants or auditors: see s 909(4) Companies Act 2006 (UK); § 11 Umwandlungsgesetz and § 319 Handelsgesetzbuch (Germany); L236–10 Code de commerce (France); Art. 2501-VI Civil code (Italy). In the case of closed companies member states may adopt a more relaxed regime. For example, an expert assessment is required for a merger of closed companies in Germany only if a shareholder asks for this: § 48 Umwandlungsgesetz.
[77] Tokyo Stock Exchange, Listing Rules, Art. 417(8)e.
[78] See, e.g., *Smith v. Van Gorkom*, 488 ATLANTIC REPORTER (A.2d) 858 (Delaware Supreme Court 1985) (sale of a company without valuation report and with little deliberation is grossly negligent despite premium price).
[79] Even in schemes where there are no experts' reports the court is not likely to intervene substantively if the meetings have been properly conducted and the requisite level of shareholder approval obtained: Gower and Davies, *op cit* para. 29–8.

the case of significant changes in the articles of public companies will catch some mergers.[80] Appraisal may be made available expressly where the merger involves a revolution in legal form or some other unusual restriction on shareholders' rights.[81] As a side benefit, the appraisal remedy also protects shareholders as a class by making unpopular decisions more expensive for management to pursue.[82] The cost of these protections, of course, is that this same remedy may harm shareholders if the need for cash to satisfy appraisal demands scuttles a transaction that would otherwise have increased the company's value.[83]

The scope of the appraisal remedy varies widely among U.S. states and the handful of non-U.S. jurisdictions that offer this exit right. In practice, however, cumbersome procedures, delay, and uncertainty discourage small shareholders from seeking appraisal in the jurisdictions that offer it. For example, shareholders seeking to perfect their appraisal rights in Delaware must first file a written dissent to the objectionable transaction before the shareholders meeting in which it will be considered; they must refrain from voting for the transaction at the meeting; and they may be forced to pursue their valuation claims in court for two years or more before obtaining a judgment. In addition, many U.S. states, including Delaware and RMBCA jurisdictions, further limit appraisal rights by introducing a so-called 'stock market exception' to their availability in corporate mergers.[84] Under this 'exception', shareholders do not receive appraisal rights if the merger consideration consists of stock in a widely-traded company rather than cash, debt, or closely-held equity—apparently on the theory either that appraisal rights ought to protect the liquidity rather than the value of minority shares, or that the valuation provided by the market, while imperfect, is unlikely to be systematically less accurate than that provided by a court.[85] As a result, appraisal

---

[80] See *supra* text attached to note 34 and Viandier, *supra* note 34, paras. 2595–8. The UK has a mechanism whereby a company in liquidation can transfer its assets to another company in exchange for securities in the transferee which are distributed in specie to the shareholders of the liquidating company. Unlike a scheme, court approval is not required but an appraisal right is provided instead (Insolvency Act 1986, ss 110 and 111) It is used only in family companies (where the take-up of the appraisal right can probably be accurately gauged in advance) and investment companies. Italy provides a similar remedy for mergers involving SRLs and for mergers of a listed company into a non-listed one: see 2505-IV (SRLs) and Art. 2437-V (listed company into non-listed company), Civil Code. See *infra* 6.2.2.2.

[81] See Reg. Gen. AMF Art. 236–5 (France); Unwandlungsgesetz (Germany) § 29. For example, shareholders have much less influence over the management of a *société en commandite par actions* than over that of a company and are less likely to receive a takeover offer. See Viandier, *supra* note 34, paras. 2570, 2571, 2502.

[82] See Hideki Kanda and Saul Levmore, *The Appraisal Remedy and the Goals of Corporate Law*, 32 UCLA LAW REVIEW 429 (1985).

[83] See Bayless Manning, *The Shareholder's Appraisal Remedy: An Essay for Frank Coker*, 72 YALE LAW JOURNAL 223 (1962).

[84] § 13.02 RMBCA; § 262 DGCL.

[85] Of course this theory does not explain why appraisal rights are available when shareholders receive cash, the most liquid merger consideration possible.

rights are of little use to shareholders who wish to challenge the price they receive in stock mergers between public corporations.[86]

These difficulties may explain why most European jurisdictions have never turned to the exit strategy—appraisal rights—as a general remedy to protect minority shareholders in uncontrolled mergers. Instead, as we have seen, EC law relies on a decision rights strategy (shareholder approval) and on the gatekeeper strategy as well, to the extent that EC law requires valuation by independent experts who are liable to shareholders for their misconduct.[87]

Note, however, that some individual member states go beyond the minimum required by Community law and provide individual shareholders with a right to challenge the fairness of merger prices, a right that resembles the appraisal remedy in spirit if not in form. This is the case in both Germany and Italy where shareholders of merged companies may sue the surviving companies for the difference between the value of the shares they previously owned and the value of those they received in exchange.[88] Indeed, the ability of individual shareholders to challenge the merger decision has proved so effective in Germany that it has acted as a considerable deterrent to mergers in that country.[89] In the U.S., class actions permit aggrieved shareholders to claim damages in a similar way.[90]

7.4.2 The majority-minority shareholder conflict in mergers (including freeze-out mergers)

Many of the mechanisms that limit manager/shareholder conflicts, for example independent assessment of the merger terms or appraisal rights, operate to protect minority shareholders against majority shareholders as well. That is, they provide protection for non-controlling shareholders against company

---

[86] See Paul G. Mahoney and Mark Weinstein, *The Appraisal Remedy and Merger Premiums*, 1 AMERICAN LAW AND ECONOMICS REVIEW 239 (1999) (analysing 1,350 mergers involving publicly-held firms from 1975–1991); Joel Seligman, *Reappraising the Appraisal Remedy*, 52 GEORGE WASHINGTON LAW REVIEW 829 (1984) (only about 20 mergers from 1972–1981 resulted in appraisal proceedings).

[87] Art. 20 Third Company Law Directive (liability of managers vis-à-vis their shareholders) and Art. 21 (liability of independent experts vis-à-vis shareholders); Art. 18 Sixth Company Law Directive (liability of managers and of independent experts vis-à-vis shareholders). See also Matthias Habersack, EUROPÄISCHES GESELLSCHAFTSRECHT (3rd ed., 2006) Rn 16–20.

[88] § 15 Umwandlungsgesetz; Art. 2504-IV Civil Code; see also Schmidt, *supra* note 52, 390; Pierre-Henri Conac, Luca Enriques, and Martin Gelter, *Constraining Dominant Shareholders' Self-Dealing: The Legal Framework in France, Germany, and Italy*, 4 EUROPEAN COMPANY AND FINANCIAL LAW REVIEW 491, 525 (2007). The particular difficulty with the German system is that it may result in an adjustment of the merger terms after the merger has been carried into effect. Contrast Art. 25.3 of the Regulation for a European Company (2157/2001/EC) which makes the application of this mechanism to a German company involved in the creation of an Societas Europaea by merger dependent on the consent of the involved companies from other member states which do not use this particular type of standard.

[89] See *infra* 7.4.2.3.1 and 8.4.

[90] See, e.g., *Smith v. Van Gorkom*, 488 A.2d 858 (Supreme Court of Delaware, 1985).

controllers, whether those controllers are management or majority shareholders (or, of course, both). However, some of the techniques, notably shareholder approval (even on a supermajority basis) will be less effective in such a situation. Majority/minority conflicts are particularly acute in a freeze-out merger, where a controlling shareholder, using the merger structure, eliminates the non-controlling shareholders either for cash or stock. Management buyouts, in which managers team up with a financial sponsor to acquire the company, present many of the same problems.

All of our major jurisdictions strengthen the protection of minority shareholders when controlling shareholders stand on both sides of an organic change, such as a merger. In particular, standards play a more important role in regulating conflicted transactions.[91] European jurisdictions offer minority shareholders the right to sue under a variety of protective standards. In France, for example, controlled mergers can be invalidated under the *abus de majorité* doctrine,[92] while, in the UK the 'unfair prejudice' remedy is at least potentially available to provide an exit right for the minority at a fair price.[93] Although in the U.S. standards play a relatively small role in the regulation of most arm's-length organic changes (except when the company is being sold for cash or broken up[94] or a merger or other transaction promises to create a new controlling shareholder where there had been none before),[95] they become prominent in controlling shareholder transactions.[96]

7.4.2.1 *When the parent has more than 90%*

In an attempt to balance the interests of minority and controlling shareholders, jurisdictions generally facilitate minority buyouts when a controlling shareholder owns more than 90% of a company's shares. For example, EC merger law allows member states to substitute the equivalent of appraisal rights for expert assessment of the merger plans and to dispense with the need for a vote by the shareholders of the acquiring company when an acquiring corporation owns more than 90% of a target company—an option inspired by Germany's *Konzernrecht*.[97] More dramatically, a parent company holding more than 90% of a subsidiary can unilaterally merge the subsidiary into itself without a shareholders meet-

---

[91] See *supra* 6.2.5.

[92] For France, see Art. 1382 Code Civil (France); mergers are one of the instances where the *abus de majorité* remedy is available: Cozian et al., *supra* note 21, para. 1362, note 9.

[93] On the 'unfair prejudice' remedy see Gower and Davies, Ch. 20.

[94] *Revlon, Inc. v. MacAndrews & Forbes Holdings, Inc.* 506 A.2d 173 (Del. 1986).

[95] See, e.g., *Paramount Communications, Inc. v. QVC Network, Inc.,* 637 A.2d 34 (Delaware Supreme Court 1994).

[96] See Mahoney and Weinstein, *supra* note 86, 272–4; compare *Weinberger v. UOP, Inc.,* 457 A.2d. 701 (Delaware Supreme Court 1983); *Kahn v. Lynch Communications Systems, Inc.,* 638 A.2d 1111 (Del. 1994). Robert B. Thompson, *Squeeze-out Mergers and the 'New' Appraisal Remedy,* 62 WASHINGTON UNIVERSITY LAW QUARTERLY 415 (1984).

[97] See Arts. 27–29 Third Company Law Directive. See also Volker Emmerich, Jürgen Sonnenschein, and Mathias Habersack, KONZERNRECHT 136–44 (8th ed., 2005).

ing of the transferring company (a so-called 'short-form' merger) in most U.S. jurisdictions—with minority shareholders entitled to appraisal rights in lieu of a shareholder vote.[98] Japanese law is similar.[99]

7.4.2.2 When the parent has less than 90%

U.S. law also permits freeze-outs in situations in which the controlling shareholders own less than 90% of a subsidiary's shares, but at the price of providing additional minority shareholder protection beyond what would be available in an uncontrolled merger or other organic change. Japanese law is similar.[100] U.S. securities regulation requires public corporations that go private to make disclosures relating to the fairness of the transaction and to any discussions with third parties who may be interested in acquiring the company,[101] whilst in France the market regulator may require the appraisal remedy to be made available in the case of the merger of a public subsidiary into a controlling company where the AMF thinks one is necessary to protect the minority's interests.[102]

In addition, the Delaware courts generally review these (< 90%) freeze-out mergers under the rigorous 'entire fairness' standard that applies to related-party transactions generally, with the burden on the controlling shareholder to prove fair price and fair process.[103] The Delaware case law, developed in the intensely fact-specific application of fiduciary duties, strongly encourages the use of a special committee comprised of independent directors, advised by independent counsel and an independent investment banker, and supplemented by approval by a majority of the minority shareholders. When these steps are taken, the burden of proof in challenging the transaction shifts to the minority shareholders, and, while the standard formally remains 'entire fairness', the standard as applied seems more deferential.[104]

The law in EU jurisdictions is less clear-cut with respect to controlled mergers and freeze-outs in which the controlling shareholder holds less than 90% of the issuer. Certainly the minimum requirements established by the Third and Sixth Company Law Directives are applicable to such transactions, but beyond this, EU member states have generally adopted a 'neutral' approach in their national laws

---

[98] See, e.g., § 253 DGCL.   [99] Art. 784(1) Companies Act (Japan).

[100] In such cash-out mergers (or more generally mergers in which the consideration is other than the stock of the surviving company), disclosure of additional information is required. See Arts. 182 and 184 MOJ Companies Act Implementation Regulation (2006).

[101] Rule 13e-3 1934 Securities Exchange Act.

[102] General Regulation of the AMF, Art. 236–6, control being undefined but probably being based on the definition in Art. 233–3 Code de commerce, requiring a 40% holding of voting rights in absence of other significant shareholders. For Japan, see METI, the Report of the Corporate Value Study Group on MBOs (August 2007) (providing best practices for the fair treatment of minority shareholders).

[103] See *Weinberger v. UOP, Inc.*, 457 A.2d 701 (Delaware Supreme Court 1983).

[104] Some controlling shareholders seek to avoid the rigorous entire fairness standard by coupling a tender offer to get above 90% with a short-form merger. Guhan Subramaniam, *Post-Siliconix Freezeouts: Theory and Evidence*, 36 JOURNAL OF LEGAL STUDIES 1 (2007).

that, in contrast to U.S. jurisdictions, does not actively facilitate freeze-outs.[105] There are no special disclosure rules for freeze-out transactions in listed companies. In France, a company's charter *may* provide that its minority shareholders can be cashed out in well-defined circumstances, although the terms of such a buy-out would be subject to a Delaware-like fairness review by the courts.[106] Without an authorizing provision in the charter, however, it does not seem that a controlling shareholder may squeezeout even abusive minority shareholders.[107] By contrast, the more liberal German law does recognize the right of a controlling shareholder to cash out an abusive minority shareholder, but neither the German statutes nor the German courts acknowledge a general right of controlling shareholders with under 95% of an issuer's shares to freeze out its minority share holders.[108] In Italy, absent an absolute right to cashout (abusive) minorities, a squeeze-out may only take place for shareholders with a number of shares lower than is needed to receive one share in the resulting company.[109]

7.4.2.3 Squeeze-outs through non-merger techniques

7.4.2.3.1 Compulsory share sales

Many jurisdictions also provide squeeze-out techniques which are not based formally on the merger. As we shall see in the next chapter,[110] under Community law an acquirer which ends up with 90 to 95% of a target's shares after a public offer is able to squeeze out the non-accepting shareholders on the terms of the public offer (or something near it)—and the minority has a similar right to be bought out. In some jurisdictions the same facility is made available, whether or not the 90 or 95% threshold is reached via a public offer. In this case, fixing the price is a more sensitive matter. In France, a shareholder group holding 95% or more of voting rights in a listed company may eliminate the minority by making a public offer to acquire their shares, followed by a compulsory acquisition of the shares of the non-accepting shareholders.[111] The price in the compulsory acquisition has to be approved *ex ante* by the market regulator, which operates on the basis of a proposal prepared by the acquirer's investment bank,

---

[105] Regarding the '*Wertneutralität*' of the German approach, see BUNDESVERFASSUNGSGERICHT (BVerfGE) 14, 263 [*Feldmühle*]: Schmidt, *supra* note 52, 348.

[106] Cozian et al., *supra* note 21, paras. 329–30.

[107] See *Cour de Cassation Commerciale,* 1996 REVUE DES SCOCIÉTÉS 554 (squeeze-out is prohibited unless permitted by statute or the corporation's charter).

[108] See Schmidt, *supra* note 52, 803 (AG), 1058–64 (GmbH); BUNDESGERICHTSHOF ZIVILSACHEN (BGHZ) 129, 136 [*Girmes*].

[109] See Luigi A. Bianchi, LA CONGRUITÀ DEL RAPPORTO DI CAMBIO NELLA FUSIONE 101 (2002).

[110] See *infra* 8.4. If, however, an existing 90% majority mount a bid for the company simply in order to squeeze out the minority, UK scrutinizes the reason for the squeeze-out by reference to a standard akin to that applied to charter amendments to that end. See *Re Bugle Press Ltd* [1961] Ch 270, CA.

[111] Reg. Gen. of the AMF, Arts. 236–3, 236–4 and 237–1. Again, there is a parallel right for the minority to be bought out.

the report of an expert commissioned by the target and its own judgment.[112] Since 2002 Germany has also provided a squeeze-out procedure at the 95% level for all public companies in a procedure which tracks merger rules (including the need for a report from the 95% shareholder and a report from a court-appointed expert on the adequacy of the compensation).[113] Unlike in the French procedure, the price is not approved *ex ante* but is subject to *ex post* challenge by any individual minority shareholder before a court, whose decision will apply to all the minority shareholders (*Spruchverfahren*). Although the challenge does not normally prevent the squeeze-out from being effected immediately, the post squeeze-out procedure can be protracted (even up to ten years), which generates a strong incentive for the 95% shareholder to settle the minority's claim and an equally strong incentive for arbitrageurs to acquire the minority's shares in order to take advantage of the court challenge.[114]

In jurisdictions (such as the UK) which lack explicit procedures for squeezing out minorities (other than post-bid), a variety of substitute corporate procedures may be available. The issue is whether these more general procedures provide adequate safeguards against majority opportunism when used to effect a squeeze-out. The simplest form of these non-specific squeeze-out mechanisms is a charter amendment requiring the minority to transfer their shares to the majority or to the company. Because the standard supermajority requirement for charter changes may seem inadequate minority protection in the squeeze-out situation, UK courts, under their general power to review charter amendments,[115] have developed a requirement for a good corporate reason for even a fair-price squeeze-out, in contrast with the simple requirement for good faith in respect of other changes to the charter. In Australia, from a similar doctrinal starting-point, the High Court has barred such compulsory acquisitions except in very limited circumstances.[116]

---

[112] Ibid. Arts. 237–2, 261–1(II), and 262–1. See generally Viandier, *supra* note 34, paras. 2780 ff. In Italy, the market regulator, when determining the price of the compulsory acquisition, takes into account the market price of shares over the previous half-year, the price of previous bids (if any), the issuer's equity capital adjusted to its current value and the issuer's results and outlook (Art. 108 Consolidated Law on Finance and Art. 50 Consob Regulation on Issuers).

[113] §§ 327a–f AktG. The 95% figure relates to the share capital as a whole, not to the shares carrying voting rights. The 95% may be held by shareholders acting in partnership, but a mere voting agreement cannot be used to pass the threshold: T. Stohlmeier, GERMAN PUBLIC TAKEOVER LAW (2nd ed., 2007) 139.

[114] Stohlmeier, 145. The post-bid squeeze-out procedure does not suffer from this defect, because of the strong presumption that the bid price is the appropriate price. See *infra* 8.4. German law (AktG §§ 320–320b) also contains an older procedure, which served as a model for the one described in the text) for the 'integration' of a 95%-held subsidiary into the parent company, but in this case the minority are not fully squeezed out but become shareholders in the parent, which makes the procedure attractive only if parent is a publicly traded company.

[115] See *supra* note 32.

[116] Gower and Davies, Ch. 19–4ff .and *Gambotto v. WCP Ltd* (1995) 127 AUSTRALIAN LAW REPORTS 417 (High Court of Australia). The latter seems to accept compulsory acquisition to protect the company from harm but not to confer a benefit on it. See generally R. P. Austin and I. M. Ramsay, FORD'S PRINCIPLES OF CORPORATIONS LAW (12th ed., 2005) 618ff.

7.4.2.3.2 Other squeeze-out techniques

A charter amendment is not, however, the only, or even the typical, way of eliminating a small minority in the absence of an explicit procedure for so doing. A reverse stock split, a sale of all the assets of the company followed by its dissolution[117] or, in those jurisdictions still attaching importance to legal capital, a reduction of capital, may all be used to this end. Again, since these procedures are not designed for squeeze-outs, the protection against opportunism lies mainly in the deployment of standards strategies governing the majority's decision.[118]

The delisting of a traded company may also operate as a squeeze-out. As discussed in Chapter 9, securities regulation and stock exchange rules provide a wide variety of protections for shareholders against both managers and controlling shareholders. Delisting and deregistration deprive shareholders and creditors of the benefits of extended mandatory disclosure, in addition to vastly reducing the shares' liquidity. In light of this, exit from either regulatory structure is a fundamental change in the firm.

Firms may choose to delist when the costs of being a public corporation exceed the benefits. This may be because of the costs of complying with the mandatory disclosure system, or because of other mandatory provisions of the public company regulatory structure.[119] Firms may sometimes be forcibly delisted if their stock price drops below an exchange's minimum required.[120]

On the other hand, delisting, and the threat of delisting, can be used opportunistically. A self-tender offer for preferred stock, for example, was held to be actionably coercive because the issuer indicated that it intended to seek delisting of the securities.[121] The prospect of holding shares that were no longer listed, the court held, forced shareholders to tender. Finally, even when not used opportunistically, delisting/deregistration may interfere with investors settled expectations as to the indefinite duration of the protections afforded by securities regulation and listing rules.

---

[117] A procedure explicitly provided for in § 179a AktG (Germany), on a 75% vote of the shareholders, but in fact not taken up often in practice for a number of reasons, including the ability of the minority to delay the transaction for long periods by challenging the price for the transfer of the assets. Consequently, the more recently introduced general squeeze-out procedure (*supra* 7.4.2.3.1) is typically employed. See Stohlmeier, *supra* note 113, at 150.

[118] See *Rock Nominees Ltd v. RCO (Holdings) plc* [2004] 2 BCLC 439 (CA—UK): bidder, which had fallen just short of the 90% threshold for a post-bid squeeze-out, proposed to sell the business of the new subsidiary to another group company, liquidate the vendor and distribute its assets to the shareholders. The Court of Appeal refused to regard this proposal as infringing the 'unfair prejudice' standard for reviewing controllers' decisions (see *supra* note 32) where the price obtained in the sale was 'the best price reasonably obtainable'. It was also clear that the minority opposed the deal because it hoped to obtain a 'ransom price' through a voluntary sale of its shareholding to the new parent.

[119] See *infra* 9.2.2.

[120] E.g., the NASDAQ requires that shares trade at a minimum bid price of $1.

[121] *Eisenberg v. Chicago Milwaukee Corp.*, 537 A.2d 1051 (Del. Ch. 1987).

A variety of mechanisms are used to protect shareholders from the opportunistic use of delisting and deregistration.[122] First, it is often quite difficult to delist or deregister. In the U.S., an issuer, once subject to the SEC mandatory disclosure system, may only deregister if the number of shareholders is reduced to fewer than 300.[123] Even where delisting is not subject to rule of this type, a variety of other techniques are used by exchanges, market regulators and legislators to regulate the delisting process. The New York Stock Exchange requires a board resolution and notice,[124] while the Main Market of the London Stock Exchange requires supermajority shareholder approval.[125] Germany, by contrast, requires shareholder approval (albeit by ordinary resolution) coupled with an exit right for the minority at a fair price for their shares, with the possibility of appeal to the court over the pricing issue (but without the delisting itself being delayed).[126] In Italy, delisting not deriving from mergers or other corporate finance operations is admitted only to the extent that shares are contextually admitted to trading on another stock exchange; where delisting is admitted, Italy grants dissenting shareholders the exit right at the average share price in the previous six months.[127]

7.4.3 The protection of non-shareholder constituencies in mergers

Several of our major jurisdictions seek to protect non-shareholder constituencies (creditors and/or employees) in mergers and other consolidations in addition to addressing the agency problems between managers and shareholders and between controlling and minority shareholders.

7.4.3.1 The protection of creditors

As we noted in Chapter 5, the European jurisdictions and Japan are relatively more creditor-friendly than the U.S.[128] In keeping with this tradition, EC and Japanese law offer special protections to creditors when firms undergo mergers and similar organic changes. Although creditors lack the power to stop mergers,

---

[122] See, generally, Edward Rock, *Securities Regulation as Lobster Trap: A Credible Commitment Theory of Mandatory Disclosure*, 23 Cardoxo Law Review 675 (2002).

[123] § 12(g)(4), Securities Exchange Act. See, also, rule 12g-4 (less than 300 or less than 500 where total assets are less than $10 million).

[124] NYSE Listed Company Manual § 806.00. It should be noted that previously it was far more difficult to delist, with the longstanding rule requiring a vote of two-thirds of the shareholders in favor and not more than 10% against. Rock *supra* note 122 at 683. The change to a rule permitting easier exit was in response to pressure from foreign private issuers who wished to leave the NYSE in the wake of Sarbanes-Oxley.

[125] FSA, Listing Rule 5.2.5. Unless the delisting follows a control shift or merger carried out under the relevant procedures or the company's financial situation is precarious.

[126] These principles are derived from the *Macrotron* case (BGH, Az. II ZR 133/01, ZIP 2003, 387).

[127] Art. 133 Consolidated Law on Finance and Art. 2437-V Civil Code.

[128] See *supra* 5.4.

they are entitled to demand adequate safeguards when a merger puts their claims at risk.[129] These safeguards often extend to a requirement that their claims be secured by the surviving or emerging company or that their claims be discharged before the merger, which may act as a significant disincentive to the merger.[130] These issues are discussed further in Chapter 5.

7.4.3.2 *The protection of employees*

There are two main issues here. First, to what extent do employees have a 'voice' (whether through collective bargaining or legal rules providing for workforce-based works councils or board-level representation) in the merger decision and to what extent will those voice arrangements be carried over to the resulting company? This goes to the likely impact of the merger, either immediately or in the future, on the development of terms and conditions of employment and the availability of job and promotion opportunities. The second issue is whether employees have the option to transfer their existing terms and conditions of employment (which, depending on the situation, may be located in a collective agreement or in an individual contract of employment) to the corporation which results from the merger.

Voice may be provided through general governance provisions relating, for example, to board-level representation of employees, as discussed in Chapter 4. Or voice may be injected through a mechanism independent of the board and applying only to certain categories of corporate decision. Here, Community law adopts a strong stance. On a transfer of a business (of which the merger is a prototypical example) the Acquired Rights Directive[131] mandates consultation on the part of both transferor and transferee employers with the representatives of the employees (unionized or non-unionized) prior to the transfer of the business. The focus of the consultation is on the implications of the merger for the employees.[132] Given the stately and public procedure of the merger (production of a merger plan, its public filing, the experts' report, the shareholder meeting), it is not normally too demanding to fit consultation with employee representatives into this timetable.[133]

---

[129] See Art. 13 Third Company Law Directive.
[130] Umwandlungsgesetz (Germany) § 22 (AktG § 321 to similar effect).
[131] Directive 2001/23/EC, Chapter III.
[132] Art. 7, i.e., 'the legal, economic and social implications of the transfer for the employees' and 'any measures envisaged in relation to the employees' though the employer must also state 'the reasons for the transfer'. In some member states, for example France, the employee representatives have more extensive rights to review the business reasons for the transfer.
[133] However, for analysis of a case where the transfer of a business (not a merger) to one of two competing acquirers was significantly influenced by the consultation obligation (BMW's disposal of a large part of its UK assets in 2000) see John Armour and Simon Deakin, *The Rover Case— Bargaining in the Shadow of TUPE* (2000) 29 INDUSTRIAL LAW JOURNAL 395. Subsequent experience, i.e., the collapse of the successful acquirer a few years later, suggests, however, that the more modest plans of the originally preferred but unsuccessful acquirer were the better bet.

U.S. law is more cautious. There is no general consultation duty on transferor or transferee companies. If both parties to the merger are unionized, then the effects of themerger are a mandatory topic of bargaining. If one party is unionized and the other is not, the only way to implement the merger is to put the companies into separate subsidiaries because the union component has bargaining rights that can prevent any sensible integration of the operation.

The quality of the voice mechanisms after the merger will normally depend on the rules applying to the surviving or emerging company. This has proved to be a particular problem in cross-border mergers in the European Community, since voice requirements, especially in terms of board-level representation, vary significantly from member state to member state. We discuss this issue further under 'Relocations' in Section 7.6. For purely domestic mergers, the Acquired Rights Directive has a limited provision preserving the voice arrangements existing within the transferor after the transfer.[134] However, since in most member states the provision of employee voice at enterprise or establishment level is a matter of legal requirement, the rules applicable to the surviving or emerging company will lead to the transferred business being covered by equivalent voice arrangements.

US law is again considerably more cautious, applying only in the unionized sector. When operations are transferred by merger or stock sale, both the collective bargaining agreement and the statutory duty to bargain carry forward automatically. By contrast, when operations are transferred by a sale of assets and the rehiring of employees, the collective bargaining agreement only carries forward when the asset purchaser explicitly or constructively adopts it, while the presumption of continued majority support and related statutory duty to bargain carry over when more than 50% of the asset purchaser's bargaining unit employees worked for the seller.[135]

As to the second point—protection of acquired rights—the 'universal transmission' mechanism of the statutory merger procedure may operate so as to transfer the individual entitlements of the employees to the surviving or emerging entity.[136] In any event the Community Directive requires that on a transfer of a business the contracts of employment of workers employed in the transferor company are automatically transferred in an unaltered form to the surviving or emerging entity.[137] It also makes the fact of the transfer an unacceptable ground

---

[134] Art. 6. This operates only if (a) if the undertaking transferred 'preserves its autonomy' and (b) 'the conditions necessary for the reappointment of the representatives' after the transfer are not met.

[135] Rock and Wachter, *Labor Law Successorship: A Corporate Law Approach*, 92 MICHIGAN LAW REVIEW 203, 212–32 (1993).

[136] Though in the UK the courts found automatic statutory transfer of employment contracts to be inconsistent with the personal nature of the relationship embodied in them: See *Nokes v. Doncaster Amalgamated Collieries Ltd* [1940] AC 1014, HL.

[137] Directive 2001/23/EC, Chapter II, replacing an earlier directive of 1977. As a result of interpretation by the European Court of Justice, employees have the right to opt out of automatic

for dismissal. These two rules put the burden of any subsequent lay-off compensation on the transferee employer, but this can normally be allowed for in the price paid for the transferor's business. The more problematic rule from an economic perspective is that transferred employees who remain on the job also retain the pre-existing terms and conditions of their employment. This makes it difficult for the transferee to integrate the transferred employees into a common structure of terms and conditions of employment for its enlarged workforce, since even changes subsequently negotiated by the transferee with the representatives of the employees are at risk of legal challenge.

By contrast, the United States adheres to the common law doctrine of the personal nature of the contract of service[138] and does not provide for automatic transfer of the contract of employment in the non-unionized area. Even in the unionized area the same approach has influenced judicial interpretation of the U.S. National Labor Relations Act. The extent to which collectively agreed terms and conditions will be carried over to the transferee employer depends on the form of the transaction, as described above.[139]

7.5 Corporate Divisions and Sales of Assets

A corporate division is the transactional inverse of a merger: it divides the assets and liabilities of a single corporation into two or more surviving corporations, one of which may be the dividing corporation itself. Despite logical similarities between mergers and divisions, however, jurisdictions differ on whether they are as closely regulated as mergers. The U.S. only regulates divisions on an ad hoc basis when opportunism appears unless the corporation sells all or substantially all of its assets, and Japan regulates divisions only perfunctorily.[140] At first glance, the EC seems different. The provisions of the Sixth Company Law Directive[141] regulating divisions are a virtual mirror-image of the Third Directive dealing with mergers, including its provisions on minority and creditor protection.

transfer to the transferee employer (though whether it is an attractive option is left to the member states to determine by defining the non-transferring workers' rights against the transferor); and the principle of automatic transfer on unaltered terms and conditions is softened to some degree where the transferor is insolvent. The principle of automatic transfer on the same terms can be traced back to the 1930s in the case of some member states (France, Italy).

[138] See *supra* note 136.

[139] Rock & Wachter, *supra* note 135; *Howard Johnson Co. v. Detroit Local Joint Executive Bd* 417 U.S. 249 (1974). In an asset sale or a shift of work, if the transferee simply ends up rehiring a substantial proportion of the transferor's employees, it may be under a duty to bargain with the union, but need not preserve the transferred employees' terms and conditions, i.e., it need not bargain to impasse before changing them.

[140] See Arts. 783, 784, 795, 796, 804, 805 Company Act (Japan).

[141] Directive 82/891/EEC (Sixth Company Law Directive) [1982] O.J. L 378/47 (applicable to open companies).

In practice, however, even the Community member states do not scrutinize divisions as closely as mergers. Although French and German national law, following the directive, closely regulate the division of both public and private corporations, the reach of these regulations can be avoided.[142] In particular, corporations can sidestep Germany's detailed (and ostensibly mandatory) division provisions by adopting alternative transactional forms.[143] Avoiding France's division regime—that is the model for division in the EU's Sixth Company Law Directive[144]—is more difficult because French law does not provide any other convenient way to split a dividing company's debt, in addition to its assets. Nevertheless, both French and German companies can choose to remain outside the division framework if they find the requirements too onerous.[145]

Perhaps the most attractive way to avoid the Community's division rules is for the transferor company to remain in existence carrying on the non-transferred businesses.[146] Only in France does this transaction seem to be regulated in the same way as a division, but with the crucial difference that those proposing the *apport partiel d'actif* may choose whether to submit the transaction to the rules governing divisions.[147] Elsewhere asset sales are left within the purview of the board alone, except when in some jurisdictions they reach the level of a disposal of substantially the whole of the company's assets, at which point a shareholder vote is required. Thus for Italian private companies, where operations (including the sale of assets) result in a substantial change in the business scope, shareholder approval is required.[148]

---

[142] In Germany and in France, as in Japan, division requirements apply to 'total' transfer (§ 123 Umwandlungsgesetz: '*Übertragung… als Gesamtheit*'), not individual transfer of assets and debts. Individual transfer of an asset requires normal legal procedure (perfection of title, etc.), and individual transfer of a debt requires consent of the creditor. By contrast, in France, Germany, and Japan, total transfer avoids these requirements—and also ensures that any transfer of assets is tax advantageous (see *supra* note 24).

[143] For example, the sale of specific assets for stock or cash is not subject to division regulation. Regarding the availability of substitutes in German law, see Schmidt, *supra* note 52, 366–7. Also, if the transfer is of assets which do not amount to a 'business' the Community's employee protection provisions will not apply either.

[144] Arts. 236–22 Code de commerce; Marcus Lutter, EUROPÄISCHES UNTERNEHMENSRECHT 196 (4th ed., 1996).

[145] In France, as in Germany, division enjoys tax advantages over other ways of dividing assets. See Cozian et al, *supra* note 21, para. 1401; Schmidt, *supra* note 52, 366–7. Note, however, that German and French tax law recognize a 'division' only when an entire 'business' is transferred rather than an individual asset.

[146] Arts. 1–2 and 21 of the Sixth Directive make it clear that it applies only where the transferor company is wound up without liquidation after the transfer of all of its assets to other existing or newly-formed companies.

[147] Code de commerce, Art. L236–22. The advantage of this otherwise unattractive choice is that a transfer subject to the division rules benefits from universal transfer of the relevant assets and liabilities. It should also be noted that in the *apport partiel* the shares in the transferee are held by the transferor, not the transferor's shareholders, though the *apport partiel* may be a prelude to the sale of the shares to a third party. See Cozian, *supra* note 21, paras. 1390ff.

[148] Art. 2479 Civil Code (Italy). See also AkgG § 179a (Germany); Art. 467(1) Companies Act (Japan); § 271 DGCL (US). As with mergers the German rule requires three-quarters approval of the

Nevertheless, overall, even European shareholders are accorded less protection in divisions than in their inverse, corporate mergers. We suspect the reason lies in the functional characteristics that make corporate actions 'significant' in the first instance. To begin, a division is a 'smaller' transaction than most mergers, insofar as it merely restructures the existing assets and liabilities of a company instead of adding to the company's existing assets and liabilities. In addition, and most significantly, the risk of conflict of interests in a corporate division—or at least conflict between the shareholders and managers—is lower than the parallel risk of conflict in mergers. Empire dismantling is less prone to create management/shareholder conflicts than empire building. One reason is that it is easy to monitor the fairness of the consideration received by shareholders after a division: shareholders must receive their proportionate amount in the continuing companies. A second reason is that the final period problem is less severe in a division: the managers and directors from the dividing firm usually stay on to manage the continuing firms.

As we discuss below, the main focus of corporate law is on the two most significant agency cost problems presented by divisions and asset sales: the risk that a division will be used to entrench managers, and the risk that creditors' and other stakeholders' claims will be impaired.

7.5.1 The manager-shareholder conflict in divisions

Divisions can be used to entrench management. For example, ITT, in response to a tender offer by Hilton, sought to divide itself into three new entities, each of which would have significant antitakeover provisions, and to do so without obtaining shareholder approval.[149] The U.S. relies on a standards strategy to control this problem.[150] In Europe the requirement for shareholder approval (at least in the transferring company) after full disclosure of the division proposal operates to chill management entrenchment.

7.5.2 The protection of non-shareholder constituencies in divisions

7.5.2.1 The protection of creditors

Creditor protection is particularly necessary in case of corporate divisions.[151] The risk is that creditors' claims will be impaired because the division of assets and

---

voting shareholders, Japanese law does two-third and Delaware does simple majority approval of the outstanding stock. See also *infra* 7.8.

[149] *Hilton Hotels Corp. v. ITT Corp.*, 978 F.Supp. 1342 (D.Nev. 1997). For a similar attempt, see also *Robert Bass Group v. Evans*, 552 A.2d 1227 (Del. Ch. 1988).

[150] *Id.*

[151] See Habersack, *supra* note 87, No 251 (emphasizing the creditor protection aspects of the Sixth Company Law Directive).

liabilities (which is determined in the division contract) is not pro rata as between the receiving companies. Thus, EC law makes companies receiving assets through a division jointly and severally responsible to pre-division creditors, though the liability of the receiving companies other than the one to which the debt was transferred may be limited to the value of the assets transferred.[152] Japanese law adopts a similar approach.[153]

7.5.2.2 The protection of employees

Employees can also be affected by corporate divisions. For example, the assets may be transferred to an entity that seeks to avoid obligations under a collective bargaining agreement. As discussed above, under U.S. labor law, the rights of employees depend on the mode by which operations are transferred.[154] By contrast, the employee protection provided by Community law, as discussed in Section 7.3.3.2, turns on whether there has been a 'transfer of a business' from one employer to another, a phrase which is apt to cover divisions as much as mergers and indeed sales of assets, unless they are 'bare' sales of assets, so that the legal form of the transaction is less central to the application of the rules.[155]

In Japan, the general rule is that divisions transfer debts without consent of individual creditors (though they can object and get payment or collateral, as noted above), but employees are given special rights to voice and generally, unless they agree, their employment contracts are not transferred.[156]

7.6 Reincorporation

The migration of a corporation between jurisdictions can also fundamentally transform the relationship among the participants. If the new home has corporate law that is more pro-management or pro-controlling shareholder, such a migration can aggravate the management-shareholder or controlling-non controlling

---

[152] Art. 12 Sixth Company Law Directive. The joint and several liability of the transferee companies may be dispensed with entirely if, as is the case in the UK, the division requires the approval of a court (as a 'scheme of arrangement') and is dependent upon the consent of the three-quarters of each class of creditor.

[153] Arts. 759(2)(3), 764(2)(3) Companies Act (rule is complex, but principally the transferee is liable only against tort creditors who were not notified).

[154] See *supra* note 135.

[155] Crucially, however, the EC Directive does not cover a control shift effected by a transfer of shares, as discussed in the next chapter, because there is no change in the identity of the employer. In such a case individual and collective contractual obligations of the employer are not formally affected, whilst the consultation obligations which the directive would otherwise impose are now applied under the provisions requiring employers to consult generally on matters likely to have a significant impact on their employees. See Directive 2002/14/EC establishing a general framework for informing and consulting employees in the European Community.

[156] See Act for the Succession of Employment Contracts in Corporate Divisions (2000) (Japan).

shareholder agency problems. If the new home has corporate law that is less protective of non-shareholder interests, such a migration can be a means by which shareholders and managers escape those limitations. These problems are controlled using different tools.

Consider the mechanics of corporate migration. The easiest process is to allow companies, by declaration, to change their jurisdiction of incorporation. In Canada, for example, a corporation can move its jurisdiction while preserving legal personality (i.e., all its legal rights and obligations), upon a two-thirds vote of shareholders, so long as the corporate body will, inter alia, remain liable to creditors in the new jurisdiction.[157] When a corporation fulfills these straightforward requirements, it ceases to be, for example, an Ontario corporation and starts to be an Alberta or federal corporation. This simple, direct approach is highly unusual.[158]

A more common mechanism allows a corporation to migrate by merger. In the United States, for example, the mechanism commonly used to transform, say, a California corporation into a Delaware corporation is to merge the original California corporation and a newly-established, wholly-owned Delaware subsidiary, in which the Delaware corporation is designated to be the surviving corporation. Shareholders of the California corporation typically receive the same percentage of ownership in the Delaware corporation as they previously had in the California corporation. Elsewhere, a scheme of arrangement—which requires a shareholder vote and court approval—has been used to effect a migration.[159] In addition, there are more complex mechanisms involving asset or stock sales that can arrive at the same destination, although sometimes with different tax consequences.[160]

---

[157] Douglas J. Cumming and Jeffrey G. MacIntosh, *The Rationales Underlying Reincorporation and Implications for Canadian Corporations*, 22 INTERNATIONAL REVIEW OF LAW AND ECONOMICS 277, 279 (2002).

[158] A similar procedure is available to the European Company (see below) to move between Community jurisdictions, except that, at the moment, a reincorporation also requires a shift in the location of its head office: Council Regulation 2157/2001/EC on the Statute for a European Company, Arts. 7, 8 and 69. For the argument that the requirement for the head office to be located in the state of incorporation is an infringement of the right to freedom of establishment created by the EC Treaty see Wolf-Georg Ringe, *The European Company Statute in the Context of Freedom of Establishment* (2007) 7 JOURNAL OF CORPORATE LAW STUDIES 185. The Company Law Review (UK) proposed a similar procedure for British companies to move both between the UK jurisdictions and to jurisdictions outside the UK, but the proposal was not taken up in the 2006 reforms, evidently because of Treasury fears of loss of tax revenues. See CLR, *Final Report* (2001), Ch. 13 (URN 01/942).

[159] For an account of News Corp's migration from Australia to Delaware by a scheme of arrangement, see Jennifer G. Hill, *The Shifting Balance of Power between Shareholders and the Board: News Corp's Exodus to Delaware and Other Antipodean Tales* 27–45 (January 2008). Sydney Law School Research Paper No. 08/20, available at SSRN: http://ssrn.com/abstract=1086477.

[160] For an analysis of the intersection of charter competition and tax considerations, see Mitchell Kane and Edward Rock, *Corporate Taxation and International Charter Competition*, 106 MICHIGAN LAW REVIEW 1229 (2008).

In the common migration-by-merger structure, the interests of minority shareholders and creditors are safeguarded primarily by piggy-backing on the protections provided by the merger form detailed above. However, protection of non-shareholder constituencies apart from creditors—principally employees— must come from elsewhere.

Historically, the principal protection for non-shareholders came from block-ing cross-border mergers and functional equivalents.[161] Thus, in Germany, codetermination was protected, in part, by not providing for cross-border mer-gers in the relevant corporate law, reinforced by use of the real seat choice of law rule. Together, these provisions meant that a corporation which migrated to, say, the UK would be deemed to have liquidated itself, with all of the unpleasant busi-ness and tax consequences that follow on liquidation.[162]

More recently, developments in EC law have seemed to undermine this strat-egy for protecting employees. Thus, one of the purposes of the creation of the European Company (SE)[163] was to facilitate cross-border mergers.[164]

A second route for cross-border mergers involves the merger of entities from different member states so as to produce a surviving or resulting com-pany formed under a member state's domestic law (something now provided for by the Cross-Border Merger Directive[165]). In both cases the shareholder and creditor-protection provisions contained in these instruments are derived

---

[161] In many jurisdictions, cross-border mergers are not provided for in the local corporate law. Joseph A. McCahery and Erik P.M. Vermeulen, *Understanding Corporate Mobility in the EU: Towards the Foundations of a European 'Internal Affairs Doctrine'* 9 (27 June 2007), avail-able at http://www.bdi-online.de/Dokumente/Recht-Wettbewerb-Versicherungen/Panel_I_ WorkingPaper_UnderstandingCorpMob.pdf.

[162] For excellent treatments of traditional modes of corporate migration in the EU context, see R.R. Drury, *Migrating Companies*, 24 European Law Review 354 (1999); Karsten Engsig Sorensen and Mette Neville, *Corporate Migration in the European Union: An Analysis of the Proposed 14th EC Company Law Directive on the Transfer of the Registered Office of a Company from One Member State to Another with a Change of Applicable Law*, 6 Columbia Journal of European Law 181 (2000). As discussed below, recent developments in EU law have rendered these analyses somewhat out of date.

[163] The SE was established by the European Company Statute in 2001 (Council Regulation 2157/2001/EC) and the accompanying Directive 2001/86/EC supplementing the Statute with regard to the involvement of employees. It can be created by merger, the creation of a holding company, creation of a joint subsidiary, or conversion of an existing company set up under the laws of a member state. It cannot be created from scratch, and has a minimum capitalization requirement of €120,000. While it must have its real seat in its place of registration, it allows an SE from a real seat jurisdiction to migrate without dissolution and reincorporation. See Eric Engle, *The EU Means Business: A Survey of Legal Challenges and Opportunities in the New Europe*, 4 DePaul Business Law Journal 351, 398 (2006). For further description of the SE, see Europa— Glossary: European Company, http://europa.eu/scadplus/glossary/eu_company_en.htm (last accessed 26 Jan. 2008).

[164] Eidenmueller et al, *Incorporating under European Law: The Societas Europaea as a Vehicle for Legal Arbitrage*, http://papers.ssrn.com/sol3/papers.cfm?abstract_id=1316430.

[165] Council Directive 2005/56/EC, on Cross-Border Mergers of Limited Liability Companies, 2005 O.J. (L 310) 1 [hereinafter Cross-Border Merger Directive]. To some extent the ECJ jumped the gun by holding in the *SEVIC* case that Germany violated Arts. 43 (Freedom of Establishment) and 48 of the EC Treaty by permitting the registration of domestic mergers without also

from the Community and national rules applicable to domestic mergers. Both instruments, however, involve a novel set of rules for the safeguarding of employees' interests in not having their pre-merger 'voice' arrangements at board level undermined by the merger.

For cross-border mergers under either of these Community instruments, the normal principle operative in mergers, that post-merger voice requirements should be determined by the national rules applicable under the laws of the state in which the surviving or resulting company is located,[166] has been extensively qualified. When one or more of the merging companies or companies forming an SE is subject to employee board-level influence requirements, those requirements will be carried over to the surviving or resulting company, even if the laws of the state of incorporation of the latter company would not otherwise require board level influence for employees.[167] This is a default rule, but a strong default rule, since it can be modified only if the merging entities and representatives of the employees negotiate a different solution in advance of the merger.[168] This approach is intended to prevent cross-border mergers from undermining existing board-level voice requirements but not to extend such requirements to companies not previously subject to them (e.g., in a cross-border merger of companies, none of which was previously subject to mandatory board-level employee voice).

Despite this policy, however, German companies have been over-represented in the admittedly small number of SEs formed to date and seem to have been able thereby to obtain what they regard as attractive modifications of their national employee representation systems, even if they have been unable to avoid the principle.[169] A further and more radical question is whether it is possible for a

---

permitting equivalent registration of cross-border mergers (Case C-411/03, *SEVIC Sys. AG* [2005] ECR I-10805, paras. 16–19).

[166] See above.

[167] Voice provided otherwise than via board level influence (principally via mandatory consultation of employee representatives outside the board) is subject to the rules of the jurisdiction of the resulting or emerging entity in the case of a cross-border merger and to rules modeled on the European Works Councils Directive (Directive 94/45/EC) in the case of an SE.

[168] This summarizes a very complicated set of provisions (see Davies, *Workers on the Board of the European Company?* (2003) 32 INDUSTRIAL LAW JOURNAL 75); and the provisions themselves vary slightly according to whether the cross-border merger is effected by formation of an SE under the Cross-Border Mergers Directive. The requirement for pre-merger settlement of the board influence issue through negotiations with the employee representatives is likely significantly to slow down the formation of SEs. In a merger effected under the Directive the merging companies can opt for the 'fall-back' rules on board level representation without entering into any negotiations with the employee representatives.

[169] For example, a reduction in the size of the board (required under domestic German law to be at least 21 for large companies: Mitbestimmungsgesetz § 7) or a 'freezing' of the domestic level of representation (for example, a German company about to go through the employee threshold which would trigger the domestic requirement to move from one-third to parity representation can form an SE which will be (and will remain) affected only by the German rules applicable to the merging company as of the date of formation of the SE). See B. Keller and F. Werner, *The Establishment of the European Company: The First Cases from an Industrial Relations Perspective* (2008) 14 EUROPEAN JOURNAL OF INDUSTRIAL RELATIONS 153.

company to escape entirely from its domestic board-level requirements by a two-step process involving moving to a jurisdiction without such requirements for its domestic companies and then a subsequent merger within that jurisdiction. For example, under the European Company Statute, could a German corporation merge with a wholly-owned UK company to form a UK-registered SE (to which, as indicated above, the German board level representation rules would apply), and then transform the UK SE to a domestic UK company, to which they might not? A number of barriers may limit this gambit. First, at least two years must pass before the UK-registered SE may transform again.[170] Second, the directive accompanying the European Company Regulation requires member states to take measures to prevent misuse of the European Company procedure 'for the purpose of depriving employees of rights to' board-level representation.[171] This set of moves may be somewhat easier in relation to a cross-border merger.[172]

7.7 Voluntary Liquidation

No change in the relationship of the participants in the firm is as fundamental as the final, complete termination of those relationships, as in voluntary liquidation.[173] Moreover, as with other fundamental transformations, agency costs can arise. For example, a firm can be liquidated by a controlling shareholder who wishes to take corporate opportunities for itself or the shareholders as a whole may wish to rid themselves of a contingent liability.

The protection of creditors is the core rule of liquidations: that creditor claims be met before any distribution is made to the shareholders. However, this rule may prove under- or over-protective of contingent creditors whose claims are normally accepted in the liquidation on the basis of a negotiation between liquidator and creditor.[174] In some jurisdictions, protections specific to voluntary liquidation are added. Thus, in the UK the directors are required to support the shareholders' resolution for voluntary liquidation with a solvency declaration to the effect that the company will be able to meet its debts in full within

---

[170] The subsequent transformation of the UK-registered SE into a UK domestic company cannot occur until two years after the registration of the UK SE (Art. 66).

[171] Directive 2001/86/EC, art. 11.

[172] Here the company resulting from the second merger will be subject to the same board-level voice requirements as the first UK company, if the second merger takes place within three years of the cross-border merger: Cross-Border Mergers Directive, Art. 16(7). However, the Cross-Border Merger Directive contains no general anti-avoidance language akin to that found in the European Company Directive.

[173] Sometimes referred to as 'solvent' liquidation. The bankruptcy of companies, whether voluntary or involuntary, is dealt with in Chapter 5.

[174] For the difficulties in handling the contingent claims of potential tort victims (who had inhaled asbestos) and future pensioners in the trans-Atlantic insolvency of T&N Ltd and its U.S. parent, Federal Mogul, see *Re T&N Ltd* [2005] 2 BCLC 488, *ibid (No. 2)* [2006] 2 BCLC 374 and *ibid (No. 3)* [2007] 1 BCLC 563.

a year of the commencement of the winding-up of the company.[175] The negligent making of such a declaration is sanctioned by criminal penalties. The function of this rule, however, is to ensure that shareholders are properly allocated control of the liquidation—rather than creditors, as would be the case if the solvency declaration could not be made. Other jurisdictions achieve the same result by funneling all liquidations of insolvent companies via the court and providing for the court's procedure to take precedence over that initiated by the members.

As to minority shareholder protection, U.S. and European law differ in much the same way as they do in the amendment of corporate charters. While a voluntary liquidation in Delaware typically requires approval of both the board and of a simple majority of all the outstanding stock,[176] in Europe a decision of the shareholders alone suffices.[177] In both systems, controlling shareholders are not 'locked in' because they control the liquidation decision. The European jurisdictions, having abandoned the board as a trustee for the minority shareholders, require supermajority approval for the dissolution resolution and rely on standards to do the remainder of the work.[178] The UK provides some additional protection of the minority shareholders by not permitting the existing management (and, by extension, the controlling shareholders) to act as liquidator of the company. Requiring the appointment of a professional insolvency practitioner, even in a solvent liquidation,[179] places an obstacle in the way of corporate controllers seeking to acquire the business or assets of the company in the liquidation at a favorable price.

A voluntary liquidation may impact adversely on the position of the employees. Although their accrued entitlements will be protected by virtue of their status as creditors, as will the financial entitlements they may have as a result of being laid off by the company, their future job prospects may be at risk. The employees may have some opportunity to exercise 'voice' in relation to the liquidation decision, as a result of general provisions providing for employee involvement in the company's decision-making, though such provisions tend to be more demanding in respect of open (as opposed to closed) companies. If the liquidation takes the form of a sale of the company's business or part of it (rather than a break-up sale of assets), then in Europe the Community provisions discussed above[180] in relation to both consultation and transfer of employment will apply.

---

[175] Insolvency Act 1986, s 89.
[176] DGCL §275. A shareholder-only dissolution is possible only if it is based on a unanimous decision of the shareholders.
[177] Insolvency Act 1986 (UK) s 84; AktG § 262 (Germany); Commercial Code L225–246 (France) Art. 2484 Civil Code (Italy). However, the requirement for a solvency declaration (above) makes the decision in effect a joint one of the board and the shareholders in the UK.
[178] *Abus de majorité* in France (see Cozian et al, *supra* note 21, para. 447) and *abuso della maggioranza* in Italy (see Cass. 5–5-1995, n. 4923); Italy also requires a supermajority for the approval of winding-up in non-listed public companies (two-thirds majority representing one-third of the outstanding capital); BGHZ 76, 352 (Germany—to similar effect) or unfair prejudice in the UK.
[179] Insolvency Act 1986 (UK) ss 388(1) and 389.   [180] Section 7.4.3.2.

7.8 General Provisions on Significant Transactions

Given the penumbra of uncertainty about what corporate decisions are 'fundamental', and so should not be left entirely to the board, it is understandable that legal systems seek to remove particular types of transaction from unilateral board control, rather than laying down general tests to identify significant transactions. The downside of the transaction-by-transaction approach is that it can be side-stepped, as we have seen,[181] by the adoption of a non-regulated transaction which achieves the same functional goal. To be sure, in some jurisdictions, strongly enforced directors' duties operate as powerful general standards across transactional types. This is particularly the case in Delaware. However, where a decision rights strategy is thought to be appropriate, the problem of identifying the fundamental corporate decisions and transactions is particularly acute.

Both Germany and the UK have developed general criteria for the identification of situations in which shareholder consent for a transaction is required, though in neither case as a result of legislative action.[182] In Germany the doctrine was developed by the highest civil court for company law (the Second Senate of the *Bundesgerichtshof*), despite the provision in the open company law restricting the powers of the shareholders to a list of matters and otherwise providing that 'the shareholders' meeting may decide on matters concerning the management of the company only if required by the management board.'[183] In its famous *Holzmüller*[184] decision, later restricted and somewhat clarified in its *Gelatine I* and *II* decisions,[185] the BGH turned this provision on its head in the case of a spin-off of a major part of the company's operations into a separate subsidiary. In principle, it required shareholder approval for such a restructuring on the grounds that the rights which the shareholders of the parent previously had in relation to these assets would be exercisable in future in relation to the new subsidiary by the management board of the parent alone, as the representative of the new subsidiary's only shareholder. The decision caused enormous uncertainty as to when the management had to seek the approval of the shareholders in corporate restructurings. Although the *Gelatine* cases somewhat restrict the scope of

---

[181] See *supra* note 104.

[182] In Italy, some decisions entailing a substantial change of the company's business require shareholder approval: see Art. 2361 Civil Code (acquisition of shareholdings by public companies to be approved whenever it results in a substantial change of company's business); Art. 2479 Civil Code (in private companies, transactions causing a substantial change in the company's business require shareholder approval).

[183] AktG § 119(2).   [184] BGHZ 83,122 (1982).

[185] BGH ZIP 2004, 993 and BGH ZIP 2004, 1001. See generally Marc Löbbe, *Corporate Groups: Competences of the Shareholders' Meeting and Minority Protection* (2004) 5 German Law Journal 1057; Florian Möslein, *Towards an Organisational Law of the Polycorporate Enterprise? A Comparative Analysis. Corporate Ownership and Control* (forthcoming). Available at SSRN: http://ssrn.com/abstract=887281.

the doctrine, by confining it to decisions affecting a major part (probably around 80%) of the company's assets and having a highly significant impact on the practical value of the shareholders' rights, uncertainty still exists in relation to the scope of the doctrine.[186]

In the UK the Financial Service Authority's 'significant transactions' rules,[187] which apply to companies with a primary listing on the main market in London, aim at a similar objective, but do so in a more mechanical way.[188] In principle, any transaction (by the company or its subsidiary undertakings) of certain size, relative to the listed company proposing to make it, requires *ex ante* shareholder approval, unless it is within the ordinary course of the company's business or is a financing transaction not involving the acquisition or disposal of a fixed assets of the company.[189] The requisite size is 25% or more of any one of the listed company's assets, profits or gross capital or where the consideration for the transaction is 25% or more of value of the ordinary shares of the listed company.[190]

France does not make use of the decision rights strategy in general, although the market regulator may accord an exit right to minority shareholders under the provisions discussed above,[191] that is, when a listed company's controllers propose to 'reorient the company's business'.[192] This, as we have seen, is part of a set of provisions empowering the regulator to protect minority interests through the buy-out requirement where the majority propose significant legal or financial changes to the business by way of significant amendments to the company's charter, merger of the company into its controller, disposal of all or most of its assts or a prolonged suspension of dividend payments, as well as reorientation of the business. As such, the French approach, besides its different remedy, seems to fall in between the German one of trying to identify a general principle and the British one of using a single financial criterion for triggering the minority protections, by laying down a list of circumstances, albeit a quite extensive one, in which a buy-out may be required.[193]

---

[186] As a result of the *Gelatine* cases it is now clear that, where shareholder approval is required, three-quarters of those voting must consent, by analogy with what is needed to change the constitution of the company. See 7.2 above. Under Delaware law, dropping assets into a subsidiary does not require a shareholder vote, even if they amount to all or substantially all of the assets. DGCL § 271(c).

[187] Listing Rules, Chapter 10.

[188] 'This chapter is intended to cover transactions that are outside the ordinary course of the listed company's business and may change a security holder's economic interest in the company's assets or liabilities...' (LR 10.1.4.)

[189] LR 10.1.3.

[190] LR 10.2.2, 10.5, and 10 Annex 1. A reverse takeover (LR 10.2.3) and an indemnity (LR 10.2.4) are included in the covered transactions in certain circumstances, but the rules can be waived in restricted circumstances if the listed company is in financial difficulty (LR 10.8).

[191] Section 7.2.2.

[192] Reg Gen AMR 236–6. See Viandier, *OPA*, paras. 2603–09.

[193] There is some doubt about the power of the AMF to make regulation 236–6, which seems to have arisen out of the practice of the regulator without clear legislative sanction: Viandier, OPA, para. 2591.

7.9 Explaining Differences in the Regulation of Significant Corporate Changes

The most striking conclusion to emerge from our review of fundamental corporate changes is how uniform major jurisdictions are in their distinctions between the bulk of corporate actions that are fully delegated to the board, and the handful of corporate changes in which the board's authority is limited, by a shareholder vote requirement or direct regulation. In all jurisdictions, mergers, charter amendments, reincorporations and dissolutions fall outside the scope of (complete) delegation to the board of directors, and require shareholder approval by an extraordinary resolution. In no jurisdiction does the investment of capital in firm projects or the incurring of debt require shareholder approval, no matter how large these transactions are.

Despite widespread consensus about which corporate changes ought to be regulated and which ought to be left to the board, jurisdictions nonetheless differ in certain familiar respects. In general, these differences do not track the common law/civil law divide. Although continental European jurisdictions rely less on judicially-enforced standards to regulate mergers than do the Anglo-American jurisdictions, merger transactions are atypical of the broader class of significant corporate actions. Over the entire class, France and Germany rely as heavily on standards as the U.S. or the UK.

Rather than following the common law/civil law divide, differences in the regulation of significant corporate actions among our jurisdictions appear to reflect a broader pattern of divergences in governance structures. EC law and, to some extent Japanese law, accord more attention to management-shareholder conflict in regulating corporate decisions than does the law of U.S. jurisdictions. In Europe, shareholder approval is more limited in time (e.g., for authorized capital or the repurchase of shares) or required for a wider range of decisions (e.g., reductions in legal capital) than in the U.S. In Japan, shareholders must approve large acquisitions, even when acquiring companies pay for these acquisitions in cash. European shareholders (except, as noted above, in Italy) may also initiate organic changes, including mergers and major restructurings, by extraordinary resolution, whereas in U.S. jurisdictions shareholders can only veto them, after such organic changes have been proposed by the board.

The greater power of the general shareholders meeting to make significant corporate decisions in EU jurisdictions reflects the stronger legal position of European shareholders and coincides—as we noted in Chapter 3—with the well-known differences in ownership structure between U.S. and European companies.[194] The different allocation of power may be evidence that 'the allocation

---

[194] See *supra* 3.1.1.5, 3.1.2.5, and 3.2.5.

of power backs up the prevailing ownership structures' and grants the effective controllers the right to exercise and retain control.[195] In the U.S., where shares tend to be widely held and management is dominant, only the board can initiate fundamental changes. In Europe, where controlling shareholders are dominant, shareholders have greater power to initiate major changes.

But if the U.S. provides less protection to shareholders as a class, it offers more protection to minority shareholders. As noted above, boards must approve important decisions in the U.S., which modestly limits the power of controlling shareholders. In addition, both the U.S. and Japan provide an exit strategy, in the form of appraisal rights, for minority shareholders who vote against mergers or (in Japan and most U.S. states) other organic transactions. U.S. jurisdictions also provide a standard of entire fairness, backed by the threat of a class action lawsuit, for significant transactions between entities controlled by a single shareholder. By contrast, EU boards generally do not limit the power of controlling shareholders, appraisal rights are uncommon in the EU, and shareholders suing for violations of standards face significant enforcement obstacles.[196] In general, the European jurisdictions focus their efforts on protecting minority shareholders from changes in legal capital. For example, unlike the U.S. or Japan, all major European juris-dictions grant at least default preemptive rights in case of new issues of shares and share repurchases.

The differences among jurisdictions also seem roughly to map the differences in permitted transactional flexibility: in the U.S. and the UK, where there are a variety of alternative transactional forms with different requirements but which arrive at the same goal, the systems are forced to adopt *ex post* standards strategies. By contrast, where transactional flexibility is limited, more regulation can be *ex ante*. While France, Germany, Italy, and Japan have legislated detailed merger procedures to safeguard shareholder decision rights, the UK and U.S. rely heav-ily on the judiciary to screen mergers under the aegis of a basic fairness standard, with the UK also addressing mergers in the City Code.[197] Indeed, the transac-tional flexibility provided by UK law allows public corporations to pursue one species of mergers (termed 'amalgamations') without complying with the provi-sions that were inserted in the UK Companies Acts in order to implement the EC Merger Directive.[198] Further, the UK preference for *ex post* standards is reflected in the treatment of mergers between private companies: the UK regulates such mergers by means of informal judicial screening, while France, Germany, Italy, and Japan impose similar statutory merger procedures on both closely held

---

[195] Luca Enriques and Paolo Volpin, *Corporate Governance Reforms in Continental Europe*, 21 Journal of Economic Perspectives 117, 127 (2007).

[196] See *supra* 5.1.5 and 5.2.3.3.

[197] See Chapter 8 for discussion of the City Code.

[198] See Paul Davies, Gower and Davies' Principles of Modern Company Law (8th ed., 2008) para. 29–10.

and public companies.[199] While this divergence between the UK and U.S. and continental Europe may be due in part to differences in ownership structure, and in part to the fact that mergers are more common on the continent than in the UK (where business planners favor tender offers[200]), it surely also reflects a more basic difference in the permitted transactional flexibility as well as views on the relative value of judicially-enforced standards on the one hand, and *ex ante* rules and decision rights on the other.[201]

Finally, the protection of non-shareholder constituencies in significant corporate actions resembles that offered by corporate governance more generally. As compared with U.S. law, EC and Japanese law are more protective of creditors, both in general (through capital maintenance rules) and when firms embark on mergers and other organic changes. Moreover, not surprisingly, EC law provides workers with substantially more protection in mergers and other restructurings than U.S. law does.

---

[199] See Company Law Review Steering Group, *Modern Company Law, For a Competitive Economy, Final Report* I281 (2001) (a majority of consultees thought it would be inappropriate to create a broader statutory merger procedure without court supervision for private companies).

[200] Of course, the absence of more general merger provisions may also have led to a preference for tender offers in the UK.

[201] Unsurprisingly, academics also debate the benefits and determinants of Mergers & Acquisitions (M&A) activity. See, e.g., Gegor Andrade, Mark Mitchell, and Erik Stafford, *New Evidence and Perspective on Mergers*, 15(2) JOURNAL OF ECONOMIC PERSPECTIVES 103 (2001); Marina Martynova and Sjoerd Oosting, *The Long-Term Operating Performance of European Mergers and Acquisitions, in International Mergers and Acquisitions Activity since 1990: Recent Research and Quantitative Analysis* (G. Gregoriou and L. Renneboog (eds.), 2007), at 79–116.

8

Control Transactions

Paul Davies and Klaus Hopt

8.1 Agency Problems in Control Transactions

8.1.1 Control transactions

In this chapter we consider the legal strategies for addressing the principal/agent problems which arise when a person (the acquirer) attempts, through offers to the company's shareholders, to acquire sufficient voting shares in a company to give it control of that company.[1] The core transaction in this chapter is one between a third party (the acquirer)[2] and the company's shareholders,[3] whereby the third party aims to acquire the target company's shares to the point where it can appoint its nominees to the board of that company. This is what we mean in this chapter by 'control transactions'. Of course, control may also pass to a new share-holder or set of shareholders as a result of transactions between *the company* and its shareholders or the investing public (as when a company issues or re-purchases shares). However, such control transactions involving corporate decisions can be analysed in the same manner as other corporate decisions, a task we undertake elsewhere in this book. The absence of a corporate decision and the presence of a new actor, in the shape of the acquirer, give the agency problems of control trans-actions (as defined) a special character which warrants separate treatment in this chapter.[4]

---

[1] Note that we will use the terms 'company' and 'corporation' interchangeably.

[2] Of course, the acquirer may, and typically will, already be a shareholder of the target company, but it need not be and the relevant rules (other than shareholding disclosure rules) do not turn on whether it is or not. The bidder may also be or contain the existing management of the target company (as in a management buy-out (MBO)). This situation generates significant agency problems for the shareholders of the target company which we address below.

[3] More precisely, its vote-holders. As we see below, addressing effectively both the main sets of agency problems in this area is made more problematic where voting rights and cash-flow rights in a company are not proportionately distributed.

[4] The special character of control transactions is also reflected in the increasing number of juris-dictions which have adopted sets of rules, separate from their general company laws, to regulate them.

More challenging for analysis is the distinction between shifts in control through statutory mergers[5] and control transactions. In terms of end result, there may not be much difference between a statutory merger and a friendly takeover bid, at least where the successful bidder avails itself of a mechanism for the compulsory purchase of non-accepting minorities. However, in terms of the legal techniques used to effect the control shift, there is a chasm between the two mechanisms. A merger involves corporate decisions, certainly by the shareholders and usually by the board as well. Control transactions, by contrast, are effected by private contract between the acquirer and the shareholders individually. Nevertheless, at least in friendly acquisitions, the acquirer often has a free choice whether to structure its bid as a contractual offer or as a merger proposal. This creates a regulatory dilemma. In some jurisdictions the regulation of takeovers is confined to control shifts, as defined above.[6] Others, the minority, adapt the rules for control shifts and apply them, at least in part, to acquisitions through statutory mergers, on the grounds that many of the principles applicable to contractual offers (for example, the equality rules governing the level of the required consideration, some of the timing rules and even the 'no frustration' principle) can be applied to control shifts by means of statutory mergers. Moreover, not to do so might provide an incentive for acquirers to structure their offers that way. Where this latter approach is adopted, the rules on control transactions act as an additional layer of regulation of the statutory merger, whose significance depends upon the extent to which the rules for statutory mergers have not already occupied the regulatory ground.[7]

Control transactions, not implemented as statutory mergers, may be effected in a variety of ways which can be used singly or, more likely, in combination: via private treaty with a small number of important shareholders; via purchases of shares on the market; or by way of a general and public offer to all the shareholders of the target company. In the case of the public offer it may be either 'friendly'

---

[5] See *supra* 7.4.

[6] Thus, the definition of a takeover in Art. 2.1(a) of the Directive of the European Parliament and of the Council on takeover bids (2004/25/EC, O.J. L 142, 30.4.2004—hereafter 'Takeover Directive') excludes statutory mergers.

[7] Thus, in the UK, the City Code starts from the principle that the Code applies equally to the peculiar UK version of the statutory merger (the 'scheme of arrangement': see *supra* 7.4), except to the extent that the statutory merger procedure regulates a particular issue or the nature of the statutory merger procedure makes a particular Code provision inapplicable. (The Panel on Takeovers and Mergers, The Takeover Code (9th ed., 2009) § A3(b) and Appendix 7—hereafter 'City Code'). This recently introduced Appendix results from the Panel's decision further to specify how the Code applies to mergers in the light of the 'significant increase in recent years in the use of schemes of arrangement in order to implement transactions which are regulated by the Code': see Panel Consultation Paper 2007/1. By contrast, the acquisition of Bank Austria AG by Bayerische Hypo Vereinsbank was effected by a merger in order to avoid the new Austrian takeover legislation. See 4 Neue Zeitschrift für Gesellschaftsrecht 282 (2001).

(i.e., supported by the management of the target company) or 'hostile' (i.e., made over the heads of target management to the shareholders of the target).[8]

Of the three acquisition methods, the second and third are clearly facilitated if the target's shares are traded on a public market. For this reason, companies with publicly traded shares are at the centre of attention in this chapter. In fact, legislation specific to control transactions is usually (though not always) confined to companies whose securities are traded on public markets (or some sub-set of these, such as the top-tier markets).[9] Not only are hostile bids difficult to organize other than in relation to publicly traded companies, but also the shareholders' agency and coordination problems (discussed below) are less pronounced in closely held companies. Nevertheless, the control transaction is not logically confined to such companies and we make some reference to non-traded[10] companies as well. In jurisdictions which rely on general corporate standards, such as fiduciary duties, rather than rules specific to control transactions, to regulate the behavior of target management or the target's controlling shareholders, the application of these standards to the managements and shareholders of non-traded companies raises no difficult boundary questions.[11]

8.1.2 Agency and coordination issues

8.1.2.1 *Where there are no controlling shareholders in the target company*

Where there are no controlling shareholders in the target company, the main focus is on the first agency relationship, i.e., that between the board and the shareholders as a class. Here, the acquirer's underlying strategy is likely to focus on a public offer to all the shareholders, preceded by pre-bid acquisition, through the market, of as large a 'toe-hold' shareholding in the target as the acquirer can manage without revealing the object of its intended offer. Unlike in the case of the

---

[8] Of course, the board's decision whether to recommend an offer, either at the outset or during the course of an initially hostile offer, will often be influenced by its estimate of the bidder's chances of succeeding with a hostile offer. Further, the number of concluded deals which remain hostile to the end is likely to be small whether or not the incumbent management is in a position effectively to block the bid: if it can, the acquirer will negotiate with it to achieve its recommendation; if it cannot, there is little point in target management opposition. Thus, it may be difficult to characterize a particular bid as 'friendly' or 'hostile' but the question of whether a particular system of rules facilitates hostile bids is of enormous importance. See *infra* 8.2.1.

[9] Thus the Takeover Directive applies only to companies whose securities are traded on a 'regulated market' (Art. 1.1)—normally a top-tier market. The City Code applies slightly more widely (to all companies which may offer their shares to the public and even to closely held companies where there has been something analogous to a public market in the private company's shares) (City Code, § A3(a)).

[10] Throughout this book, corporations whose shares do not trade freely in impersonal markets are also referred to as 'closely held' companies.

[11] See *infra* 8.3.1 for a discussion of U.S. rules on sales of shares by controlling shareholders to looters.

company with controlling shareholders, the control shift effected by a successful general offer in this case is not from those who have control (the blockholders) to the acquirer who wishes to obtain it. Rather, de facto control of the company was probably in the hands of the target board, so that control shifts from the board of the target to the (board of the) acquirer. Therefore, there is a disjunction between the parties to the dealings which bring about the transfer of control (acquirer and target shareholders) and the parties to the control shift itself (acquirer and target board).

It is precisely this disjunction which generates the agency issues which need to be addressed. The control transaction may be wealth-enhancing from the target shareholders' point of view but threaten the jobs and perquisites of the existing senior management. The incumbent management of the target may thus have an incentive to block such transfers, by exercising their powers of central management. They may seek to use those powers to make the target less attractive to a potential bidder or to prevent the offer being put to the shareholders. These steps may take a myriad of forms but the main categories are: placing a block of the target's securities in the hands of persons not likely to accept a hostile bid; structuring the rights of the shareholders and creditors, for example, through poison pills; and placing strategic assets outside the reach of even a successful bidder.

Alternatively, the transaction may not be wealth-enhancing from the shareholders' point of view but the incumbent management may have an incentive to promote it to the shareholders, because the management stand to gain from the proposed control shift, either by reaping significant compensation for loss of office or by being part of the bidding consortium. The control transaction cannot be effected without the consent of the shareholders, the transfer of whose securities is the central mechanism for effecting the shift. However, the incumbent management may use their influence with the shareholders and their knowledge of the company to 'sell' the offer to its addressees or, in the case of competing bids, they may use those factors to favour one bidder over another.

However, the rules governing control shifts need also to deal with a second matter where shareholdings in the target company are dispersed. This is the coordination problem of dispersed shareholders as against the acquirer. In particular, the acquirer may seek to induce shareholders of the target to accept an offer which is less than optimal. There are a number of ways in which this can be done,[12] but in essence they rely on information asymmetry or unequal treatment of the target's shareholders. Moreover, the agency problems of the shareholders as a class as against the incumbent management may continue even if the latter do not (or cannot) prevent an offer from being made. This is particularly likely to be the case where it is in the interests of the incumbent management to promote a deal between the acquirer and the target shareholders.

---

[12] See *infra* 8.2.5.

8.1.2.2 *Where there are controlling shareholders*[13]

Where there is an existing controlling block of shares held by one or a small number of shareholders, the acquirer is likely to come to an agreement with the blockholders first and decide whether, and on what terms, to make a general offer to the non-controlling shareholders only once such an agreement has been reached. As between the acquirer and the blockholder, it is likely that the standard provisions on commercial sales will cope well with any problems likely to arise.

However, the general rules of civil law are not likely to address effectively the coordination problems as between the acquirer and the non-controlling shareholders (at least if these are dispersed) nor the agency problems between controlling and non-controlling shareholders. The former problem is largely the same as that discussed in relation to companies with no controlling shareholder.[14] As to the latter, the controlling shareholder may engage in rent-seeking by selling control of the company to an acquirer who will 'loot' it; or, simply sell it to an acquirer who, perhaps for good commercial reasons, will be less respectful of the interests of non-controlling shareholders than the vendor had been. This is particularly so where the target, upon acquisition, will become a member of a group of companies where business opportunities, which the target has been able to exploit in the past, may be allocated to other group members. The law could seek to address this problem by focussing on the existing controlling shareholder's decision to sell or on the terms upon which the acquirer obtains the controlling block or upon the subsequent conduct of the affairs of the target by the new controller. In the last case, reliance will be placed on the general legal strategies for controlling centralized management, including group law.[15] In the first and second cases, the law is likely to develop rules or standards specific to the control transaction, though they may take a wide variety of forms, up to and including an exit right for the minority upon a change of control, via a mandatory bid requirement.[16]

8.1.2.3 *Agency problems of non-shareholders*

Finally, whatever the structure of the target company's shareholding, agency issues will arise as between the acquirer and non-shareholders, especially employees. In those countries where company law is used to address company/employee agency issues as a matter of general practice via standing employee or union representation on the board,[17] a control shift effected simply by means of a transaction between the acquirer and the target shareholders, thus by-passing the corporate organ which embodies the principle of employee representation, is

---

[13] All jurisdictions will face such situations, even if the typical pattern of shareholdings in companies in that jurisdiction is the dispersed one.

[14] *Supra* 8.1.2.1.   [15] See *supra* 4.1.

[16] See *infra* 8.3.   [17] See *supra* 4.2.1.

likely to be regarded with suspicion. Consequently, the strategy of using board composition rules to address the general agency costs of employees will argue in favour of the insertion of the board into the control shift transaction, usually via a relatively relaxed regulation of defensive measures on the part the target board. Even where company law is not normally used to address employee agency issues, the freedom of management to take defensive measures may be seen as a proxy for the protection of the interests of employees and, possibly, other stakeholders. As we shall see,[18] the closeness of the 'fit' between the ability of management to defend itself and the interests of non-shareholder stakeholders is contentious. Beyond this, regulation of the control transaction, because of its focus on the acquirer/target shareholder relationship, is unpropitious ground for dealing with the agency costs of employees, except through disclosure of information, which may be useful to stakeholders generally in the generation of political or social pressure in response to the offer,[19] or through mandatory consultation over the consequences of the takeover for the employees.

Creditors, as well as employees, may stand to lose out as a result of changes in the company's strategy implemented by the acquirer, especially changes in the company's risk profile, perhaps arising from the leveraged nature of the bid. Those most at risk, the long-term lenders, are well placed to protect themselves by contractual provisions, such as 'event risk' covenants in loans.[20] Such protections may not always be fully protective of the creditors, but adopting sub-optimal contractual protection is normally part of the commercial bargain contained in the contract. Consequently, the agency costs of creditors are not normally addressed in control-shift rules.[21]

8.1.2.4 The nature and scope of control-shift regulation

Many of the agency problems of control transactions are familiar from earlier chapters of this book. However, they appear in this chapter in a novel context. A central feature of that context is the tension between a commitment to the free transferability of shares and a recognition that sales of shares sufficient to produce a control shift have consequences for the policies of the company which would normally call for a decision of either the board or the general meeting (or, of course, both). This point applies as much to transfers from existing controlling shareholders as to transfers of control from the board of the target. Moreover, the control transaction brings onto the scene a new actor, namely the acquirer, whose

---

[18] *Infra* 8.5.

[19] Trade unions and management in some countries may be able to form an effective, if implicit, coalition to oppose a proposed acquisition.

[20] William W. Bratton, *Bond Covenants and Creditor Protection*, 7 European Business Organization Review 39 especially at 58ff (2006).

[21] It is sometimes difficult to distinguish covenants whose aim is to protect the lender and those which aim to protect target management ('poison debt'); in fact, both groups may have an interest in inserting provisions which make debt repayable upon a change of control. However, this point relates to the agency costs of the shareholders, not the creditors.

activities both generate new problems (arising, for example, out of the manner in which the offer to the shareholders of the target is formulated) and reveal the traditional agency problems (for example, that between shareholders and management of the target) in a novel and more complicated setting.

A major question which then arises is whether the element of novelty in the control transaction leads to the fashioning of rules specific to control shifts or whether the agency and coordination issues inherent in control transactions can be handled by the application of the established principles of corporate and securities law, albeit in this new context. All our jurisdictions utilize to some degree both types of approach, but the balance between them can vary considerably. Towards one end of the spectrum stands the law applicable where the target company is incorporated in Delaware. Although both federal law (in the shape of the Williams Act)[22] and Delaware law (in the shape of rules governing access to the short-form, squeeze-out merger)[23] contain some rules specific to control transactions, the main weight of the rules on control shifts (for example, dealing with the allocation of decision rights over the offer)[24] is to be found in the application to the directors of the target company of the general fiduciary standards governing board decision-making.

By contrast, in the member states of the European Community rules specific to control shifts are more important (though not to the complete exclusion of general rules of corporate and securities law). Thus, the Takeover Directive lays down an extensive set of rules which is confined to control shifts. Further, the directive reflects the long-standing leaning towards extensive control-shift specific rules in some of the member states, notably France, Italy, and the UK. Japan sits somewhat between these two models, though it is difficult to classify as its rules are still in a state of development. It has legislation specific to control shifts,[25] but, on the central issue of the allocation of decision rights over the offer, court-developed general standards applying to directors' decisions are still central.[26]

The line between a rule specific to control transactions and the application of a general corporate law principle to control shifts may be a fine one, especially if the general principle is applied frequently in the specific context and begins to form a jurisprudence of its own. Nevertheless, it is a significant one. First, the type of body responsible for the application of the rules is likely to be different. The application of the body of specific rules is likely to be a task given to a specialized agency. The Takeover Directive requires member states to 'designate the authority or authorities competent to supervise bids for the purpose of the rules which

---

[22] 1968, 82 Stat. 454, codified at 15 U.S.C. §§ 78m(d)–(e) and 78n(d)–(f), adding new §§ 13(d), 13(e), and 14(d)–(f) to the Securities Exchange Act of 1934.
[23] *Infra* 8.4.   [24] *Infra* 8.2.3.
[25] See Art. 27–2(1)(5) of the Financial Instruments and Exchange Act 2006.
[26] *Infra* 8.2.2—coupled in this case with non-binding guidelines issued by the government.

they make or introduce pursuant to this Directive.'[27] This will generally be the financial markets regulator but may be a specific regulator for takeovers.[28] The application of general corporate law principles, by contrast, is likely to be a task which falls to the courts, so that the core of control shift regulation in Delaware is judge-made. Second, as noted,[29] specific control shift rules tend to apply only in respect of target companies whose shares are publicly traded, whereas general principles can be adapted by the courts for all types of control shift. Third, it has been argued that the 'judicialization of US takeover regulation made it easier for a pro-management approach to emerge' because, on the one hand, case law precedents are relatively free from interest group influence and, on the other, the courts can decide only the cases which come before them and management (and their lawyers) are in a good position to control the flow of litigation and appear as repeat players before the courts.[30] Of course, this does not mean that specific regulation is necessarily pro-shareholder: that depends on how interest group pressures play out in any particular case. As we shall see, a variety of patterns of specific regulation across jurisdictions can be found.

However, takeover-specific rules do not often address the agency problems which arise as between the shareholders of the *acquiring* company and their board in relation to the decision to acquire the target; and we shall follow that lead in this chapter. This issue is but an example (albeit an important one) of the general agency problems existing between shareholders (and creditors) and boards in relation to setting the corporate strategy, which have been fully analysed in earlier chapters.[31] However, it is central to this chapter to consider the extent to which regulation purportedly designed to address the agency and coordination costs of *target* shareholders (both as a class and as non-controlling shareholders) impacts upon the incentives for potential bidders actually to put forward an offer.[32]

---

[27] Art. 4.1.

[28] The former is by far the more common choice but the UK, for largely historical reasons, gives the supervision of takeovers to a body (City Panel on Takeovers and Mergers) different from the general financial market regulator (Financial Services Authority (FSA)).

[29] *Supra* 8.1.1.

[30] J. Armour and D. Skeel, *Who Writes the Rules for Hostile Takeovers, and Why?—The Peculiar Divergences of U.S. and U.K. Takeover Regulation*, 95 GEORGETOWN LAW JOURNAL 1727, 1793 (2007).

[31] See *supra* Chapters 3 and 5.

[32] On this issue in general see Athanasios Kouloridas, THE LAW AND ECONOMICS OF TAKEOVERS: AN ACQUIRER'S PERSPECTIVE (2008). The empirical literature is virtually unanimous in concluding that target shareholders capture nearly all of the gains from takeovers and that the gains for bidders' shareholders are small or non-existent (even negative for hostile takeovers). See M. Martynova and L. Renneboog, MERGERS AND ACQUISITIONS IN EUROPE (2006) 5.1 and 5.2 (available on http://www.ssrn.com/abstract_id=880379)—confirming the U.S. empirical studies in relation to the European takeover wave of 1993 to 2001. Acquirer shareholders thus seem to have strong incentives to control their management's misjudgments in this area.

8.2 Agency Problems Where There is No Controlling Shareholder

8.2.1 The decision rights choice: shareholders only or shareholders and board jointly

The central issue is the extent to which the bidder is provided with access to the target shareholders to make and maintain an offer for their shares without the consent of the incumbent management. Theoretically, the available solutions range from allocating the decision on the control shift exclusively to the shareholders by depriving the management of any role in the interactions between acquirer and target shareholders, to designing the control shift decision as a joint one for incumbent management and shareholders, as if it were a statutory merger. In the former case, the shareholders' agency problems as against the management are resolved by terminating the agency relationship for this class of decision: the principal is protected by becoming the decision-maker[33] and the principle of free transferability of shares is made paramount. In the latter case, both management and target shareholders must consent if the control shift is to occur. The acquirer is forced to negotiate with both groups. The potential gains from the control shift may now have to be split three ways (acquirer, target shareholders, target management) and, to the extent that the benefits to management of their continuing control of the target company exceed any share of the gain from the control shift which the acquirer is able or willing to allocate to them, fewer control shifts will occur.

8.2.2 The 'no frustration' rule

The choice of vesting the decision on the offer in the shareholders alone is most prominently illustrated by the UK Code on Takeovers and Mergers, which, since its inception in 1968, has contained a 'no frustration' injunction addressed to the board of the target company. This provides that 'during the course of an offer, or even before the date of the offer if the board of the offeree company has reason to believe that a bona fide offer might be imminent, the board must not, without the approval of the shareholders in general meeting, take any action which may result in any offer or bona fide possible offer being frustrated or in shareholders being denied the opportunity to decide on its merits . . .'[34] This is an effects-based rule, not one dependent on the intentions or motives of the board. Action on the

---

[33] Typically, the shareholders determine the fate of the offer by deciding individually whether to accept the offer or not, but in some cases the shareholders' decision may be a collective one, as where the shareholders decide in a meeting whether to approve the taking of defensive measures by the incumbent management or where the shareholders vote to remove a board that will not redeem a poison pill. *Infra* 8.2.2 and 8.2.3.

[34] Rule 21.1.

part of the incumbent management which might 'frustrate' an offer an acquirer wishes to put to the target shareholders is legitimate under this rule only if the shareholders themselves, through a collective decision, have approved it, i.e., have in effect rejected the offer. The 'no frustration' rule recognizes that effectively to implement a strategy of exclusive shareholder decision-making in relation to public offers requires rules which ensure, not only that shareholders are free to accept offers which are put to them, but also that offerors are free to put offers to the shareholders. In other words, the law must provide entry rules for acquirers as well as exit rules for shareholders.

The 'no frustration' (or 'board neutrality')[35] rule was proposed by the European Commission as a central element in the Takeovers Directive, but it proved controversial (especially in Germany) and agreement among the member states was possible in the end only on the basis that it became a rule the member states could choose not to make mandatory in their jurisdictions.[36] Nevertheless, the 'no frustration' rule became widely adopted in the European Union during the long process of negotiation over the directive (though not in Germany).[37]

It is clear in both the City Code and the directive that shareholder approval means approval given during the offer period for the specific measures proposed and not a general authorization given in advance of any particular offer. A weaker form of the shareholder approval rule is to permit shareholder authorization of defensive measures in advance of a specific offer. This is a weaker form of the rule because the choice which the shareholders are making is presented to them less sharply than under a post-bid approval rule.[38] On the other hand, rendering pre-bid approval of post-bid defensive measures ineffective makes it more difficult for shareholders to commit themselves to handling future offers through board negotiation with the bidder.[39] Pre-bid shareholder approval is one way of legitimizing defensive action in Germany[40] and also in Japan. In the latter the

---

[35] The Community-level discussion normally uses the term 'board neutrality' but we prefer the term 'no frustration' as more accurately indicating the scope of the rule. See *infra* 8.2.2.1.

[36] Directive 2004/25/EC, Arts. 9.2 and 12.1. Even if a member state does not impose the rule, a company must be given the right to opt into the 'no frustration' rule: Art. 12.2. The same solution was adopted in relation to the 'break-through rule': *infra* 8.3.2.

[37] Commission of the European Communities, *Report on the implementation of the Directive on Takeover Bids*, SEC(2007) 268, February 2007, p.6, indicating that 17 of the 25 member states had a 'no frustration' rule in place before the adoption of the directive.

[38] This point is well captured in the French terminology which refers to advance authorization as approval given '*à froid*' and authorization given after the offer as given '*à chaud*': *Cf* David Kershaw, *The Illusion of Importance: Reconsidering the UK's Takeover Defence Prohibition*, 56 INTERNATIONAL AND COMPARATIVE LAW QUARTERLY 267 (2007), arguing that the 'no frustration' rule of the Code adds little or nothing to UK company law, but on the basis that pre-bid and post-bid approval are functionally equivalent.

[39] On pre-commitment see *supra* 7.2. For the possible use of pre-bid defensive measures to this end see *infra* 8.2.3.

[40] § 33(2) *Übernahmegesetz*. Such permission may be given for periods of up to 18 months by resolutions requiring the approval of three-quarters of the shareholders, though the constitution of a particular company may set more demanding rules. However, approval may also be given post-bid by the supervisory board without shareholder approval (§ 33(1) *Übernahmegesetz*, last sentence)

governmental guidelines favor pre-bid approval of defensive action 'to allow the shareholders to make appropriate investment decisions'.[41] However, court decisions are unclear whether pre-bid approval will always legitimize defensive measures.[42] Like Germany, Japan also contemplates the legality in certain situations of defensive measures taken by the board unilaterally, and to that extent the two countries embrace the joint decision-making model.[43]

8.2.2.1   No frustration, passivity, and competing bids

The 'no frustration' rule, even though it allocates the decision on the acceptance of the bid to the target shareholders, does not impose a 'passivity rule' on the incumbent management. There are a number of situations in which the target board, consistently with the 'no frustration' rule, may take action which may significantly influence the outcome of the offer. To this extent the board does not have to be neutral towards the offer. First, incumbent management remains free to persuade shareholders to exercise their right of choice in a particular way and, indeed, in most jurisdictions the target board is required to provide the shareholders with an opinion on the offer. This recognizes the role of the incumbent management in addressing the information asymmetry problems of the target shareholders. The question of whether the 'no frustration' rule should give way in a more fundamental sense to the need to address target shareholders' coordination problems is addressed below.[44]

Second, the management may appeal to the competition authorities to block the bid, presumably the rationale being that this is an efficient way of keeping the public authorities informed about potential competition concerns, whilst the public interest in competitive markets must trump the private interest of shareholders in accepting the offer made to them.

Third, the rule is usually understood as a negative one and not as requiring incumbent management to take steps to facilitate an offer to the shareholders

---

and so pre-bid approval by shareholders seems unimportant in practice. See K.J. Hopt, *Obstacles to corporate restructuring. Observations from a European and German perspective*, in M. Tison, H. De Wulf, C. Van der Elst and R. Steennot (eds.), Perspectives in Company Law and Financial Regulation: Essays in Honour of Eddy Wymeersch, pp. 373–95 (2009).

[41] METI and Ministry of Justice, *Guidelines Regarding Takeover Defense*, 27 May 2005, p.2. These guidelines are not legally binding in themselves but seek to capture court decisions and best practice.

[42] See the warrants issued as a defensive measure in the recent *Bulldog Sauce* case, which both the District and Supreme Courts upheld on the main ground that the action had been approved by the shareholders after the bid had been launched and acquirer was treated fairly in respect of its pre-bid holdings (if not in the same manner as the other shareholders of the target): S. Osaki, *The Bulldog Sauce Takeover Defense*, 10 Namura Capital Markets Review No. 3, 1 (2007).

[43] Guidelines, p.3, though even these should be removable at the will of the shareholders. For Germany see *supra* note 40.

[44] See *infra* 8.2.5.

(except in some cases where a facility has already been extended to a rival bidder). Thus, the no-frustration rule is not interpreted as requiring the target management to give a potential bidder access to the target's books in order to formulate its offer. In the case of private equity, and even some trade, bidders, this may give the management of the target something approaching a veto over the control transaction or, at least, give it significant negotiating power with the bidder as to the terms of the offer.[45]

Moreover, developments elsewhere in company and securities law may enhance the possibilities noted in the previous paragraph. Recent developments in requirements for disclosure of the beneficial ownership of voting shares, although primarily aimed at the prevention of false markets, in fact help incumbent management by increasing the time available to them to prepare the defensive steps permitted to them. Most jurisdictions now have rules requiring the beneficial holders of shares in listed companies, whether acting alone or in concert, to disclose that fact to the company and the market when certain minimum levels are exceeded.[46] The beneficial owner may also be required to disclose, not just the fact of the ownership, but also its intentions in relation to control of the company.[47] Some jurisdictions employ a further technique and permit the *company* to trigger a disclosure obligation.[48]

8.2.2.2 *White knights and competing bids*

Finally, the 'no frustration' rule does not normally prevent an incumbent management from seeking to enlarge the shareholders' choice, for example, by seeking a 'white knight'. Whether or not sought by the incumbent management, a competing bidder may emerge. This event may seem unproblematic because it

---

[45] Given the leveraged nature of the typical private equity offer, the acquirer needs to be very sure about the target's income-generating potential. Of course, the shareholders may pressurize the board to open the company's books to the potential bidder, even if the management are reluctant to do so, but the management do not require shareholder approval to stand pat.

[46] Most national laws require disclosure at the 5% mark. There is also the beginnings of a trend towards mandatory disclosure of economic interests in shares, whether or not accompanied by an ownership interest. See, for example, *CSX Corp v. The Children's Investment Fund (UK) LLP* 562 F. Supp 511 (2008) bringing equity swaps within § 13(d) of the Securities Exchange Act 1934; FINANCIAL SERVICES AUTHORITY (UK), *Disclosure of Contracts for Difference*, CP 08/17, October 2008, proposing extended disclosure rules from September 2009. *Cf* the acquisition by Schaeffler of an undisclosed 28% stake in Continental via CfDs before announcing a takeover in May 2008; and the undisclosed increase in the same way of Porsche's stake in Volkswagen from 43% to 74% in October 2008, which led to a severe short squeeze in Volkswagen's shares, given that 20% of the shares were held by the State of Saxony and were not available for sale. See http://www.thehedge-fundjournal.com/research/sj-berwin/fm-alert-the-volkswagen-case.pdf.

[47] § 13(d) Securities Exchange Act 1934 (US); Art. L. 233–7.VII Code de commerce (France)—but this additional information is required only at the 10% and 20% levels; Risk Limitation Act 2008 (*Risikobegrenzungsgesetz*), again at the 10% level (Germany); Art. 27–23 et seq. of the Financial Instruments and Exchange Act 2006 (Japan).

[48] Companies Act 2006, Part 22 (UK)—this is not tied to any particular level of shareholding and involves an obligation to respond to the company's request, in default of which the company may seek an order from the court suspending the right to transfer or vote the share.

appears not to constrain the shareholders' choices but rather to enlarge them. The wealth-enhancing impact of competing bids as far as target shareholders are concerned is well established in the empirical literature. However, this may be true in relation to a particular offer, but not in relation to the universe of offers. The cost associated with rules which facilitate competing bids is that they reduce the incentives for first offers to be made. First bidders often lose out if a competitor emerges, and in that situation the search and other costs incurred by the first bidder will be thrown away. This will discourage first bidders generally and so reduce the number of offers.[49] It is thus significant whether the 'no frustration' rule permits the seeking of a 'white knight' and, more generally, whether other rules on the conduct of a bid in fact help or hinder competing bidders.

As Romano has remarked,[50] 'any regulation that delays the consummation of a hostile [or even a friendly] bid... increases the likelihood of an auction by providing time for another bidder to enter the fray, upon the target's solicitation or otherwise.' Thus, rules ostensibly aimed at other problems may have a significant impact on the chances that an alternative offer will be forthcoming. An example is rules which require the bid to remain open for a certain minimum period of time (in order that shareholders shall not be pressurized into accepting the offer before they have had a chance to evaluate it). Another is rules, just discussed, requiring disclosure to the market of the beneficial ownership of shareholdings above a certain size[51] which may give a potential competitor advance warning that an offer for a particular target company is likely to be forthcoming.[52] If a competitor does emerge, whether through the actions of the target management or not, its task is facilitated in those systems which permit acceptors to withdraw their acceptance of the first offer, unless it has been declared unconditional, either for any reason or if a competing offer emerges.[53] To the same effect are rules giving competing bidders equal treatment with the first bidder as far as information is concerned.[54]

There are a number of techniques which can be used to mitigate the downside to the first bidder of rules which facilitate competing bids.[55] Where the directors of the potential target judge that it is in the shareholders' interests that a bid

---

[49] Frank H. Easterbrook and Daniel R. Fischel, *The Proper Role of a Target's Management in Responding to a Tender Offer*, 94 HARVARD LAW REVIEW 1161 (1981). The debate is examined by Romano, Roberta Romano, *A Guide to Take-overs: Theory, Evidence and Regulation*, in Klaus J. Hopt and Eddy Wymeersch (eds.), EUROPEAN TAKEOVERS: LAW AND PRACTICE 3 (1992) 27–38.
[50] *Ibid* at 28.   [51] See *supra* note 46.
[52] Securities Exchange Act 1934, § 13(d)(1)(C) (US); Art. L. 233–7.VII Commercial Code (France);
[53] This is the predominant rule in takeover regulations, even in the U.S. (see § 14(d)5 1934 Securities Exchange Act and Rule 14d-7)—though not in the UK (Code on Takeovers and Mergers, Rule 34, allowing withdrawals only more narrowly). The bidder may seek to avoid this rule by obtaining irrevocable acceptances outside the offer (and usually before it is made)—though the acceptor may choose to make the acceptance conditional upon no competing bidder emerging.
[54] *Infra* 8.2.5.1.
[55] For further analysis see Kouloridas, *supra* note 32, Chs. 6 and 7.

be made for their company and that an offer will not be forthcoming without some protection against the emergence of a competitor, the directors of the target could be permitted to contract not to seek a white knight.[56] More effective from the first offeror's point of view would be a financial commitment from the target company in the form of an 'inducement fee' or 'break fee', designed to compensate the first offeror for the costs incurred if it is defeated by a rival. Such fees are common in the U.S., but treated with reserve in the UK because of their potential impact upon the principle of shareholder decision-making.[57] They could be used to give a substantial advantage to the bidder preferred by the incumbent management. Finally, the first offeror could be left free to protect itself in the market by buying shares inexpensively in advance of the publication of the offer, which shares it can sell at a profit into the competitor's winning offer if its own offer is not accepted. Although pre-bid purchases of shares in the target (by the offeror) do not normally fall foul of insider dealing prohibitions,[58] rules requiring the public disclosure of share stakes limit the opportunity to make cheap pre-bid purchases of the target's shares.[59]

Overall, in those jurisdictions which do not permit substantial inducement fees, the ability of the first bidder to protect itself against the financial consequences of a competitor's success are limited.

8.2.3 Joint decision-making

Where management is permitted unilaterally to take effective defensive measures in relation to an offer, the process of decision-making becomes in effect a joint one involving both shareholders and management on the target company's side. Unless the target board decides not to take defensive measures or to remove those already implemented, the offer is in practice incapable of acceptance by the shareholders. Perhaps the best known of such measures is the 'poison pill' or shareholders' rights plan, as developed in the United States. Here, the crossing by an acquirer of a relatively low threshold of ownership triggers rights for target shareholders in relation to the shares of either the target or the acquirer, from

---

[56] This is the situation in the UK: see *Dawson International plc v. Coats Patons plc* [1990] Butterworths Company Law Cases 560. Self-interested use of this power is then policed by subjecting its exercise to court review by reference to the board's fiduciary duties. Even so, if, despite the contractual undertaking, a competing bidder does emerge, the target board may not contract out of its fiduciary duty to advise its shareholders about which bid is in their interests.

[57] They are usually in the 2–5% range in the U.S., whilst rule 21.2 of the City Code sets an upper limit on inducement fees of 1% of the offer value. It also requires the arrangement to be disclosed in the offer document and the offeree board and its financial adviser to confirm to the Panel that they believe the inducement fee is in the best interests of the target shareholders.

[58] See, e.g., Recital 29 to the Directive of the European Parliament and of the Council on insider dealing and market manipulation (2003/6/EC, [2003] OJ L 096/16). Details are controversial, *cf.* Klaus J. Hopt, *Takeovers, Secrecy and Conflicts of Interests*, in Jennifer Payne (ed.), Takeovers in English and German Law 9 (2002) 33, 38–50.

[59] See *supra* note 46.

which the acquirer itself is excluded and which render the acquisition of further shares in the target fruitless or impossibly expensive.[60] Whilst the poison pill is not mandatory, the ease with which it can be adopted by management of potential target companies renders it widespread in practice in U.S. companies. It is also a powerful legal technique, apparently putting the incumbent management is a position where they can 'just say no' to a potential acquirer.[61]

The success of the poison pill defence depends, it should be noted, not simply upon its effect on the acquirer but also upon the target management having power under general company law and the company's constitution to adopt the plan containing these contingent rights without the approval of the shareholders and upon the courts' holding it not to be a breach of the directors' duties to adopt or to refuse to remove the plan in the face of a bid. In the absence of these features, a shareholders' rights plan will not necessarily produce joint decision-making by shareholders and target management. Thus, although allegedly modelled on the poison pill, the power given to target companies in the recent French reforms to issue share warrants does not have by any means the same potential for management entrenchment. Under the French rules, the decision must be taken by the shareholders, either themselves to issue the warrants or to authorize management to do so; and this decision must be taken during the bid period. Only if the acquirer's management would not be subject to a neutrality rule, were it a bid target (i.e., if there is no 'reciprocity'), may the shareholders authorize the management to issue warrants in advance of a bid.[62] Thus, under the French rule, while the legal mechanism is similar to the U.S. one, it is firmly under the control of the shareholders, at least in cases of reciprocity.[63] Where there is no reciprocity, the rule constitutes the weak form of the 'no frustration' rule.[64]

More generally, the possibilities for the incumbent board to insert itself into the decision-making process on the bid (whether through a shareholder rights

---

[60] This definition of a poison pill is taken from Lucian A. Bebchuk and Allen Ferrell, *Federalism and Corporate Law: The Race to Protect Managers from Takeovers*, 99 COLUMBIA LAW REVIEW 1168 (1999) (citing, in their footnote 35, the chief economist for the Securities and Exchange Commission). See also, by the same authors, *On Takeover Law and Regulatory Competition*, 57 THE BUSINESS LAWYER 1047 (2002).

[61] 'The passage of time has dulled many to the incredibly powerful and novel device that a so-called poison pill is. That device has no other purpose than to give the board issuing the rights the leverage to prevent transactions it does not favor by diluting the buying proponent's interests (even in its own corporation if the rights "flip-over").' Strine V-C in *Hollinger Int'l v. Black*, 844 A.2d 1022 (2004, Del. Ch.) at para.111.

[62] Art. L. 233–32.II and 33 of the Commercial Code, inserted by law no. 2006–387 of 31 March 2006 concerning public offers, Arts. 12 and 13. Also the warrants (*bons d'offre*) must be issued to all the shareholders, including the acquirer in respect of its pre-bid shareholding (though the shares which it has agreed to acquire through the bid do not count for entitlement to the warrants). Subject to this partial exception, the boards of French companies are now subject to an explicit neutrality rule (Art. L. 233–32.I), though the prior law, which was much less clear, was interpreted in this way as well.

[63] For further discussion of the reciprocity rule see *infra* 8.3.2.

[64] See *supra* 8.2.2.

plan or in some other way) will depend, in the absence of a 'no frustration' rule, upon the extent to which shareholder approval is required, whether by general corporate law or the company's articles, for particular decisions.[65] Normally, the powers of centralized management are extensive in the relation to the handling of the company's assets, but in many jurisdictions they are more constrained where issues of shares or securities convertible into shares are concerned, because of their dilution potential for the existing shareholders. Yet, in principle, defensive measures which focus on the company's capital rather than its business assets may be more attractive to incumbent management, because they are less disruptive of the underlying business or a more powerful deterrent of the acquirer. Thus, in the European Community general rules requiring shareholder approval for increases in capital inhibit, though do not completely rule out, shareholder rights plans adopted unilaterally by incumbent management.[66] Equally, the recent development of share warrants as a defensive measure in Japan was premised upon changes in general corporate law (not aimed specifically at the control shift situation but at implementing a more general deregulation programme) which expanded the board's share-issuing powers. In particular, the board was empowered to issue stock options without having to seek shareholder approval, though the court may prevent 'unfair issuance'.[67] Whether it is legitimate for the board to use its powers to defeat a takeover is, of course, a separate question, but without the power, the question does not even arise.

8.2.3.1 Strategies for controlling the board's powers to take defensive measures

Although the 'no frustration' rule is not a fully-fledged passivity rule, it nevertheless operates so as to put the shareholders in the driving seat as far as decision-making on the offer is concerned. Putting the shareholders in a position where they can deal with their coordination problems as against the acquirer then becomes a significant concern of the rules applying to control shifts which are based on the 'no frustration' principle. By contrast, joint decision-making strategies permit the incumbent management to negotiate on behalf of the shareholders and to take other steps in their interests, such as rejecting bids which undervalue the company. If, within a joint decision-making system, it is possible to secure that the incumbent management's decision-making power is used in the shareholders' interests rather than to promote the self-interest of the management in retaining their positions, it can be argued that the outcome is superior to

---

[65] See *supra* 3.4 and 7.

[66] The Second Company Law Directive [1977] O.J. L 26/1, requires shareholder approval for increases in capital (Art. 25). See in general Guido Ferrarini, *Share Ownership, Takeover Law and the Contestability of Corporate Control* (2002), available on http://ssrn.com/abstract=265429, and *supra* 7.2.

[67] Arts. 210 and 247 of the Companies Act .

that achieved by lodging the decision right wholly with the shareholders, because the shareholders' coordination problems are circumvented where incumbent management negotiates on their behalf.[68] However, to achieve this result, a joint decision-rights strategy needs to be accompanied by one or more other strategies, if the risk of self-serving use by the management of its veto power is to be avoided. There is a range of strategies which could be deployed to this end: standards, trusteeship, removal rights, and reward strategies.

8.2.3.2 Standards

Ex post scrutiny by a court of the exercise of the veto power by management is the most obvious additional legal strategy to apply, since the decisions of centralized management, whether in relation to control transactions or not, are routinely subject to such review in most jurisdictions. It has been argued[69] that in the 1980s the Delaware courts applied fiduciary duties to directors in such a way as indeed to sustain refusals to redeem poison pills only where the bid was formulated abusively as against the target shareholders. At this time, therefore, it could be argued that the poison pill was generating an efficient set of responses to the agency and coordination problems of the target shareholders: directors could exercise their discretion to block the opportunism of acquirers but not to further their own interests in the preservation of their jobs. However, with the development by the Delaware courts of the 'just say no' rule, the impact of the poison pill changed significantly. The starting point of this new approach was the adoption of the view that decisions on the fate of a bid are in principle as much a part of the management of the company, and thus within the province of the directors, as any other part of the board remit.[70] Sole decision-making had to be given to the shareholders (and indeed a policy of neutrality adopted among the competing bidders) only if the incumbent management, as part of its strategy, had reached a decision to sell control of the company or to dispose of its assets.[71] But the decision to maintain the business as a going concern in the hands of the incumbent management was one that the board was in principle free to take, whether or not it thought the offer to be wealth maximizing from the shareholders' point of view. Thus, from a shareholders' perspective, joint decision-making over control shifts

---

[68] The attractiveness of this argument depends, of course, on (a) how easily the shareholders' coordination problems can be addressed if management is sidelined (*infra* 8.2.5) and (b) how much scope for negotiation is left to the incumbent board under the no-frustration rule (*supra* 8.2.2.1).

[69] Lucian Bebchuk, *The Case Against Board Veto in Corporate Takeovers* 69 University of Chicago Law Review 973 at 1184–8 (2002). See also R. Gilson, *UNOCAL Fifteen Years Later (and What We Can Do About It)*, 26 Delaware Journal of Corporate Law 491 (2001).

[70] *Paramount Communications Inc. v. Time Inc.*, 571 Atlantic Reporter Second Series (hereafter A.2d) 1140 (1989); *Unocal Corp. v. Mesa Petroleum Co.*, 493 A.2d 946 (1985); *Unitrin Inc. v. American General Corporation*, 651 A. 2d 1361 (1995).

[71] *Revlon Inc. v. MacAndrews & Forbes Holdings Inc.*, 506 A.2d 173 (1986); *Paramount Communications v. QVC Network*, 637 A.2d 34 (1994).

will have a significant downside if the courts' approach to review of board decisions is essentially managerialist.[72]

In Japan as well, in the absence of shareholder approval, the governmental guidelines and court decisions anticipate that defensive action by target management will be lawful only where it enhances 'corporate value' and promotes the shareholders' interests. Consequently, defensive measures not approved by the shareholders will stand a greater chance of meeting this standard if the bid is coercive, animated by greenmail or based on information asymmetry as between acquirer and target shareholders.[73] However, the flexibility, perhaps the unreliability, of this standard is demonstrated by the characterization by the Tokyo High Court of the bidder in the *Bulldog Sauce* case as 'abusive' simply because it was a shareholder with purely financial interests in the target.[74]

In general, in all jurisdictions there will be overarching duties applying to decisions of the board—such as the duty to act in the best interests of the company or to exercise powers only for a proper purpose—from which even a specific legislative mandate to take defensive measures will not normally relieve the management. However, there is little evidence that the courts are willing to scrutinize rigorously over long periods of time the discretion vested in management under the dual decision-making model.[75]

8.2.3.3 Trusteeship

An alternative to going outside the company for review of defensive measures proposed by management is to seek approval within the company from independent directors. Thus, in Germany the managing board has two possibilities for taking defensive action but both turn on the action being approved by the supervisory board.[76] This strategy depends for its effectiveness (from the shareholders' point

---

[72] In many U.S. states the managerialist approach was adopted legislatively through 'constituency statutes' which, whilst appearing to advance the interests of stakeholders, in particular labor and regional interests, in practice operated—and were probably intended to operate—to shield management from shareholder challenge. Romano, *supra* note 49, at p. 40 and 8.5 *infra*.

[73] METI and MoJ Guidelines, *supra* note 41, at pp.1–2 and see the discussion of the *Livedoor* and other cases by Kozuka, *infra* note 95, at pp. 12–16.

[74] Osaki, *supra* note 42 at pp.7ff.

[75] Thus, in Germany the managing board's power to take defensive action with the consent of the shareholders and/or the supervisory board will not relieve it of its duty to act in the best interests of the company. There is much academic discussion of what this limitation means, but it is doubtful whether it prevents management entrenchment except in egregious cases. The same appears to be true of Italy which in 2008 repealed its 'no frustration' rule but left boards subject to the laws on directors' duties. However, there is some evidence that the Delaware courts have done a better job with the standards strategy when it has been deployed to control managerial promotion of (rather than resistance to) control shifts. See Robert B Thompson and Randall S. Thomas, *The New Look of Shareholder Litigation: Acquisition-Oriented Class Actions*, 57 Vanderbilt Law Review 113 (2004).

[76] The managing board may seek the advance approval of the shareholders for defensive measures but then any exercise of the power must be approved by the supervisory board (§ 33(2) *Übernahmegesetz*) or it may take defensive measures simply with the approval of the supervisory board (§ 33(1) *Übernahmegesetz*, last sentence). Only the last-minute amendments to § 33 in the

of view) heavily on the ability of the supervisory board to play a genuinely independent role. This may be questionable in the case where the board is codetermined, since the employee representatives on the supervisory board will typically favor the management's rather than the shareholders' standpoint.[77] Equally, to the extent that board decisions in the U.S. to redeem or not a poison pill are taken by the independent members of the board, that jurisdiction makes use of a trustee strategy. Here there are no complications arising from codetermination but the independence of the non-executives is still an open issue.[78]

8.2.3.4 Removal rights

As management's decisions to turn away potential offers were upheld in the U.S. courts, shareholders responded by seeking to replace the existing board with those who would look on the bid more favorably. The effect of this development was to channel takeover bids into battles at the general meeting to replace the incumbent board with nominees of the bidder, who would remove the pill. In effect, this strategy gives greater emphasis to the role of collective shareholder decision-making, which is also to be found when post-bid defensive measures are subject to shareholder approval under the no frustration rule. In the latter case, however, a collective decision of the shareholders is a pre-condition for defensive measures to be taken by incumbent management; in the former, it is a pre-condition for the offer to be put to the shareholders of the target where the board will not deal with the bidder. The burden of obtaining shareholder approval falls on the target board under the former set of rules and on the bidder in the latter. This makes a crucial difference. The requirement to obtain shareholder approval before the offer is put to the shareholders, is restrictive of the acquirer.[79] The momentum behind the offer may well have been dispersed before the conditions for launching it have been realized. This is especially so if the vote can be obtained only at the end of the director's term of office or if more than one vote is needed because the company has a staggered board.[80] It has been argued that it is the combination of the poison pill with the staggered board which puts the management of

---

legislative process explain this oddity. In practice, there seems little value to the management in obtaining prior approval of the shareholders.

[77] Hopt, *supra* note 40 at III,A,b.

[78] For an assessment of supervisory boards in two-tier board structures, see *supra* 3.2.

[79] On the advantages of the bid over a proxy fight see Louis Loss and Joel Seligman, FUNDAMENTALS OF SECURITIES REGULATION 562 (4th ed., 2001). Lucian Bebchuk and Oliver Hart, *Takeover bids versus proxy fights in contests for corporate control* (Harvard Law and Economics Discussion Paper No. 336; and ECGI—Finance Working Paper No. 04/2002. Available at SSRN: http://ssrn.com/abstract=290584) argued that in principle a speedy shareholder vote binding on all the shareholders is preferable to individual acceptances of a general offer as a way of deciding upon a bid, though they recognized that the American rules fall short of this scheme. In effect, this is an argument in favor of using the statutory merger procedure to effect a control transaction. See *supra* 8.1.1.

[80] This is where a proportion only—normally one-third—of the board can be removed at each annual shareholders' meeting.

the target in a powerful defensive position in the U.S., rather than the poison pill on its own, i.e., that the removal strategy would effectively constrain the board's use of the poisoned pill, if it were available.[81]

8.2.3.5 Reward strategy

Under this strategy the self-interest of the incumbent management in retaining their jobs is replaced by self-interest in obtaining a financial reward which is dependent upon surrendering control of the company to the acquirer.[82] This may arise because rewards under general incentive remuneration schemes for managers are triggered upon a transfer of control;[83] or because payments can be claimed under the management's contracts of service;[84] or because, less often, ad hoc payments are made to the incumbent management, either by the acquirer or the target company, in connection with a successful control shift. Such payments are widely available in the U.S.; and it has been argued that the reward strategy has succeeded in bringing about, in terms of incentives not to invoke the poison pill, what the removal strategy failed to achieve.[85] Outside the U.S., however, it is often unacceptable or unlawful to make payments of a sufficient size to amount to a significant counter-incentive for the managers, at least without the consent of the shareholders, which, in the context we are considering, undermines the reward strategy.

Thus, in the *Mannesmann* case, a payment to the CEO of a German target company, after the successful takeover of that company by a (foreign) acquirer, led to criminal charges against him for corporate waste. Although the case was ultimately settled without admission of liability, the test laid down by the top civil court for criminal liability for waste was a tough and objective one.[86] It is possible to avoid this criminal liability by contracting in advance for the payment of compensation for loss of office, but it is difficult to believe that this decision will not chill

---

[81] Bebchuk, Coates, and Subramanian, *The Powerful Antitakeover Force of Staggered Boards*, 54 Stanford Law Review 887 (2002). More recent evidence suggests incumbent management is subject to shareholder pressure and financial incentives to de-stagger the board: M. Ganor, *Why do Managers Dismantle Staggered Boards?*, 33 Delaware Journal of Corporate Law 149 (2008).

[82] M. Kahan and E. B. Rock, *How I Learned to Stop Worrying and Love the Pill: Adaptive Responses to Takeover Law* 69 University of Chicago Law Review 871 (2002); J. Gordon, *American Experience and EU Perspectives* in G. Ferrarini et al. (eds), Reforming Company and Takeover Law in Europe (2004).

[83] For example, because of accelerated stock options.

[84] For example, contractual golden parachutes.

[85] L. Bebchuk and J. Fried, Pay Without Performance (2004) 89–91; Alessio M. Pacces, Featuring Control Power (2007) Ch. 6.3 (welcoming such a result on theoretical grounds as enabling a manager/entrepreneur to be compensated for idiosyncratic private benefits of control on a control shift, at a lower level of ownership of the company than s/he would aim for if such side-payments were not available); B. Holmstrom and S. Kaplan, *Corporate Governance and Merger Activity in the US: Making Sense of the 1980s and 1990s*, MIT, Department of Economics, Working Paper No. 01–11 (available at http://www.ssrn.com).

[86] BGH 21 December 2005, NJW 2006, 522.

the levels of both contractual compensation thought to be appropriate for pre-bid agreement and gratuitous payments post-acquisition. Even in the UK gratuitous payments in connection with loss of office after a takeover require shareholder approval, in the absence of which the payments are regarded as held on trust for the shareholders who accepted the offer.[87] This remedy nicely underlines the fact that strengthening the role of incumbent management in control shifts is likely to lead to the diversion to them of part of the control premium.[88] More generally, the moves in the UK towards greater shareholder scrutiny of executive director remuneration have constrained even contractual rewards dependent upon a successful takeover.[89] Since the financial incentives needed to compensate management for the monetary, reputational and psychological losses arising out of their removal from office are likely to be substantial, jurisdictions which regard such payments with suspicion are not likely to achieve any re-balancing of the incentives arising out of the adoption of joint decision-making on control transactions.

Overall, one can say that the initial decision-rights choice is likely to be highly significant. Whilst in some jurisdictions, notably the U.S., the deployment of additional strategies, especially the reward strategy, may produce a result in which the outcomes of the joint decision-making process are not significantly different (in terms of deterring value-enhancing bids) from those arrived at under the 'no frustration' rule, this conclusion is highly dependent upon those additional strategies being available and effective. In the absence of pro-shareholder courts with effective review powers, easy removal of incumbent management or the ability to offer significant financial incentives to management to view the bid neutrally, rejection of the 'no frustration' rule is likely to reduce the number of control shifts.[90]

8.2.4 Pre-bid defensive measures

It has often been pointed out that a major limitation of the 'no frustration' rule is that the requirement for shareholder approval of defensive tactics applies only once a bid is in contemplation,[91] even though management may well be

---

[87] Companies Act 2006, §§ 219 and 222(3). Contractual payments are also caught by this rule (§ 220), if agreed in connection with the bid.

[88] Referring to golden parachutes and accelerated stock options Gordon says: 'One way to understand these devices is as a buyback by shareholders of the takeover–resistance endowment that managers were able to obtain from the legislatures and the courts during the 1980s.' Gordon, *supra* note 82 at 555.

[89] Thus, it has been reported that, after the introduction of the shareholders' advisory vote on directors' remuneration, clauses providing for automatic vesting of directors' stock options on a change of control virtually ceased to be part of directors' remuneration packages: Deloitte, *Report on the Impact of the Directors' Remuneration Report Regulations* (November 2004) p. 19.

[90] Gordon, see *supra* note 82 at 555, making these points in relation to Germany, where neither easy removal of the board not high-powered incentives to accept offers is available.

[91] See Paul Davies, *The Regulation of Defensive Tactics in the United Kingdom and the United States,* in Hopt and Wymeersch, *supra* note 49, 195. If a defence put in place pre-bid, requires

able to act effectively against potential offers in advance of any particular offer materializing. The European Commission's High Level Group identified five categories of pre-bid defensive measures,[92] consisting of barriers to (a) the acquisition of shares in the company (for example, ownership caps or poison pills[93]); (b) exercising control in the general meeting (voting caps; multiple voting shares); (c) exercising control of the board of directors (codetermination, staggered boards, special appointment rights for some shareholders); and (d) exercising control of the company's assets (lock-ups); and creating (e) financial problems for the acquirer as a result of the acquisition (poison debt); or (f) regulatory issues (defensive acquisitions creating anti-trust problems if further consolidation).

The availability of pre-bid defenses does not simply create a gap in the regulation of management opposition to value-enhancing control shifts; it promises to undermine the 'no frustration' rule entirely. The situation becomes one where the board has a strong incentive to simply shift its defensive actions to the pre-bid period. However, because the 'no frustration' rule seeks to alter the normal allocation of decision-making powers as between shareholders and the board once a bid is imminent, to apply the 'no frustration' rule at all times, at least on the basis of an 'effects' test, would be too great an interference with the operation of centralized management.[94] Any commercial decision which might have the effect of deterring a future bidder for the company would have to be put to the shareholders for their approval. This issue arises in relation to the joint decision-making model as well, but in a less strong form. Since the board has much more influence under that model over the success of the offer, once it is made, it has a lesser incentive to put defensive measures in place pre-bid. Further, if there is an effective rewards strategy in place to induce management to accept offers which are wealth-enhancing for the shareholders, then that incentive structure actually discourages management from putting non-removable barriers in place pre-bid. The question of how to regulate pre-bid defences thus arises most acutely in the context of the adoption of a 'no frustration' rule.

---

action on the part of the board post-bid to be effective, then it will be caught by the no-frustration rule, for example, the issuance of shares by the board which the board has previously been authorized to issue.

[92] *Report of the High Level Group of Company Law Experts Issues Related to Takeover Bids*, Brussels, January 2002, Annex 4. Some of these defensive steps could be taken, of course, post-bid as well.

[93] A poison pill may be adopted pre- or post-bid, normally the former. However, there is still a post-bid issue, namely, whether the directors redeem the pill (i.e., remove the shareholder rights plan), their unilateral power to do this being a central part of the scheme.

[94] Of course, the precise point at which the line between pre- and post-periods is drawn can be the subject of some debate. The City Code draws it once the board 'has reason to believe that a bona fide offer might be imminent' (see *supra* 8.2.2), whilst the Takeover Directive's (default) no frustration rule applies only when the board is informed by the bidder of its decision to make an offer (Arts. 9.2 and 6.1)

8.2.4.1 *Strategies for controlling pre-bid defensive measures*

However, as with post-bid defensive decisions by incumbent management under the joint decision-making model, pre-bid defensive tactics are subject to other legal strategies. The most general of these are the standards applied by company law to all board decision-making (duties of care and loyalty). These standards are necessarily less constraining than the 'no frustration' rule, for the reasons just given, i.e., in order to preserve the benefits of centralized management. Typically, some form of a 'primary purpose' rule is used to distinguish legitimate from illegitimate decisions taken pre-bid which have defensive qualities as well as commercial rationales. Such rules necessarily give management considerable freedom to take action for which there is a plausible commercial rationale, even if that action has defensive qualities of which the directors are aware and welcome, for example, an acquisition of assets which will create competition problems for a future bidder or which will put a block of shares into friendly hands.[95]

Rules dealing with specific decisions may be more constraining, but are necessarily also of less general impact. Rules on significant transactions may require shareholder approval of certain types of pre-bid corporate action with defensive qualities.[96] Thus, we have also noted that the Community rules on shareholder consent to capital issues have placed obstacles in the way of the straightforward adoption of 'poison pills' in Europe.[97] Here, pre-bid, the joint decision-making process is the more pro-shareholder choice, since the available alternative is not unilateral decision-making by shareholders but unilateral decision-making by the board. However, these veto rights for shareholders are generally driven by more general corporate law concerns than the control of pre-bid defensive measures and, hence, have a somewhat adventitious impact on control shifts.

Overall, management is necessarily given greater freedom to entrench itself pre-bid than post, and the legal strategies used to control managerial opportunism pre-bid are simply the general strategies used to protect the shareholders as principals and against the management as agents which are discussed elsewhere in this book.[98]

---

[95] Even post-bid the courts may have difficulty applying the proper purpose rule so as to restrain effectively self-interested defensive action. See the discussion of the *Miyairi Valve* litigation by S.Kozuka in Zeitschrift Für Japanisches Recht No. 21, 10–11 (2006) and *Harlowe's Nominees Pty Ltd v Woodside (Lake Entrance) Oil Co.* 42 Australian Law Journal Reports 123 (High Court of Australia) (1968).

[96] See *supra* Chapter 7 for a discussion of the extent to which significant decisions require shareholder approval.

[97] See *supra* 8.2.3.

[98] The 'break-through rule' is an exception to this statement, since it is a rule fashioned specifically to deal with the impact of a certain class of pre-bid defenses (mainly from category (b) on the High Level Group's list). However, we discuss this rule *infra* 8.3.2, since it addresses principally situations where there is a controlling shareholder.

8.2.5 Agency and coordination problems of target shareholders when there is no controlling shareholder

When an offer is put to the shareholders of the target company, they face, potentially, two sets of problems. As against the acquirer, they face significant coordination problems. This is because the decision to accept or reject the bid is normally made by the shareholders individually, rather than by way of a collective decision which binds everyone, and so there is considerable scope for a bidder to seek to divide the shareholder body. As against the target management, the shareholders still face agency issues, since the board's recommendation to them (for or against the offer) may not be disinterested. This issue can arise even under the joint decision-making model, where the board recommends the offer to the shareholders. Indeed, that endorsement (under either model) may constitute the manifestation of the agency problem: the offer may not be the best available or may not be wealth-enhancing for the shareholders, but the management may recommend it because it is the best offer from their point of view. This is particularly likely to be the case where the incumbent management are part of the bidding team, as in an MBO supported by a private equity fund. Laws specific to control transactions tend to concentrate on the target shareholders' coordination problems as against the acquirer, with the solution of their agency problems as against the target management as a subsidiary theme.

The coordination problems of shareholders may be mitigated to some degree through the board's negotiations with the potential acquirer. Under the joint decision-making model, the board is in a strong position to negotiate in this way (though it may prefer to negotiate in its own interests),[99] whilst even under the no frustration rule, the board retains a not-insignificant negotiating potential, as we have seen.[100] However, if there is effective specific regulation of the shareholders' coordination problems, the benefits from entrusting the target board with the task of protecting the shareholders against coercive offers are reduced, perhaps eliminated, whilst it becomes less necessary to incur the costs arising from the risk of board entrenchment.

We now turn to examine the legal techniques which can be deployed to reduce target shareholders' coordination and agency costs. We need to note that all these techniques have costs, in particular by reducing incentives to potential bidders to make offers. The strategies are: mandatory disclosure of information; the trustee strategy; and, above all, requiring shareholders to be treated equally, both substantively and in terms of being afforded an exit right.

8.2.5.1 Information asymmetry

Provision of up-to-date, accurate, and relevant information can help target shareholders with both their coordination and agency problems. In particular,

---

[99] *Supra* 8.2.3.1.   [100] *Supra* 8.2.2.1.

disclosure of information by target management reduces the force of one of the arguments in favor of the joint decision-making model, i.e., that manager's have information about the target's value which the market lacks.[101] However, does the law need to stipulate what information shall be made available? Even without regulation, the target management and the acquirer are likely to generate a lot of information about both companies—and, in a hostile bid, to point out the weaknesses in each other's presentations. However, both sides are under strong incentives to hide unfavorable, and to exaggerate favorable, information. By controlling the types of information which can be distributed and the channels by which it is disseminated, such regulation may discourage unsubstantiated and unverifiable claims.

Company law, of course, contains information disclosure provisions which operate independently of control transactions. However, annual financial statements are often out of date and, despite the continuing reporting obligations applied to listed companies in most jurisdictions,[102] it is likely that both the target board and the acquirer will be better informed about their respective companies than the target shareholders. Thus, it is not surprising to discover that a centrepiece of all specific control shift regulation, whether it is aimed that the target shareholders' coordination or agency problems, is an elaborate set of provisions mandating disclosure by both the target board and the acquirer for the benefit of the target shareholders. It is routine to find rules requiring the disclosure of information on the nature of the offer, the financial position of the offeror and target companies, and the impact of a successful offer on the wealth of the senior management of both bidder and target. Even if the regulation does little else, it will tackle the issue of information disclosure.

In an agreed bid, incentives for reciprocal criticism will be lacking, especially for MBOs, where the management of bidder and target is common—or, at least, significantly overlapping. Here incumbent management appears in a dual role: as fiduciaries for the shareholders and as buyers of their shares. In this context, rules requiring the board of the target to take independent advice on the merits of the bid and to disclose it to target shareholders acquire a particular importance.[103] Equally, where an MBO is on the table, but a competing bid emerges, a requirement that all the information given to (potential) external providers of finance to the MBO team must also be given to a competing bidder reduces the scope for target management to favor their own bid.[104] In jurisdictions without takeover-specific regulation on the matter, it may be possible to leave the issue to general

---

[101] Ronald J. Gilson and Reinier Kraakman, *The Mechanisms of Market Efficiency Twenty Years Later: the Hindsight Bias* in John Armour and Joseph A. McCahery (eds.), AFTER ENRON (2006) 57, noting, however, that target management may have a difficulty making the disclosed information credible.

[102] This matter is discussed more fully in Chapter 9.   [103] City Code Rule 3.1 (Note 1).

[104] City Code Rule 20.2 (Note 3).

corporate law, notably the rules on self-dealing transactions.[105] Even where there is no MBO, the target directors may prefer one offer over the other and thus soft-pedal their comments on the preferred offer. Further, mandatory disclosure requirements can help the process by providing the materials on the basis of which gatekeepers such as investment bankers can evaluate the bid.

In addition, information rules in control transactions are usually premised on the view that information disclosure is ineffective unless shareholders are given enough time to absorb the information (or other people's analyses of the information) before they have to act on it. All takeover regulation requires offers to be open for a certain minimum time (practice seems to coalesce around the 20-day mark) and revised offers to be kept open for somewhat shorter periods.[106] The main counter argument against very generous absorption periods is the need to minimize the period during which the target's future is uncertain and, in particular, during which the normal functioning of the centralized management of the target is disrupted. In addition, mandatory minimum offer periods increase the chances of the emergence of a white knight, imposing a cost on acquirers and, possibly, upon shareholders of potential targets through the chilling effect upon potential bidders.[107] Given the role played by arbitrageurs in takeover bids and their ability to absorb information quickly, it is likely that the main practical effect of the minimum periods is to facilitate competing bids rather than understanding of the information disclosed.

8.2.5.2 *Trusteeship strategy*

Target shareholders face the risk that the incumbent management will exaggerate the unattractive features of an offer they oppose and vice versa with one they support. As we have seen immediately above, a common response is to require the incumbent management to obtain 'competent independent advice' on the merits of the offer (usually from an investment bank) and to make it known to the shareholders. This is partly a disclosure of information strategy and partly a trusteeship strategy: the investment bank does not take the decision but it provides an assessment of the offer to which the shareholders must receive, the accuracy of which has reputational consequences for the bank. Where there is an MBO, the

---

[105] See Werner F. Ebke, *The Regulation of Management Buyouts in American Law: A European Perspective,* in Hopt and Wymeersch, *supra* note 49, 304–6—though it should be noted that the transaction here is technically one between the director (or associated person) and the shareholders, not the company. In the case of MBOs of close companies common law jurisdictions may deal with the grosser information disparities by imposing a duty on the directors to disclose information to the shareholders as an element of their fiduciary duties (see, for example, *Coleman v. Myers* [1977] 2 New Zealand Law Reports 225, NZCA.).

[106] The Williams Act (*supra* note 22) in the U.S. was motivated in particular by the desire to control 'Saturday night specials' i.e., offers to which the shareholders had an unreasonably short time to respond, the term being apparently used originally to refer to inexpensive hand-guns popular for use on Saturday nights.

[107] See a discussion of competing bids and the passivity rule, *supra* 8.2.2.2.

directors involved in the bidding team may be excluded from those responsible for giving the target's view of the offer, thus allocating that responsibility to the non-conflicted directors of the target.[108]

8.2.5.3 *Reward (sharing) strategy*

A notable feature of laws aimed at the solving target shareholders' coordination problems is their adoption of the rule of equality of treatment of the shareholders of the target company—though this principle can be implemented with various degrees of rigour. The principle is aimed mainly at controlling acquirer opportunism: it stands in the way of acquirers which wish to put pressure on target shareholders to accept the offer, by promising some (normally those who accept early) better terms than others.[109] In general, systems which place decision-making on the bid in the hands of the shareholders alone have developed the equality principle more fully than those which have adopted the model of joint decision-making.

All systems recognize the equal treatment principle to some degree. It can be applied, first, within the offer (i.e., to require those to whom the offer is addressed to receive the same[110] terms); second, as between those who accept the offer and those who sell their shares to the offeror outside the offer, whether before or after a formal offer is launched; and, third, as between those who sell their shares to an acquirer as part of a control-building acquisition and those who are left as shareholders in the company. In this third case, implementation of the equality principle goes beyond a sharing strategy and involves providing an exit right for the target shareholders.

The first level of equality is recognized in all our jurisdictions. Thus, 'front-end loaded' offers are ruled out; and prior acceptors receive the higher price if the offer is later increased. However, instead of formulating differential offers, the acquirer may seek to offer some target shareholders preferential terms by obtaining their shares outside the offer. One solution is to prohibit purchases outside the offer, though this rule can be sensibly applied only to purchases during the offer period.[111] An alternative strategy is to require the offer consideration to be raised to the level of the out-of-bid purchases. Where such purchases are permitted during the offer period, the imposition of a sharing rule seems universal. More difficult is the issue of whether pre-bid purchases should be subject to a sharing rule. The Takeovers Directive does not explicitly deal with this point,

---

[108] City Code, Rule 25.1 (Notes 3 and 4).

[109] Paul Davies, *The Notion of Equality in European Takeover Regulation,* in Jennifer Payne (ed.), TAKEOVERS IN ENGLISH AND GERMAN LAW 9 (2002).

[110] Or equivalent terms, where the offer covers more than one class of share.

[111] See, for example, the French rule in Art. 232–14 of the General Regulation of the Autorité des Marchés Financiers (AMF). However, the latter prohibits market purchases of the target shares during the offer period only in share exchange offers, presumably on the grounds that the offer is not for cash.

but some jurisdictions impose a strict sharing rule triggered by recent pre-bid purchases.[112]

8.2.5.4 Exit rights: mandatory bid rule and keeping the offer open

The strongest, and most controversial, expression of the sharing principle is the requirement that the acquirer of shares make a general offer to the other shareholders once it has acquired sufficient shares by private contract (whether on or off market) to obtain control of the target. Control is usually defined as holding around one third of the voting shares in the company.[113] This is the mandatory bid rule.[114] It is a particularly demanding rule if, as is common, it requires that the offer be at the highest price paid for the controlling shares[115] and to give the shareholders the option of taking cash.[116] Here the law, in imposing a duty on the acquirer to make a general offer, provides the shareholders with something they rarely have, namely, a right to exit the company and at an attractive price. The mandatory bid rule does not simply structure an offer the acquirer wishes in principle to make, but requires a bid in a situation where the acquirer might prefer not to make one at all.

Such a requirement might be defended on two grounds. First, although the rule cannot be explained on the basis of pressure to accept a general offer (the assumption is that there would not be one in the absence of the rule), the absence of a mandatory bid rule would permit the acquirer to put pressure on those to whom offers are made during the control acquisition process to accept those offers. Absent a mandatory bid rule, the acquirer is free to make the following statement, explicitly or implicitly: 'I offer you an attractive price for your shares. If you do not accept it now, you may lose the benefit of the offer and, in addition, find that your shares have declined in value because I will be prepared to make only a lower offer (or none at all) once I have obtained control of the company.' Where the offer is value-decreasing or its impact on the target is just unclear, use of the mandatory

---

[112] Rules 6 and 11 City Code (but requiring cash only where the pre-bid purchases for cash reach 10% of the class in question over the previous 12 months); § 31 Übernahmegesetz and § 4 Übernahmegesetz-Angebotsverordnung (Germany) (requiring cash at the 5% level but only where that percentage was acquired for cash in the 3 months prior to the bid).

[113] The Takeovers Directive leaves the triggering threshold to be decided by the member states. The Commission's Report on implementation (*supra* note 37), Annex 2, confirms the 'one third' choice by most member states but also shows that Latvia, Malta, and Poland have set it at 50% or higher.

[114] The additional issues arising when a mandatory bid rule is imposed upon an acquirer who obtains the control block from an existing controlling shareholder controlling shareholder are discussed *infra* 8.3.1.

[115] The Takeover Directive, Art. 5(4), imposes a highest price rule, subject to the power of the supervisory body to allow dispensations from this requirement in defined cases.

[116] The Takeover Directive permits the mandatory offer to consist of 'liquid securities' but some members states (e.g., City Code rule 9) require the offer to be in cash or accompanied by a cash alternative.

bid rule to remove pressure to tender addresses a significant coordination issue of the shareholders as against the acquirer.[117] However, where the bid is value-increasing, as far as the target company is concerned, it can be argued that the value of shares held by the non-accepting shareholders will be higher after the control shift than before, even if they remain in the company, so that providing the non-accepting shareholders with an exit right is not necessary, given the costs of the mandatory bid rule in reducing the number of control shifts (below). However, it may be difficult to identify *ex ante* which category of offer is in question, so that the choice in practice is between applying or not applying the mandatory bid rule across the board.

Moreover, though the offer may be value-increasing for the target company's shareholders as a whole, the non-controlling shareholders may not obtain in the future their pro-rata share of that value. The leads to the second rationale for the mandatory bid rule. It could be said that permitting the acquisition of control over the whole of the company's assets by purchasing only a proportion of the company's shares would encourage transfers of control to those likely to exploit the private benefits of corporate control. On this view, the mandatory bid rule constitutes a preemptive strike at majority oppression of minority shareholders and proceeds on the basis that general corporate law is not adequate to police the behavior of controllers. The mandatory bid rule thus anticipates that there is a strong likelihood of majority/minority conflicts after the acquisition of control, and gives the minority the option to exit the company before such problems manifest themselves.[118] On this rationale, the mandatory bid rule should be accompanied by a prohibition on partial offers, even where, assuming a pro rata acceptance rule, all target shareholders are treated equally. By extension, one would expect to find a rule requiring comparable offers to be made for all classes of equity share in the target, whether those classes carry voting rights or not.[119]

Mandatory bid rules are now quite widespread. The Takeovers Directive requires member states to impose a mandatory bid rule (whilst leaving a number of crucial features of the rule, including the triggering percentage, to be determined at national level).[120] However, the mandatory bid rule is not part of U.S.

---

[117] Burkhart and Panuzi, *Mandatory Bids, Squeeze-Outs and Similar Transactions* in Ferrarini et al. (eds.) (*supra* note 82) at 748–53 prefer a mechanism based on a shareholder vote where a bidder is 'seeking to buy a controlling stake'. It is not clear how this would operate where the bidder is assembling a controlling holding but no acquisition of controlling stake is involved.

[118] It constitutes, in the concept developed by German law, an example of *Konzerneingangskontrolle* (regulation of group entry). See A. Pacces, above note 85, at ch. 10.4.5, arguing for reliance on fiduciary duties to control future diversionary private benefits of control rather than a mandatory bid rule, but cf. Caroline Bolle, A Comparative Overview of the Mandatory Bid Rule in Belgium, France, Germany and the United Kingdom (2008), at 279–80, suggesting that the mandatory bid is the more effective European rule.

[119] The City Code contains both such rules: see Rules 14 (offers where more than one class of equity share) and 36 (partial offers).

[120] Takeover Directive, Art. 5. The Commission's implementing report (Annexes 2 and 3) shows: that, whilst most states have put the triggering percentage near 30%, there are a number of

federal law nor the law of Delaware, perhaps because the shareholders' coordination problems are intended to be dealt with by target management.[121]

Whilst the mandatory bid rule effectively addresses the coordination problems of target shareholders as against acquirers in the context of particular transactions, it runs the risk of reducing the number of control transactions which occur. This is so for a number of reasons. First, the implicit prohibition on partial bids makes control transactions more expensive for potential bidders: either the bidder offers for the whole of the voting share capital and at a high price or it does not offer for control at all.[122] Second, the mandatory bid rule may also require the bidder to offer a cash alternative when otherwise it would have been free to make a wholly paper offer. Third, the rules fixing the price at which the acquirer must offer for the outstanding shares may expose the acquirer to adverse movements in the market between the acquisition of de facto control and the making of a full offer. As we see below,[123] these costs of the mandatory bid rule to minority shareholders are particularly high where there is a controlling shareholder, but they exist also where the acquirer builds up a controlling stake by acquisitions from non-controlling shareholders. On the other hand, the mandatory bid rule discourages acquisitions driven by the prospect of private benefits of control, in the form of diversion of corporate assets and opportunities to the controller, through the risk to the acquirer that it will end up with all or nearly all of the shares.[124]

Some, but by no means all, takeover regimes have responded to these concerns, either in the formulation of the rules relating to the fixing of the price for the general offer or by extending the list of exceptions to the rule. Thus, Swiss law requires only that the offer be at not less than the higher of the market price when the mandatory offer is launched and 75% of the highest price paid for the shares over the previous 12 months.[125] The Takeovers Directive[126] permits the supervisory authorities to identify specific situations in which the mandatory bid

---

states with much higher triggers; that, apparently, there are variations over the meaning of 'holding securities', notably how far having an interest in securities is equated with holding securities; that derogation provisions vary considerably from state to state; and that most states do not deal with consolidation of control.

[121] In any event partial bids are in fact rare in the U.S.

[122] See, e.g., Clas Bergström, Peter Högfeldt, and Johan Molin, *The Optimality of the Mandatory Bid*, 13 JOURNAL OF LAW, ECONOMICS AND ORGANIZATION 433 (1997); S. Rossi and P. Volpin, *Cross-Country Determinants of Mergers and Acquisitions* 74 JOURNAL OF FINANCIAL ECONOMICS 277 (2004), showing that takeover premia are higher in countries with strong shareholder protection, especially those with mandatory bid rules.

[123] *Infra* 8.3.1.

[124] Thus, the mandatory bid rule discourages inefficient transfers of control. The balance between that effect and its discouragement of efficient transfers of control is disputed. See L. Bebchuk, *Efficient and Inefficient Sales of Corporate Control* 109 QUARTERLY JOURNAL OF ECONOMICS 854 (1994); M. Kahan, *Sales of Corporate Control* 9 JOURNAL OF LAW ECONOMICS AND ORGANIZATION 368 (1993).

[125] Art. 32(4) Loi sur les bourses (Switzerland).

[126] Art. 5.4. Italian law previously had provided for a discount from the highest price rule, but the directive caused this provision to be dropped.

rule many be set aside.[127] Italy permits partial bids for at least 60%. of the shares, provided the shareholders other than the offeror and connected persons approve the offer by majority vote and the offeror has not acquired more than 1% of the shares over the preceding 12 months.[128]

Japan addresses some of the above problems through a mandatory bid rule which also permits partial offers. Someone seeking to obtain more than one third of the shares of a listed company may not do so by private purchase but only via purchase over the exchange or by means of a regulated pro-rata offer (called a tender offer) to all the shareholders. Only if the aim is to acquire two thirds or more of the shares must the offer be to purchase all the outstanding shares.[129] In effect, the mandatory bid rule is triggered only at the two-thirds threshold. This rule facilitates control shifts and equal treatment of shareholders but without fully providing protection for minority shareholders.[130]

Switzerland permits shareholders of potential target companies to choose between the protection of the mandatory bid rule in its full form or modifying it to encourage changes of control. The Swiss regulation permits the shareholders to raise the triggering percentage from one-third (the default setting) to up to 49% or to disapply the obligation entirely.[131] Of course, such provisions still leave the burden of proof on those arguing against the mandatory bid rule.

The need to tailor the initial rigour of the mandatory bid rule, as described above, adds considerably to its complexity. So also does the need to close obvious avoidance loopholes. Thus, the rule will usually apply to those 'acting in concert' to acquire shares,[132] not just to single shareholders. This idea has been implemented in a variety of ways in jurisdictions.[133] The rule can also be avoided if it does not include both the acquisition of economic as well as legal interests in shares.[134]

---

[127] Member states have made use of this flexibility to grant exemptions where other policy objectives override that of minority shareholder protection, for example, where dispensation from the mandatory bid rule is required to facilitate the rescue of a distressed corporation.

[128] Legislative Decree No. 58 of 24 February 1998 (as amended) Art. 107.

[129] Arts. 27–2(1) and 27–2(5) of the Financial Instruments and Exchange Act; Art. 8(5)(iii) of the Ordinance for Implementing the Act.

[130] And it must chill sales of controlling blocks, because the existing controller will not be sure to dispose of the whole of the shareholding.

[131] Arts. 22(2) and 32(1) Loi sur les bourses. These provisions must be contained in the company's constitution. In the case of total disapplication this rule cannot be introduced after the company has become listed.

[132] Takeovers Directive, Art. 5. There is a considerable danger that the acting in concert extension will chill shareholder activism, a development which policy-makers may or may not welcome. Contrast the Risk Limitation Act 2008 in Germany (discussed by Hopt, *supra* note 40 at III.B) with the City Code, Note 2 to Rule 9.1.

[133] Leading to proposals for greater harmonisation with the EU: see European Securities Markets Expert Group, *Preliminary Views on the Definition of Acting in Concert between the Transparency Directive and the Takeover Bids Directive*, November 2008.

[134] The City Code includes both extensions to the notion of acquisition of shares. See Rule 9.1 and the definition of 'interests in securities'. The extension to long economic exposures is recent and results from recognition that a person in this position can normally control the voting rights

The exit right in control transactions is associated above all with the mandatory bid rule, just discussed. However, a minor form of the exit right can be found in the obligation, imposed in some jurisdictions, upon an offeror to keep the offer open for acceptance, even after it had closed under the terms attached to the offer by the bidder. As Bebchuk has demonstrated, pressure to tender can be generated without breaching the equality principle in the formulation of the offer or by making purchases at a higher price outside the offer. Shareholders may still come under pressure to accept a uniform offer, which they regard as less than optimal and therefore wish to reject, for fear of being locked into the target as minority shareholders if the majority of the shareholders take a different view.[135] However, the solution to this problem is relatively simple, namely, the extension of the limit for acceptance of the offer to embrace a short period after it has become clear that a majority of the shareholders have accepted the offer.[136] In other words, a dissenting shareholder is given the opportunity to change his or her mind in favor of the offer once the crucial piece of information previously lacking—the decision of the majority of the other shareholders—has been provided.[137]

8.3 Agency Issues upon Acquisition from an Existing Controlling Shareholder

Where there is a controlling shareholder or shareholding group the allocation of the decision on the offer as between the shareholders alone and shareholders and target board jointly loses much of its significance, for, on either basis, the controlling shareholder is likely to determine whether the control shift occurs.[138]

---

attached to or acquire on settlement the shares bought by the counterparty as a hedge. See also *supra* note 46. The City Code is also unusual in applying the mandatory bid rule to any acquisition of voting shares by a shareholder holding between 30 and 50% of the voting shares. Many jurisdictions either have no 'creeping control' provisions or grant exemptions for acquisitions of up to 2% in any one year. See Commission Report, *supra* note 37.

[135] Lucian A. Bebchuk, *Pressure to Tender: An Analysis and a Proposed Remedy,* 12 DELAWARE JOURNAL OF CORPORATE LAW 911 (1987). See however Subramanian, *A New Takeover Defense Mechanism: Using an Equal Treatment Agreement As an Alternative to the Poison Pill,* in 23 DELAWARE JOURNAL OF CORPORATE LAW 375, 387 (1998).

[136] See, e.g., Rule 31.4 City Code (UK) (but qualified by Rule 33.2); § 16(2) Übernahmegesetz (Germany), both adopting a two-week period.

[137] For a less effective alternative, because pitched at a higher level of shareholding, see the 'sell-out right' *infra* 8.4.

[138] This depends, of course, on the board being immediately responsive to the wishes of the majority (see 3.1.1). If it is not, even a majority holder may not be able to assert its will. For a striking example see *Hollinger Int'l v. Black,* 844 A.2d 1022 (2004, Del. Ch.), where the Delaware Court of Chancery upheld the power of the board of a subsidiary to adopt a shareholders' rights plan in order to block a transfer by the controller of the parent of his shareholding in the parent to a third party. This case involved egregious facts. In particular, the controller of the parent was in breach of contractual and fiduciary duties (as a director of the subsidiary) in engaging in the transfer, and the transferee was aware of the facts giving rise to the breaches of duty.

However, the shareholder/board agency issues are here replaced by minority/majority agency problems. As with shareholder/board issues, since minority/majority conflicts are not unique to control transactions, it is possible to leave their resolution to the standard company law techniques analysed in previous chapters. However, laws dealing with control shifts have tended to generate more demanding obligations for controlling shareholders which arise only in this context. There are two central issues. First, are the selling controlling shareholder and the acquirer free to agree the terms of sale of the controlling block without offering the non-controlling shareholders either a part of the control premium or an opportunity to exit the company? Second, may the controlling shareholder, by refusing to dispose of its shares, prevent the control shift from occurring?

8.3.1 Exit rights and premium-sharing

In relation to the first issue, the central question is, again, whether the law imposes a sharing rule when there is a sale of control.[139] This question may be approached either from the side of the selling controlling shareholder (i.e., by imposing a duty on the seller to share the control premium with the non-selling minority (sharing of the consideration), or, from the side of the acquirer (i.e., by imposing a duty upon the purchaser of the controlling block to offer to buy the non-controlling shares at the same price as that obtained by the controlling shareholder (sharing of both the consideration and the exit opportunity).

Looking first at obligations attached to the selling controlling shareholder, some jurisdictions in the U.S. have used fiduciary standards to impose a sharing rule.[140] These duties may impose an obligation upon the controlling seller either to compensate the remaining shareholders for foreseeable harm caused by the sale[141] or to share the premium with the non-controlling shareholders when the sale can be identified as involving the alienation of something belonging to all shareholders.[142] However, these cases do not state the general rule. Despite some academic argument to the contrary,[143] U.S. courts have not adopted a general equality principle which might have led them to generate an unqualified right for non-controlling shareholders to share in the control premium. The law is probably best stated from the opposite starting point: 'a controlling shareholder has the same right to dispose of voting equity securities as any other shareholder,

---

[139] See *supra* 8.2.5.3–4.

[140] See also *supra* Chapter 6 (discussing controlling shareholders' fiduciary duties in the context of related party transactions).

[141] As in the looting cases: see *Gerdes v. Reynolds* 28 New York Supplement Reporter 2nd Series 622(1941).

[142] *Perlman v. Feldman* 219 Federal Reporter 2d Series 173 (1955); *Brown v. Halbert*, 76 California Reporter 781 (1969).

[143] William Andrews, *The Stockholder's Right to Equal Opportunity in the Sale of Shares*, 78 Harvard Law Review 505 (1965). For an incisive general discussion of this area see Robert Clark, Corporate Law 478–98 (1986).

including... for a price that is not made proportionally available to other share-holders' but subject to a requirement for fair dealing.[144] Provided self-dealing is effectively controlled, permitting sales at a premium price gives both seller and acquirer an appropriate reward for their extra monitoring costs.[145] It is worth noting that, since the U.S. rules are a development of general fiduciary duties, they are apt to catch sales of control in closely held companies as well as in publicly traded ones.

As far as duties on the acquirer are concerned, many of the sharing rules discussed above will operate in favour of minority shareholders against a shareholder purchasing a controlling block, for example, the rules determining the level of the consideration.[146] Consequently, an acquirer that wishes to obtain an equity stake in the target beyond that which the purchase of the controlling block will provide may find it difficult to offer a sufficiently high price to the controlling shareholder to secure those shares if the rules require the subsequent public offer to reflect the price paid outside or prior to the bid. The greatest controversy, however, revolves around the question of whether the mandatory bid rule[147] should be applied to a transfer of a controlling position, so as to require the acquirer to make a public offer, where it would otherwise not wish to do so, and on the same terms as those accepted by the controlling seller.

It can be argued that there is a vital difference between sales of control and acquisitions of control, because, where the sale is by an existing controlling share-holder, the minority is no worse off after the control shift than they were previously. However, such a view ignores the risks which the control shift generates for the minority. The acquirer, even if it does not intend to loot the company, may embark upon a different and less successful strategy; may be less respectful of the minority's interests and rights; or may just simply use the acquired control systematically for implementing a group strategy at the expense of the new group member company and its minority shareholders.[148] It is very difficult to establish *ex ante* whether the minority shareholders will be disadvantaged by the sale of the controlling block, so that the regulatory choice is between reliance on general corporate law to protect the minority against unfairness in the future and giving the minority an exit right at the time of the control shift.[149]

---

[144] American Law Institute, Principles of Corporate Governance, 5.16.

[145] For the argument that in general the controlling shareholder should be free to transfer control, whether directly or indirectly, for the reason given in the text, see R. Gilson and J. Gordon, *Controlling Controlling Shareholders* 152 University of Pennylvania. Law Review (2003–4) at 811–16.

[146] *Supra* 8.2.5.3. In most cases these rules can be avoided if the acquirer is prepared to wait long enough before launching an offer for full control.

[147] See *supra* 8.2.5.4.

[148] These are, of course, the arguments in favor of the mandatory bid rule, even where the seller is not a controlling shareholder. See *supra* 8.2.5.4. In the last case mentioned, it may be beneficial for the shareholders of the holding company to allocate business opportunities to another group member, but in that situation the minority shareholders in the new subsidiary will lose out.

[149] For a general discussion of this issue, see Jürgen Reul, Die Pflicht zur Gleichbehandlung der Aktionäre bei Privaten Kontrolltransaktionen 277 et seq. (1991).

Nevertheless, the costs of the mandatory exit right are potentially much greater in a situation of transfer of control from a controlling shareholder than where control is transferred from the management of the target through acquisitions of non-controlling shares. In the latter case, transferors of the shares which become the controlling block have nothing more to sell the acquirer than any other shareholder (but for being first in line). In the case of a transfer from a controlling shareholder, on the other hand, a mandatory exit rule, based on a public offer at the same price, requires the transferor to give up the private benefits of control for a price that does not reflect those advantages. Thus, if private benefits of control are high, the disincentive effect of a mandatory sharing of bid premiums will be significant.[150] Fewer control shifts will occur because not only must the acquirer bid for the whole share capital, but also it is unable to offer the transferor any premium for control (or at least cannot do so without overpaying for the share capital taken as a whole). In countries where controlling shareholders, especially in families, are common, this may be seen as a strong objection to the mandatory bid rule.[151] In such cases, 'it is far from certain that the benefits to minority shareholders from protection against value-decreasing acquisitions (in the worst scenario, by looters) are greater than the costs of lost opportunities for value-increasing acquisitions, the increased agency costs of reduced market discipline upon incumbent managers and blockholders, and the efficiency loss deriving from the lesser adaptability of the industrial system to environmental changes.'[152] The adverse impact of the mandatory bid rule is further enhanced if it applies to indirect acquisitions of control.[153]

---

[150] John C. Coffee, *Regulating the Market for Corporate Control*, 84 COLUMBIA LAW REVIEW 1145, 1282–9 (1984) and L. Bebchuk, *supra* note 124.

[151] See Alexander Dyck and Luigi Zingales, *Private Benefits of Control: An International Comparison* 59 JOURNAL OF FINANCE 537 (2004) (sample of 412 control transactions in 39 countries: control premia vary between -4% and 65%); Rolf Skog, DOES SWEDEN NEED A MANDATORY BID RULE? A CRITICAL ANALYSIS (1995) (Sweden in the end did adopt the mandatory bid rule in 1999. As to the reasons for the adoption, see Klaus J. Hopt, *Common Principles of Corporate Governance*, in Joseph McCahery, Piet Moerland, Theo Raaijmakers, and Luc Renneboog (eds.), CORPORATE GOVERNANCE REGIMES, CONVERGENCE AND DIVERSITY 175, 180 (2002)). On the other hand, the mandatory bid rule will prevent all inefficient transfers of control: the price demanded by the incumbent controller, when generalized across all the shares, will exceed the current value of the firm, thus preventing inefficient transfers.

[152] Luca Enriques, *The Mandatory Bid Rule in the Proposed EC Takeover Directive: Harmonization as Rent-Seeking?* in Ferrarini et al. (eds.), *supra* note 82, at 785. See further A. Pacces, *supra* note 85, at 653f, arguing for the abandonment of the mandatory bid rule and for permitting the acquirer of the controlling block to make a post-acquisition bid at the higher of the pre- and post-acquisition market price of the target's shares. A further consequence of this analysis is that a harmonized rule on mandatory bids within the EU, even if there is complete uniformity in the formulation of the rule across the member states, will in fact produce very different impacts according to whether block-holding is a prevalent form of ownership.

[153] Sometimes referred to as the 'chain principle', i.e., a person acquiring control of company. A also acquires control of company B. Must the acquirer make a general offer to the outside shareholders of company B? Perhaps reflecting the British penchant for wholly-owned subsidiaries, the City Code starts from the presumption that an offer is not required (Rule 9.1, Note 8), German law, as befits its commitment to group law, starts from the opposite presumption but allows the

However, although the above may constitute strong objections to a rule requiring prorata sharing of the premium, it is not necessarily a strong objection to the mandatory bid requirement, if the price may be fixed at a lower level than the price paid for the controlling shares. As we have seen, some systems do allow variations between the price offered to the minority and that paid for the controlling shares or permit partial bids in certain cases.[154] However, other systems are committed to the principle of equality of treatment even in the case of sales of controlling blocks and the Takeovers Directive has made this choice.[155]

8.3.2 Facilitating bids for controlled companies

The existence of controlling blocks of shareholders in public companies clearly constitutes a structural barrier to control shifts, if the controllers are unwilling to relinquish their position. However, there is not much company law can do about such barriers—other than refrain from designing rules which, like the full-price mandatory bid, reinforce the reluctance of controllers to sell out. 'Concentrated patterns of ownership represent … simply the existing condition of the economic environment.'[156] By contrast, 'technical' barriers to control shifts—which constitute 'part of the formal structure of the corporate governance environment'[157]—may be susceptible to regulation through corporate law. The recent adoption by the European Community of a Break-Through Rule (BTR) constitutes an example—ultimately only very partially successful—of a legislative attempt to address technical barriers to control shifts.

The break-through rule (BTR), embodied in the directive after a number versions of it had been canvassed by the Commission's High Level Group of Company Law Experts[158] and in various drafts of the directive, aims to prevent boards and controlling shareholders from structuring the rights of shareholders pre-bid in such a way as to deter bids. Subject to the payment of compensation, it mandatorily removes (some) restrictions on shareholders' transfer and voting rights once a bid is made, whether the restrictions are found in the company's constitution or in contracts among shareholders (to which contracts the company may or may not be party).[159] Restrictions on rights to transfer shares (more likely to found in shareholder agreements than the constitutions of public companies)

---

supervisory authority to dispense with the obligation if the assets of the subsidiary are less than 20% of the assets of the parent (§ 35 WpÜG).

[154] See *supra* 8.2.5.4. However, it is not clear on what basis the discount from the highest price rule has been identified.

[155] Art. 5.

[156] Ronald J Gilson, *The Political Ecology of Takeovers* in Hopt and Wymeersch (eds.), *supra* note 49 at 67, discussing the difference between 'structural' and 'technical' barriers to takeovers.

[157] *Ibid*, p.65.

[158] Report of the High Level Group of Company Law Experts on Issues Related to Takeover Bids, Brussels, January 2002 at 28–36.

[159] Art. 11,

are not permitted to operate during the offer period. More important, restrictions on voting rights are not permitted, and multiple voting shares will be reduced to one vote per share, at any shareholder meeting called to approve defensive measures under the 'no frustration' rule[160] *and* at the first general meeting called by a bidder who has obtained 75% of the capital carrying voting rights. At this meeting any 'extraordinary right' of shareholders in relation to the appointment and removal of directors, contained in the company's constitution, shall not apply either.[161] The break-through of voting restrictions during the offer period might be thought to be necessary to make the no frustration rule work effectively. The post-acquisition break-through is potentially more significant and gives the successful bidder an opportunity to translate its control of the share capital into control of the company by placing its nominees on the board and by amending the company's constitution so that its voting power reflects its economic interest in the company. The overall impact of the BTR, if implemented, is to render contestable the control of companies where control has been created through (some) forms of departure from the notion of 'one share one vote' or by shareholder agreements.

However, adoption of the BTR was made optional for member states in the final version of the Takeover Directive.[162] Very few of the member states have adopted the BTR in full, as set out in the directive, apparently only some of the Baltic States,[163] and a few have opted for partial adoption.[164] Thus, the overall response of the member states has been to take only a very limited interest in introducing a significant version of the BTR into their national systems. In particular, it was rejected by 13 states which nevertheless choose to apply the ban on post-bid defences.[165]

Why should this be? First, the BTR does not attack blockholding as such but only situations where the controlling position results from the misalignment of

---

[160] *Supra* 8.2.2.

[161] Thus rights of codetermination (see *infra* 8.5) are not affected because these are normally not shareholder rights of appointment and will be contained in legislation rather than the company's articles.

[162] Art. 12, just as the 'no frustration' rule was made optional.

[163] Commission Implementation Report 2007, p. 7. One state, Hungary, which previously had a mandatory partial BTR, removed it upon implementation of the Directive. For Italy, which initially adopted the BTR on implementation, see *infra* 8.6.

[164] Thus in France restrictions on the transfer of shares found in the company's constitution (but not those in shareholder agreements) do not apply in relation to a takeover offer (Art. L. 233–34 of the Commercial Code), whilst at the first general meeting after a bid, where the offeror has succeeded in obtaining acceptances from two-thirds of the capital carrying voting rights, voting caps in the articles do not apply (Art. L. 225–125 of the Commercial Code and General Regulation of the AMF, Art. 231–43). In some member states, notably Germany, voting caps have been removed as part of general corporate law reforms, not restricted to takeovers (§ 134 I Aktiengesetz, amendment of 1998, applying to listed companies).

[165] Including the UK, which has traditionally relied on a market, rather than a legal, solution to 'one share, one vote' issue, namely, the reluctance of institutional investors to buy restricted voting shares, unless they are convinced there are good reasons for the restrictions. Davies, *supra* note 41.

control rights and cash-flow rights (or restrictions on transfer) and, even then, only where, the misalignment is sufficient to trigger the BTR's threshold. Thus, a person holding just over 25% of shares of a company which have been issued on a 'one share; one vote' basis would not be affected by the post-bid BTR; nor would a person holding shares carrying just over 25% of the cash-flow rights, even if that person has voting rights which are disproportionately excessive to his cash-flow rights. In consequence, the control position in rather few public companies in the Community was potentially affected by the BTR—but enough to generate aggressive lobbying by those which were.[166] Second, the arguments for and against controlling positions not based on proportionate holdings of control and cash-flow rights were thought to be inconclusive, a deficiency which undermined the later Community initiative towards the imposition of a mandatory 'one share; one vote' rule in public corporations across the board.[167] Third, the limited member state take-up of the BTR could be seen as a response to the inadequacy of the BTR as stated in the directive: it left many pre-bid shareholder structures with defensive qualities in place (non-voting shares, extra voting rights given to long-term holders of shares, preference shares, pyramids, cross-holdings, splitting the holders of the voting and the economic rights in the shares so as to put the former in friendly hands,[168] controlling blocks exceeding 25% of the voting capital). On the other hand, picking up all possible shareholding structures with defensive qualities would lead to an extensive curtailment of the freedom of companies to adopt what they see as appropriate capital arrangements.[169]

Even if a member state chooses not to impose the BTR, as most have so chosen, each member state is obliged to permit companies incorporated in its jurisdiction to opt into the BTR.[170] The directive requires opting in and out to be effected in the same way as a change to the company's constitution, i.e., in Europe by

---

[166] See John C. Coates IV, *The Proposed 'Break-Through' Rule* in Ferrarini *et al* (eds.), *supra* note 82, Ch. 10, summarizing the available data. These suggested only a maximum of 4% of public firms in the EU would be affected, and the controlling shareholders in some of those might be able to avoid the impact of the BTR by increasing their holdings of cash-flow rights or moving to equivalent structures not caught by the BTR, such as pyramid structures and/or cross-holdings.

[167] Commission of the European Communities, IMPACT ASSESSMENT ON THE PROPORTIONALITY BETWEEN CAPITAL AND CONTROL IN LISTED COMPANIES (Staff Working Document), SEC (2007) 1705.

[168] A technique frequently employed in the Netherlands.

[169] The non-adoption by the UK of the BTR is particularly interesting in this regard. The British government gave as its main reason that 'market forces have reduced the number of companies with differential share structures without legislative intervention.' Department of Trade and Industry, COMPANY LAW IMPLEMENTATION OF THE EUROPEAN DIRECTIVE ON TAKEOVER BIDS, January 2005, para 3.9. This is a reference above all to the attitudes of the institutional shareholders whose opposition to buying non-voting and restricted-voting stock is strong and of long standing. See Davies, *The Regulation of Defensive Tactics in the United Kingdom and the United States* in Hopt and Wymeersch (eds.), *supra* note 49, Ch. 7. The Government was also alive to the desirability of not driving listings out of London. Those companies which had survived this market pressure probably had good reasons for their differential voting structures and so it would be undesirable to impose a BTR on them.

[170] Art. 12.2.

shareholder vote alone. In that decision the voting restrictions and multiple voting rights to which the BTR would apply, if adopted, will still be in force. The incentives for a controlling shareholder to opt in and thus partially dismantle the defences the company has put in place do not seem to be strong. In particular, they will depend substantially on the take-up of a further option given by the Directive to the member states, i.e., whether to permit companies which opt into the BTR to do so on the basis of the 'reciprocity rule'. This permits an opting-in company to do so on the basis that the BTR will not operate in relation to a bid from a company which is not itself subject to the equivalent of the BTR.[171]

A potential acquirer company, which is already BTR compliant, might choose to opt in, because, as a potential acquirer, it protects itself against a target relying on the reciprocity exception where that option has been taken up in the target company's state of incorporation. The strength of the incentive in this case thus depends upon how many member states (containing potential target companies) permit the reciprocity exception.[172] Even where the potential acquirer is not BTR compliant, it might see some advantage in putting itself in this position, in order to obtain the advantage just indicated. The strength of this incentive is somewhat increased by the fact that opting into the BTR is a reversible decision.

Where the state of incorporation of the company considering opting in has adopted the reciprocity rule, the BTR might generate an additional effect. The reciprocity exception might make the controllers somewhat more willing to comply with pressure from institutional shareholders to opt into the BTR, because the company will be required to do so only on the basis of a level playing field with other companies (whether domestic or foreign). Overall, however, the incentives for companies to opt into the BTR do not look strong.

8.4 Acquisition of Non-Accepting Minorities

The absence, in a control shift, of a corporate decision which binds all the shareholders means that shareholder decision-making under a general offer can operate so as to confer hold-up powers on minority shareholders who do not accept the offer, despite the fact that the majority of the shareholders have chosen to do so. This issue can arise whether the new controller has acquired that position from dispersed shareholders or from an existing controlling shareholder, provided, of course, that it is important to the acquirer to obtain complete control. Minority shareholders may decide not to accept the offer in the hope of negotiating more favorable terms with the acquirer after the bid has closed or because they wish to

---

[171] Art. 12(3). Despite some ambiguity the better view is that the reciprocity option is available when a company opts into the BTR and not only where the member state imposes it.

[172] The Commission's Implementing Report (*supra* note 37) suggests just over half the member states allow reciprocity.

maintain their opposition to the control shift or they may simply have failed to respond to the offer. Most jurisdictions provide, in one way or another, for the squeeze-out of minorities on the terms accepted by the majority, but only where a very high proportion of the shareholders have accepted the offer. Even more significant, the squeeze-out right facilitates the initial fixing of the level of the offer at less than the post-acquisition price of the shares. It achieves this result by eliminating the free-rider incentives of target shareholders, which the acquirer may otherwise be able to counter only by equating the offer with the post-acquisition price of the shares, thus reducing the acquirer's incentive to bid at all.[173]

In most jurisdictions, minority hold-ups or incentives not to tender are directly addressed by rules which give the acquirer compulsory purchase powers over the non-accepting minority.[174] In Delaware the acquisition is effected through the short-form squeeze-out merger available to the holder of 90% of each class of stock in a Delaware corporation and without, in principle, a review by the courts of the fairness of the merger.[175] The importance of the squeeze-out to acquirers is reflected in the way in which control of access to the short-form merger is used as a takeover control device in Delaware.[176]

The squeeze-out mechanism may be specific to control shifts, in which case the issue of price can be settled by entitling those whose shares are compulsorily acquired to the same consideration as was offered in the general offer. Where the squeeze-out mechanism is general (i.e., permitting a large majority shareholder to acquire compulsorily the remaining shares, no matter whether the majority was acquired in a bid), the rules for fixing the price may be more contestable.[177] However, the compulsory buy-out threshold, whether the mechanism is specific or general, is set at a high level, normally the 90% or 95% level.[178] Control shifts

---

[173] Burkhart and Panunzi, in Ferrarini, *supra* note 82, at 753–6.

[174] The Takeover Directive (Art. 15) requires member states to provide such a mechanism and some half a dozen states (mainly small but including Spain) introduced it in consequence: Commission Report, *supra* note 37 at 9.

[175] DGCL § 253. And see *supra* 7.4.2.

[176] Delaware's statutory 'anti-takeover' provision relies precisely on restricting access to business combinations (especially the short-form squeeze-out merger) between a bidder and the target in the three years after the acquisition of control: § 203 DGLC. These restrictions can be avoided if there has been either approval by the previous board of the target or a high level of acceptance (85%) of the offer by the target shareholders. See generally Y. Amihud, M. Kahan, and R. Sundaram, *The Foundations of Freezeout Laws in Takeovers* 59 JOURNAL OF FINANCE 1325 (2004).

[177] Some jurisdictions have both types of rule. In Germany the introduction of the squeeze-out power specific to control shifts was important precisely because of its presumption that the bid price is fair (§ 39a(3) WpÜG), in contrast to endless opportunities to challenge the price under the general merger procedure (§ 327b AktG). Under both specific and general squeeze-out mechanisms the courts are likely to be worried if the threshold is (to be) reached as a result of a bid by an already controlling shareholder. See *Re Bugle Press* [1961] Ch 279, CA (UK) and *Re Pure Resources Inc* 808 A.2d 421 (Del. Ch. 2002)—both in effect requiring the acquirer to show the offer to be fair.

[178] However, it is important to see whether this is a percentage of the shares offered for or a percentage of the issued shares of the class. In the former case, shares held by the offeror before the bid do not count.

might be facilitated by setting the squeeze-out threshold lower. In fact, one of the attractions of using the statutory merger procedure[179] to effect a control shift, rather than deploying it as a tidying-up mechanism after a high threshold of ownership has been achieved through a general offer, is that complete control of the target is achieved at a lower level of acceptances from the shareholders than that needed to trigger a post-bid squeeze-out. The decision of the shareholders, acting as the company, makes the statutory merger binding on all the shareholders (perhaps subject to court approval or appeal to the court)[180] at a consent level of something like two-thirds or three-quarters of those voting at the meeting.

In many countries the right of the offeror at the 90%-plus level to acquire minority shares compulsorily is 'balanced' by the right of minorities to be bought out at that level, a right which, again, may be tied to a preceding take-over offer or not.[181] However, functionally, the two are very different. Within control transactions, the effect of a right to be bought out is to reduce the pressure on target shareholders to tender, though that objective is in fact better achieved by rules requiring the bid to be kept open for a period after it has become unconditional, because the latter rule is not linked to any particular level of acceptances.[182]

8.5 Agency Problems of Non-Shareholder Groups

Some have argued that a substantial proportion of the gains to acquirers from takeovers are the result of wealth transfers from non-shareholder groups, especially the employees of the target.[183] The responses of control transaction regulation to this issue can be put, broadly, into one of three classes. First, those systems which allocate to the shareholders of the target the exclusive power to approve the offer find it difficult to fit into that structure a significant mechanism for the protection of non-shareholder interests, other than via disclosure of

---

[179] *Supra* 8.1.1. British courts have treated the acquirer as having a free hand to structure the deal as a take-over or a merger (and even to change horses in the middle of a transaction) on the grounds that court approval in a merger is a substitute for the high level of acceptances required for the squeeze-out: *Re National Bank* [1966] 1 WEEKLY LAW REPORTS 819.

[180] Other squeeze-out techniques may be available to the acquirer at a lower level of acceptances, for example, delisting the company's shares. See *supra*. 7.4.2.3.2.

[181] Both types of rule are discussed in greater detail in Forum Europaeum Corporate Group Law, *Corporate Group Law for Europe*, 1 EUROPEAN BUSINESS ORGANISATION LAW REVIEW 165, 226 et seq. (2000). The Takeover Directive requires both a squeeze-out and a sell-out right.

[182] See *supra* 8.2.5.4. An offeror may be satisfied with a controlling stake short of the 90% level and thus not be subject to the sell-out right, whereas the 'keep it open' requirement applies at whatever level the acquirer declares the bid to be unconditional.

[183] Margaret M. Blair, OWNERSHIP AND CONTROL (1995); Andrei Shleifer and Lawrence H. Summers, *Breach of Trust in Hostile Takeovers*, in Alan J. Auerbach (ed.), CORPORATE TAKEOVERS: CAUSES AND CONSEQUENCES 33 (1988).

information.[184] This strategy is heavily adopted by the Takeover Directive,[185] but the disclosure obligation sits in a vacuum, dependent for its effectiveness upon rules and institutions existing outside corporate law. In some jurisdictions such structures—usually some form of works council—do exist and may be built into the takeover process by national legislation.[186]

Where, however, the board is given a significant role in the takeover process, a second pattern can be discerned, which is to regard the survival of target management as a proxy for the furtherance of the interests of non-shareholder groups. Thus, in the U.S., one popular form of state anti-takeover statute ('constituency statutes') consists of expanding widely the range of interests beyond the shareholders' interests which management is entitled (but not bound) to take into account when responding to a takeover bid.[187] It is doubtful, however, whether, by itself, relieving directors of liability to the shareholders if they act to promote non-shareholder interests encourages anything more than self-interested behavior on the part of the target board. The greater the range of interests which directors are entitled to take into account when exercising their discretion, the more difficult it will be to demonstrate in any particular case that the standard has been breached. If this is a correct analysis, non-shareholder constituencies will benefit from such rules only to the extent that their interests happen to coincide with those of the target board.[188]

The third pattern involves taking the step of giving the non-shareholders a decision-making role, though it is a pattern to be found in practice only in relation to employee interests. In those jurisdictions (notably Germany) in which company law is used in a significant way to regulate the process of contracting

---

[184] Of course, non-shareholder interests may be protected through mechanisms existing outside company law which deal with some of the possible consequences of a control shift, for example, mandatory consultation over lay-off, under Council Directive 98/59/EC on collective dismissals. See *supra* 7.4.3.2.

[185] The extent to which the employees should be informed or be influential in the takeover process was one of the contentious issues in the deadlock over the Commission's Proposal for a Takeover Directive. The Parliament's attempt to ride all possible horses can be seen in one of its proposed amendments to the effect that 'the board of the offeree is to act in the interests of the company as a whole, in particular in the interests of corporate policy and its constitution, shareholders and staff, and with a view to safeguarding jobs, and must not deny the holders of securities the opportunity to decide on the merits of the bid.' As enacted the directive requires the target board to 'act in the interests of the company as a whole and must not deny the holders of securities the opportunity to decide on the merits of the bid.'

[186] Thus, French law (Code du Travail, Art. L. 432–1) requires an immediate meeting between the CEO of the target and the works council when the bid becomes public and, if requested by the works council, a second meeting within fifteen days of the publication of the offer document, which a representative of the acquirer must attend. Non-compliance may result in the target's shares acquired by the bidder losing their voting rights. For an analysis of the potential of such mechanisms for employee involvement in the decision-making on control shifts see Final Report of the Project AgirE (2008), available at http://www.fse-agire.com/.

[187] See, e.g., § 717(b) New York Business Corporation Law.

[188] See also Mark J. Roe, Political Determinants of Corporate Governance 45 (2002) (employee influence is indirect and weak, constituency laws are made by and for managers).

for labor,[189] the presence of employee representatives on the supervisory board and the relative insulation of the board from the direct influence of the shareholders may enable those representatives to have a significant input into takeover decisions (perhaps to the point where control shifts which are unacceptable to the employee representatives are hard to achieve). This strategy depends upon the law adopting a model of joint board/shareholder decision-making over the bid. Moreover, in this situation the disclosure requirements of takeover laws and general corporate law provisions defining 'the company' so as to include non-shareholder interests operate in an entirely different institutional context and may have real bite.[190]

In jurisdictions in which decision-making is placed in the hands of the shareholders exclusively, ad hoc examples of significant employee influence may be found, usually in relation to the acquirer's willingness to offer. Thus, in the UK, the new-found and still ill-defined rights of the Pensions Regulator[191] and by extension the trustees of employee pension schemes, which are in deficit, to require a new owner of the company to make substantial contributions to the fund, especially if it is proposing to make significant alterations to the risk profile of the company's business (likely if a private equity bid is in question), has been an important factor in a number of recent proposed bids either not emerging or emerging on terms more favorable to the employees. Equally, a generally disorderly industrial relations climate in a particular company may discourage bidders from emerging: the potential acquirer may not think it can solve all the difficult problems of the target company which the present owners have singularly failed to address.

8.6 Explaining Differences in the Regulation of Control Transaction

We have analysed control shift regulation along two main and one minor dimension. The major dimensions were the location of decision-making on the offer and the protection of target shareholders (especially non-controlling shareholders) against opportunism on the part of the acquirer or target management. The minor dimension was the responsiveness of the regulation to non-shareholder constituencies.

Two immediate conclusions can be drawn from our analysis. The first and negative conclusion is that none of the systems puts the goal of maximizing the number of control shifts at the centre of their regulatory structures. The maximum

---

[189] See *supra* 4.1.1.

[190] For information provisions in Germany see § 11(2) Übernahmegesetz and § 2 Übernahmegesetz- Angebotsverordnung (Germany). For the inclusive definition of the interests to be considered in Germany, see Michael Kort, N852–78 § 76, in Klaus J. Hopt and Herbert Wiedemann (eds.), GROSS-KOMMENTAR ZUM AKTIENGESETZ (4th ed., 2003).

[191] Under the Pensions Act 2004.

number of takeovers is likely to be generated by a system which enjoins upon target management a rule of passivity in relation to actual or threatened take-overs (the first dimension) and which gives the acquirer the maximum freedom to structure its bid (the second dimension), whilst non-shareholder interests are ignored. None of our jurisdictions conforms to this pattern: the regulation of agency and coordination issues is a better, if more complex, explanation of the goals and effects of national regulatory systems than the maximisation of the number of bids.

The second is that there are important tradeoffs involved in the placing of a particular system along the three (two major, one minor) dimensions. Thus, pro-visions aimed, at least ostensibly, at protecting target shareholders, may oper-ate indirectly so as to protect target management.[192] A system which rigorously controls defensive tactics on the part of management may nevertheless still chill takeovers by, say, strict insistence upon equality of treatment of the target share-holders by the acquirer or the prohibition of partial bids. Indeed, it is probably no accident that those systems which, historically, most clearly favor shareholder decision-making in bid contexts (France, UK) also have the most developed rules protecting target shareholders against acquirer opportunism. Deprived of the protection of centralized management, the target shareholders need explicit regulatory intervention as against acquirers, but that intervention—notably the mandatory bid rule—may also protect indirectly incumbent management. Thus, comprehensive control shift regulation of the type found in the UK may both make it difficult for incumbent management to entrench themselves against ten-der offers which do emerge and reduce the incidence of such offers. Which effect is predominant in practice is an empirical question.[193]

It is clear that the most sensitive question in relation to control transactions is whether they can be implemented over the opposition of the incumbent board. The hostile takeover dramatizes the conflict between shareholders and managers (and other stakeholders) in a more effective way than any other corporate event. Facilitating or hindering hostile takeovers thus often becomes the central issue in debates over whose interests the boards of companies are required to promote. In tussles between shareholders and managers over the design of takeover legisla-tion, the management often stands as proxy for the interests of the employees and of local communities and perhaps even of the national economy.

So, the crucial dividing line might seem to be between those systems which place the decision on the control transaction wholly in the hands of the target shareholders and those which give to each of the target shareholders and target

---

[192] See also Sanford J. Grossman and Oliver Hart, *An Analysis of the Principal-Agent Problem*, 51 ECONOMETRICA 7 (1983).

[193] Martynova and Renneboog *supra* note 32 show that in the European merger wave of the 1990s 58% of all hostile takeovers within Europe (29 countries) involved UK or Irish targets as did 68% of all tender offers (hostile or friendly) (Table 4), whilst the takeover premium paid for UK targets 'towered above' that paid for Continental targets (Figure 23).

board a veto over the transaction. This is the major fault-line in the design of control-shift rules. However, there are reasons for thinking that this division may be an over-simplification. First, it is possible, though not straightforward, for a jurisdiction which allocates the decision on the control shift jointly to target shareholders and target boards to develop adaptive mechanisms which, to a greater or lesser extent, reproduce the effects of an allocation wholly to the shareholders of the target company. As we have seen,[194] the U.S. demonstrates the possibilities for a development of this kind. Thus, Armour and Skeel have argued that, whilst the proportion of hostile bids in the U.S. is smaller than in the UK,[195] which allocates the decision entirely to the shareholders, the overall level of control shifts is not much different.[196] This suggests that the strategies for controlling the exercise by incumbent management of their decision rights over the control shift have had the effect of moving the U.S. towards the UK position. In other words, a combination of legal strategies and institutional facts may permit the shareholders to reap the benefits of joint decision-making over control shifts (shareholders overcome their coordination problems by using management to negotiate with the bidder on their behalf) without incurring the costs of this arrangement (notably management entrenchment). Where those legal strategies are not available or the institutional facts do not obtain, however, the initial allocation of the decision right will indeed be crucial.

One may wonder why the UK and the U.S. have taken such different doctrinal paths to achieve an arguably similar result. Doctrinal path-dependency would seem to explain a lot here. The UK system of company law has always been strongly shareholder-centred—the board's powers derive from the company's constitution, not the legislation, and the constitution is, formally, wholly under the control of the shareholders;[197] and directors can be removed at any time by ordinary shareholder vote—whilst U.S. law has been more protective of the prerogatives of centralized management,[198] whilst preserving the ultimate control of the shareholders.[199] For the UK, allocating decision-making on control shifts wholly to the shareholders fitted well with established patterns of corporate governance, whilst in the U.S. shareholder influence over control shifts was established in a more convoluted and, perhaps, less stable way, but one doctrinally consistent with its managerial orientation.[200]

---

[194] See *supra* 8.2.3.1.   [195] Armour and Skeel, *supra* note 30, Table 1.

[196] *Ibid*, p. 16. Whether the two systems are functionally absolutely equivalent is not clear (see Armour and Skeel, *supra* note 30 at 1742–3, arguing that the U.S. system has costs which the straightforward adoption of a 'no frustration' rule avoids).

[197] *Supra* 7.2.   [198] *Supra* 3.1.3.   [199] *Supra* 3.7.

[200] Armour and Skeel, *supra* note 30 at 1767–8 point out that the traditional doctrinal pro-shareholder orientation of British corporate law was reinforced by the rise of institutional shareholding during the precise period that modern takeover regulation was being developed in the UK, i.e., in the 1960s, whereas this coincidence did not occur in the U.S. Equally, one might speculate that, if managerial stock option plans were to become a less significant part of compensation in the U.S., then U.S. institutional investors might begin to agitate for shareholder-friendly control-shift regulation.

There is a further, and very different but important, sense in which the initial allocation of decision rights is less important than it might seem. In jurisdictions where corporate control is typically concentrated in the hands of blockholders, the notion of a hostile takeover (one accepted by the shareholders over the opposition of the incumbent board) seems beside the point, since the directors in all likelihood will be the nominees of the controlling shareholder (except to the extent that employees have appointment rights). Yet, blockholding regimes dominate the international landscape, with dispersed or semi-dispersed shareholding patterns being the exception.[201] However, here too some qualification is called for. The average size of the largest block varies from jurisdiction to jurisdiction,[202] so that in jurisdictions with smaller average blocks, whilst hostile takeovers may be more difficult, they are not ruled out entirely. Further, there is evidence, in important jurisdictions, of a weakening of the grip of blockholders.[203] Finally, even in jurisdictions dominated by large blockholders, shareholdings in particular companies atypically may be dispersed. Thus, there are very few jurisdictions in which hostile takeovers are fully ruled out on shareholder structure grounds. More important, over the last decade the hostile bid has become a significant event in a number of jurisdictions where previously it was virtually unknown.[204]

Again, the desire of rule-makers to fit regulation of the hostile takeover into the existing parameters of corporate law explains much of the responses in these jurisdictions. In the European Community the legislative response was crystallized around the design and implementation of the Takeover Directive, with the European Commission pushing for a liberal response as an important tool for promoting an integrated 'single market' within the Community,[205] whilst some

[201] M Becht and C Mayer, *Introduction* in F. Barca and M. Becht (eds.), THE CONTROL OF CORPORATE EUROPE (2001).

[202] *Ibid*, Table 1.1, reporting that in the late 1990s the median size of the largest voting block in listed companies varied from 57% in Germany to 20% in France.

[203] Franks, Meyer, Volpin, and Wagner, *Evolution of Family Capitalism: A Comparative Study of France, Germany, Italy and the UK* (http://ssrn.com/abstract=1102475) p. 13 and Table 2, show an increase in the proportion of widely held listed companies between 1996 and 2006 (from 21% to 48% in Germany; from 16% to 37% in France; and from 19% to 22% in Italy; the UK figures were 91% in both years). 'Widely held' is defined as a company where the largest vote-holder had less than 25% of the voting rights—a relatively generous definition of 'widely held'. For Japan see Tokyo Stock Exchange, SHARE OWNERSHIP SURVEY (2007). See also Martynova and Renneboog *supra* note 193, Table 4 showing that 42% of European hostile takeovers in the 1990s occurred outside the UK and Ireland, notably in France, Sweden, and Norway.

[204] Franks *et al*, *supra* note 202, Appendix A.3 report that the average number of listed companies which were the target of an unsolicited bid expressed as a percentage of all listed companies increased between the periods 1992–1996 and 2002–2006 from 0% to 0.19% in Germany; from 0% to 0.22% in Italy; and from 0.03% to 0.15% in France. The UK figures were 0.18% and 0.93%. It must be remembered, however, that the proportion of the largest 1000 companies (by sales) which is listed in those three jurisdictions is smaller that in the UK (in the UK about half; in the other countries between 15% and 30%). The same general trend can be found in Japan, as the litigation it has generated attests. See *supra* note 42.

[205] For which policy there was considerable empirical support. See, for example, Martynova and Renneboog, *supra* note 32 at 4 stating that the European merger boom of the 1990s 'boiled down to business expansion in order to address the challenges of the European market'.

member states (and the European Parliament) responded to current popular fears of globalization and its impact.[206] With the abandonment of the 'no frustration' and 'break-through' rules as mandatory rules at Community level,[207] the protectionist forces may be said to have had the better of the argument with the liberals at Community level. This trend was repeated in the transposition of the directive, where, overall, there was a less liberal approach on the part of the member states than had obtained previously.[208]

Turning to specific national level actions, German opposition to the hostile bid can be said to reflect the general weakness of shareholder interests in that traditionally bank-financed economy,[209] whilst the protection of employee interests within and outside the corporate structure (through various forms of codetermination) is perceived in that country as a particularly important way of securing social cohesion, which might be undermined by control shifts decided on solely by shareholders. In any event, after the successful hostile takeover of Mannesman, a German company with, unusually, a fairly dispersed shareholding body, by Vodafone, a British one, and the fear of such a takeover of the national champion, Volkswagen, the German government mobilized its resources to defeat at the last moment in the European Parliament the draft Takeovers Directive which, in its then form, would have made the 'no frustration' rule mandatory and which had previously been approved by all the member states, including Germany.[210] This permitted the government to proceed with its strategy of allocating approval of defensive measures to the supervisory board, on which in the largest companies the employees hold half the seats.[211]

---

[206] See Hopt, *supra* note 40 at III.A on the spread of economic nationalism within the Community.

[207] *Supra* 8.2.2 and 8.3.2.

[208] Commission Report, *supra* note 37, p 6. Transposition of the Directive was taken as the opportunity in some member states to qualify an existing 'no frustration' rule, usually through adoption of the reciprocity exception. Only one member state previously without a 'no frustration' rule adopted it upon implementation of the directive. Nevertheless, the overwhelming majority of member states have the 'no frustration' rule and had adopted it before the Directive was passed, probably in anticipation of the directive's adoption of it as a mandatory rule. As pointed out above in this section, however, the significance of this statistic is somewhat undercut by the presence of controlling blockholders in most member states.

[209] Of course, the extensive reforms from the 1990s onwards, under the general rubric of promoting *Finanzplatz Deutschland*, have altered this traditional bank orientation considerably but the hostile takeover tested the limits of the reform movement. See A Börsch, GLOBAL PRESSURE, NATIONAL SYSTEM (2007) Ch. 3.

[210] Hopt, *supra* note 40, at III.A.b. See also the heated discussion of 'shareholder activism' in the Netherlands in the wake of the pressure exerted on the board by the shareholders of the Dutch bank, ABN-Amro, to put the business up for sale—a step which led to a prolonged battle between rival takeover consortia led by the British banks, Barclays, and the Royal Bank of Scotland in 2007. See also *supra* note 75.

[211] See *supra* 8.2.3.3. Note that even where the power to take defensive measures has been conferred on the management board in advance by the shareholders, supervisory board approval of the exercise of that power is required, so that the employee representatives will have an input into that decision by the management board.

In France, which has a longer, if low-level, exposure to hostile takeovers and to their regulation,[212] the response to the increase in hostile takeover offers was more muted. The 'no frustration' rule was confirmed in the implementation of the directive, subject to the possibility of adopting defensive warrants against acquirers not subject to that rule.[213] In France employee representation within the corporate structure is a much less significant policy goal than in Germany.[214] France has traditionally relied more on state than managerial action to protect non-shareholder interests in the company.[215] In consequence, such protection has traditionally been delivered outside the framework of rules regulating agency and coordination issues between the parties in control shifts. Thus, at the same time as the Takeover Directive was being implemented in France, the foreign investment rules were strengthened so as to expand the areas of the economy in which non-EU acquirers could obtain control only with the consent of the French state.[216]

Finally, Italy is difficult to read. Having initially adopted, unusually among the member states, both the 'no frustration' and the 'breakthrough' rules, it reversed both decisions in late 2008, apparently in response to fears of the takeover of Italian 'national champions' by foreign companies and sovereign wealth funds in the wake of the 'credit crunch' of 2008.[217]

---

[212] Explicit regulation of takeovers in France dates from the late 1960s, as in the UK. See Viandier, OPA, OPE ET AUTRES OFFRES PUBLIQUES (3rd ed., 2006), paras. 71ff.

[213] See *supra* 8.2.3.

[214] See *supra* 4.2.1.

[215] Vivien A Schmidt, THE FUTURES OF EUROPEAN CAPITALISM (2002) at 117–18. See also Martynova and Renneboog *supra* note 32 at n 1: 'It is believed that French and Italian governments are rather successful in protecting their national champions. In these countries, hostile cross-border acquisitions hardly ever succeeded in the 1990s. The French and Italian governments encouraged (often inefficient) mergers between national firms to create larger national corporations…'

[216] See Decree No. 2005–1739 made under Art. L. 151–3 of the Monetary and Financial Code, requiring state approval for acquisitions in areas affecting 'public order, public safety and national defence' but interpreted widely so as to include gaming and private security provision. More generally in France, the state maintains controlling stakes, either directly or indirectly, in industries seen as important for the development of the French economy, so that in these areas a 'French solution' to a mooted control shift is normally implemented. Of course, France is not alone in taking such steps. In the United States, particular control shifts have generated strong opposition in Congress (such as the acquisition of the rights to manage major ports by a Dubai-based company) whilst the Foreign Investment and National Security Act 2007 somewhat extended Congressional control over control shifts in industries thought to have national security implications. Even in the traditionally liberal UK the government exercises a strong influence over control shifts in the defence industry (where it is a substantial customer).

[217] For the initial Italian implementation see Legislative Decree 19 November 2007, no. 229; and for the revised implementation Decree-Law 29 November 2008, no. 185, Art. 13. In effect, the boards of Italian public companies are free to adopt defensive measures, both pre- and post-bid, unless the company in its constitution has opted into either or both of the 'no frustration' or 'breakthrough' rules. In view of the fact that Italy had initially implemented both rules on the basis of reciprocity (see *supra* 8.3.2) it is doubtful whether this change was needed to provide protection against bids from most foreign companies and sovereign wealth funds.

Particularly intriguing in this context is the case of Japan, which has only recently become a jurisdiction in which hostile takeovers are feasible and which is currently seeking an appropriate set of rules to govern them, being fully aware of the regulatory patterns adopted in other countries. Thus, the Report of the quasi-official Corporate Value Group (2008) adopted a shareholder value line but did not equate this wholly with exclusive shareholder decision-making on defensive measures.[218] The ultimate shape of Japanese takeover legislation remains to be seen.

Given the range of potential opponents to a shareholder-centred regime of control-shift regulation—management, employees, some versions of national economic policy—it is perhaps surprising that the policy of allocating the decision on the control shift wholly to the shareholders of the target company has been adopted in any jurisdiction. The UK has done so since the introduction of formal regulation in this area in the late 1960s and the rule, although subject to academic criticism, is little contested in debates on public policy.[219] Elsewhere, the position is more contested. The principle of shareholder decision-making was widely adopted in the EU (outside Germany) in the years running up to the adoption of the Takeover Directive, but, ironically, there has been some retreat from this position in the actual implementation of the directive.[220] In the U.S. assessment of the overall effect of the rules varies with the attitudes of the courts, the development of executive compensation schemes and the willingness of shareholders to be active in opposing staggered boards. Japan is still making up its mind in this area. Looking at control shift rules, more broadly, however, there seems to be general agreement on the need to address shareholders' coordination problems through equality rules of greater or less rigour;[221] on the need for extensive disclosure of information from both acquirer and target management (the latter being especially important where the control shift is being promoted by the incumbent management);[222] and on the need to facilitate squeeze outs once an acquirer has obtained an overwhelming level of control.[223]

---

[218] Corporate Value Study Group, Takeover Defense Measures in the Light of Recent Environmental Changes, June 2008. The Group accepts (1) that in 'obviously detrimental' bids (which concept it tries to limit) the board may unilaterally take defensive measures and (2) that even where this is not the case the board may implement defensive measures provided these are reasonable and proportionate. Shareholder approval is an important but not conclusive factor in whether defensive measures are lawful in this case. This qualification seems partly aimed at protecting minority shareholders, but it also implies that defensive measures in this second category might be lawful even if shareholders have not approved them and even if there were evidence that the shareholders did not approve them.

[219] Department of Trade and Industry, Implementation of the European Directive on Takeover Bids, January 2005, para. 3.6.

[220] See *supra* note 37.   [221] *Supra* 8.2.5.3.

[222] *Supra* 8.2.5.1.   [223] *Supra* 8.3.2.1.

9

Issuers and Investor Protection

Gerard Hertig, Reinier Kraakman, and
Edward Rock

'Investor protection', as we use the term, denotes legal support for investors in the public trading markets[1] through, inter alia, committing listed (or registered) companies to measures, ranging from mandatory disclosure to governance reforms and regulatory constraints. Accordingly, 'investors' are passive shareholders (or debtholders) who enter and exit the market by purchasing and selling securities. Roughly speaking, investor protection seeks first to ensure the informed pricing of publicly-traded securities. In addition, however, the goal of investor protection leads all jurisdictions to take the additional step of attempting to control the quality of publicly-traded securities by screening out low-quality issuers from the public markets.[2]

Given that much of the discussion in previous chapters centered on the law of publicly-traded companies, one might ask: why devote a separate chapter to these companies and their investors? The answer is that we have not yet explored the profound importance that the *capital markets* have had in shaping legal controls over publicly-traded firms across jurisdictions. In this chapter, we focus principally on legal devices that fall outside our earlier commentary because they aim at least in part at fostering investor confidence in capital markets. Like the corporation's devices discussed in previous chapters, these devices address agency problems. But they go beyond traditional corporate law by also addressing the protection of small or unsophisticated investors, and by explicitly recognizing that one firm's opportunism or deception in the public trading market imposes negative externalities on other firms and the market as a whole.

---

[1] By public trading markets we refer to organized capital markets that trade standardized financial instruments ('securities') and are generally accessible to investors. See also *supra* 1.2.3 and 1.3.2.

[2] For example, 1933 Securities Act Rule 114A and Art 3(2) Prospectus Directive [2003] O.J. L 345/64 limit trading of non-complying securities to institutions and other 'qualified' investors. See also *infra* 9.2.1.4.1.

As we noted in Chapter 1, all jurisdictions provide the legal infrastructure for public trading markets—which law makers often refer to as 'securities' markets.[3] These markets are traditionally organized as *stock exchanges*, but they may also be structured as a *network of dealers*[4] and—increasingly today—as *multilateral trading systems*.[5] A corporation's decision to register on securities markets can confer valuable benefits on its investors by enhancing the liquidity of their shares and bonds and expanding their ability to diversify their portfolios.[6] Moreover, as the discussion in Chapters 2, 3, and 8 notes, public markets also strengthen corporate governance by allowing equity-based compensation for managers, by providing a useful measure of firm performance (share and bond prices), and by providing a useful currency for takeovers (i.e., the acquirer's shares).[7]

The law of investor protection targets two general issues: regulation of the public trading market as a whole, and the behavior of the firm and insiders toward its outside investors. Examples of the first class include regulating *margin requirements* for investors, the registration and conduct of *broker-dealers*, and the structure and performance of stock exchanges. We do *not* address systemic 'market' law of this sort here. Instead, we focus on the regulation of the actions of the firm and its insiders towards investors. These controls protect investors—and advance the goal of efficient pricing—by mandating the release of credible information about issuers, which also limits the trading advantages of corporate insiders, and by shaping the attributes and governance of publicly-traded firms.

9.1 The Objectives of Investor Protection

As noted above, the goal of protecting public investors has at least two overlapping components: informing share prices, and safeguarding the quality of publicly-traded issuers. In a hypothetical world of savvy investors, unlimited arbitrage, and low-cost information, benevolent lawmakers would have little reason to move beyond facilitating informed pricing, since disclosure would reveal differences in quality among issuers and ensure that they were fully priced in the market. But we know that real markets do not meet these strong conditions.

---

[3] See, for the U.S., Louis Loss, Joel Seligman, and Troy Paredes, FUNDAMENTALS OF SECURITIES REGULATION (5th ed., 2004 and 2009 Supplement); for Europe, Niamh Moloney, EC SECURITIES REGULATION (2nd ed., 2008).

[4] One good example is the NASD Automated Quotation System ('Nasdaq') set-up in the U.S. by the National Association of Securities Dealers.

[5] See Ruben M.G. Lee, WHAT IS AN EXCHANGE? (1998).

[6] Liquidity is the ease with which shareholders can liquidate their holdings at a reasonably efficient price. Shareholders benefit from the ability to sell their shares at efficient prices as their personal circumstances and views of the corporation dictate. Public markets also permit shareholders to diversify their investments by buying shares in numerous companies with only small transaction costs.

[7] See *supra* 2.2.1.2, 3.5, and 8.1.1.

This is the justification for controlling the quality of issuers directly. In principle, excluding 'lowest quality' issuers that are most likely to be mispriced increases the accuracy of market pricing as well as the protection of public investors. All of our core jurisdictions pursue both quality control and mandatory disclosure in the cause of protecting investors.

To return to the question of why the law generally accords more protection to investors in firms that trade on the public markets than to other shareholders, the answer turns on the economies of scale and the nature of the publicly-trading markets. First, the costs of enhanced investor protection are lower as percentage of revenue for large firms (which often tap public trading markets) than for small firms. Second, investors in small firms often have first-hand knowledge about their companies, managers, and fellow shareholders, and are thus less in need of forced disclosure. Third, and most important, an unexpected failure or fraud at one publicly-traded company typically reduces the prices of independent (if similar) companies in the same public trading market, and may reduce the process of firms across the entire market.[8] By contrast, failure or fraud among private companies is likely to be internalized to a failing firm's stakeholders without spillover effects on other companies.

9.2 Investor Protection and Legal Strategies

All legal strategies designed to protect investors are, by definition, conjoined with the entry strategy. More precisely, investor protection measures are conditions for entering—and remaining in—the public markets, even if entering these markets may not be entirely voluntary (as when U.S. companies are deemed to enter the public market when they cross certain shareholder and asset thresholds, regardless whether they are exchange-listed[9]). This said, it is convenient to group the legal strategies employed in the service of investor protection into three categories. The first is the paradigmatic exemplar of the entry strategy: mandatory disclosure in all of its dimensions, including the prescription of accounting methodologies. The second and third categories include governance and regulatory strategies respectively, which are also contingent on participating in the public markets.

9.2.1 The paradigmatic entry strategy: mandatory disclosure

All of our core jurisdictions condition entry into the public trading markets on compliance with extensive mandatory disclosure regimes. A threshold question,

---

[8] See Angela Maddaloni and Darren Pain, *Corporate 'Excesses' and Financial Market Dynamics,* Occasional Papers (2004), at http://www.ecb.europa.eu; Solomon Tadesse, *The Economic Value of Regulated Disclosure: Evidence from the Banking Sector,* JOURNAL OF ACCOUNTING AND PUBLIC POLICY 25 (2006) 32.

[9] See *infra* 9.2.1.4.

then, is whether the law must impose such requirements and, if so, to what extent.

9.2.1.1 *The underproduction of information*

The case for mandatory disclosure assumes that firms will not disclose sufficient, or sufficiently comparable, information without it. Several theoretical arguments support this view.

First, there are the familiar agency problems within corporations. Corporate insiders often prefer to suppress bad news for reasons that range from managements' desire for additional compensation, to shareholders' desire to sell high or raise additional capital at 'low' prices. Of course, such biased disclosure need not harm *diversified* investors if prices anticipate it across the market.[10] But not all public investors are diversified. Moreover, biased disclosure raises the cost of capital and distorts the allocation of capital when real-world market conditions prevent companies from signaling their true value. Tying mandatory disclosure to legal liability provides an alternative way to assure the market about the quality of a company's disclosure and the credibility of its commitments to continue honest disclosure in the future.[11]

A second justification for mandatory disclosure is that, even apart from internal agency problems, disclosure's firm-specific and market-wide benefits may diverge. Sensitive disclosures might damage any given firm in the market, while the same disclosures required from all firms might generate a net benefit for shareholders holding a diversified portfolio of all firms in the market. Put differently, diversified public investors care less about individual firms than about the informational effects on the market as a whole. Arguably, disclosure is justified whenever it leads to increased aggregate returns and lower price volatility across the market.[12]

Finally, a third justification for mandatory disclosure is the value of standardized substance, format, and quality. At bottom, this is a coordination problem

---

[10] Indeed, even outright theft of corporate assets by insiders does not 'harm' diversified shareholders to the extent that its effects are anticipated by market prices *ex ante*. Nevertheless, it harms undiversified shareholders and imposes serious *social* costs by raising the cost—and distorting the allocation—of capital.

[11] Ronald J. Gilson and Reinier H. Kraakman, *The Mechanisms of Market Efficiency*, 70 VIRGINIA LAW REVIEW 549 (1984); John C. Coffee, *The Future as History: The Prospects for Global Convergence in Corporate Governance and its Implications*, 93 NORTHWESTERN UNIVERSITY LAW REVIEW 641 (1999).

[12] There is a rich corporate law literature on the divergence between the private and public benefits of disclosure. See, e.g., Merritt B. Fox, *Securities Disclosure in a Globalizing Market: Who Should Regulate Whom*, 95 MICHIGAN LAW REVIEW 2498 (1997); Marcel Kahan, *Securities Laws and the Social Costs of Inaccurate' Stock Prices*, 41 DUKE LAW JOURNAL 977 (1992); John C. Coffee, Jr., *Market Failure and the Economic Case for a Mandatory Disclosure System*, 70 VIRGINIA LAW REVIEW 717 (1984); and Frank H. Easterbrook and Daniel R. Fischel, *Mandatory Disclosure and the Protection of Investors*, 70 VIRGINIA LAW REVIEW 669 (1984). For a sceptical view, see Roberta Romano, *Empowering Investors: A Market Approach to Securities Regulation*, 107 YALE LAW JOURNAL 2359 (1998).

among firms. Standardization through mandatory disclosure improves comparability, and thus increases the value of information to investors. Although firms have surmounted this collective action problem in the past—for example, through accounting and stock exchange rules—mandatory disclosure accelerates the standardization process.

9.2.1.2 *The empirical evidence*

Despite the foregoing arguments, legal scholars continue to debate how far issuers should be given discretion over disclosure in public markets.[13] In our view, recent scholarship supports the conventional view that publicly-traded firms under-report information without legal compulsion, especially negative information about their firms.

We acknowledge that early studies of the U.S. mandatory disclosure regime suggested otherwise, at least for exchange-traded companies.[14] More recent studies, however, provide increasing evidence of benefits. One investigation finds that large over-the-counter U.S. firms realized highly significant positive abnormal returns when they were first subject to continuous mandatory disclosure requirements in 1964.[15] Another study finds, in addition, that mandatory disclosure is associated with a dramatic reduction in the volatility of stock returns.[16] Addressing the issue from a different perspective, a third recent study finds that firms increase disclosure in response to unexpected disclosure crises (such as the collapse of Enron), and that such increased disclosure reduces the impact of transparency concerns on the firms' cost of capital.[17] Moreover, non-U.S. studies point in the same direction. Several cross-jurisdictional comparisons suggest the efficiency of mandating disclosure.[18] For example, one investigation demonstrates a strong tie between mandatory disclosure and private enforcement on the one hand, and the growth of stock markets on the

[13] For the U.S., see Merritt B. Fox, *The Issuer Choice Debate*, 2 THEORETICAL INQUIRIES IN LAW (Online Edition) No. 2, Art. 2 (2001); Roberta Romano, *The Need for Competition in International Securities Regulation*, 2 THEORETICAL INQUIRIES IN Law (Online Edition) No. 2, Art. 1 (2001); for Europe, where the debate is not as fierce, see Wolfgang Schön, *Corporate Disclosure in a Competitive Environment—The Quest for a European Framework on Mandatory Disclosure*, 6 JOURNAL OF CORPORATE LAW STUDIES 259 (2006); Hanno Merkt, *European Company Law Reform: Struggling for a More Liberal Approach*, 1 EUROPEAN COMPANY AND FINANCIAL LAW REVIEW 1 (2004).

[14] See Christian Leuz and Peter D. Wysocki, *Economic Consequences of Financial Reporting and Disclosure Regulation: A Review and Suggestions for Future Research*, Working Paper (2008), available at http://www.ssrn.com (providing a rich survey of the theoretical and empirical literature).

[15] See Michael Greenstone, Paul Oyer, and Annette Vissing-Jorgensen, *Mandated Disclosure, Stock Returns and the 1964 Securities Acts Amendments*, 121 QUARTERLY JOURNAL OF ECONOMICS 399 (2006).

[16] See Allen Ferrell, *Mandated Disclosure and Stock Returns: Evidence from the Over-the-Counter Market*, 36 JOURNAL OF LEGAL STUDIES 213 (2007).

[17] Christian Leuz and Catherine Schrand, *Disclosure and the Cost of Capital: Evidence from Firms' Responses to the Enron Shock*, Working Paper (2008), at http://www.ssrn.com.

[18] See also Allen Ferrell, *The Case for Mandatory Disclosure in Securities Regulation Around the World*, 2 BROOKLYN JOURNAL OF BUSINESS LAW 81 (2007).

other.[19] Another study concluded that more extensive disclosure requirements coupled with stricter enforcement mechanisms significantly lowered the cost of equity capital.[20]

Given these academic results and the widespread support mandatory disclosure enjoys from policymakers and participants alike, we conclude that it is the most important device for protecting public investors. The question today is not whether to implement mandatory disclosure, but how vigorously to extend and enforce it.[21]

9.2.1.3 The benefits of information

Mandatory disclosure functions principally, though not exclusively, to inform share prices. The familiar yet remarkable fact is that the disparate traders in modern markets—uninformed investors, savvy stock pickers, arbitrageurs, computers trading on autopilot, short sellers, 'technical' traders, etc.—often impound new information into price extremely rapidly. This not only protects public investors but also allows companies to use market prices as benchmarks of performance, to guide investment decisions, acquire other companies, and compensate managers.[22] Similarly, lenders and other financial intermediaries employ corporate disclosure to reduce monitoring costs and engage in profitable signaling.[23] In short, issuers, sophisticated traders, and public investors alike rely on well-informed public market prices.[24]

But mandatory disclosure confers protection on public investors beyond informing share prices. Disclosure also greases the wheels for all other legal strategies in corporate law. On the governance side, informed shareholders can better exercise their decision and appointment rights. Thus, the requirement in most of our jurisdictions that public issuers disclose the individual rather than

---

[19] Rafael La Porta, Florencio Lopez-de-Silanes, and Andrei Shleifer, *What Works in Securities Laws?* 61 JOURNAL OF FINANCE 1 (2006).

[20] Luzi Hail and Christian Leuz, *International Differences in the Cost of Equity Capital: Do Legal Institutions and Securities Regulation Matter?*, 44 JOURNAL OF ACCOUNTING RESEARCH 485 (2006).

[21] See Benjamin E. Hermalin and Michael S. Weisbach, *Information Disclosure and Corporate Governance*, Working Paper (2008), available at http://www.ssrn.com; Leuz and Wysocki, *supra* note 14.

[22] See W. Steve Albrecht et al., MANAGEMENT ACCOUNTING (2nd ed., 2002); Anat R. Admati and Paul Pfleiderer, *Forcing Firms to Talk: Financial Disclosure Regulation and Externalities*, 13 REVIEW OF FINANCIAL STUDIES 479 (2000); Ronald A. Dye, *Mandatory versus Voluntary Disclosure: The Cases of Real and Financial Externalities*, 65 ACCOUNTING REVIEW 1 (1990).

[23] See Anjan V. Thakor, *An Exploration of Competitive Signaling Equilibria with 'Third Party' Information Production*, 37 JOURNAL OF FINANCE 717 (1982) (selling of insurance signals default probability of covered firm to third parties); Tim S. Campbell and William A. Kracaw, *Information Production, Market Signaling, and the Theory of Financial Intermediation*, 35 JOURNAL OF FINANCE 863 (1980) (the market will believe the signals of those who have a sufficient stake in the market).

[24] Curiously better information may increase the volatility of share prices in individual firm under some circumstances. Compare Kenneth West, *Dividend Innovations and Stock Price Volatility* 56 ECONOMETRICA 37 (1988); Randall Morck, Bernard Yeung, and Wayne Yu, *Information Content of Stock Markets: Why do Emerging Markets Have Synchronous Stock Price Movements?*, 58 JOURNAL OF FINANCIAL ECONOMICS 215 (2000); but see Ferrell, *supra* note 16.

the aggregate compensation of senior managers is almost certainly intended to counter a perceived agency problem rather than to enhance price efficiency. On the regulatory side, information crucially affects the enforcement of rules and standards.[25] To take an obvious example, investors might never discover related-party transactions if large companies and outside auditors were not required to disclose these deals. The enforcement role of mandatory disclosure is particularly clear in the U.S. As we noted in Chapter 6,[26] issuers must report transactions with insiders involving sums as low as $120,000—an amount that is seldom material to share prices but might well indicate a duty of loyalty violation. (By contrast, the EC Transparency Directive refers to the disclosure of *major* related-party transactions, which are presumably deals that are material for informing share prices.[27])

9.2.1.4 The scope of disclosure requirements

In general terms, disclosure regimes require the release of similar information across our core jurisdictions. All jurisdictions impose disclosure duties on companies whose 'securities' trade on public trading markets within their borders. To be sure, jurisdictions differ in their regulatory definitions of 'securities' and, therefore, in financial instruments that fall within the scope of investor protection laws.[28] However, publicly-traded shares and debt instruments are generally subject to securities regulation.[29]

Despite academic calls for deregulation,[30] no jurisdiction currently allows firms to choose their own disclosure regimes.[31] Jurisdictions differ, however, in the quantity and content of information that they require companies to disclose. More precisely, disclosure regimes can be distinguished along two

---

[25] See *supra* 2.4 and Paul G. Mahoney, *Mandatory Disclosure as a Solution to Agency Problems*, 62 University of Chicago Law Review 1047 (1995).

[26] See *supra* 6.2.1.1.

[27] EC accounting law requires, however, listed groups of companies to disclose annually any transaction with directors, senior executives and controlling shareholders.

[28] See, for the U.S., Loss et al., *supra* note 3, 231–315; for Europe, Moloney, *supra* note 3, 132–5.

[29] In this chapter, references to 'securities' and shares are interchangeable unless otherwise specified.

[30] See, e.g., Stephen J. Choi and Andrew T. Guzman, *Portable Reciprocity: Rethinking the International Reach of Securities Regulation*, 71 Southern California Law Review 903 (1998). See also *supra* note 13.

[31] In theory, the EC allows for mutual recognition of national disclosure requirements and permits member states to delegate some disclosure issues to stock exchanges. See Art. 2 Prospectus Directive; Art. 2 Transparency Directive [2004] O.J. L 390/38. In practice, the approach has yet to give issuers a realistic regulatory choice. Compare Inter-institutional Monitoring Group, *Final Report Monitoring the Lamfalussy Process* (2007), at http://www.europa.eu.int; Centre for Strategy and Evaluation Services, *Study on the Impact of the Prospectus Regime on EU Financial Markets, Final Report* (2008), at http://www.europa.eu.int; Luca Enriques and Tobias H. Tröger, *Issuer Choice in Europe*, 67 Cambridge Law Journal 521 (2008).

dimensions: (1) the range of securities issues and issuers[32] that trigger their disclosure obligations, and (2) the informativeness of their disclosure requirements.

9.2.1.4.1 The threshold(s) for disclosure

Consider first the mandatory disclosure threshold for *new issues* of securities. All of our core jurisdictions adjust the level of required disclosure—from extensive to minimal—according to the number and presumed sophistication of the investors to whom the securities are sold. This is a straightforward effort to balance the costs and benefits of disclosure.

U.S. securities law, for example, distinguishes explicitly between public and private offerings of securities on the one hand, and sophisticated and unsophisticated investors who purchase securities on the other. A local offer of shares in a closed corporation does not trigger any affirmative disclosure duties. Moreover, even a geographically diverse share issue triggers only minimal disclosure obligations if shares are offered to fewer than 35 investors who are either 'accredited' (i.e., are presumptively sophisticated[33]) or have sufficient business savvy to evaluate the merits and risks of the investment.[34] Securities issued pursuant to such 'private placements' cannot be resold to the general public, but they may be resold to 'qualified institutional buyers',[35] which has given rise to an active 'private' institutional market for these securities.

Japanese and EC requirements are similar in effect. The Japanese Financial Instruments and Exchange Act (FIEA) does not require a filing with the Financial Services Agency (JFSA) for a small issue—i.e., an offering of less than 100 million yen—or for a private placement, i.e., an offering that is restricted to less than 50 persons *or* to qualified institutional investors.[36] The EC Prospectus Directive exempts securities offers from its prospectus requirement if they are made to fewer than 100 investors per member state, to 'qualified' investors, to investors who make significant purchases (worth at least a €50,000 per investor),

---

[32] Traditionally, most jurisdictions have maintained parallel disclosure requirements for public *issues* of securities and public *issuers* of securities (with shares that continue trading in the secondary markets after their initial issue). But the wisdom of this distinction is dubious, since a single issuer-oriented disclosure regime could do it all.

The U.S. has made significant progress toward a unified, issuer-oriented regime over the past two decades, a trend that is also noticeable in Japan. The EC has unified initial disclosure requirements for both issues and issuers (see Art. 1 Prospectus Directive), while maintaining a post-issuance disclosure regime that differentiates between issues that are traded on a 'regulated market' and those that are not (see Art. 1 Transparency Directive; Art. 9 Market Abuse Directive [2003] O.J. L 96/16).

[33] An accredited investor is defined to include institutional investors, officers, and directors of the issuer, and individuals with a net worth in excess of $1 million (1933 Securities Act, Rule 501).

[34] An investor who is not accredited has sufficient business savvy if he has sufficient knowledge and experience in financial and business matters to evaluate the merits and risks of his prospective investment (1933 Securities Act, Rule 506).

[35] 1933 Securities Act, Rule 144A.

[36] Art. 4 Financial Instruments and Exchange Act. An administrative statement must also be filed with the Financial Services Agency for issues above 10 million yen.

or for a total amount of less than a €100,000.[37] Like the U.S., then, the EU and Japan calibrate an issuer's burden of disclosure to the sophistication or presumed knowledge of its investors.

In contrast to the regulation of new issues of securities, *continuing disclosure* requirements for public issuers vary more among our core jurisdictions.[38] The EC's minimal requirements are narrow, since they only extend to firms traded on 'regulated markets'.[39] Disclosure requirements in non-EU jurisdictions are broader. In Japan, public companies subject to continuing disclosure duties include not only issuers of exchange-listed securities, but also issuers of securities registered with the Japan Securities Dealers Association (JSDA), issuers that have previously registered securities under the FIEA, and companies with 500 or more shareholders.[40] The U.S. has virtually the same requirements as Japan. In particular, U.S. firms must register under the 1934 Securities Exchange Act, which subjects them to a continuing reporting requirement, if they are listed on a national securities exchange, have more than 750 shareholders and assets exceeding $10 million (whether or not they are exchange-listed),[41] or have previously issued securities that were registered under the 1933 Securities Act.[42] (In effect, this last rule requires private firms with publicly-traded debt to comply with continuing disclosure requirements.)

9.2.1.4.2 The content of disclosure

The content of mandatory disclosure, like its scope, is broadly similar across jurisdictions. The registration statement or prospectus that accompanies new public issues of securities must describe them in detail, as well as the intended use of the proceeds from their issuance. It must also include a comprehensive set of financial statements prepared in accordance with national accounting practices.[43]

---

[37] Art. 3(2) Prospectus Directive.

[38] See *infra* 9.2.2.2 for a discussion of the impact of these differences in terms of investor protection and compliance costs.

[39] See Art. 1 Transparency Directive; Art. 6 Market Abuse Directive. Art. 4(1)(14) of the Markets in Financial Instruments Directive [2004] O.J. L 145/1) defines a 'regulated market' as an authorized system which functions regularly and brings together multiple third-party buying and selling interests in financial instruments admitted to trading under its rules. For the less stringent requirements applicable to financial instruments traded on so-called 'multilateral trading facilities' (MTF), see Herbert Harrer and Roger Müller, *The New Entry Standard of the Frankfurt Stock Exchange—A Comparison with the Alternative Investment Market and Alternext*, 2006 BUTTERWORTHS JOURNAL OF INTERNATIONAL BANKING AND FINANCIAL LAW 109 and 165 (March).

[40] Art. 24(1) Financial Instruments and Exchange Act; Art. 3–6(2) Financial Instruments and Exchange Ordinance.

[41] § 12(g) 1934 Securities Exchange Act and Rule 12g-1.

[42] § 15(d)1934 Securities Exchange Act. Note that issuers that are not required to register under § 12 may elect to do so voluntarily. Voluntary registration makes sense in several contexts. First, shares must be registered in order to be included in the Nasdaq. Second, shares must be registered under § 12 for shareholders to resell restricted securities under the 1933 Securities Act, Rule 144.

[43] Major non-U.S. firms increasingly comply with International Financial Reporting Standards (IFRS), which have replaced national accounting standards for groups of companies traded on exchanges in the EU. See also *supra* 5.2.1.2, 5.2.1.3, and *infra* 9.2.1.5.

Moreover, all major jurisdictions require an extensive description of the nature and performance of an issuer's business and of the identity of its management and large securities holders.

Notwithstanding these similarities, however, our core jurisdictions differ in their commitment to disclosure as a means of protecting public investors. To see why, consider that information subject to disclosure falls into three categories. The first is a basic description of the company, ranging from an inventory of its assets to an accurate statement of its current financial position and past cash flows. This is the hard, 'benchmark' data that would allow an investor to value the firm as a going concern *if* the future were exactly like the past.

All jurisdictions require substantial disclosure of such benchmark data. However, jurisdictions still differ with respect to the detail they require as accounting methodologies have yet to be fully harmonized or implemented in uniform ways.[44]

A second category of disclosure mandated in some jurisdictions encompasses 'soft', 'projective', or 'forward-looking' information. This category includes management's predictions about likely price changes in each of the multiple markets in which the firm operates (i.e., product, supply, capital, and labor markets), as well as management's best estimates of likely changes in demand for the firm's products, including any new products or cost-saving technologies that the firm plans to introduce. This 'scenario' information (if accurate) permits investors to estimate future changes in a firm's cash flows. Thus it is critical for valuing firms with conventional financial methodologies such as discounted cash flow analysis.

Despite the importance of projective data, however, it accounts for only a tiny fraction of mandated disclosure in our core jurisdictions.[45] The U.S. pioneered the reporting of soft information by requiring managers to complete a 'Discussion and Analysis of Financial Condition and Results of Operations' ('MD&A')[46] for their companies, and encouraging (but not requiring) companies to disclose forward-looking financial projections by shielding such projections from shareholder lawsuits.[47] Japan followed suit by introducing MD&A reporting in 2003.[48] The EC also mandates the disclosure of soft and projective information, but in such a general way that public investors are unlikely to derive much guidance from it.[49] The U.S., then, has been the leader in forcing the disclosure of

---

[44] See *infra* 9.2.1.5.

[45] Or put differently, 95% of mandated financial and descriptive disclosure falls into the historical category described above.

[46] Regulation S-K, Item 303. The MD&A report requires extensive discussion of 'known trends or uncertainties' that might have a favorable or unfavorable impact on future financial performance.

[47] 1933 Securities Act, Rule 175.

[48] JFSA Regulation for Issuer Disclosure, Notes on the Forms (amended in 2003).

[49] Art. 4(2)(c) and Art. 5(4) Transparency Directive merely require that firms traded on a regulated market to report 'principal risks and uncertainties that they face' on an annual and semi-annual basis.

soft and future-oriented information, but even U.S. firms have been reluctant to reveal projections prior to the last decade.[50]

Finally, the third category of disclosure information relates directly to governance issues and agency problems. This category includes information about top management compensation (salaries, bonuses, equity compensation, and severance payments), as well as information about the cash flows that find their way to controlling shareholders. In some respects, U.S. disclosure is more extensive than that of other jurisdictions here too. For example, registered U.S. companies must provide detailed reports on the background of their directors, the compensation of the top five individual managers, and direct and indirect related-party transactions between the firm and corporate insiders.[51] In addition, U.S. corporations must report all changes in accounting practices and disagreements with their auditors,[52] while corporate insiders must file monthly reports on purchases and sales of the firm's shares.[53] (As we have seen in Chapter 6, EU member states and Japan appear to be gradually moving toward requiring these disclosures as well.[54])

In other respects, however, such as in educating shareholders about the issues at stake in shareholder votes, UK disclosure is more revealing than that in other jurisdictions, including the U.S.[55]

9.2.1.5 *Accounting methodologies*

The global convergence of accounting methodologies over the past decade has been striking.

Historically, financial reporting regimes—the provision of information about a firm's past and current financial position—evolved from two different models.[56] The first, the 'continental European' model, originated in 17th century France with the goals of protecting creditors and facilitating the taxation of firms.

---

[50] The reluctance to prepare forward-looking statements has been attributed to liability concerns should the estimates prove wrong. Whether this is the case has yet to be empirically answered (see Loss et al., *supra* note 3, 165), but there is evidence of an increase in MD&A reporting in recent years. See Marilyn F. Johnson, Ron Kasznik and Karen K. Nelson, *The Impact of Securities Litigation Reform on the Disclosure of Forward-Looking Information by High Technology Firms*, 39 JOURNAL OF ACCOUNTING RESEARCH 297 (2001) (finding a significant increase in both the frequency of firms issuing forecasts and the mean number of forecasts issued following the adoption of the safe-harbor rule); Jeffrey N. Gordon, *The Rise of Independent Directors in the United States, 1950–2005: Of Shareholder Value and Stock Market Prices*, 59 STANFORD LAW REVIEW 1465 (2007) (finding that the average length of MD&A disclosure among the sampled firms grew from two pages in 1974 to six pages in 1990 to 24 pages in 2004).

[51] Regulation S-K, Items 401, 402, and 404.   [52] *Id.* Item 304.

[53] § 16(a) 1934 Securities Exchange Act (as amended by §403 Sarbanes-Oxley Act).

[54] See *supra* 6.2.1.1. See also Art 46a Fourth Company Law Directive [1978] O.J. L 222/11, as amended in 2006 (listed companies must include a corporate governance statement in their annual report).

[55] See Paul L. Davies, GOWER AND DAVIES' PRINCIPLES OF MODERN COMPANY LAW 385–9 (8th ed., 2008).

[56] See Barry J. Epstein and Eva K. Jermakowicz, IFRS 2007 2–3 (2007).

The second, the 'Anglo-Saxon' model, developed in the UK during the 19th century to enhance the ability of equity holders to monitor their investments. Put differently, the interests of creditors, insiders, and the state strongly influenced a continental European model of accounting, while the interests of equity holders informed the Anglo-Saxon accounting model.[57]

These disparate interests point toward different valuation methodologies. Traditionally, valuation has looked either to historical cost, which captures the conservative thrust of continental accounting, or to 'fair market value', which tracks the interests of equity-holders.[58] Both accounting methodologies report assets on the balance sheet at the lower of historical cost or market value.[59] However, traditional continental accounting makes much broader use of historical cost, which yields easily verifiable data but also allows firms to defer profits over time (which may delay disclosure of bad performance), and, in inflationary periods, undervalues non-financial assets and overvalues fixed-interest financial assets.[60]

By contrast, the fair value approach relies on current market prices as its metric (especially for financial assets), and is therefore more likely to correlate with the stock market valuation of firms.[61] However, if financial assets lack an active market, fair value accounting requires that they be 'marked to [a] model' of what their market value 'should' be[62]—a hazardous undertaking indeed. Moreover, fair value accounting increases the volatility of financial reporting and may not reflect the going-concern value of firm-specific assets.[63] Indeed, as we write today, some commentators, even in the U.S., criticize the pro-cyclic effects of marking

---

[57] Indeed, even today the U.S. and UK distinguish between financial and tax accounting, while most European jurisdictions employ the same accounting methodology for both tax and financial reporting purposes.

[58] See Steven J. Kachelmeier, *International Accounting*, in A. Rashad Abdel-Khaluik (ed.), ENCYCLOPEDIC DICTIONARY OF ACCOUNTING, 189–94 (1997).

[59] See also Marcus Lutter, EUROPÄISCHES UNTERNEHMENSRECHT 141 (4th ed., 1996); Epstein and Jermakowicz, *supra* note 56, 46; Barry J. Epstein, Ralph Nach, and Steven M. Bragg, GAAP 2008 41 (2007).

[60] See also Alexander Bleck and Xuewen Liu, *Market Transparency and the Accounting Regime*, 45 JOURNAL OF ACCOUNTING RESEARCH 229 (2007) (historical costs gives management a veil under which they can potentially mask a firm's true economic performance).

[61] Fair value is defined as the price for which an asset or a liability can be exchanged between knowledgeable, willing parties in an arm's length transaction. Note that the empirical evidence on the share price relevance of fair value accounting is mixed. See e.g. Jochen Zimmermann and Jörg-Richard Werner, *Fair Value Accounting under IAS/IFRS: Concepts, Reasons, Criticisms*, in Greg N. Gregoriou and Mahamed Gaber (eds.), INTERNATIONAL ACCOUNTING 127 (2006).

[62] See FAS 157: for the Financial Accounting Standards Board, a fair value measurement is based on market data reporting (observable inputs) and, to the extent market data is unavailable, on the best information available (unobservable inputs).

[63] See Guillaume Plantin, Haresh Sapra, and Hyun Song Shin, *Marking-to-Market: Panacea or Pandora's Box*, 46 JOURNAL OF ACCOUNTING RESEARCH 435 (2008) (marking to market is especially problematic when assets are long-lived, illiquid, and senior).

assets to market when market prices are purportedly 'distressed', and therefore undervalue the 'true' hold-to-maturity value of complex financial assets.[64]

Nevertheless the divergence between the Continental and Anglo-Saxon approaches toward accounting should not to be exaggerated. As indicated above, both models have always used historical cost to value non-financial assets.[65] In addition, accountants are conservative by profession, which discourages them from overvaluing financial assets under fair value accounting.[66] With the (admittedly very large) exception of financial institutions during the 2004–2007 period, post-Enron managers, auditors and regulators have come to recognize that prudent accounting is the best defense against personal liability for overstating earnings.[67] Finally, EC harmonization, coupled with the growing importance of global capital markets, has prompted continental European jurisdictions to accept a wider role for fair value.[68] Even Germany, which has traditionally favored a 'precautionary approach' (*Vorsichtsprinzip*) to valuing balance-sheet items, has edged toward accepting the fair value model.[69] As a result, financial reporting methodologies are converging.

Although the extent to which current accounting methodologies are 'equivalent' remains subject to debate,[70] there is no doubt that the standard-setting

---

[64] See Franklin Allen and Elena Carletti, *Mark-to-Market Accounting and Liquidity Pricing*, 45 Journal of Accounting and Economics 358 (2008); Guillaume Plantin, Haresh Sapra, and Hyun Shin, *Marking-to-Market: Panacea or Pandora's Box*, 46 Journal of Accounting Research 435 (2008). See also International Monetary Fund, *Global Financial Stability Report* 58–66 (2008).

[65] See e.g. Janice Loftus, *A Fair Go to Fair Value*, in Gregoriou and Gaber, *supra* note 61, 41. Note that historical cost is one of the seven principles U.S. GAAP is built upon, with the fair value principle only growing in importance since the 1970s. See Stanley Stiegel, *The Coming Revolution in Accounting: The Emergence of Fair Value as the Fundamental Principle of GAAP*, 42 Wayne Law Review 1839 (1996).

[66] Sudipta Basu, *The Conservatism Principle and the Asymmetric Timeliness of Earnings*, 24 Journal of Accounting and Economics 3 (1997); see also Sugata Roychowdhuroy and Ross L. Watts, *Asymmetric Timeliness of Earnings, Market-to-Book and Conservatism in Financial Earnings*, 44 Journal of Accounting and Economics 2 (2007).

[67] See generally Ross L. Watts, *Conservatism in Accounting*, 2003 Accounting Horizons 207 (Part I) and 287 (Part II).

[68] See A. Lewitt, *The Importance of High Quality Standards*, 12 Accounting Horizons 79 (1998) (arguing that, to get global acceptance, accounting methodology must be investor-oriented). The European Court of Justice stated in *Tomberger* [1996] European Court Reports I 3145 that Art. 2 Fourth Company Law Directive posits 'true and fair view' as the overriding EU accounting principle. Note that the directive does not explicitly override other principles, such as the German 'Vorsichtsprinzip' (precaution principle): see Mathias Habersack, Europäisches Gesellschaftsrecht § 8 No. 29 (3d ed., 2006).

[69] See Klaus J. Hopt, *Common Principles of Corporate Governance in Europe*, in Basil S. Markesinis (ed.), The Coming Together of the Common Law and the Civil Law 105, 114 (2000); Werner F. Ebke, *Rechnungslegung und Publizität in europarechtlicher und rechtsvergleichender Sicht*, in Werner F. Ebke, Claus Luttermann and Stanley Siegel (eds.), Internationale Rechnungslegungsstandards für börsenunabhängige Unternehmen? 67 (2007).

[70] According to the European Commission's Regulation EC/1569/2007 of 21 December 2007 (establishing a mechanism for the determination of equivalence of accounting standards applied by third country issuers of securities, O.J. L 340/66), there is equivalence if the financial statements enable investors to make a similar assessment of the assets and liabilities, financial position, profit

authorities in all of our core jurisdictions favor further coordination.[71] However, even 'equivalent' accounting methodologies do not necessarily imply uniform accounting practices.[72] Institutional differences in ownership regimes and regulatory structures will remain a source of divergence.[73] For example, GAAP relies on detailed rules to reduce the risk of shareholder litigation alleging faulty accounting—an interest that is more salient in the U.S. than elsewhere. Conversely, jurisdictions with low litigation risk, such as the European ones, have embraced the principle-oriented IFRS, which leaves more room for managerial discretion. Ironically, flexibility may help to explain the global popularity of IFRS, even though flexibility reduces the comparability of financial statements between IFRS jurisdictions. But comparability across or within jurisdiction can also be difficult under rule-oriented accounting systems, insofar as rules cannot anticipate all cases and must be supplemented by standards.[74]

Overall, investors continue to get better information under Anglo-Saxon financial reporting rules. U.S. and UK GAAP are relatively well settled, whereas it is too early to assess how (uniformly) IFRS will be implemented in Japan and continental Europe. Some countries may conform to IFRS as closely as possible to their former (relatively uninformative) national standards while others may need years to adjust to the new accounting environment.[75] In addition, financial

and losses and prospects of the issuer as financial statements drawn up in accordance with IFRS, with the result that investors are likely to make the same decisions about the acquisition, retention or disposal of securities of an issuer.

[71] Compare *Roadmap for the Potential Use of Financial Statements Prepared in Accordance with International Financial Reporting Standards for U.S. Issuers*, SEC RELEASE Nos. 33–8982, 34–58960 (2008 European Commission, Decision on the use by third countries' issuers of securities of certain third country's national accounting standards and International Financial Reporting Standards to prepare their consolidated financial statements [2008] O.J. L 340/112 and Commission Regulation No. 1289/2008 [2008] O.J. L 340/17; Accounting Standards Board of Japan and International Accounting Standards Board, *Tokyo Agreement on Achieving Convergence of Accounting Standards by 2011* (8 August 2007, at http://www.asb.or.jp).

[72] Not reaching uniformity may also have its advantages: see Shyam Sunder, *IFRS and the Accounting Consensus*, Working Paper (2008), at http://www.ssrn.com (arguing that uniformity will discourage discovery of better methods of financial reporting).

[73] Yuan Ding, Ole-Christian Hope, Thomas Jeanjean, and Hervé Stolowy, *Differences Between Domestic Accounting Standards and IAS: Measurement, Determinants and Implications*, 26 JOURNAL OF ACCOUNTING AND PUBLIC POLICY 26 (2007); Ross L. Watts and Jerold L. Zimmerman, *Towards a Positive Theory of the Determination of Accounting Standards*, 53 ACCOUNTING REVIEW 112 (1978).

[74] See William W. Bratton, *Enron, Sarbanes-Oxley and Accounting: Rules Versus Principles Versus Rents*, 48 VILLANOVA LAW REVIEW 1023 (2003).

[75] See Holger Daske, Luzi Hail, Christian Leuz, and Rodrigo Verdi, *Mandatory IFRS Reporting around the World*, 46 JOURNAL OF ACCOUNTING RESEARCH 1085 (2008) (mandatory IFRS reporting results in higher market liquidity and cost of capital benefits in jurisdictions where firms have an incentive to be transparent); Christopher S. Amstrong, Mary E. Barth, Alan D. Jagolinzer and Edward J. Riedl, *Market Reactions to the Adoption of IFRS in Europe*, Working Paper (2008), at http://www.ssrn.com (investors react less positively to the adoption of IFRS in member states generally thought to have weaker accounting standards enforcement).

analyst coverage is denser for U.S. and the UK listed firms, a factor which empirical studies have found to correlate with the quality of financial reporting.[76]

An uncomfortable issue raised by the 2008–2009 financial crisis is whether *any* of the converging accounting methodologies capture the risks associated with firms heavily invested in financial derivative products. Particularly in the case of financial institutions which have unexpectedly disclosed extraordinarily large liabilities, all current accounting methodologies may fail to give an accurate account of firms' risk profiles, which can literally change overnight.[77]

9.2.2 Quality controls: governance and regulatory strategies

In addition to mandating disclosure, lawmakers and stock exchanges also impose 'quality' restrictions on companies with securities traded on public markets. Indeed, all law that exclusively targets 'listed' or 'public' companies—i.e., much of the law that we have discussed in earlier chapters—protects public investors by bolstering the quality of publicly-traded corporations. In general terms, the case for these quality controls resembles the case for mandatory disclosure. Unlike the failure of a closely held firm, the failure of a publicly-traded firm harms distant investors and raises capital costs for other companies trading in the same market. Moreover, imposing a more uniform regime on publicly-traded companies increases their transparency, reduces information costs for investors, and may even be viewed as a kind of 'delegated contracting'.[78]

9.2.2.1 *Governance strategies*

Consider governance strategies first. Most mandatory features of shareholder appointment rights target publicly-traded companies exclusively. These include the hard and soft law that structure shareholder voting rights and nomination procedures, director tenure, the committee structure of boards, the conduct of proxy fights, and disclosure requirements.[79] To a lesser extent, stock exchange

---

[76] See Robert M. Bushman, Joseph D. Piotroski, and Abbie J. Smith, *What Determine Corporate Transparency*, 42 JOURNAL OF ACCOUNTING RESEARCH 207 (2004); Richard Frankel, S. P. Kothari, and Joseph Weber, *Determinants of the Informativeness of Analyst Research*, 41 JOURNAL OF ACCOUNTING AND ECONOMICS 29 (2006); Donal Byard, Ying Li, and Joseph Weintrop, *Corporate Governance and the Quality of Financial Analysts' Information*, 25 JOURNAL OF ACCOUNTING AND PUBLIC POLICY 609 (2006).

[77] See, e.g., *Report of the High Level Group on Financial Supervision in the EU* (de Larosiere Report) (2009), at http://www.europa.eu); *Report of the Group of Thirty, Financial Reform: A Framework for Financial Stability* (2009, at http://www.group30.org); *Report of the Financial Stability Forum on Enhancing Market and Institutional Resilience* (2008, at http://www.fsforum. org); Brian W. Nocco and René M. Stulz, *Enterprise Risk Management: Theory and Practice*, 18 APPLIED CORPORATE FINANCE 8 (2006).

[78] See Henry Hansmann, *Corporation and Contract*, 8 AMERICAN LAW AND ECONOMICS REVIEW 1 (2006) (corporations save on charter amendment costs by relying on state default law and, thus delegate charter amendment to lawmakers). See also *supra* 9.2.1.1.

[79] See *supra* 3.1, 3.3, and 3.4.

listing rules mandate direct decision making rights for shareholders, as in the U.S., where the New York Stock Exchange (NYSE) and NASDAQ mandate shareholder approval of certain equity compensation plans and any transaction that permits companies to issue new shares with voting rights exceeding 20% of shares that are already issued and outstanding.[80] And, of course, both hard and soft law mandate extensive use of the trusteeship strategy, in the form of adding independent directors to the board, for publicly-traded companies.[81]

But there is another variation of the trusteeship strategy that is targeted directly at investor protection. Most major jurisdictions maintain at least vestigial screening by regulators or stock exchanges of companies eligible for public trading.

In the U.S. vernacular, this form of trusteeship strategy is termed 'merit regulation'. In past decades, many U.S. states permitted state regulators to refuse to approve an issue that failed to conform to certain guidelines, or appeared—to the officials—to be particularly risky without offsetting economic merit. In practice, U.S. state officials rarely bar initial public offerings, although the practice still occurs.[82]

European jurisdictions also engage in merit regulation when they allow regulators to screen applications for exchange listings in the interest of protecting the investing public.[83] Thus, the UK's Financial Services and Markets Act 2000 (FSMA) authorizes the UK Listing Authority (UKLA) to refuse a listing application that it considers detrimental to the interests of investors.[84] Similarly, the French supervisory authority may oppose exchange listings that appear to violate applicable laws, while German stock exchanges are required to withhold listings that fail to comply with provisions enacted to protect the public.[85] However, quality-control provisions have recently fallen from favor among regulators.[86]

9.2.2.2 Affiliation strategies: entering and exiting public markets

As we have noted throughout this book, publicly-traded companies are far more heavily regulated than closely held companies. The familiar legal distinction between 'open' companies, such as the German *Aktiengesellschaft* or the French *sociétés anonymes,* and 'closed' companies such as the GmbH and the SARL, arguably serves as a device for subjecting publicly-traded companies to tighter

---

[80] New York Stock Exchange Listing Company Manual § 312.03; Nasdaq Marketplace Rule 4350(i)(1)(A). Note that most of our major jurisdictions impose much more restrictive requirements on shareholder approval of new share issues: see *supra* 4.1.3.2. and, especially, 7.3.2.

[81] See *supra* 3.2.

[82] Regarding the limited coverage of merit regulation, see, e.g., Roberta Romano, THE GENIUS OF AMERICAN CORPORATE LAW 108–12 (1993).

[83] See Art. 11 Consolidated Admission and Reporting Directive, [2001] OJ L 184/1, applicable to 'official' listed segments.

[84] § 75 Financial Services and Markets Act.

[85] Art. L 421–4 Code Monétaire et Financier and Art. 214–2 Règlement Général de l'Autorité des Marchés Financiers (AMF) (France); § 30 Börsengesetz (Germany).

[86] See also Moloney, *supra* note 3, 72–7.

regulatory control. Of course, the overlap between 'open' and publicly-traded companies is spotty (not all open companies are publicly traded).[87] Nevertheless, a straightforward justification for limiting regulation to 'open' companies is that closed companies are, by definition, insulated from public investors and trading markets. In addition, of course, there is a second web of rules specifically geared to trading status which governs publicly-traded companies. These rules, which are addressed in earlier chapters, range from controls on the allocation of voting rights and board structure to regulating tender offers.

But if much of our earlier discussion implicitly focuses on publicly-traded companies, we have yet to address the listing rules for entering the public market and the delisting and 'deregistration' rules for escaping regulation as a public company.

Listing requirements are designed to exclude presumptively low-quality or illiquid issuers from particular public markets. 'Official' or 'first-tier' markets typically mandate a minimum size for corporate issuers, a minimum float for listed securities, and a minimum history of published accounts. For example, the NYSE requires a pre-tax corporate income of between $2 million and $4.5 million,[88] net tangible assets of $40 million, and a float of publicly-held shares that—depending on market conditions—must exceed $40 million. It also requires a minimum of 1.1 million shares of publicly-held common stock, and a minimum number of shareholders (between 500 and 2,200, depending on trading volume). Other exchanges, with the exception of the Tokyo Stock Exchange,[89] impose less rigorous listing requirements. For example, the EC minimum for an exchange listing is €1 million in 'foreseeable' market capitalization (or, if this cannot be assessed, in legal capital and reserves), and financial accounts covering the company's prior operating history for at least three years.[90]

---

[87] See also *supra* 1.2.3 and 1.3.1.

[88] More precisely, the NYSE generally requires: either $2.5 million in income before federal income taxes for the most recent year and $2 million pre-tax income for each of the preceding two years, or an aggregate for the last three fiscal years of $6.5 million together with a minimum in the most recent fiscal year of $4.5 million (all three years must be profitable).

[89] For its so-called first section, the Tokyo Stock Exchange requires: at least 20,000 unit shares; at least 4 billion yen in shareholders' equity; at least 2,200 shareholders; and a high minimum pre-tax profit calculated over a two- or three-year period.

[90] Arts. 43 and 44 Consolidated Admission and Reporting Directive. Member states may provide for admission even if these conditions are not fulfilled, provided that the competent authorities are satisfied there will be an adequate and informed market for the shares concerned. EU member states have generally chosen not to add to these requirements, as is shown by the German (minimum foreseeable market capitalization of €1.25 million) and UK listing rules (a minimum expected aggregate market value of £700,000). For Germany, see § 2 Börsenzulassungsverordnung 38(1); for the UK, § 2.2.7 Listing Rules (although the UK Listing Authority may admit a lower float if satisfied that there will be an adequate market for the securities concerned: § 2.2.8). The Italian Stock Exchange has set a much higher requirement for the admission to the main market (the required foreseeable market capitalization is €40 millions), but shares with a smaller market capitalization may be admitted if the Stock Exchange is satisfied that an adequate market for such shares will develop: see Art. 2.2.2 Listing Rules for the markets set up and managed by Borsa Italiana SpA.

Although the conditions for entering even top-tier markets are modest, the rules governing 'delisting' and 'deregistration' are less so. Easy exit from pub-licly-traded and listed company regulation might encourage firms to bait and switch—to attract investors with the implicit promise of full disclosure, and then 'go dark' by abandoning their status as public companies. Thus, difficult exit rules serve as a commitment device for publicly-traded firms, and as a protective device for public investors.[91]

Two kinds of legal regimes govern the withdrawal of a company from public reporting obligations in our core jurisdictions. First, all jurisdictions establish objective criteria for allowing companies to cease complying with public report-ing obligations. In some jurisdictions, these criteria are quantitative. For example, U.S. securities law ceases to mandate disclosure when the number of a com-pany's shareholders drops below 300 (or, in some circumstances, 500),[92] whereas Japanese public registration requirements cease to apply when the number of an issuer's shareholders falls below 300 or its legal capital drops below 500 million yen.[93] In some jurisdictions that distinguish between the closed and open cor-porate forms, the choice of the latter form with freely transferable shares triggers disclosure obligations that remain in force until shareholders choose to revert to the closely held form. One example is Germany, where the *Aktiengesetz*—the corporation code—imposes disclosure obligations aimed at protecting invest-ors in addition to those of the *Wertpapierhandelsgesetz*, a U.S.-style securities code applicable to listed firms.[94] France provides another example of this hybrid approach, combining the disclosure obligations of a continental company law and an Anglo-Saxon-style code of securities regulation.[95]

Second, public companies that are exchange-listed must also comply with the rules governing voluntary delisting.[96] For example, the NYSE permits securities

---

[91] See Edward Rock, *Securities Regulation as Lobster Trap: A Credible Commitment Theory of Mandatory Disclosure*, 23 CARDOZO LAW REVIEW 675 (2002).

[92] §§ 12(d), 15(d) 1934 Securities Exchange Act (holders of records being the relevant ones).

[93] The exact rules are more complex. See Art. 24(1) Financial Instruments and Exchange Law and Art. 3–6(1) Financial Instruments and Exchange Ordinance.

[94] See Rüdiger von Rosen, *Die Rechtliche Ordnung des geregelten Kapitalmarkts*, in Heinz-Dieter Assmann and Rolf A. Schütze, HANDBUCH DES KAPITALANLAGERECHTS § 2 No. 285 (3d ed., 2007) (investors are protected directly by the *Aktiengesetz*); Karsten Schmidt, GESELLSCHAFTSRECHT 842–7, 1147–8 (4th ed., 2002) (information rights are mandatory, and shareholders in *Aktiengesellschaften* benefiting from 'smaller firms' accounting simplifications may ask for accounts reflecting 'larger firms' requirements); Uwe Hüffer, AKTIENGESETZ, § 131 No. 1 (8th ed., 2008) (limited discretion for charter provisions).

[95] See Art. 215–1 Règlement Général de l'AMF (firms may stop complying with requirements applicable to public issuers when the number of shareholders drops below 100); Thierry Bonneau and France Drummond, DROIT DES MARCHÉS FINANCIERS No. 464 (2d ed. 2005). Italy has a similar regime for non-listed companies with widely distributed securities (i.e. with 200 sharehold-ers or more): these companies are subject to ongoing disclosure duties (see Art. 2-II Consob Issuers Regulation).

[96] Delisting may also be involuntary, for failure to meet listing thresholds, mergers, or rule violations. See Shinhua Liu, *The Impact of Involuntary Foreign Delistings: An Empirical Analysis*, Working Paper (2004), at http://www.ssrn.com (out of a sample of 158 involuntary

to be delisted only upon approval of (1) the company's audit committee and (2) a majority of the company's full board of directors; and only after providing shareholders with at least 45 (but no more than 60) days' written notice.[97] In other jurisdictions, the law specifically empowers listing or supervisory authorities to oppose delisting applications when it is in the interests of investors to do so.[98] This form of investor protection has, in particular, the advantage of reinforcing the effectiveness of delisting-related company law requirements. For example, German delisting authorities will take into account whether the Aktiengesetz shareholder majority and minority exit rights have been complied with.[99]

Particularly since enactment of the U.S. Sarbanes-Oxley Act, scholars have closely investigated the regulatory costs associated with registration as a publicly-traded company. In the U.S., the concern has been that firms might withdraw from the disclosure regime to avoid these costs.[100] While firms have not left the NYSE to list on, say, the London Stock Exchange (LSE) main market,[101] many foreign firms cross-listed on U.S. exchanges have delisted or are considering delisting.[102] In addition, many small U.S. public companies have gone dark—i.e., ceased to file with the Securities and Exchange Commission (SEC) while continuing to trade on the Over-the-Counter (OTC) market. The relative importance of factors influencing firms' decisions to go dark is unclear, however. No doubt regulatory costs play an important role.[103] But there is also evidence

---

delistings between 1990 and 2003, 100 were threshold related and 29 due to mergers and similar transactions).

[97] *Self-Regulatory Organizations; Notice of Filing of Proposed Rule Change and Amendment No. 1 Thereto by the New York Stock Exchange, Inc. To Amend its Rule 500 Relating to Voluntary Delistings by Listed Companies*, SEC Release No. 34–39394 (3 December 1997, at http://www.sec.gov).

[98] See Art. L 421–4 Code Monetaire et Financier (France); § 39 Börsengesetz (Germany); Art. 64 Consolidated Law on Finance (Italy); Art. 112 Financial Instruments and Exchange Act (Japan).

[99] See *supra* 7.4.2.3.2.

[100] Whether these concerns are founded is another matter. See Robert Prentice, *Sarbanes-Oxley: The Evidence Regarding the Impact of SOX 404*, 29 CARDOZO LAW REVIEW 703 (2007); Luigi Zingales, *Is the U.S. Capital Market Losing its Competitive Edge?*, Working Paper (2007), at http://www.ssrn.com.

[101] Joseph D. Piotroski and Suraj Srinivasan, *The Sarbanes-Oxley Act and the Flow of International Listings*, Working Paper (2007), at http://www.ssrn.com.

[102] See Committee on Capital Market Regulation, *The Competitive Position of the U.S. Public Equity Market* (2007); Geoffrey Peter Smith, *What are the Effects of Sarbanes-Oxley on Cross-Listed Companies*, Working Paper (2008), at http://www.ssrn.com. To discourage delistings and encourage new listings, the SEC has facilitated deregistration by foreign issuers with low average U.S. trading volumes as compared to their worldwide average trading volumes. See *Termination of a Foreign Private Issuer's Registration of a Class of Securities under 12(g)*, Exchange Act Release No. 34–55540, 72 Federal Register 16,934 (5 April 2007, at http://www.sec.gov).

[103] Compare Stanley Block, The *Latest Movement to Going Private: An Empirical Study*, 14 JOURNAL OF APPLIED FINANCE 36 (2004) (cost of being public is top reason); William J. Carney, *The Costs of Being Public after Sarbanes-Oxley: The Irony of 'Going Private'*, 55 EMORY LAW JOURNAL 141 (2006) (it is difficult to tell why firms go private); Christian Leuz, *Was the Sarbanes-Oxley Act of 2002 Really This Costly? A Discussion of Evidence from Event Returns and Going-Private Decisions*, 44 JOURNAL OF ACCOUNTING AND ECONOMICS 146 (2007) (there is not much evidence of SOX imposing substantial costs); Ehud Kamar, Pinar Karaca-Mandic, and Eric L. Talley,

that firms may deregister for other reasons, including poor investment prospects, financial distress, or the desire by their controllers to withhold uncomfortable information from shareholders and regulators.[104] Moreover, the costs of complying with SOX seem to be highly variable across companies.[105]

By contrast, scholarly concern in our other core jurisdictions—France, Germany, Italy, Japan, and the UK—has centered on the risk that investors may be misled by overly lax disclosure by firms traded on so-called 'second-tier' trading systems.[106] Firms that can easily shift from the rigorous disclosure required by a first-tier (or 'official') listing to the more relaxed requirements of a second-tier (or 'alternative') listing, have the power to degrade their own regulatory regimes at will. In effect, shifting from a first-tier to a second-tier listing is going dusky if not entirely dark. The UK's Financial Services Authority has been particularly aggressive in alerting investors to the significance of the distinction between these two sorts of listings.[107] Other European jurisdictions rely on classifying main trading systems as 'regulated markets' to signal that these markets mandate high quality disclosure.[108]

9.3 Enforcement of Investor Protection Strategies

The area of investor protection, and of mandatory disclosure in particular, provide numerous examples of the enforcement devices outlined in Chapter 2—namely,

---

Sarbanes-Oxley's Effects on Small Firms: What is the Evidence?, Working Paper (2007), at http://www.ssrn.com (SOX seems to have a disproportionately negative impact on smaller firms, at least at its initial implementation, but the evidence is not conclusive).

[104] Andrew G. Karolyi, *The World of Cross-Listings and Cross-Listings of the World: Challenging Conventional Wisdom*, 10 Review of Finance 99 (2006); Christian Leuz, Alexander J. Triantis and Tracy Yue Wang, *Why do Firms Go Dark? Causes and Economic Consequences of Voluntary SEC Deregistrations*, Working Paper (2007), at http://www.ssrn.com; Craig Doidge, G. Andrew Karolyi and René M. Stulz, *Why Do Foreign Firms Leave U.S. Equity Markets? An Analysis of Deregistration under SEC Exchange Act Rule 12b-6*, Working Paper (2008), at http://www.ssrn.com (providing evidence that delisting is related to vanishing growth opportunities).

[105] Michel Maher and Dan Weiss, *The Costs of Complying with the Sarbanes-Oxley Act*, Working Paper (2008), at http://www.ssrn.com.

[106] See, e.g., the contributions in Guido Ferrarini (ed.), European Securities Markets (1998); Guido Ferrarini and Eddy Wymeersch (eds.), Investor Protection in Europe (2006); see also Moloney, *supra* note 3, 67–72.

[107] While the total number of foreign listings have increased in the UK in recent years, this is because of an impressive number of small firms listing on the Alternative Investment Market (which has less stringent listing requirements than U.S. exchanges)—foreign listings on the LSE having fallen during the same period. See Craig Doidge, G. Andrew Karolyi and René M. Stulz, *Has New York Become Less Competitive in Global Markets? Evaluating Foreign Listing Choices Over Time*, 91 Journal of Financial Economics 253 (2007).

[108] See Ellís Ferran, Principles of Corporate Finance Law 424–5 (2008); Annotated presentation of regulated markets and national provisions implementing relevant requirements of ISD [2007] J.O. C 38/5. The list of 'regulated markets' is changing so rapidly that the European Commission is updating it on a continuous basis instead of annually, as originally planned.

private, public, and gatekeeper enforcement.[109] Yet jurisdictions differ dramatically in the mix of the enforcement devices that they employ as well as in the severity of these enforcement measures.

9.3.1 Private enforcement

The chief private enforcement device in the area of investor protection is the shareholder lawsuit for monetary damages, brought against managers, issuing companies, audit firms, and other public 'speakers', such as financial analysts and their employers, whose credibility can materially influence market prices. But for Japan subjecting issuers to strict liability, the law in all of our major jurisdictions imposes liability under a negligence standard when it mandates the disclosure of specific information, as in audited financial statements.[110] In the U.S., Germany, and other jurisdictions, however, the law employs the weaker liability standard of 'knowing misconduct' when misrepresentations affect market trading in general.[111] Thus, a negligent misstatement in a company's press release would not trigger liability under SEC Rule 10b-5 (a catch-all provision targeting untrue statements of material facts), while a knowing misstatement of a material fact would.[112]

If the substantive standards of misconduct are similar in the U.S. and Europe, however, reliance on *formal* private enforcement (i.e., shareholder litigation) varies greatly. In the U.S., the shareholder class action is one of the most important mechanisms for enforcing mandatory disclosure requirements, notwithstanding recent legislative efforts to cabin it.[113] Such actions are typically brought by a specialized 'plaintiff's law firm' in the wake of a SEC investigation or merely the disclosure of bad news unanticipated by the market.[114] As with bounty hunters in the (U.S.) 'Old West', a law firm that successfully prosecutes or settles a shareholder class action (settlements far outnumber trials) earns lucrative attorney's

---

[109] See *supra* 2.3.2.

[110] For the U.S., see for example, §§ 11 and 12(2) of the 1933 Securities Act; for the UK, § 90 Financial Services and Market Act 2000; for France, Germany and Italy, see Klaus J. Hopt and Hans-Christoph Voigt (eds.), PROSPEKT- UND KAPITALMARKTINFORMATIONSHAFTUNG (2005).

[111] See Klaus J. Hopt and Hans-Christoph Voigt, *Grundsatz- und Reformprobleme der Prospekt- und Kapitalmarktinformationshaftung*, in Hopt and Voigt, *supra* note 110, 9, 125–6 (contrasting this approach with the one adopted in other European jurisdictions). See also *Final Report, Davies Review of Issuer Liability* (2007, at http://www.hm-treasury.gov.uk).

[112] See also Richard A. Booth, *The Future of Securities Litigation*, 4 JOURNAL OF BUSINESS AND TECHNOLOGY LAW 129 (2009).

[113] See, e.g., Private Securities Litigation Reform Act (1995), codified at 15 U.S. Code §§ 77–8.

[114] During the 1990s, around 200 securities fraud cases seeking class-action status were filed every year in federal court, with a significant increase to 498 in 2001 and a return to the 200 level in 2002–2008 (2006 being an outlier, with 119 cases): see the data provided by Stanford Law School, Securities Class Action Clearing House, at http://www.securities.stanford.edu. See also James D. Cox and Randall S. Thomas, SEC *Enforcement Actions for Financial Fraud and Private Litigation: An Empirical Inquiry*, 53 DUKE LAW JOURNAL 737 (2003) (finding that private suits with parallel SEC actions settle for significantly more than private suits without such proceedings).

fees well in excess of their out-of-pocket expenses.[115] Outside the U.S., procedural rules and the law governing attorneys' fees (still) makes the private lawsuits for monetary damages a much less important tool for enforcing the mandatory disclosure regimes on publicly-traded companies.[116] The incidence of private law suits relating to disclosure violations is (still) modest in France, Germany, and Italy[117]—and, somewhat surprisingly, almost non-existent in the UK.[118] Japan is the exception, with strictly liable issuers facing increasing litigation.

The law also provides for *informal* private enforcement of investor protections, however, by using mandatory disclosure itself to encourage the reputational sanctioning of publicly-traded firms that fail to reveal material information or deviate from 'best practices' and other informal quality-control recommendations. The significant business penalties (cost of capital, unemployment) markets impose on firms and managers that have been the target of SEC financial misrepresentation investigations are one example of informal enforcement.[119] Another example is provided by the codes of best practices adopted by EU member states, which are backed by a mandatory 'comply or explain' rule.[120] As discussed in Chapter 3, these codes govern much of the governance structure of European listed companies, including board composition and committee structure.[121] In theory, at least, such soft enforcement encourages firms to adopt recommended practices unless they have very good reasons not to, or face a penalty of investor mistrust

---

[115] See, e.g., Roberta Romano, *The Shareholder Suit: Litigation Without Foundation?*, 7 JOURNAL OF LAW, ECONOMICS, AND ORGANIZATION 55 (1991). See also *supra* 6.2.5.4 (discussing shareholder lawsuits).

[116] For recent overviews of collective action mechanisms in Europe, see Nikki Tait and Bob Sherwood, *Class Actions Across the Atlantic*, FINANCIAL TIMES, 16 June 2005, at 9; Peter Mattil and Vanessa Desoutter, *Class Action in Europe: Comparative Law* (2008) BUTTERWORTHS JOURNAL OF INTERNATIONAL BANKING AND FINANCIAL LAW 484; Christopher Hodges, THE REFORM OF CLASS AND REPRESENTATIVE ACTIONS IN EUROPEAN LEGAL SYSTEMS (2008).

[117] See Hopt and Voigt, *supra* note 111, 99–103 and 140. European mass litigation may, however, be in the making. See, in general, European Commission, *Green Paper on Consumer Collective Redress*, COM(2008) 794 final; more specifically, *Deutsche Telekom, Bad Connection*, THE ECONOMIST, 12 April 2008 at 68 (reporting on the €80 million case involving 16,000 Deutsche Telekom investors); Cleary Gottlieb, *The Shell Settlement and the Dutch Act on Collective Settlement of Mass Damages*, 16 April 2007 (at http://www.clearygottlieb.com).

[118] See John Armour, *Enforcement Strategies in UK Corporate Governance: A Roadmap and Empirical Assessment*, in John Armour and Jennifer Payne (eds.), *Rationality in Company Law: Essays in Honour of D.D. Prentice* 71 (2009). Indices that list the U.K. (as well as Japan) as very high on a scale of 'liability standards' as compared to Italy, France, and Germany are at best referring to substantive standards, not private (or public) enforcement. See, e.g., La Porta et al., *supra* note 19, Table II.

[119] Jonathan M. Karpoff; D. Scott Lee, and Gerald S. Martin, *The Cost to Firms of Cooking the Books*, JOURNAL OF FINANCIAL AND QUANTITATIVE ANALYSIS (forthcoming); *id.*, *The Consequences to Managers for Financial Misrepresentation*, JOURNAL OF FINANCIAL ECONOMICS (forthcoming).

[120] See, for the UK, Listing Rules 9.8.6; for Germany, § 161 Aktiengesetz. See, more generally, Luca Enriques and Paolo Volpin, *Corporate Governance Reforms in Continental Europe*, 21 JOURNAL OF ECONOMIC PERSPECTIVES 117 (2007) (the vast majority of recently adopted codes include a significant number of investor-friendly provisions).

[121] See *supra* 3.3.2.

in the market.[122] The U.S. and Japan do not rely on this kind of informal private enforcement although some U.S. disclosure requirements seem to come close.[123]

9.3.2 Public enforcement

Public enforcement contrasts with private enforcement insofar as it is initiated by organs of the state (e.g., market regulators or public prosecutors) or private institutions with quasi-governmental powers such as stock exchanges.[124] All of our major jurisdictions devote significant resources to public enforcement of securities laws including mandatory disclosure regimes.

Two resource-based measures provide a rough indication of the intensity of enforcement by market regulatory authorities in our major jurisdictions.[125] Looking at public enforcement *staff* relative to population, the UK and the U.S. stand out: these two Anglo-Saxon jurisdictions devote at least three times the staff to public securities enforcement (adjusted for population) as any one of our remaining four jurisdictions.[126] Enforcement *budgets* adjusted for jurisdictional GDP yield much the same result. The adjusted enforcement budgets of the UK and U.S. exceed those of France, Germany, and Japan by ratios of three or four.[127]

As nearly as we can determine, however, the balance between formal and informal public enforcement between the two Anglo-Saxon regimes differs dramatically. U.S. civil and criminal authorities bring many more *formal* enforcement actions than their UK counterparts, while UK authorities—especially the Financial Services Authority (FSA) and the City—appear to be able to accomplish much more informally, with the proverbial 'raise of the regulator's eyebrow'.[128]

These results do not include many aspects of public enforcement, such as criminal prosecutions and enforcement undertaken by exchanges. But here, too, U.S. formal public enforcement seems more intense, since it imposes 'real' prison sentences on top executive or dominant shareholders in high profile cases such as

---

[122] See also Armour, *supra* note 118, Part V.

[123] See *supra* 3.3.1. For the U.S., see SEC Rule 13e-3, and Regulation M-A, Item 1014, which govern disclosure in going-private transactions and could be considered an implicit form of 'comply or explain'. These provisions require controlling shareholders to report on the 'fairness' along a number of procedural and substantive dimensions, including whether unaffiliated security holders (such as minority shareholders) were represented by independent professionals and offered an opportunity to vote on the transaction.

[124] For a more elaborated definition of public enforcement, see *supra* 2.3.2.1.

[125] See Howell E. Jackson and Mark J. Roe, *Public and Private Enforcement of Securities Regulation: Resource-Based Evidence*, JOURNAL OF FINANCIAL ECONOMICS (forthcoming). The data is adjusted for population and GDP, but not for per capita market capitalization. Note also that the evidence consolidates issuer behavior and market trading enforcement.

[126] Jackson and Roe, *supra* note 125, Table 2 (also showing that, by comparison, France, Italy, Germany, and Japan have roughly the same population-adjusted enforcement staff).

[127] *Id.* The exception is Italy, where the enforcement budget is closer to U.S.-UK levels, but staffing remains far below U.S.-UK levels.

[128] See Armour, *supra* note 118.

Enron, Worldcom, and Holliger International. Such harsh treatment contrasts with the occasional sentence of 'at-home confinement' in equivalent European cases, such as Parmalat.[129] Moreover, as discussed in Chapter 6, higher levels of U.S. private enforcement go hand-in-hand with higher levels of public enforcement.[130] Vibrant private litigation should prompt public enforcers to be more active themselves while, conversely, private litigation feeds on evidence gathered by public enforcers.[131]

On the other hand, the level of U.S. criminal prosecution of issuers and their managers may not differ as markedly as it appears from the analogous level in jurisdictions such as France or Japan, especially in recent years. As discussed in Chapter 6, managers of French corporations face a significant risk of criminal prosecution should they engage in self-dealing without proper disclosure and approval by shareholders.[132] French corporations also face a high risk of criminal liability for misrepresentations.[133] For example, in 2007 the AMF seems to have referred about as many misrepresentation-based fraud cases to French public prosecutors as the comparable number of misrepresentation cases referred by the SEC to the U.S. Department of Justice for criminal prosecution during the same period.[134] Similarly, the JFSA's increasing imposition of administrative fines upon Japanese issuers may achieve an enforcement level that may functionally compare with U.S. criminal prosecution activity.

9.3.3 Gatekeeper enforcement

We term the hybrid mode of enforcement, in which the law co-opts a third party to assist in compelling disclosure or other forms of compliance by corporate issuers, 'gatekeeper enforcement'.[135] In screening financial information, auditors, credit rating agencies, and financial analysts enhance the trustworthiness of the information by implicitly pledging their reputational capital, which they may have accumulated over many years and many clients.[136] However, reputational

---

[129] Compare Stephanie Kirchgaessner and Hal Weitzman, *Black Sentenced to Six and a Half Years*, FINANCIAL TIMES, 11 December 2007, at 1; *Première Condamnation dans l'Affaire Parmalat*, LE TEMPS, 20 December 2008, at 28.

[130] See *supra* 6.2.5.4.

[131] See James D. Cox, Randall S. Thomas, and Dana Kiku, *SEC Enforcement Heuristics: An Empirical Enquiry*, 53 DUKE LAW JOURNAL 737, 761 (2003).

[132] See *supra* 6.2.5.1.

[133] See Hubert de Vauplane and Jean-Pierre Bornet, DROIT DES MARCHÉS FINANCIERS No. 1050–4 (3rd ed., 2001).

[134] Compare AMF, RAPPORT ANNUEL 2007, 190–4 and Eric Lichtblau, *Federal Cases of Stock Fraud Drop Sharply*, NEW YORK TIMES, 25 December 2008 at A1.

[135] See *supra* 2.3.2.3.

[136] See Reinier Kraakman, *Gatekeepers: The Anatomy of a Third-Party Enforcement Strategy*, 2 JOURNAL OF LAW, ECONOMICS, AND ORGANIZATION 53 (1986); John C. Coffee, GATEKEEPERS: THE PROFESSIONS AND CORPORATE GOVERNANCE (2006); Alexander Dyck, Adair Morse, and Luigi Zingales, *Who Blows the Whistle on Corporate Fraud*, Working Paper (2008), at http://www.ssrn.com.

capital is an illusive commodity. Thus, the law has intervened in all jurisdictions to encourage gatekeepers to police disclosure—and the quality of market information more generally—by imposing liability. As in the case of encouraging compliance by firms, the law may attempt to motivate gatekeepers by providing for privately-imposed liability, public sanctions, or both.

Historically, audit firms were the first gatekeepers to be regulated, since all major jurisdictions have traditionally required publicly-held companies to use outside auditors to verify their financial statements and subjected these auditors to auditing standards and potential liability.[137] Financial analysts have been targeted more recently, as they have been subjected to organizational and conduct rules on conflict of interest in the wake of the Enron-related scandals.[138] Regulation of credit rating services has been much more limited thus far. The U.S. confers benefits on registered Nationally Recognized Statistical Rating Organizations (NRSROs) and imposed limited conflict of interest requirements on these agencies. Other jurisdictions merely recommended the adoption of a self-regulatory code of conduct.[139] However, the current financial crisis—and especially the sub-prime mortgage bubble—in resulting in more interventionist regulation of gatekeepers in general and credit rating agencies in particular.[140]

Regulatory intervention has gone hand-in-hand with an increase in gatekeeper liability to private parties. As is indicated in Chapter 5, expansion of auditor liability, especially in the U.S., has prompted both courts and legislatures to attempt to rein in this form of liability.[141] Even so, the recent wave of corporate scandals in Europe, Japan, and the U.S. has led to an increase of suits against auditors, especially when investors were foreseeable users of financial statements, which may bring a new round of statutory limitations on auditor liability.[142]

Financial analysts have not escaped private litigation either. Major U.S. investment banks have paid enormous sums to settle suits alleging misrepresentations

---

[137] See *supra* 5.2.1.4. The definition of 'outside' auditors has, however, differed across jurisdictions and over time. See, for Japan, Zenichi Shishido, *The Turnaround of 1997: Changes in Japanese Corporate Law and Governance*, in Masahiko Aoki, Gregory Jackson, and Hideaki Miyajima (eds.), CORPORATE GOVERNANCE IN JAPAN 310 (2007).

[138] For the U.S., see § 501 Sarbanes-Oxley Act and Regulation Analyst Certification; for the EU, Market Abuse Directive; for Japan, International Council of Securities Associations, *Principles and Regulation for Research-Related Conflicts of Interest* (2005) (comparing the EU, Japan, the UK and the U.S.).

[139] For the U.S., see Credit Rating Agency Reform Act (2006). There are more than 130 credit-rating agencies in the U.S., but only five have been recognized by the SEC as of June 2007; for other jurisdictions, see International Organization of Securities Commissions, Code of Conduct Fundamentals for Credit Rating Agencies (October 2004).

[140] See *supra* 5.2.1.4.

[141] See *supra* 5.2.1.4. But see *Central Bank of Denver, N.A. v. First Interstate Bank of Denver, N.A.* 511 U.S. 164 (1994) (no aiding and abetting liability under Rule 10b-5) and other 'anti-gatekeeping' cases cited *infra* note 145.

[142] See the European Commission's Recommendation of 5 June 2008 concerning the limitation of the civil liability of statutory auditors and audit firms [2008] O.J. L 162/39.

by their securities analysts.[143] Moreover, private lawsuits have not been limited to the U.S. In France, for example, LVMH has brought a well-publicized case against Morgan Stanley, which claims that that the bank's financial analysts were neither independent nor objective towards LVMH, and this favored Gucci—a bank client and LVMH competitor.[144]

Generally speaking, however, gatekeeper enforcement has been limited to situations in which public investors might reasonably be expected to rely on the certification or information that gatekeepers provide.[145] What is less clear is whether gatekeeper enforcement—or the other modes of enforcement—measurably increase the quality of financial reporting across our limited set of highly-developed core jurisdictions.[146]

9.3.4 The informativeness of financial reports

One might say that the proof of whether intensive enforcement raises the quality of financial reporting is in the pudding. But the problem is, which pudding? The U.S. still mandates the world's most extensive public reporting requirements (although our other core jurisdictions are rapidly catching up), employs one of the world's most trusted accounting methodologies, and deploys unparalleled private and public enforcement measures in the cause of investor protection. It is natural to expect, therefore, that accounting scandals in the U.S. ought to be fewer and more benign than elsewhere. In fact, however, Enron, WorldCom, and a host of other accounting scandals have sullied the reputation of U.S. accounting reports in particular and its mandatory disclosure regime more generally.[147] Perhaps reporting requirements in the U.S. style only marginally affect the quality of financial reporting even in the presence of strong public and private enforcement.

---

[143] See Global Research Analysts Settlement (April 2003), discussed in Loss et al., *supra* note 3, 838–41.

[144] See *Morgan Stanley Ltd v. SA LVMH* [2006] Semaine Juridique 303479 (Cour d'Appel de Paris 2006) (clearing the bank from most charges). Note, however, that this is a case brought by an issuer, not investors or on their behalf.

[145] See, for the U.S., *Regents of the University of California v. Merrill Lynch Pierce Fenner & Smith Inc. et al*, 128 Supreme Court 1120 (2008); *Stoneridge Investment Partners LLC v. Scientific Atlanta Inc. and Motorola Inc.*, 128 Supreme Court 761 (2008); for the UK, *Hedley Byrne & Co v. Heller & Partners* [1964] Appeal Cases 465 (House of Lords 1963); for Switzerland, *X. Corporation v. Q.*, Amtliche Sammlung 122 III 176 (Federal Tribunal 1966).

[146] See also Hamid Mehran and René M. Stulz, *The Economics of Conflicts of Interest in Financial Institutions*, 85 Journal of Financial Economics 267 (2007) (empirical evidence is mixed on the relationship between analysts' conflicts of interests and the value of their forecasts and recommendations); Anup Agrawal and Mark A. Chen, *Do Analyst Conflicts Matter? Evidence from Stock Recommendations*, 51 Journal of Law and Economics 503 (2008) (conflicted analysts make optimistic recommendations but do not systematically mislead investors).

[147] See, e.g., Baruch Lev, *Corporate Earnings: Facts and Fiction*, 17 Journal of Economic Perspective 27 (2003) (providing an anatomy of earnings manipulation).

We are hesitant to draw this conclusion, however. The cost of U.S.-style disclosure appears to be low: more than 90% of eligible non-U.S. firms that forgo a U.S. listing claim that the burden of increased transparency did not influence their decision not to list.[148] Moreover, the evidence suggests that the relatively rigorous U.S. disclosure and enforcement rules can raise the value of foreign equity by increasing the informational quality of share prices.[149] The more recent amendments to the U.S. disclosure regime, which include enhanced regulatory and gatekeeper enforcement under the Sarbanes-Oxley Act, ought to make price increases even more likely,[150] even if they cannot settle the question whether increased transparency is worth the candle.[151]

9.4 Ownership Regimes and Investor Protection

All our major jurisdictions build on the entry and exit strategies to protect public investors by mandatory disclosure and quality control measures, ranging from governance requirements to basic qualifications for trading on exchanges. Both attach as soon—and as long—as publicly-traded companies cross certain thresholds (for example, counting a minimum number of investors or listing on a particular market). Significant differences remain, of course, in the extent of mandatory disclosure. As we noted earlier, however, the disclosure gap between the Anglo-Saxon jurisdictions and the civil law jurisdictions is narrowing. The chief differences among our jurisdictions concern enforcement.

The unique feature of U.S. enforcement is that private lawsuits for monetary damages are, as a first guess, of roughly equal importance to civil and criminal actions brought by the state. For better or worse, other jurisdictions lack a full class action device to threaten companies and their managers with massive private monetary damages for knowing, or sometimes negligent, misrepresentations or omissions in public disclosures. As far as private enforcement is concerned,

---

[148] Craig Doidge, *Why are Foreign Firms Listed in the U.S. Worth More?* 71 JOURNAL OF FINANCIAL ECONOMICS 205 (2004). See also *supra* 9.2.2.2.

[149] See also Nuno Fernandes and Miguel A. Ferreira, *Does International Cross-Listing Improve the Information Environment*, 88 JOURNAL OF FINANCIAL ECONOMICS 216 (2008) (providing evidence of an increase in share price informativeness for firms incorporated in developed markets).

[150] See also Daniel A. Cohen, Aiyesha Dey, and Thomas Lys, *Real and Accrual-based Earnings Management in the Pre- and Post-Sarbanes Oxley Periods*, 83 THE ACCOUNTING REVIEW 757 (2008); Doidge et al. *supra* note 107.

[151] Empirical studies on the compliance costs imposed by Sarbanes-Oxley have produced mixed results. See *supra* note 103 and John C. Coates, *The Goals and Promises of the Sarbanes-Oxley Act*, 21 JOURNAL OF ECONOMIC PERSPECTIVES 91 (2007). There are also diverging views on the Act's impact on corporate risk-taking. Compare Coates, *supra*, and Kate Litvak, *Defensive Management: Does the Sarbanes-Oxley Act Discourage Corporate Risk-Taking*, Working Paper (2008), at http://www.ssrn.com.

they rely chiefly on listing requirements and codes of best practices, backed by the reputational sanction implicit in the disclose-or-explain rule.

As nearly as we can determine, the public enforcement of investor protection law breaks down in a slightly different way. The U.S. and UK invest more resources in the public enforcement of investment protection than our remaining core jurisdictions, while U.S. authorities put the emphasis on formal enforcement and their UK counterparts operate much more informally. France, Germany, Italy, and Japan invest similar amounts in public enforcement, whereas criminal prosecution seems more developed in France than in our other continental European jurisdictions.

Strikingly, the legal regimes of investor protection seem roughly to match the size and maturity of national capital markets.[152] Where capital markets are large and highly developed, as in the U.S. and UK, the scope and enforcement of investor protection is aggressive. Where capital markets are still relatively small, as in Germany, France, and Italy, investor protection is less aggressively pursued. This correlation seems robust, even if it is not perfect.

Its explanation, however, is not nearly so clear. The most straightforward possibility is that jurisdictions with more developed capital markets have both a greater need to protect investors and market infrastructure (including confidence), and greater experience in how to do so. Of course ever-increasing mandatory disclosure and enforcement must at some point generate greater costs than benefits for capital markets. Indeed, a sceptic might argue that where capital markets are *already* highly developed, with intermediary actors who process information and a tradition of voluntary disclosure, legal intervention is less necessary to protect public investors than it is in undeveloped capital markets, where there are few informal enforcement institutions to supplement the law. Conversely, however, jurisdictions with underdeveloped markets rely on other modes of financing, such as bank and intra-group financing, that bypasses public markets.

Another possibility is that differences in investor protection mirror differences in ownership regimes, albeit less directly than when it comes to the basic governance structure, related-party transactions, fundamental changes or control transactions.[153] The correlation is strongest in the UK, where a moderately aggressive approach towards investor protection is in line with the interests of institutional investors. But the correlation also exists in our other jurisdictions. While managers and controlling shareholders are likely to favor a less aggressive approach, they also have an interest in some degree of investor protection. Hence, managers may benefit in that it ensures dispersed ownership (allowing them to keep control

---

[152] See also Rafael La Porta, Florencio Lopez-de-Silanes, and Andrei Schleifer, *The Economic Consequences of Legal Origins*, 46 JOURNAL OF ECONOMIC LITERATURE 285 (2008); La Porta et al., *supra* note 19; Rafael La Porta, Florencio Lopez-de-Silanes, Andrei Schleifer, and Robert W. Vishny, *Legal Determinants of External Finance*, 52 JOURNAL OF FINANCE 1131 (1997).

[153] Compare *supra* 5.4 and 6.3. On differences in ownership regimes, see also *supra* 1.6.1.

over the firms) and allows equity-based compensation. Similarly, investor protection benefits controlling shareholders insofar as it reduces the cost of external finance and makes it easier to sell their stake in the firm or diversify their assets.

However, the aggressiveness of investor protection is not a simple function of ownership regimes. First, labor (in continental Europe) and retail investor (in the U.S.) interests also play a role.[154] Second, the development of capital markets should go hand-in-hand with an increase of the political clout of market intermediaries and gatekeepers.[155] Third, capital markets are regularly plagued by financial crises that result in regulatory change shaped by political entrepreneurs tapping into broad public sentiments for reforms.[156]

These factors undoubtedly contribute to the severity of U.S. disclosure requirements, even if managers might prefer less transparency. Market intermediaries and financial analysts in particular, have a strong interest in getting firm-specific information. Moreover, the U.S. federal government generally enacts significant securities legislation in times of market crisis, i.e. when managerial influence is weakest. By contrast, the existence of demanding substantive disclosure standards in the UK reflects both the preferences of institutional investors and a convergence of their interests with those of financial intermediaries.

In continental Europe and Japan, controlling shareholders, blockholders, and financial intermediaries had direct access to company information and the public equity markets were not a major source of capital. However, increasing equity ownership by (domestic and foreign) institutional investors and the maturing of capital markets are pressing substantive disclosure requirements in these jurisdictions closer to those of the Anglo-Saxon jurisdictions.

Ownership regimes might also explain in part the increasing importance of governance strategies that specifically target publicly-traded companies. These strategies, including the EU codes of best practices, reflect increasing (domestic and foreign) institutional ownership in continental Europe and Japan, and SOX-like regulatory reforms undertaken in the wake of financial scandal in the U.S.

Even enforcement policies can be explained in terms of ownership regimes. In the U.S., formal enforcement has limited impact on managers while serving the interests of market intermediaries, such as security analysts and lawyers, who have grown politically powerful in the shadow of the markets.[157] The UK has strong if often informal public enforcement because the interests of institutional investors dominate the government administrators of the law of capital markets for public companies, including the City and the FSA. By contrast, France, Germany,

---

[154] See Mark J. Roe, Political Determinants of Corporate Governance (2003).
[155] See Franklin Allen and Douglas Gale, Comparing Financial Systems (2000).
[156] See Mark J. Roe, *Delaware's Politics*, 118 Harvard Law Review 2491 (2005); Roberta Romano, *The Sarbanes-Oxley Act and the Making of Quack Corporate Governance*, 114 Yale Law Journal 1521 (2005).
[157] See, e.g., Jonathan R. Macey and Geoffrey P. Miller, *Toward an Interest-Group Theory of Delaware Corporate Law*, 65 Texas Law Review 469 (1987).

Italy, and Japan do not, as yet, dedicate the same resources to investor protection, in part because the stock market is less important to corporate finance than it is in the U.S. and the UK, and in part, because outside institutional investors, who can be expected to champion aggressive regulation of public investors, are still weak relative to inside blockholders, friendly shareholders, and entrenched managers.

10

Beyond the Anatomy

Paul Davies, Luca Enriques, Gerard Hertig,
Klaus Hopt, and Reinier Kraakman

A short book deserves a short conclusion. The preceding chapters map the corporate law of our core jurisdictions in areas ranging from basic governance structure to investor protection. They focus on a handful of legal strategies that all jurisdictions deploy to address the agency problems inherent to corporations: the conflicts between managers and shareholders, between minority and controlling shareholders, and between non-shareholder constituencies and shareholders as a class. We do not summarize the contents of earlier chapters here. Instead we address the surprisingly complex relationship between corporate law and the ownership structure of publicly-traded firms in our core jurisdictions.

From that perspective, it is helpful to recall that the corporate form has the same fundamental legal features around the world: legal personality, limited shareholder liability, transferable shares, centralized (and delegated) management, and investor ownership.[1] These features shape the agency problems that corporate law must address, and they create the domain in which a functional framework for comparative corporate law makes sense. We do not believe that all of corporate law is functional or 'efficient'. As we noted in Chapter 1, the political economy of corporate law reflects not only market forces but history and the distributional interests of powerful political actors, including controlling shareholders, managers, employees, and the state.[2] But even if the corporate law of particular jurisdictions is shaped by history and distributional interests as well as market forces, a functional framework helps to unravel these multiple influences. For example, the law's weak response to a particular agency problem may hint at the distributional interests of powerful corporate stakeholders.

Political economy is especially important for corporations with publicly-traded shares—our main focus in this book. Although all jurisdictions provide company forms for closely-held businesses whose shares do not trade on the public markets, these forms are highly flexible. The actual governance of such closely-held firms may depend more on contract—in the form of customized charter provisions,

---

[1] See *supra* 1.2.   [2] See *supra* 1.6.1.

shareholder agreements, etc.—than on corporate law. By contrast, the governance of publicly-traded firms is more likely to be set within one corporate form and fixed by capital market regulations that are designed to protect investors and ensure confidence in the trading market. Thus the governance of publicly-traded firms is more likely to be homogenous within jurisdictions and to be framed by law, even for fine-grained matters such as board structure and internal procedures. In addition, publicly-traded companies are typically the largest and most politically salient firms in every jurisdiction.

Throughout this book, we rely on the ownership structure of publicly-traded corporations as one source of legal differences among our core jurisdictions. We are not alone in this respect. The correlation between ownership structure and corporate law has been a common theme in academic literature for the past three decades, if not since the publication of Berle and Means' celebrated book[3] on the separation of ownership from control in large U.S. companies. The simplest conjecture is that managers, as an interest group, dominate corporate law reform and capital market regulation where shareholders are dispersed and weak, while controlling shareholders (or large blockholders) dominate the law where shareholdings in listed firms are concentrated. Variations on this story reverse the direction of causality. For example, commentators have argued that it is the law protecting minority shareholders from managers and controlling shareholders that allows diffuse ownership structures to emerge in the first instance.[4] Or, alternatively, others have argued that powerful stakeholders, such as labor in social democratic jurisdictions, may require powerful shareholders to contain stakeholder influence and ensure the survival of the firm.[5]

Given the academic centrality of the distinction between jurisdictions characterized by dispersed and concentrated ownership of publicly-traded corporations, a natural point of conclusion is to ask how far this distinction correlates with legal and governance differences across our core jurisdictions. This question is surprisingly difficult to answer.

Our three continental European jurisdictions—France, Germany, and Italy—are blockholder jurisdictions by all accounts. Single shareholders or blockholder coalitions control a majority of the largest firms in these jurisdictions, as well as almost all small listed firms. In our remaining jurisdictions—Japan, the U.S., and the UK—most large companies lack a controlling shareholder. Thus, for the purpose of this chapter, we can treat half of our jurisdictions as 'dispersed' and half as 'controlled' jurisdictions, albeit this division already oversimplifies. (In fact, many large companies have dispersed ownership in continental Europe—particularly in Germany and France—just as significant numbers of

---

[3] Adolf A. Berle and Gardiner C. Means, THE MODERN CORPORATION AND PRIVATE PROPERTY (1932).

[4] See, e.g., Rafael La Porta, Florencio Lopez-de-Silanes, Andrei Shleifer, and Rober Vishny, *Law and Finance*, 106 JOURNAL OF POLITICAL ECONOMY 1113 (1998).

[5] See Mark J. Roe, POLITICAL DETERMINANTS OF CORPORATE GOVERNANCE (2003).

listed companies in Japan, the U.S., and the UK have controlling shareholders.[6] Moreover shareholder coalitions play an important role in 'dispersed' jurisdictions, although in a less structured way than in 'controlled' jurisdictions; hence, institutional investors often act in concert in the UK, whereas manager-friendly collations of shareholders are common in Japan.)

Given this distinction between ownership structures, we first ask the hypothetical question, what *should* a jurisdiction's corporate law look like were it *dominated* by either corporate managers or controlling shareholders? We then draw impressionistically from prior Chapters to determine how well these expectations are met. As an organizing device, we use the corporation's three principal agency problems: the conflict between managers and shareholders as a class, the conflict between controlling and minority shareholders, and the conflict between all shareholders and non-shareholder constituencies. While this is an ad hoc exercise, it nevertheless provides useful insights into the complex relationship between ownership structure and law.

10.1 Ownership Structures and Agency Problems

10.1.1 The managers-shareholders conflict

Controlling shareholders (or coalitions of blockholders) have both the incentive to monitor corporate managers and the power to control them. A corporate law dominated by these shareholders would need little more than strong appointment and decision-making rights to control managerial opportunism. One might expect such a law to pay close attention to voting rules and veto thresholds for large minority shareholders, particularly in the realm of charter amendments and fundamental transactions. But one would not expect it to detail voting regimes or proxy rules, or to include the kinds of reforms that are currently favored by international codes of best practices: for example, minimal numbers of independent directors on the audit, nomination, and remuneration committees of the board. Similarly, controlling shareholders have no need for elaborate mandatory disclosure provisions or well-developed investor protections, since they have the power to inform and protect themselves. Indeed, too much public disclosure would limit their ability to self-deal, particularly in corporate groups, where the controlling shareholder is a parent company that holds a stable of partially-owned subsidiaries. Enforcement—apart from the enforcement of property rights and creditors' rights—might also receive minimal attention, given that controlling shareholders should have little use for class actions or derivative suits.

By contrast, the law of dispersed-shareholder jurisdictions should track the interests of corporate managers. Such a law would minimize attempts to contain

---

[6] See *supra* 1.6.1.

the manager-shareholder agency conflict. Its first priority would be to insulate boards of directors from both shareholder pressure and hostile takeover attempts. Thus, a managerial law would support strong takeover defenses while circumscribing shareholder decision and appointment rights (for example, by making proxy fights costly). Dominant managers might be more open-minded towards today's corporate governance reforms as long as they do not destabilize managerial control. For example, independent directors can force management to explain itself clearly, screen related-party transactions with the firm and its managers, and spot suspect financial reports with the help of outside auditors. Consequently, they might legitimate management by protecting disaggregated shareholders from rogue managers without jeopardizing the positions of honest managers—especially if independent directors have little time to spend and little knowledge about the companies that they direct. Similarly, while managers might not gain directly from mandatory disclosure, they would understand that a regime of dispersed share ownership depends on a liquid share market, which in turn requires market regulation, access to information, and even mechanisms for punishing rogue managers who attempt to steal outright, or engage in other forms of highly deviant behavior. It follows that a robust regime of mandatory disclosure is consistent with managerialist corporate law, as are shareholder suits and regulatory enforcement.

How well do these caricatures fit the legal regimes of our core jurisdictions? As hypothesized above, our controlled jurisdictions do provide shareholders with strong appointment and decision-making rights. French and Italian law enables powerful shareholders to exercise corporate oversight and even operational direction through the board. German law distinguishes between the legal competences of the supervisory board and those of the management board. Thus German law limits the power of shareholder directors on the supervisory board from meddling in firm operations or business planning. Nevertheless, even in Germany, controlling shareholders decisively influence the supervisory board's shareholder members and the selection of its chairman. Moreover, until the past decade, there has been little takeover regulation among our controlled jurisdictions, presumably because hostile takeovers were rare. Finally, while continental European jurisdictions provide for criminal and regulatory enforcement against corporate officers and directors, private avenues for shareholder suit are only now developing. So far, so good.

The catch lies with our dispersed-shareholder jurisdictions, which are all over the map. By hypothesis, law in these jurisdictions should insulate managers from shareholder pressure and provide for strong anti-takeover measures. In fact, only one dispersed jurisdiction—the U.S.—comes close to fitting the stereotype. Delaware law does insulate managers and is self-consciously *board centric*. The litmus test is Delaware's strong support for takeover defenses. By contrast, Japanese and UK law are best described as *shareholder centric*. Both

urisdictions accord significant appointment and decision rights to sharehold-
rs. As for the litmus test of takeover defenses, UK directors must comply with
he 'non-frustration' rule in the face of a takeover offer. Japanese managers, for
heir part, have long relied upon friendly coalitions of shareholders to preclude
iostile takeovers. In recent years, Japanese managers have become more vul-
ierable to pressure from outside shareholders and it is unclear how far Japanese
:ourts will allow them to deploy poison pill defenses. Although they may not
;o as far as U.S. courts in permitting takeover defenses, we note, in a nod to the
mportance of ownership structure, that the U.S. takeover cases are well-known
imong Japanese regulators and corporate lawyers.

The distinction between controlled and dispersed jurisdictions is also only a
iartial fit with the law of disclosure and governance reforms, but this is due to
levelopments related to the controlling-minority shareholders conflict.

10.1.2 The controlling-minority shareholders conflict

\s with the conflict between managers and shareholders as a class, the distinc-
ion between controlled and dispersed jurisdictions leads to *a priori* expect-
itions about how corporate law might intervene in conflicts between controlling
ind minority shareholders. We would naturally expect controlled jurisdictions
o police related-party transactions lightly, since these are among the principal
hannels through which controlling shareholders can extract private benefits
rom their firms. Conversely, jurisdictions in which widely-held firms domin-
te might be expected to police self-dealing more closely, not only because their
op managers generally lack the means to engage in tunneling (management
ompensation aside), but also because increasing the private benefits available to
ontrolling shareholders undermines the stability of board-centered governance
iy encouraging investors to seek control blocks.

By and large, the historical legal differences among our core jurisdictions seem
o confirm these expectations. U.S. corporate law and securities regulation have
igorously policed self-dealing transactions with controlling shareholders since
he end of the 1970s if not before. The UK City Code originated a tough man-
latory bid rule, which ensured that minority shareholders would participate
iro rata in any premia following the aggregation or sale of corporate control.
\nd Japan has long subscribed to a strong equal-treatment norm, which limits
he opportunities for controlling shareholders to exploit minority shareholders.
Iowever, here again, only the U.S. closely fits the stereotype of a self-consciously
ioard-centric jurisdiction, with the UK and Japan being better described as
hareholder centric. The UK's mandatory bid rule essentially reflects the interests
nd influence of institutional investors holding large but non-controlling stakes,
vhereas the Japanese equal treatment norm caters to the friendly coalitions of
hareholders upon which managers rely to secure their grip on the firm.

By contrast, France, Germany, and Italy have traditionally been less keen to police related-party transactions with controlling shareholders. Even in Germany, which is well-known for its regulation of corporate groups through *Konzernrecht*, the effectiveness of minority protection against tunneling is debatable. The same is true for France, even though it relies primarily on criminal prosecution—rather than civil actions by minority shareholders—to deter opportunism by controlling shareholders. While criminal prosecution may be a powerful deterrent in some circumstances, it is inherently limited to only the most flagrant cases of opportunism by controlling shareholders.

On the other hand, the match between ownership structure and mandatory disclosure has been weakened significantly over the past decade. We conjectured that mandatory disclosure and shareholder-friendly accounting methodologies were consistent with—and perhaps even essential for—a dispersed jurisdiction, while a controlled jurisdiction would oppose them. Historically, this prediction was on the mark. Mandatory disclosure regimes developed earlier and more rapidly in the U.S., UK, and Japan than they did in continental Europe. The same is true for 'fair value' accounting methodologies. Today, however, the disclosure gap between our controlled and dispersed jurisdictions has narrowed. The U.S. retains an edge in the scope and enforcement of disclosure obligations, but the global accounting methodologies in use today—IFRS and U.S. GAAP—both derive from an Anglo-Saxon tradition of shareholder friendliness.

What weakened the link between ownership structure and disclosure law? We suspect that the rise of domestic and global equity markets made expanded disclosure attractive, even to controlling shareholders. While disclosure has constrained their ability to extract private benefits from firms, it has also enhanced the liquidity of their holdings and lowered the cost of attracting additional (minority) equity capital for their firms.

The match between ownership structure and minority protection has been weakened much like the link between ownership structure and mandatory disclosure. Italy now mandates the right of minority shareholders to elect a director to the board of listed firms. In Germany, minority shareholders have been able to make increasingly aggressive use of their right to challenge shareholder resolutions that appear to harm minority shareholders.

A similar story may explain the widespread embrace of governance reforms by controlled jurisdictions. We conjectured earlier that independent directors with limited time budgets pose little threat to entrenched managers while possibly legitimizing them. Do we expect independent directors to fulfill a similar function for controlled companies? They can be dismissed at the whim of the controlling shareholder. But personal liability can inspire even independent directors to rise against abusive controlling shareholders. Thus, controlled jurisdictions are no more likely than dispersed jurisdictions to resist the imposition of independent directors. The gain is a better price for publicly-traded minority shares and therefore, a reduction in the cost of capital; the loss is the possible exit of public arkets by firms controlled by abusive shareholders, a result that is likely to e supported by the great majority of controlling shareholders. Germany and pan, which seem to have at least partially rejected the current orthodoxy of ood corporate governance are really exceptions. Independent directors play a ·sser role in these jurisdictions mainly because these jurisdictions approach the 1areholder-non shareholder agency problem differently—through codetermin-tion in Germany and by continuing to allow boards dominated by managers 1 Japan.

0.1.3 The shareholders-non shareholders conflict

inally, consider the most plausible connection between ownership structure and 1e protection of non-shareholder constituencies—assuming, as before, that cor-orate law mirrors the interests of either managers or controlling shareholders.)ne might naturally suppose that the latter are more likely than managers to ehave opportunistically towards other stakeholders. In contrast to shareholder iterests, managerial incentives often coincide with those of non-shareholder)nstituencies. Managers, creditors, employees, and the state all share an interest i safeguarding the firm's ability to meet its fixed obligations—interest, wages, 1d taxes—but none of these parties benefits directly from firm revenue beyond hat is needed to meet fixed obligations.

Thus, controlled jurisdictions should generally offer only limited protection • stakeholders, just as they offer limited protection to minority shareholders. By)ntrast, stakeholder protection should be more developed in dispersed jurisdic-ons. How does this prediction compare to our finding in previous chapters?

As with other corporate agency problems, the answer is mixed. Mandatory editor protection is strong in continental European jurisdictions, Japan, and 1e UK—especially if insolvency law is included. It is arguably weaker in the '.S., insofar as U.S. law provides little *ex ante* protection for corporate credit-·s, minimal director liability toward creditors, and a debtor-in-possession bank-1ptcy regime.

Two controlled jurisdictions—Germany and, to a lower degree, France— :ovide for employee participation on boards of directors. Codetermination and two-tier board structure make the selection of independent directors to the)ard unusually sensitive in Germany, where the law presumes that supervis-·y board members are either shareholder representatives or labor representatives. idependent directors are neither, which explains the resistance to corporate gov-nance reforms aiming at fostering their role, since the defection of any share-)lder or labor director would transform the balance of power in the boardrooms : large German firms. None of our dispersed-shareholder jurisdictions directly :ovides for employee participation, but one cannot fail to notice that an over-helming majority of listed Japanese companies have not opted to appoint a sig-ificant number of independent directors as they are encouraged to do by recent reforms. Instead, they prefer to keep the traditional Japanese board structure in which past or present corporate officers constitute a large majority of directors.

And if one steps outside the domain of corporate law, it is clear that non-shareholder constituencies (other than creditors) receive far more legal and political protection in controlled than in dispersed jurisdictions. Germany, France, and Italy, for example, strongly regulate terms of employment contracts in the labor market, and their governments also hold large and influential shareholdings in many of their countries' largest companies.

Clearly, the naïve expectation that corporate law—or law generally—will minimize the protection accorded to non-shareholder constituencies in controlled jurisdictions is wrong. Non-shareholder constituencies do not resemble minority shareholders. As others have pointed out, the most likely reason is that employee and state interests in our controlled jurisdictions carry more political punch than the interests of minority shareholders do—and perhaps more punch than even the interest of controlling shareholders carry.[7]

10.2 Looking Forward

As the discussion above suggests, a careful review of the preceding chapters shows that there is some correlation between corporate law and ownership structure among our core jurisdictions, but that it is far weaker today than it was a decade ago—or than it is often assumed to be in the academic literature.

We conjecture that at least three factors in our core jurisdictions have influenced the declining correlation between ownership structure and corporate law over the last decade. First, the attractions of a liquid equity market, together with the EC's push toward harmonization, have led our controlled jurisdictions to accommodate the interests of minority shareholders in their corporate law. Long-standing distinctions in ownership structure across jurisdictions remain intact. However, they are no longer as sharply defined as they once were. Even during the brief period since our first edition of this book, ownership structures in controlled jurisdictions have become more dispersed. Correlatively, equity markets have grown and market regulation—including the regulation of disclosure and accounting methodologies—has converged significantly across our core jurisdictions. Whatever costs this has imposed on controlling shareholders appears to have been more than offset by the benefits of increased liquidity and access to global capital markets.

Second, there are significant discrepancies between corporate law on the books and the institutional reality of corporate practice. Changes in corporate law or best practices that do not immediately challenge the dominant corporate interest group (i.e., top managers or controlling shareholders) diffuse easily across

---

[7] See Roe, *supra* note 5.

jurisdictions. When a corporate governance reform poses a real challenge to a controlling interest group—for example to the push toward shareholder decision-making in the U.S. or toward independent directors in Germany and Japan— a jurisdiction is unlikely to impose it on listed companies. Correlatively, it seems that a number of 'best practices' in corporate governance that have been accepted by jurisdictions dominated by different ownership structures are in fact a sort of fausse convergence. For example, independent directors are less likely to be change agents when they are vetted by controlling shareholders than when they are not. Thus, what begins as a sincere effort to reform corporate governance in dispersed shareholder jurisdictions may become a purely cosmetic reform in controlled jurisdictions.

Lastly—and most importantly—history, economics, and political economy cause corporate law to differ across jurisdictions regardless of ownership structure. An extremely powerful example is the stark contrast between U.S. and UK corporate law. The UK offers what is arguably the most shareholder-centered corporate law of any of our core jurisdictions, while U.S. law is more board-centric than that of any other jurisdiction. Why? The answer is not ownership structure but history and political economy. In the U.S., populism and financial collapse, particularly during the Great Depression, facilitated the rise of managerial capitalism. In the UK, institutional investors became the dominant shareholders during and after the Second World War. They inherited a shareholder-centric company law, and developed strong shareholder-centric self-regulatory institutions—particularly the City Code—to decide important issues of corporate governance.

We expect the correlation between ownership structure and corporate law to continue to evolve during the coming years, albeit at a pace and in a direction that may differ from what we observed during the past decade. Until recently, one might have predicted disclosure requirements and trusteeship strategies to continue to converge, and expected to see shareholder appointment and decision rights increase across jurisdictions. This, in turn, might have correlated with increasing accountability of managers to shareholders in the U.S. and Japan, and of controlling shareholders to institutional investors in continental Europe.

These, however, are extrapolations from 'normal times' that may no longer hold in view of the current global credit crisis. Its causes are hard to tie down and its consequences even harder to predict.[8] But financial crises regularly provoke massive governmental intervention and regulatory reform.[9] As just mentioned, major changes in corporate governance are often generated by external shocks such as financial scandals, economic crises, or wars. Reforms brought by the Enron/Parmalat cohort of financial debacles are the most recent regulatory example. Impressive as they may have seemed thus far, they may turn out to be

---

[8] See e.g. John Kenneth Galbraith, THE GREAT CRASH, 1929 (1954).
[9] See Charles P. Kindleberger and Robert Aliber, MANIAS, PANICS AND CRASHES, A HISTORY OF FINANCIAL CRISIS (5th ed., 2005); see also Paul Krugman, THE RETURN OF DEPRESSION ECONOMICS AND THE CRISIS OF 2008 (2009).

just of secondary magnitude in comparison with the post-crisis reforms policy-makers around the world are busy crafting as we are writing.[10]

What do newly emerging proposals tell us about possible changes in corporate governance in the future? As it is often the case, they include several items that have been on the political agenda even before the current crisis. One example is whether executive remuneration should be constrained, perhaps in order to deter managers from accepting excessive short-term risks.[11] Another example is whether the responsibilities and professional competences of auditors and credit rating agencies should be subject to better regulation and supervision.[12] A third issue is whether accounting methodologies should be improved, in particular to avoid the pro-cyclic effects of mark-to-market accounting.[13] Finally, hedge funds and private equity, despite having been arguably among the crisis' casualties rather than among its causes, will no longer have the chance to deflect long-standing proposals for stricter regulation.

However, one can also expect developments that are less in line with the political agenda of 'normal times'. The breakdown in securitization markets may not only lead to disclosure, rating and compensation reforms,[14] but it may also bring about substantive regulation of financial products and reinstate some of the 'quality' restrictions that used to apply to the issue of securities.[15] In addition, increased regulation of hedge funds and private equity may diminish their role in corporate governance. Similarly, a new wave of corporate law reforms could make shareholder activism more difficult—for example, by restricting empty voting and short-selling or by requiring investors to disclose investment strategies.[16] In this scenario, all our core jurisdictions might confine institutional investors to the limited role they traditionally have had in the U.S.—a role in which exit rather than voice is the legally preferred governance mechanism.[17]

In other words, the credit crisis affects global corporate governance to the extent that it may undermine the role of institutional investors. Assuming this will happen, will it last? It is well known that corporate law reforms adopted in the wake of financial scandals, economic crises, or wars can erode over time. This may occur because the costs of the reforms prove to be too high. For example, the regulators have relaxed constraints imposed by the Sarbanes-Oxley reforms as soon as investor confidence was restored, which may be why their often alleged

---

[10] See LEADERS STATEMENT—*The Global Plan for Recovery and Reform* (2009, available at http://www.G20.org); *Report of the High Level Group on Financial Supervision in the EU* (de Larosiere Report) (2009, available at http://www.europa.eu); *Financial Services Authority, A Regulatory Response to the Global Banking Crisis* (Turner Report) (2009, available at http://www.fsa.gov.uk); Department of the Treasury, *Blueprint for a Modernized Financial Regulatory Structure* (2008, at http://www.treas.gov).

[11] See *supra* 3.5.   [12] See *supra* 5.2.1.4.   [13] See *supra* 9.2.1.5.

[14] See Günter Franke and Jan P. Krahnen, *The Future of Securitization*, Working Paper (2008), at http://www.ssrn.

[15] See *supra* 9.2.2; Luigi Zingales, *The Future of Securities Regulation*, Working Paper (2009), at http://www.ssrn.com.

[16] See *supra* 3.1.2.   [17] See *supra* 3.1.4, 3.4, 7.2, and 7.4.

excessive costs have yet to be established empirically.[18] This may also occur because reforms are not compatible with their underlying economic or cultural environment.[19] On the other hand, regulatory erosion may take decades to become significant—as evidenced by the time it took for Dutch law to move away from reforms adopted after the Second World War or for the Glass-Steagall Act to be abolished[20]—or may not occur at all—as evidenced by the persistence of U.S. securities regulation enacted during the Great Depression.

In short, none of us has a crystal ball to predict the future—or at least none of the authors of this book has volunteered a crystal ball to share with his coauthors. We write our second edition during a major global recession. If our core jurisdictions successfully navigate it, we expect more of the same in corporate law: that is, a slow but ultimately incomplete convergence of law and practice among our core jurisdictions. Intra-jurisdictional distributions of ownership structures are unlikely to converge, but even if they did, they could not force legal convergence, given the deeply-rooted historical differences among our core jurisdictions. If this book proves nothing else, it is that convergence of ownership structures is not a sufficient condition for full legal convergence.

In the (hopefully unlikely) event that the current financial crisis deepens into a worldwide depression, all bets are off. In this case, perhaps our best guidance comes from the history of the last 'Great Reversal' in global trade and economic growth following the First World War.[21] At that time, global trade and international capital markets were devastated. Jurisdictions turned inward, and financial and legal distinctions among jurisdictions increased because they were no longer tempered by the global market. Naturally we hope for a better outcome—a continuation of the gradual convergence of corporate law and governance that we have experience over the past decade. But all this depends on fundamental economic developments and even more fundamental political decisions by our respective states.[22]

---

[18] See *supra* 9.2.2.2.

[19] See Corporate Governance Lessons from Transition Economy Reforms (Merritt B. Fox and Michael A. Heller (eds.), 2006); Katharina Pistor, Yoram Keinan, Jan Kleinheisterkamp, and Mark D. West, *Evolution of Corporate Law and the Transplant Effect: Lessons from Six Countries*, 8 World Bank Research Observer 89 (2003).

[20] See Gramm-Leach-Bliley Act of 1999, Public Law No. 106–102, 113 Statutes 1338; Edo Groenewald, *Corporate Governance in the Netherlands*, 6 European Business Organization Law Review 291 (2005).

[21] See Raghuram G. Rajan and Luigi Zingales, *The Great Reversals: The Politics of Financial Development in the 20th Century*, 69 Journal of Financial Economics 5 (2003).

[22] See also Randall K. Morck (ed.), A History of Corporate Governance Around the World (2005).

Index

accountants *see* auditors
accounting
  closely held corporations 124–5
  conflicted transactions 156–7
  conservative 125–7, 132–3, 286–7
  divergence 124–8, 285–9
  methodologies 285–9
  publicly held corporations 125–7
  group of companies 127–8
  requirements 124–8
  true and fair view 125–7, 286–7
  see also auditors, GAAP,
    gatekeepers, IFRS
actio pauliana 141–2
  see also insolvency
affiliation strategy 39, 40–2, 81–2, 99,
  123–30
  see also entry, exit
agency problems 2–3, 35–7, 153–4
  control transactions 225, 227, 233
  and legal strategies 37–9, 225
  majority-minority shareholder 2, 38,
    89, 229, 257
  manager-shareholder 2, 38, 55,
    227, 231, 232
  shareholder-non shareholder 2, 38,
    89, 100
agent incentive strategy 39, 42–4, 94–9,
  145–7, 150–1, 162–6
  see also reward, trusteeship
analyst *see* financial analyst
analytic framework 4
anti-takeover defenses
  see control transactions
appointment rights strategy 39, 42, 56,
  58–60, 90–2, 100–1, 143–4
appraisal rights 99
  see also exit
asset partitioning 10
  see also entity shielding,
    owner shielding
assets
  dilution 116, 131
  sale 74, 211
  substitution 116–18
  see also divisions, mergers, related party
    transactions
auditors 74, 81, 128, 157, 159, 287, 299
  liability 128–9, 159, 299

see also gatekeepers
authority 7, 8, 12–13

bank-centered environment
  and control transactions 271
  and creditor protection 147–51
  and investor protection 63
bankruptcy *see* insolvency
board of directors 12–14
  board approval 95, 162–6, 226
  committees 69, 90, 94,
    164–5, 173
  composition 69–72, 94–6
  de facto or shadow directors 134, 138,
    142, 176
  director disqualification 136–7
  director independence 64–6, 95, 162,
    242–3
  director liability 79–80, 95, 104,
    134–6, 166, 169, 174, 176,
    181, 295–6
  fiduciary duties 79–80, 94, 104,
    135–6, 165–6, 174–5,
    178, 241–2
  and insolvency 80, 104, 133–7, 182
  limits on board authority 72–3,
    92–3,166–9
  and operational managers 64
  removal of directors 60–2, 143–4
  self-selecting 64, 94–5, 102
  and shareholder interests 56, 64, 72,
    75, 94–6
  staggered boards 61
  size 69–70, 101
  structure 69–72
  two-tier 13
  see also agency problems, appointment
    rights, control transactions, delegated
    management, judicial review
business judgment rule 77, 79–80, 164–5,
  174, 181

capital *see* legal capital
capital markets
  and capital maintenance 133
  and issuer regulation 156, 158, 160, 302
centralized management *see* delegated
  management
charter 2 (note 2) 19, 180